131 Christians Everyone Should Know

From the Editors of
Christian History Magazine

Foreword by J.I. Packer

HOLMAN
REFERENCE

131 Christians Everyone Should Know
© 2000 Broadman & Holman Publishers
Nashville, Tennessee

ISBN 0-8054-9040-X

Dewey Decimal Classification: 270.09
Subject Heading: Christian Biography
Library of Congress Card Catalog Number: 00-040741

Editors: Mark Galli and Ted Olsen
Design: The Phanco Group

Galli, Mark.
    131 Christians everyone should know / by Mark Galli and Ted Olsen
      p. cm.   (Holman reference)
    ISBN 0-8054-9040-X (alk. paper)
  1. Christian biography. I. Title: One hundred thirty-one Christians everyone should
  know. II. Olsen, Ted, 1974- III. Title. IV. Series
  BR1700.2 .G35 2000
  270'.092'2—dc21
    [B]

Printed in the United States

4 5 04 03

D

Table of Contents

Theologians

Evangelists and Apologists

Pastors and Preachers

Musicians, Artists, and Writers

Poets

Denominational Founders

Movers and Shakers

Missionaries

Inner Travelers

Activists

Martyrs

Foreword

When Henry Ford declared that history is bunk, he no doubt thought he was uttering wisdom. But his dictum is a classic instance of —well, bunk, and bunk in its purest form. Both the processes and the characters of history have a vast amount to teach us; studying them matures our judgment and frees us from blind submission to present-day prejudices. It has often been said, if we will not learn from history, we sentence ourselves to repeat its mistakes. This is supremely true of Christian history, which shows us the conflict of God's Word with the world, in and through the lives of his servants, and sets before us the possibilities of living for God that had never before entered our minds.

Readers of the excellent journal, *Christian History*, of which Mark Galli and Ted Olsen have been editors, will know exactly what I mean when I say that, and non-readers of the journal who read the present volume will soon find out. There is not a dull line in this book; its well-chosen 131 characters come vividly to life, as our brothers and sisters in Christ; and learning the lesson of their careers is as pleasant a task as chewing candy. If you like the thought of history with edification, and without tears, this is certainly a book for you. Its authors have served you well.

J.I. Packer
Regent College
Vancouver

Acknowledgements

Some profiles were adapted from articles written in *Christian History* over the years; and first drafts of others were contributed by Kelvin Crow, Kathy Mulhern, William Martin, and Mary Ann Jeffreys. Most, however, were written by the authors, and whether as editors or authors, they take responsibility for any errors that remain therein.

Introduction

It has been said that history is biography, although you wouldn't know it by reading many history books. Too often stories, quotes, and anecdotes are replaced with analysis, statistics, grand social movements, and dates piled upon one another. No wonder people find history boring.

We don't, and that's because the nature of our work—publishing a history magazine for a general audience—continually forces us to ask a simple question: What's really interesting about this? Most of the time, the answer lies in the people who have made history happen, without whom important dates would be just numbers. Here we present 131 of those interesting, and important, people.

Why 131 exactly? We determined first some of the callings Christians have practiced through the ages, then chose the ten (or, in one case, eleven) most important and interesting for each calling. Most of our choices can be easily defended, but we admit some are arbitrary. Space constraints have forced us to leave out some key figures (like poet W. H. Auden, Pentecostal preacher William Seymour, and theologian Reinhold Niebuhr, for instance), and personal passions have dictated we include others less well-known (like theologian John of Damascus and adventist William Miller).

As for the adjective *Christian*: some of the individuals profiled here had, because of their times and circumstances, a limited understanding of the full-orbed faith. But since we see the same limitations in ourselves, it seemed only right that we err on the side of charity in determining who was "Christian."

This doesn't mean we've chosen the 131 Christians we most admire or with whom we agree. This is a book about 131 Christians everyone should know because of what they've contributed to history and because of their intrinsic interest—not 131 Christians we should all emulate. Though certainly all have something to teach us.

As such, this is not a bad place to begin research, since we've striven to remain accurate throughout, separating myth from history where necessary, and including key dates and quotes. But the book is primarily designed for those who want to have a deeper appreciation of their Christian heritage—and enjoy it.

Mark Galli
Ted Olsen
Christian History

Timeline
IMPORTANT EVENTS IN CHURCH HISTORY

THE AGE OF JESUS AND THE APOSTLES
30 Crucifixion of Jesus; Pentecost
35 Stephen martyred; Paul converted
46 Paul begins missionary journeys
48 Council of Jerusalem
57 Paul's Letter to the Romans
64 Fire of Rome; Nero launches persecutions
65 Peter and Paul executed

THE AGE OF EARLY CHRISTIANITY
70 Destruction of Jerusalem by Titus
110 Ignatius of Antioch martyred
150 Justin Martyr dedicates his *First Apology*
155 Polycarp martyred
172 Montanist movement begins
180 Irenaeus writes *Against Heresies*
196 Tertullian begins writing
215 Origen begins writing
230 Earliest known public churches built
248 Cyprian elected bishop of Carthage
250 Decius orders empire-wide persecution
270 Antony takes up life of solitude
303 "Great Persecution" begins under Diocletian

THE AGE OF THE CHRISTIAN EMPIRE
312 Conversion of Constantine
312 Donatist Schism begins
313 "Edict of Milan"
323 Eusebius completes *Ecclesiastical History*
325 First Council of Nicea
341 Ulphilas, translator of Gothic Bible, becomes bishop
358 Basil the Great founds monastic community
367 Athanasius's letter defines New Testament canon
381 Christianity made state religion of Roman Empire
381 First Council of Constantinople
386 Augustine converts to Christianity
390 Ambrose defies emperor
398 Chrysostom consecrated bishop of Constantinople
405 Jerome completes the Vulgate

410 Rome sacked by Visigoths
431 Council of Ephesus
432 Patrick begins mission to Ireland
440 Leo the Great consecrated bishop of Rome
445 Valentinian's Edict strengthens primacy of Rome
451 Council of Chalcedon
500 Dionysius the Pseudo-Areopagite writes
524 Boethius completes *Consolation of Philosophy*
529 Justinian publishes his legal Code
540 Benedict writes his monastic Rule
563 Columba establishes mission community on Iona

THE CHRISTIAN MIDDLE AGES
590 Gregory the Great elected Pope
597 Ethelbert of Kent converted
622 Muhammad's *hegira*: birth of Islam
663 Synod of Whitby
716 Boniface begins mission to the Germans
726 Controversy over icons begins in Eastern church
731 Bede's *Ecclesiastical History* published
732 Battle of Tours
750 Donation of Constantine written about this time
754 Pepin III's donation helps found papal states
781 Alcuin becomes royal adviser to Charles
787 Second Council of Nicea settles icon controversy
800 Charlemagne crowned Holy Roman Emperor
843 Treaty of Verdun divides Carolingian Empire
861 East-West conflict over Photius begins
862 Cyril and Methodius begin mission to Slavs
909 Monastery at Cluny founded
988 Christianization of "Russia"
1054 East-West Split
1077 Emperor submits to pope over investiture
1093 Anselm becomes archbishop of Canterbury
1095 First Crusade launched by Council of Clermont
1115 Bernard founds monastery at Clairvaux
1122 Concordat of Worms ends investiture controversy
1141 Hildegard of Bingen begins writing
1150 Universities of Paris and Oxford founded

1173 Waldensian movement begins

1208 Francis of Assisi renounces wealth

1215 Magna Carta

1215 Innocent III assembles Fourth Lateran Council

1220 Dominican Order established

1232 Gregory IX appoints first "inquisitors"

1272 Thomas Aquinas's *Summa Theologica*

1302 *Unam Sanctam* proclaims papal supremacy

1309 Papacy begins "Babylonian" exile in Avignon

1321 Dante completes *Divine Comedy*

1370 Catherine of Siena begins her Letters

1373 Julian of Norwich receives her revelations

1378 Great Papal Schism begins

1380 Wycliffe supervises English Bible translation

1414 Council of Constance begins

1415 Jan Hus burned at stake

1418 Thomas a' Kempis writes *The Imitation of Christ*

1431 Joan of Arc burned at stake

1453 Constantinople falls; end of Eastern Roman Empire

1456 Gutenberg produces first printed Bible

1479 Establishment of Spanish Inquisition

1488 First complete Hebrew Old Testament

1497 Savonarola excommunicated

1506 Work begins on new St. Peter's in Rome

1512 Michelangelo completes Sistine Chapel frescoes

1516 Erasmus publishes Greek New Testament

THE AGE OF THE REFORMATION

1517 Martin Luther posts his Ninety-Five Theses

1518 Ulrich Zwingli comes to Zurich

1521 Diet of Worms

1524 The Peasants' Revolt erupts

1525 William Tyndale's New Testament published

1525 Anabaptist movement begins

1527 Schleitheim Confession of Faith

1529 Colloquy of Marburg

1530 Augsburg Confession

1534 Act of Supremacy; Henry VIII heads English church

1536 John Calvin publishes first edition of *Institutes*

1536 Menno Simons baptized as Anabaptist

1540 Ignatius Loyola gains approval for Society of Jesus

1545 Council of Trent begins

1549 *Book of Common Prayer* released

1549 Xavier begins mission to Japan

1555 Peace of Augsburg

1555 Latimer and Ridley burned at stake

1559 John Knox makes final return to Scotland

1563 First text of Thirty-Nine Articles issued

1563 John Foxe's *Book of Martyrs* published

1565 Teresa of Avila writes *The Way of Perfection*

1572 St. Bartholomew's Day Massacre

1577 Formula of Concord

1582 Mateo Ricci and colleague begin mission in China

1589 Moscow becomes independent patriarchate

1598 Edict of Nantes (revoked 1685)

1609 John Smyth baptizes self and first Baptists

1611 King James Version of Bible published

1618 Synod of Dort begins

1618 Thirty Years' War begins

1620 Mayflower Compact drafted

1633 Galileo forced to recant his theories

1636 Harvard College founded

1636 Roger Williams founds Providence, R.I.

1647 George Fox begins to preach

1646 Westminster Confession drafted

1648 Peace of Westphalia ends Thirty Years' War

THE AGE OF REASON AND REVIVAL

1649 Cambridge Platform

1653 Cromwell named Lord Protector

1654 Blaise Pascal has definitive conversion experience

1667 John Milton's *Paradise Lost*

1668 Rembrandt paints *Return of the Prodigal Son*

1675 Spener's *Pia Desideria* advances Pietism

1678 John Bunyan writes *The Pilgrim's Progress*

1682 William Penn founds Pennsylvania

1687 Newton publishes *Principia Mathematica*

1689 Toleration Act in England

1707 J.S. Bach publishes first work

1707 Isaac Watts publishes *Hymns and Spiritual Songs*

1729 Jonathan Edwards becomes pastor at Northampton

1732 First Moravian missionaries

1735 George Whitefield converted

1738 John & Charles Wesley's evangelical conversions

1740 Great Awakening peaks

1742 First production of Handel's *Messiah*

1759 Voltaire's *Candide*

1771 Francis Asbury sent to America

1773 Jesuits suppressed (until 1814)
1779 John Newton and William Cowper publish *Olney Hymns*
1780 Robert Raikes begins his Sunday school
1781 Kant publishes *Critique of Pure Reason*

THE AGE OF PROGRESS

1789 French Revolution begins
1789 Bill of Rights
1793 William Carey sails for India
1793 Festival of Reason (de-Christianization of France)
1799 Schleiermacher publishes *Lectures on Religion*
1801 Concordat between Napoleon and Pius VII
1804 British and Foreign Bible Society formed
1806 Samuel Mills leads Haystack Prayer Meeting
1807 William Wilberforce succeeds abolishing slave trade
1810 American Board of Commissioners for Foreign Missions
1811 Alexander Campbell begins Restoration Movement
1816 Richard Allen elected bishop of new AME church
1816 Adoniram Judson begins mission trip
1817 Elizabeth Fry organizes relief in Newgate Prison
1819 Channing issues *Unitarian Christianity*
1827 J. N. Darby founds the Plymouth Brethren
1833 John Keble's sermon launches Oxford Movement
1834 George Mueller opens Scriptural Knowledge Institute
1835 Charles Finney's *Lectures on Revivals*
1840 David Livingstone sails for Africa
1844 First Adventist churches formed
1844 Soren Kierkegaard writes *Philosophical Fragments*
1845 John Henry Newman becomes Roman Catholic
1845 Phoebe Palmer writes *The Way of Holiness*
1848 Marx publishes *Communist Manifesto*
1851 Harriet Beecher Stowe releases *Uncle Tom's Cabin*
1854 Immaculate Conception made dogma
1854 Charles Spurgeon becomes pastor of New Park St. Church
1855 D. L. Moody converted
1857 Prayer Meeting Revival begins in New York
1859 Darwin publishes *Origin of Species*
1859 Japan reopens to foreign missionaries
1860 U.S. Civil War begins
1864 Syllabus of Errors issued by Pope Pius IX
1865 J. Hudson Taylor founds China Inland Mission
1870 First Vatican Council declares papal infallibility
1878 William & Catherine Booth found Salvation Army
1879 Frances Willard becomes president of WCTU

1880 Abraham Kuyper starts Free University
1885 Berlin Congress spurs African Independent Churches
1885 Wellhausen's documentary hypothesis
1886 Student Volunteer Movement begins
1895 Freud publishes first work on psychoanalysis
1886 Billy Sunday begins leading revivals
1901 Speaking in tongues at Parham's Bible school
1906 Azusa Street revival
1906 Schweitzer's *The Quest of the Historical Jesus*
1908 Federal Council of Churches forms
1910 Edinburgh International Missionary Conference begins
1910 *The Fundamentals* begin to be published
1912 Social Creed of the Churches adopted

THE AGE OF IDEOLOGIES

1914 World War I begins
1919 Karl Barth writes *Commentary on Romans*
1924 First Christian radio broadcasts
1931 C. S. Lewis comes to faith in Christ
1934 Barmen Declaration
1934 Wycliffe Bible Translators founded
1938 Kristallnacht accelerates Holocaust
1939 World War II begins
1940 First Christian TV broadcasts
1941 Bultmann calls for demythologization
1941 Niebuhr's *Nature and Destiny of Man*
1942 National Association of Evangelicals forms
1945 Atomic bomb dropped on Hiroshima
1947 Dead Sea Scrolls discovered
1948 World Council of Churches organized
1949 Los Angeles Crusade catapults Billy Graham
1950 Missionaries forced to leave China
1950 Assumption of Mary made dogma
1950 Mother Teresa founds Missionaries of Charity
1951 Dietrich Bonhoeffer's *Letters and Papers from Prison*
1960 Bennett resigns; charismatic renewal advances
1962 Vatican II opens
1963 Martin Luther King, Jr., leads March on Washington
1966 Chinese Cultural Revolution
1968 Medellin Conference advances liberation theology
1974 Lausanne Congress on World Evangelization
1979 John Paul II's first visit to Poland
1989 Fall of the Berlin Wall

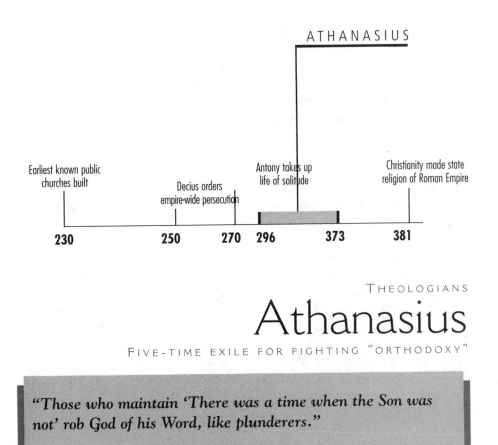

ATHANASIUS

Earliest known public churches built	Decius orders empire-wide persecution	Antony takes up life of solitude		Christianity made state religion of Roman Empire
230	**250**	**270**	**296**	**373**	**381**

Athanasius

FIVE-TIME EXILE FOR FIGHTING "ORTHODOXY"

> *"Those who maintain 'There was a time when the Son was not' rob God of his Word, like plunderers."*

"Black Dwarf" was the tag his enemies gave him. And the short, dark-skinned Egyptian bishop had plenty of enemies. He was exiled five times by four Roman emperors, spending 17 of the 45 years he served as bishop of Alexandria in exile. Yet in the end, his theological enemies were "exiled" from the church's teaching, and it is Athanasius's writings that shaped the future of the church.

Challenging "orthodoxy"

Most often the problem was his stubborn insistence that Arianism, the reigning "orthodoxy" of the day, was in fact a heresy.

The dispute began when Athanasius was the chief deacon assistant to Bishop Alexander of Alexandria. While Alexander preached "with perhaps too philosophical minuteness" on the Trinity, Arius, a presbyter (priest) from Libya announced, "If the

Father begat the Son, then he who was begotten had a beginning in existence, and from this it follows there was a time when the Son was not." The argument caught on, but Alexander and Athanasius fought against Arius, arguing that it denied the Trinity. Christ is not of a like substance to God, they argued, but the same substance.

To Athanasius this was no splitting of theological hairs. Salvation was at issue: only one who was fully human could atone for human sin; only one who was fully divine could have the power to save us. To Athanasius, the logic of New Testament doctrine of salvation assumed the dual nature of Christ. "Those who maintain 'There was a time when the Son was not' rob God of his Word, like plunderers."

Alexander's encyclical letter, signed by Athanasius (and possibly written by him), attacked the consequences of the Arians' heresy: "The Son [then,] is a creature and a work; neither is he like in essence to the Father; neither is he the true and natural Word of the Father; neither is he his true wisdom; but he is one of the things made and created and is called the Word and Wisdom by an abuse of terms.... Wherefore he is by nature subject to change and variation, as are all rational creatures."

The controversy spread, and all over the empire, Christians could be heard singing a catchy tune that championed the Arian view: "There was a time when the Son was not." In every city, wrote a historian, "bishop was contending against bishop, and the people were contending against one another, like swarms of gnats fighting in the air."

Word of the dispute made it to the newly converted Emperor Constantine the Great, who was more concerned with seeing church unity than theological truth. "Division in the church," he told the bishops, "is worse than war." To settle the matter, he called a council of bishops.

Of the 1,800 bishops invited to Nicea, about 300 came—and argued, fought, and eventually fleshed out an early version of the Nicene Creed. The council, led by Alexander, condemned Arius as a heretic, exiled him, and made it a capital offense to possess his writings. Constantine was pleased that peace had been restored to the church. Athanasius, whose treatise *On the Incarnation* laid the foundation for the orthodox party at Nicea, was hailed as "the noble champion of Christ." The diminutive bishop was simply pleased that Arianism had been defeated.

But it hadn't.

Bishop in exile

Within a few months, supporters of Arius talked Constantine into ending Arius's exile. With a few private additions, Arius even signed the Nicene Creed, and the emperor ordered Athanasius, who had recently succeeded Alexander as bishop, to restore the heretic to fellowship.

When Athanasius refused, his enemies spread false charges against him. He was accused of murder, illegal taxation, sorcery, and treason—the last of which led Constantine to exile him to Trier, now a German city near Luxembourg.

Constantine died two years later, and Athanasius returned to Alexandria. But in his absence, Arianism had gained the upper hand. Now church leaders were against him, and they banished him again. Athanasius fled to Pope Julius I in Rome. He returned in 346, but in the mercurial politics of the day, was banished three more times before he came home to stay in 366. By then he was about 70 years old.

While in exile, Athanasius spent most of his time writing, mostly to defend orthodoxy, but he took on pagan and Jewish opposition as well. One of his most lasting contributions is his *Life of St. Antony*, which helped to shape the Christian ideal of monasticism. The book is filled with fantastic tales of Antony's encounters with the devil, yet Athanasius wrote, "Do not be incredulous about what you hear of him.... Consider, rather that from them only a few of his feats have been learned." In fact, the bishop knew the monk personally, and this saint's biography is one of the most historically reliable. It became an early "best-seller" and made a deep impression on many people, even helping lead pagans to conversion: Augustine is the most famous example.

During Athanasius's first year permanently back in Alexandria, he sent his annual letter to the churches in his diocese, called a festal letter. Such letters were used to fix the dates of festivals such as Lent and Easter, and to discuss matters of general interest. In this letter, Athanasius listed what he believed were the books that should constitute the New Testament.

"In these [27 writings] alone the teaching of godliness is proclaimed," he wrote. "No one may add to them, and nothing may be taken away from them."

Though other such lists had been and would still be proposed, it is Athanasius's list that the church eventually adopted, and it is the one we use to this day.

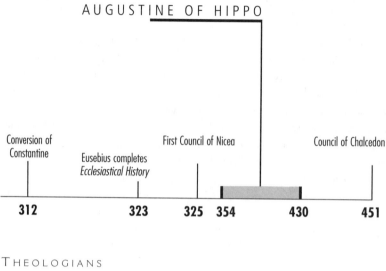

AUGUSTINE OF HIPPO

Conversion of Constantine	Eusebius completes *Ecclesiastical History*	First Council of Nicea		Council of Chalcedon
312	323	325	354 430	451

Augustine of Hippo
ARCHITECT OF THE MIDDLE AGES

> *"Mankind is divided into two sorts: such as live according to man, and such as live according to God. These we call the two cities.... The Heavenly City outshines Rome. There, instead of victory, is truth"*

Barbarians surged into the empire, threatening the Roman way of life as never before. The Christian church also faced attack from internal heretics. The potential destruction of culture, civilization, and the church was more than an occasional nightmare—it was perceived as an immediate threat. And Augustine answered with such wisdom, his responses are still considered by some to be the church's most important writings after the Bible.

Sex and fun

From his birth in a small North African town, Augustine knew the religious differences overwhelming the Roman Empire: his father was a pagan who honored the old Punic gods; his mother was a zealous Christian. But the adolescent

Augustine was less interested in religion and learning than in sex and high living—like joining with friends to steal pears from a neighbor's vineyard "not to eat them ourselves but simply to throw them to the pigs."

At age 17, Augustine set off to school in Carthage—the country boy in the jewel of North Africa. There the underachiever became enraptured with his studies and started to make a name for himself. He immersed himself in the writings of Cicero and Manichaean philosophers and cast off the vestiges of his mother's religion.

His studies completed, Augustine returned to his home town of Thagaste to teach rhetoric—and some Manichaeism on the side. (The philosophy, based on the teachings of a Persian named Mani, was a dualist corruption of Christianity. It taught that the world of light and the world of darkness constantly war with each other, catching most of humanity in the struggle.) Augustine tried to hide his views from his mother, Monica, but when she found out, she threw him out of the house.

But Monica, who had dreamt her son would become a Christian, continued to pray and plead for his conversion and followed him to Carthage when he moved there to teach. When Augustine was offered a professorship in Rome, Monica begged him not to go. Augustine told her to go home and sleep comfortably in the knowledge that he would stay in Carthage. When she left, he boarded a ship for Rome.

Darkness vanquished

After a year in Rome, Augustine moved again, to become the professor of rhetoric for the city of Milan. There he began attending the cathedral to hear the impressive oratory of Ambrose the bishop; he kept attending because of Ambrose's preaching. He soon dropped his Manichaeism in favor of Neoplatonism, the philosophy of both Roman pagans and Milanese Christians.

His mother finally caught up with him and set herself to find her son a proper wife. Augustine had a concubine he deeply loved and who had given him a son, but he would not marry her because it would have ruined him socially and politically.

Added to the emotional strain of forsaking his lover and the shift in philosophies, Augustine was struggling with himself. For years he had sought to overcome his fleshly passions and nothing seemed to help. It seemed to him that even his smallest transgressions were weighted with meaning. Later, writing about the pear stealing of his youth, he reflected, "Our real pleasure consisted in doing something that was forbidden. The evil in me was foul, but I loved it."

One afternoon, he wrestled anxiously about such matters while walking in his garden. Suddenly he heard a child's sing-song voice repeating, "Take up and read." On a table lay a collection of Paul's epistles he'd been reading; he picked it up and read the first thing he saw: "Not in reveling and drunkenness, not in lust and wantonness, not in quarrels and rivalries. Rather, arm yourselves with the Lord Jesus Christ, spend no more thought on nature and nature's appetites" (Romans 13:13–14).

He later wrote, "No further would I read; nor needed I: for instantly at the end of this sentence, by a light as it were of serenity infused into my heart, all the darkness of doubt vanished away."

From monk to bishop

Augustine's conversion sent shockwaves through his life. He resigned his professorship, dashed off a note to Ambrose telling of his conversion, and retreated with his friends and mother to a country villa in Cassiciacum. There he continued discussing philosophy and churning out books in a Neoplatonist vein. After half a year, he returned to Milan to be baptized by Ambrose, then headed back to Thagaste to live as a writer and thinker.

By the time he reached his home town (a journey lengthened by political turmoil), he had lost his mother, his son, and one of his closest friends. These losses propelled Augustine into a deeper, more vigorous commitment: he and friends established a lay ascetic community in Thagaste to spend time in prayer and the study of the Scriptures.

In 391, Augustine traveled to Hippo to see about setting up a monastery in the area. His reputation went before him. The story goes that, seeing the renowned layman in church one Sunday, Bishop Valerius put aside his prepared sermon and preached on the urgent need for priests in Hippo. The crowd stared at Augustine and then pushed him forward for ordination. Against his will, Augustine was made a priest. The laity, thinking his tears of frustration were due to his wanting to be a bishop rather than priest, tried to assure him that good things come to those who wait.

Valerius, who spoke no Punic (the local language), quickly handed over teaching and preaching duties to his new priest, who did speak the local language. Within five years, after Valerius died, Augustine became bishop of Hippo.

Orthodox champion for a millennium

Guarding the church from internal and external challenges topped the new bishop's agenda. The church in North Africa was in turmoil. Though Manichaeism was already on its way out, it still had a sizable following. Augustine, who knew its strengths and weaknesses, dealt it a death blow. At the public baths, Augustine debated Fortunatus, a former schoolmate from Carthage and a leading Manichaean. The bishop made quick work of the heretic, and Fortunatus left town in shame.

Less easily handled was Donatism, a schismatic and separatist North African church. They believed the Catholic church had been compromised and that Catholic leaders had betrayed the church during earlier persecutions. Augustine argued that Catholicism was the valid continuation of the apostolic church. He wrote scathingly, "The clouds roll with thunder, that the house of the Lord shall be built throughout the earth; and these frogs sit in their marsh and croak 'We are the only Christians!' "

In 411 the controversy came to a head as the imperial commissioner convened a debate in Carthage to decide the dispute once and for all. Augustine's rhetoric destroyed the Donatist appeal, and the commissioner pronounced against the group, beginning a campaign against them.

It was not, however, a time of rejoicing for the church. The year before the Carthage conference, the barbarian general Alaric and his troops sacked Rome. Many upper-class Romans fled for their lives to North Africa, one of the few safe havens left in the empire. And now Augustine was left with a new challenge—defending Christianity against claims that it had caused the empire's downfall by turning eyes away from Roman gods.

Augustine's response to the widespread criticism came in 22 volumes over 12 years, in *The City of God*. He argued that Rome was punished for past sins, not new faith. His life-long obsession with original sin was fleshed out, and his work formed the basis of the medieval mind. "Mankind is divided into two sorts," he wrote. "Such as live according to man, and such as live according to God. These we call the two cities…. The Heavenly City outshines Rome. There, instead of victory, is truth."

One other front Augustine had to fight to defend Christianity was Pelagianism. Pelagius, a British monk, gained popularity just as the Donatist controversy ended. Pelagius rejected the idea of original sin, insisting instead that the tendency to sin is humankind's own free choice. Following this reasoning, there is no need for divine grace; individuals must simply make up their minds to do the will of God. The church excommunicated Pelagius in 417, but his banner was carried on by young Julian of Eclanum. Julian took potshots at Augustine's character as well as his theology. With Roman snobbery, he argued that Augustine and his other low-class African friends had taken over Roman Christianity. Augustine argued with the former bishop for the last ten years of his life.

In the summer of 429, the Vandals invaded North Africa, meeting almost no resistance along the way. Hippo, one of the few fortified cities, was overwhelmed with refugees. In the third month of the siege, the 76-year-old Augustine died, not from an arrow but from a fever. Miraculously, his writings survived the Vandal takeover, and his theology became one of the main pillars on which the church of the next 1,000 years was built.

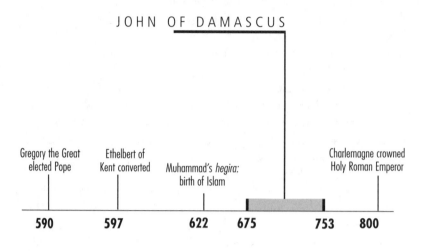

JOHN OF DAMASCUS

Gregory the Great elected Pope	Ethelbert of Kent converted	Muhammad's *hegira*: birth of Islam		Charlemagne crowned Holy Roman Emperor	
590	597	622	675	753	800

John of Damascus

IMAGE-CONSCIOUS ARAB

> *"I do not worship matter, I worship the God of matter, who became matter for my sake and deigned to inhabit matter, who worked out my salvation through matter. I will not cease from honoring that matter which works for my salvation. I venerate it, though not as God."*

Visitors to an Orthodox Church are confronted with many unfamiliar elements of worship: for example, the use of incense and Byzantine chant and the custom of standing throughout the service. But perhaps the most perplexing element is the icons, especially when Orthodox worshipers bow before and kiss them. Isn't this idolatry?

This very question raged through the Christian world in the eighth and ninth centuries, and it occupied the attention of two of the seven ecumenical (worldwide) church councils. The strongest defense of the practice came from a Christian living in the heart of the Islamic empire, John of Damascus.

Responding to the imperial volcano

He was born John Monsur, into a wealthy Arab-Christian family of Damascus. Like his father, he held a position high in the court of the caliph. About 725 he resigned his office and became a monk at Mar Saba near Bethlehem, where he became a priest. In this secluded place at the relatively advanced age of 51, John's lasting legacy began to unfold. It began when Emperor Leo III, in 726, outlawed the veneration of icons.

The conflict had been brewing for decades. It wasn't a question of bowing and kissing icons; this was a culturally acceptable way to show respect. The basic question went deeper: are Christians allowed to paint pictures of Jesus, or other biblical figures, at all? As Islam spread through the Mediterranean region, bringing its absolute interdiction of images, Christianity was feeling pressure to rid itself of images.

The main threat to icons came not from the Islamic caliph but from the heart of the Byzantine Empire. A few bishops from Asia Minor (now Turkey) believed the Bible, particularly the second commandment, forbade such images:

"You shall not make for yourself an idol in the form of anything in heaven above or on the earth beneath or in the waters below. You shall not bow down to them or worship them."

The bishops' argument convinced Byzantine Emperor Leo III, who set about to convince his subjects to abandon iconography. But a natural disaster changed his approach. In 726 a violent volcano erupted in the middle of the Aegean Sea and terrorized Constantinople, the capital. Afterward, tidal waves buffeted the shores and volcanic ash extinguished the sunlight. Leo reasoned that God was angry about icons. That's when he outlawed their use.

In 730 Leo commanded the destruction of all religious likenesses, whether icons, mosaics, or statues, and iconoclasts ("image smashers" in Greek) went on a spree, demolishing nearly all icons in the Empire.

From his distant post in the Holy Land, John challenged this policy in three works. He argued that icons should not be worshiped, but they could be venerated. (The distinction is crucial: a Western parallel might be the way a favorite Bible is read, cherished, and treated with honor—but certainly not worshiped.)

John explained it like this: "Often, doubtless, when we have not the Lord's passion in mind and see the image of Christ's crucifixion, his saving passion is brought back to remembrance, and we fall down and worship not the material but that which is imaged: just as we do not worship the material of which the Gospels are made, nor the material of the Cross, but that which these typify."

Second, John drew support from the writings of the early fathers like Basil the Great, who wrote, "The honor paid to an icon is transferred to its prototype." That is, the actual icon was but a point of departure for the expressed devotion; the recipient was in the unseen world.

Third, John claimed that, with the birth of the Son of God in the flesh, the depiction of Christ in paint and wood demonstrated faith in the Incarnation. Since the unseen God had become visible, there was no blasphemy in painting visible representations of

Jesus or other historical figures. To paint an icon of him was, in fact, a profession of faith, deniable only by a heretic!

"I do not worship matter, I worship the God of matter, who became matter for my sake and deigned to inhabit matter, who worked out my salvation through matter," he wrote. "I will not cease from honoring that matter which works for my salvation. I venerate it, though not as God."

Eastern theologian for the whole church

While the controversy continued to rage, John spent his days at Mar Saba monastery in the hills 18 miles southeast of Jerusalem. There he wrote both theological treatises and hymns; he is recognized as one of the principal hymnographers of Eastern Orthodoxy. His most important theological work, *The Fount of Wisdom,* is a summary of Eastern theology.

Tradition says that his fellow monks grumbled that such elegant writing was a distraction and prideful; so John was sometimes sent to sell baskets humbly in the streets of Damascus, where he had once been among the elite.

After more dissension and bloodshed over icons (the decade after John's death, over 100,000 Christians were injured or killed), the issue was finally settled, and icons are an integral part of Orthodox worship to this day. His other writings were major influences on Western theologians such as Thomas Aquinas. In 1890 he was named a doctor of the church by the Vatican, and in this century, his writings have become a fresh source of theological insight, especially for Eastern theologians.

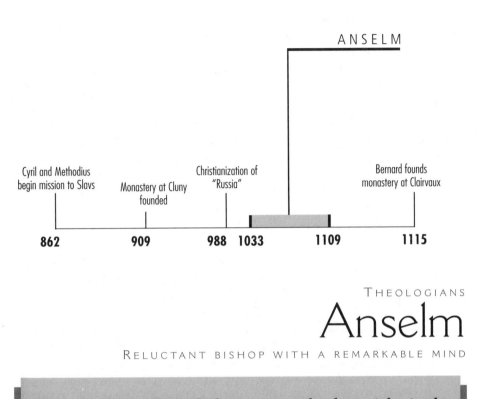

ANSELM

| Cyril and Methodius begin mission to Slavs | Monastery at Cluny founded | Christianization of "Russia" | | | Bernard founds monastery at Clairvaux |

862　　909　　988　1033　　1109　　1115

THEOLOGIANS

Anselm

RELUCTANT BISHOP WITH A REMARKABLE MIND

"No one but one who is God-man can make the satisfaction by which man is saved."

In the Middle Ages, it was customary for bishops-elect to make a show of protest to signify their modesty. When Anselm, an Italian monk from Normandy, was chosen to become archbishop of Canterbury, he protested too. The episcopal staff had to be held against his clenched fist. But his refusal was sincere: for Anselm, becoming the archbishop meant less time for his studies. His instincts, in fact, have proved correct: Anselm is remembered today not merely as a great archbishop but as one of the most profound thinkers of the Middle Ages.

Pulled to higher office

The struggle between the scholarly life and that of high office began in Anselm's earliest years. His father, Gundulf, wanted to see him in politics and forbade him from entering the local abbey. When the abbot refused to accept the 15-year-old without his father's consent, Anselm prayed to become ill: he reasoned he could enter if he was in danger of death. He actually became seriously ill but was still refused admission.

After wandering Europe for years, looking to stretch his mind, Anselm settled at Bec, Normandy, to study under Lanfranc, a renowned scholar. Anselm felt here he could live the monastic life in obscurity, since the fame of Lanfranc would outshine his possible accomplishments.

But Anselm shined nonetheless. After three years, Lanfranc left the abbey to become archbishop of Canterbury, and Anselm replaced him as prior. He spent his time reading and reflecting on theological mysteries. Under his leadership, the monastery became famous for its scholastic excellence. When administrative duties interfered with his desired calling, he begged the local bishop to relieve him of some of his duties. Instead, the bishop told Anselm to prepare himself for higher office.

A proof of God

At Bec, Anselm made his first great intellectual contribution: he attempted to prove the existence of God. He set out his famous ontological argument in his *Proslogion*. God is "that which nothing greater can be thought," he argued. We cannot think of this entity as anything but existing because a god who exists is greater than one who merely is an idea. The argument, though contested almost as soon as it was written, has influenced philosophers even into the twentieth century.

Anselm also thought deeply on the relationship of faith and reason. He concluded that faith is the precondition of knowledge (*credo ut intelligam*, "I believe in order to understand"). He didn't despise reason; in fact he employed it in all his writings. He simply believed knowledge cannot lead to faith, and knowledge gained outside of faith is untrustworthy.

Squaring off against the king

In 1066 the Normans invaded England, and William the Conqueror gave the monastery at Bec several tracts of English land. Following the invasion, Anselm was summoned across the channel three times, where he impressed the English clergy. When Lanfranc died in 1089, they pressed William II to appoint Anselm to the archbishopric (formally the prerogative of the pope, but in practice the archbishop of Canterbury was the king's appointee). Anselm was reluctant, as was William II for political reasons, and the position went unfilled for four years. Then, one day, the king fell seriously ill and, fearing hell, appointed Anselm against his repeated pleas.

Anselm immediately exerted pressure on the king: he refused to do anything priestly for William until the king restored lands to Canterbury, recognized the archbishop as supreme in spiritual matters, and pledged his allegiance to Pope Urban II (who was embroiled in a power struggle with England). The king, also called William Rufus, agreed, but reneged on his promises when he recovered from his illness. In fact, he would not even let Anselm visit Rome. When Rufus denied permission the third time, Anselm blessed him and left England anyway.

Productive in exile

Anselm no doubt felt relieved. He had hated his position at Canterbury. He had avoided getting involved in disputes and often became ill when he was required to arbitrate disagreements. On the other hand, if one of his monks drew him aside and asked a theological question, he at once became enthralled and, as he explained his answer, his spirits rose. So while in exile, he again begged the pope to relieve him, but the pope replied that he needed Anselm's theological mind.

While in exile, Anselm wrote *Why Did God Become Man?*, which became the most influential treatise on the atonement in the Middle Ages. He argued for the "satisfaction theory." Early theologians, like Origen and Gregory of Nyssa, held to the "ransom theory": humankind was held captive to sin and death by Satan, at least until Christ paid the ransom through his death, and in the Resurrection, broke the power of Satan's chains. Anselm argued instead that it wasn't Satan who was owed something but God. In Adam, all human beings had sinned against divine holiness. Furthermore, being both finite and sinful, people were powerless to make proper restitution. That could only be accomplished by Christ: "No one but one who is God-man can make the satisfaction by which man is saved."

With the ascension of Henry I in 1100, Anselm was invited back to Canterbury. But when the king demanded homage from the bishops, Anselm refused and would not consecrate bishops who had done so. The controversy raged for six years, but Anselm eventually won.

For his last two years, he was able to study in relative peace. On his deathbed, Palm Sunday, 1107, Anselm told his monks he was ready to die, but before he did, he wanted to settle Augustine's question of the origin of the soul. "I do not know of anyone who will be able to do the work if I do not," he told them. But by Tuesday morning of Holy Week, he was dead.

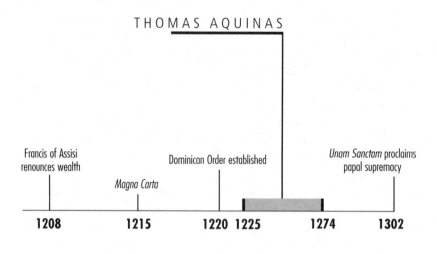

THOMAS AQUINAS

| Francis of Assisi renounces wealth | | Dominican Order established | | | Unam Sanctam proclaims papal supremacy |
| Magna Carta |

| 1208 | 1215 | 1220 1225 | 1274 | 1302 |

THEOLOGIANS

Thomas Aquinas

THE BRILLIANT "DUMB OX"

> *"In order that men might have knowledge of God, free of doubt and uncertainty, it was necessary for divine truth to be delivered to them by way of faith, being told to them as it were, by God himself who cannot lie."*

No one claimed Thomas Aquinas got famous on his looks. He was colossally fat, suffered from edema (dropsy), and one huge eye dwarfed his other. Nor was he a particularly dynamic, charismatic figure. Introspective and silent most of the time, when he did speak, it was often completely unrelated to the conversation. His classmates in college called him "the dumb ox." Today, recognized as the greatest theologian of the Middle Ages, he is called "the doctor of angels."

Temptations of a future theologian

He was born in an Italian castle to "Count Lundulf" of Aquino (though he was probably not a count) and Lundulf's wife, Theodora. At age 5, the pudgy boy was sent to the school at the nearby monastery of Monte Cassino (a community founded by

Benedict seven centuries earlier). At age 14, Thomas went to the University of Naples, where his Dominican teacher so impressed him that Thomas decided he, too, would join the new, study-oriented Dominican order.

His family fiercely opposed the decision (apparently wanting him to become an influential and financially secure abbot or archbishop rather than take a friar's vow of poverty). Thomas's brothers kidnapped him and confined him for 15 months; his family tempted him with a prostitute and an offer to buy him the post of archbishop of Naples.

All attempts failed, and Thomas went to Paris, medieval Europe's center of theological study. While there he fell under the spell of the famous teacher Albert the Great.

Wrestling with reason

In medieval Europe, all learning took place under the eye of the church, and theology reigned supreme in the sciences. Still, non-Christian philosophers like Aristotle the Greek, Averroes the Muslim, and Maimonides the Jew were studied alongside the Bible. Scholars were especially fascinated by Aristotle, whose works had been unknown in Europe for centuries. He seemed to have explained the entire universe, not by using Scripture but by his powers of observation and reason.

This emphasis on reason threatened to undermine traditional Christian beliefs. Christians had believed knowledge could come only through God's revelation, that only those to whom God chose to reveal his truths could understand the universe. How could this be squared with the obvious knowledge taught by these newly discovered philosophies?

Thomas wanted to explore this issue, and he determined to extract from Aristotle's writings what was acceptable to Christianity.

His thoughts consumed him. According to one story, he was dining with Louis IX of France (later "Saint" Louis), but while others engaged in conversation, he stared off into the distance lost in thought. Suddenly, he slammed down his fist on the table and exclaimed, "Ah! There's an argument that will destroy the Manichees!"

At the beginning of his massive *Summa Theologica* (or "A summation of theological knowledge"), Thomas stated, "In sacred theology, all things are treated from the standpoint of God." Thomas proceeded to distinguish between philosophy and theology, and between reason and revelation, though he emphasized that these did not contradict each other. Both are fountains of knowledge; both come from God.

Reason, said Thomas (following Aristotle), is based on sensory data—what we can see, feel, hear, smell, and touch. Revelation is based on more. While reason can lead us to believe in God—something that other theologians had already proposed—only revelation can show us God as he really is, the triune God of the Bible.

"In order that men might have knowledge of God, free of doubt and uncertainty," he wrote, "it was necessary for divine truth to be delivered to them by way of faith, being told to them as it were, by God himself who cannot lie."

In other words, someone looking at nature could tell that an intelligent creator exists. But that person would have no idea whether the creator was good or if he might work in history. Furthermore, though a person apart from Christianity can practice certain "natural virtues," only a believer can practice faith, hope, and love, the truly Christian virtues.

Volumes of straw

Thomas's writings (including the *Summa Contra Gentiles*, a manual for missionaries to the Muslims, which also contains several hymns) were attacked before and after his death. In 1277, the archbishop of Paris tried to have Thomas formally condemned, but the Roman Curia put a stop to the movement. Though Thomas was canonized in 1325, it took another 200 years before his teaching was hailed as preeminent and a chief bulwark against Protestantism. Four years after the Council of Trent, in which his writings play a prominent part, Thomas was declared a doctor of the church.

In 1879, the papal bull *Aeterni Patris* endorsed Thomism (Aquinas's theology) as an authentic expression of doctrine and said it should be studied by all students of theology. Today both Protestant and Catholic scholars draw upon his writings.

Thomas, however, would not necessarily be pleased. Toward the end of his life, he had a vision that forced him to drop his pen. Though he had experienced visions for years, this was something different. His secretary begged him to start writing again, but Aquinas replied, "I cannot. Such things have been revealed to me that what I have written seems but straw."

His *Summa Theologica*, one of the most influential writings of the Christian church, was left unfinished when he died three months later.

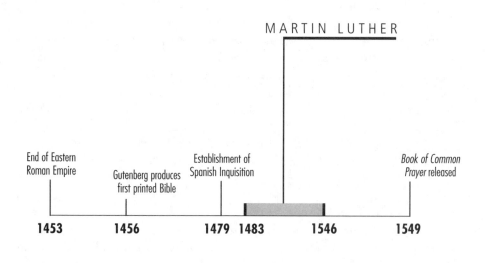

MARTIN LUTHER

End of Eastern Roman Empire	Gutenberg produces first printed Bible	Establishment of Spanish Inquisition			Book of Common Prayer released
1453	1456	1479	1483	1546	1549

THEOLOGIANS

Martin Luther

PASSIONATE REFORMER

"At last meditating day and night, by the mercy of God, I began to understand that the righteousness of God is that through which the righteous live by a gift of God, namely by faith. Here I felt as if I were entirely born again and had entered paradise itself through the gates that had been flung open."

In the sixteenth century, the world was divided about Martin Luther. One Catholic thought Martin Luther was a "demon in the appearance of a man." Another who first questioned Luther's theology later declared, "He alone is right!"

In our day, nearly 500 years hence, the verdict is nearly unanimous to the good. Both Catholics and Protestants affirm he was not only right about a great deal, but he changed the course of Western history for the better.

Thunderstorm conversion

Martin was born at Eisleben (about 120 miles southwest of modern Berlin) to Margaret and Hans Luder (as it was locally pronounced). He was raised in Mansfeld, where his father worked at the local copper mines.

Hans sent Martin to Latin school and then, when Martin was only 13 years old, to the University of Erfurt to study law. There Martin earned both his baccalaureate and master's degrees in the shortest time allowed by university statutes. He proved so adept at public debates that he earned the nickname "The Philosopher."

Then in 1505 his life took a dramatic turn. As the 21-year-old Luther fought his way through a severe thunderstorm on the road to Erfurt, a bolt of lightning struck the ground near him.

"Help me, St. Anne!" Luther screamed. "I will become a monk!"

The scrupulous Luther fulfilled his vow: he gave away all his possessions and entered the monastic life.

Spiritual breakthrough

Luther was extraordinarily successful as a monk. He plunged into prayer, fasting, and ascetic practices—going without sleep, enduring bone-chilling cold without a blanket, and flagellating himself. As he later commented, "If anyone could have earned heaven by the life of a monk, it was I."

Although he sought by these means to love God fully, he found no consolation. He was increasingly terrified of the wrath of God: "When it is touched by this passing inundation of the eternal, the soul feels and drinks nothing but eternal punishment."

During his early years, whenever Luther read what would become the famous "Reformation text"—Romans 1:17—his eyes were drawn not to the word faith, but to the word righteous. Who, after all, could "live by faith" but those who were already righteous?

The text was clear on the matter: "the righteous shall live by faith."

Luther remarked, "I hated that word, 'the righteousness of God,' by which I had been taught according to the custom and use of all teachers ... [that] God is righteous and punishes the unrighteous sinner." The young Luther could not live by faith because he was not righteous—and he knew it.

Meanwhile, he was ordered to take his doctorate in the Bible and become a professor at Wittenberg University. During lectures on the Psalms (in 1513 and 1514) and a study of the Book of Romans, he began to see a way through his dilemma. "At last meditating day and night, by the mercy of God, I ... began to understand that the righteousness of God is that through which the righteous live by a gift of God, namely by faith.... Here I felt as if I were entirely born again and had entered paradise itself through the gates that had been flung open."

On the heels of this new understanding came others. To Luther the church was no longer the institution defined by apostolic succession; instead it was the community of those who had been given faith. Salvation came not by the sacraments as such but by faith. The idea that human beings had a spark of goodness (enough to seek out God) was not a foundation of theology but was taught only by "fools." Humility was no longer a virtue that earned grace but a necessary response to the gift of grace. Faith no longer consisted of assenting to the church's teachings but of trusting the promises of God and the merits of Christ.

It wasn't long before the revolution in Luther's heart and mind played itself out in all of Europe.

"Here I stand"

It started on All Saints' Eve, 1517, when Luther publicly objected to the way preacher Johann Tetzel was selling indulgences. These were documents prepared by the church and bought by individuals either for themselves or on behalf of the dead that would release them from punishment due to their sins. As Tetzel preached, "Once the coin into the coffer clings, a soul from purgatory heavenward springs!"

Luther questioned the church's trafficking in indulgences and called for a public debate of 95 theses he had written. Instead, his 95 *Theses* spread across Germany as a call to reform, and the issue quickly became not indulgences but the authority of the church: Did the pope have the right to issue indulgences?

Events quickly accelerated. At a public debate in Leipzig in 1519, when Luther declared that "a simple layman armed with the Scriptures" was superior to both pope and councils without them, he was threatened with excommunication.

Luther replied to the threat with his three most important treatises: *The Address to the Christian Nobility, The Babylonian Captivity of the Church,* and *On the Freedom of a Christian.* In the first, he argued that all Christians were priests, and he urged rulers to take up the cause of church reform. In the second, he reduced the seven sacraments to two (baptism and the Lord's Supper). In the third, he told Christians they were free from the law (especially church laws) but bound in love to their neighbors.

In 1521 he was called to an assembly at Worms, Germany, to appear before Charles V, Holy Roman Emperor. Luther arrived prepared for another debate; he quickly discovered it was a trial at which he was asked to recant his views.

Luther replied, "Unless I can be instructed and convinced with evidence from the Holy Scriptures or with open, clear, and distinct grounds of reasoning ... then I cannot and will not recant, because it is neither safe nor wise to act against conscience." Then he added, "Here I stand. I can do no other. God help me! Amen."

By the time an imperial edict calling Luther "a convicted heretic" was issued, he had escaped to Wartburg Castle, where he hid for ten months.

Accomplishments of a sick man

In early spring of 1522, he was able to return to Wittenberg to lead, with the help of men like Philip Melanchthon, the fledgling reform movement.

Over the next years, Luther entered into more disputes, many of which divided friends and enemies. When unrest resulted in the Peasants' War of 1524–1525, he condemned the peasants and exhorted the princes to crush the revolt.

He married a runaway nun, Katharina von Bora, which scandalized many. (For Luther, the shock was waking up in the morning with "pigtails on the pillow next to me.")

He mocked fellow reformers, especially Swiss reformer Ulrich Zwingli, and used vulgar language in doing so.

In fact, the older he became, the more cantankerous he was. In his later years, he said some nasty things about, among others, Jews and popes and theological enemies, with words that are not fit to print.

Nonetheless, his lasting accomplishments also mounted: the translation of the Bible into German (which remains a literary and biblical hallmark); the writing of the hymn "A Mighty Fortress is Our God"; and publishing his *Larger* and *Smaller Catechism*, which have guided not just Lutherans but many others since.

His later years were spent often in both illness and furious activity (in 1531, though he was sick for six months and suffered from exhaustion, he preached 180 sermons, wrote 15 tracts, worked on his Old Testament translation, and took a number of trips). But in 1546, he finally wore out.

Luther's legacy is immense and cannot be adequately summarized. Every Protestant Reformer—like Calvin, Zwingli, Knox, and Cranmer—and every Protestant stream—Lutheran, Reformed, Anglican, and Anabaptist—were inspired by Luther in one way or another. On a larger canvas, his reform unleashed forces that ended the Middle Ages and ushered in the modern era.

It has been said that in most libraries, books by and about Martin Luther occupy more shelves than those concerned with any other figure except Jesus of Nazareth. Though difficult to verify, one can understand why it is likely to be true.

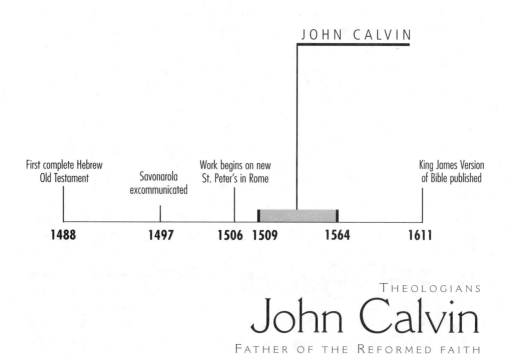

JOHN CALVIN

First complete Hebrew Old Testament	Savonarola excommunicated	Work begins on new St. Peter's in Rome			King James Version of Bible published
1488	**1497**	**1506**	**1509**	**1564**	**1611**

THEOLOGIANS

John Calvin

FATHER OF THE REFORMED FAITH

"I labored at the task [writing The Institutes] especially for our Frenchmen, for I saw that many were hungering and thirsting after Christ and yet that only a few had any real knowledge of him."

With his brother and sister and two friends, John Calvin fled Catholic France and headed to the free city of Strasbourg. It was the summer of 1536; Calvin had recently converted to the "evangelical" faith and had just published *The Institutes of the Christian Religion*, which articulated his Protestant views. He was a wanted man.

The party put up at an inn in Geneva, and word quickly passed to local church leader William Farel that the author of *The Institutes* was in town. Farel was ecstatic. He was desperate for help as he strove to organize a newly formed Protestant church in town. He rushed to the inn and pleaded with Calvin, arguing it was God's will he remain in the city.

Calvin said he was staying only one night. Besides, he was a scholar not a pastor. Farel, baffled and frustrated, swore a great oath that

God would curse all Calvin's studies unless he stayed in Geneva.

Calvin, a man of tender conscience, later reflected on this moment: "I felt as if God from heaven had laid his mighty hand upon me to stop me in my course—and I was so terror stricken that I did not continue my journey."

To this day, Calvin's name is associated, for good and for ill, with the city of Geneva. And Calvin's belief in God's election is his theological legacy to the church.

The "whole sum of godliness"

Calvin was born in 1509 in Noyon, France. His father, a lawyer, planned a career in the church for his son, and by the mid-1520s, Calvin had become a fine scholar. He spoke proficient Latin, excelled at philosophy, and qualified to take up the intensive study of theology in Paris.

Suddenly, though, his father changed his mind and decided John should achieve greatness in law. John acquiesced, and the next five or six years saw him at the University of

Orleans, attaining distinction in a subject he did not love. During these years, he dipped into Renaissance humanism. He learned Greek, read widely in the classics, and added Plato to the Aristotle he already knew. He developed a taste for writing so that by age 22, he had published a commentary on Seneca's *De Clementia*.

Then word of Luther's teaching reached France, and his life made an abrupt turn, though his own account is reticent and vague:

"He [God] tamed to teachableness a mind too stubborn for its years—for I was strongly devoted to the superstitions of the papacy that nothing less could draw me from such depths of mire. And so this mere taste of true godliness that I received set me on fire with such a desire to progress that I pursued the rest of my studies more coolly, although I did not give them up altogether."

He became marked out as a "Lutheran," and, when persecution arose in Paris (where he had returned to teach), he sought refuge in Basel. There he penned the first edition of a book that was to affect Western history as much as any other.

The Institutes of the Christian Religion was intended as an elementary manual for those who wanted to know something about the evangelical faith—"the whole sum of godliness and whatever it is necessary to know about saving doctrine." Calvin later wrote, "I labored at the task especially for our own Frenchmen, for I saw that many were hungering and thirsting after Christ and yet that only a very few had any real knowledge of him."

In *The Institutes*, Calvin outlined his views on the church, the sacraments, justification, Christian liberty, and political government. His unique and overarching theme is

God's sovereignty. He taught that original sin eradicated free will in people. Only by God's initiative can anyone begin to have faith and thus experience assurance of salvation.

In this and later editions, Calvin developed the doctrines of predestination, or election. More importantly, he argued for the indefectability of grace—that is, grace will never be withdrawn from the elect. This was Calvin's pastoral attempt to comfort new believers. In medieval Catholicism, believers remained anxious about their spiritual destinies and were required to perform more and more good works to guarantee their salvation. Calvin taught that once a believer understands he is chosen by Christ to eternal life, he will never have to suffer doubt again about salvation: "He will obtain an unwavering hope of final perseverance (as it is called), if he reckons himself a member of him who is beyond hazard of falling away."

God's city

After fleeing France to escape persecution, Calvin settled in Geneva at Farel's bidding. But after a mere 18 months, he and Farel were banished from the city for disagreeing with the city council. Calvin headed again for Strasbourg, where he pastored for three years and married Idellete de Bure, the widow of an Anabaptist, who brought with her two children.

By 1541 Calvin's reputation had spread: he wrote three other books and revised his *Institutes*. (Still more revisions came in 1550 and 1559, eventually amounting to 80 chapters.) He had become close friends with leading Reformers like Martin Bucer and Philip Melanchthon. He was asked to return to Geneva by city authorities, and he spent the rest of his life trying to help establish a theocratic society.

Calvin believed the church should faithfully mirror the principles laid down in Holy Scripture. In his *Ecclesiastical Ordinances* he argued that the New Testament taught four orders of ministry: pastors, doctors, elders, and deacons. Around these, the city was organized.

Pastors conducted the services, preached, administered the Sacraments, and cared for the spiritual welfare of parishioners. In each of the three parish churches, two Sunday services and a catechism class were offered. Every other weekday, a service was held—later on, every day. The Lord's Supper was celebrated quarterly.

The doctors, or teachers, lectured in Latin on the Old and New Testaments usually on Mondays, Wednesdays, and Fridays. The audience consisted mainly of the older schoolboys and ministers, but anyone could attend.

In every district, elders kept an eye on spiritual affairs. If they saw that so-and-so was frequently the worse for drink, or that Mr. X beat his wife, or that Mr. Y and Mrs. Z were seeing too much of each other, they admonished them in a brotherly manner. If the behavior didn't cease, they reported the matter to the Consistory, the church's governing body, which would summon the offender. Excommunication was a last resort and would remain in force until the offender repented.

Finally, social welfare was the charge of the deacons. They were the hospital management board, social security executives, and alms-house supervisors. The deacons were so effective, Geneva had no beggars.

The system worked so well for so many years that when John Knox visited Geneva in 1554, he wrote a friend that the city "is the most perfect school of Christ that ever was in the earth since the days of the apostles."

Unofficial authoritarian

Calvin, for his part, preached twice every Sunday and every day of alternate weeks. When not preaching, he lectured as the Old Testament professor three times a week. He took his place regularly on the Consistory, which met every Thursday. And he was either on committees or incessantly being asked for advice about matters relating to the deacons.

He was in no way the ruler or dictator of Geneva. He was appointed by the city council and paid by them. He could at any time have been dismissed by them (as he had been in 1538). He was a foreigner in Geneva, not even a naturalized citizen, until near the end of his life. His was a moral authority, stemming from his belief that, because he proclaimed the message of the Bible, he was God's ambassador, with divine authority behind him. As such, he was involved in much that went on in Geneva, from the city constitution to drains and heating appliances.

His role in the infamous execution of Michael Servetus in 1553, then, was not an official one. Servetus fled to Geneva to escape Catholic authorities: he had denied the Trinity, a blasphemy that merited death in the 1500s all over Europe. Geneva authorities didn't have any more patience with heresy than did Catholics, and with the full approval of Calvin, they put Servetus to the stake.

Calvin drove himself beyond his body's limits. When he could not walk the couple of hundred yards to church, he was carried in a chair to preach. When the doctor forbade him to go out in the winter air to the lecture room, he crowded the audience into his bedroom and gave lectures there. To those who would urge him to rest, he asked, "What? Would you have the Lord find me idle when he comes?"

His afflictions were intensified by opposition he sometimes faced. People tried to drown his voice by loud coughing while he preached; others fired guns outside the church. Men set their dogs on him. There were even anonymous threats against his life.

Calvin's patience gradually wore away. Even when he was patient, he was too unsympathetic sometimes. He showed little understanding, little kindness, and certainly little humor.

Calvin finally wore out in 1564. But his influence has not. Outside the church, his ideas have been blamed for and credited with (depending on your view) the rise of capitalism, individualism, and democracy. In the church, he has been a major influence on leading figures such as evangelist George Whitefield and theologian Karl Barth, as well as entire movements, such as Puritanism.

Day to day, church bodies with the names "Presbyterian" or "Reformed" (and even some Baptist groups) carry forward his legacy in local parishes all over the world.

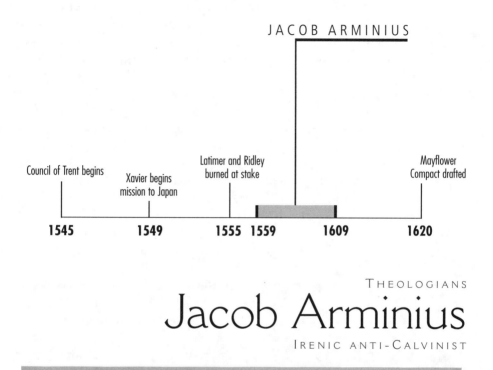

JACOB ARMINIUS

Council of Trent begins	Xavier begins mission to Japan	Latimer and Ridley burned at stake		Mayflower Compact drafted
1545	1549	1555 1559	1609	1620

Jacob Arminius

IRENIC ANTI-CALVINIST

"That teacher obtains my highest approbation who ascribes as much as possible to divine grace. . . ."

The year Jacob Arminius was born (in Oudewater, Holland), John Calvin was busy establishing the Genevan Academy to propagate his ideas of predestination. About that same time, Guido de Brès wrote the first edition of the Belgic Confession, which became one of the basic doctrinal standards of Dutch Calvinism. As Arminius grew up, arguments over Calvin's teachings interrupted those over Spanish rule. By the time Arminius was 14, William the Silent, Holland's king, was a Calvinist.

But by the time Arminius died, the theological landscape was shifting again, and Arminius's anti-Calvinist theology was spreading rapidly across Europe.

Irenic reformer

Arminius began to question Calvinism (especially its view of grace and predestination) in his early 20s, but rather than fight for his views at the Geneva Academy, where he had studied under Calvin's successor, Theodore Beza, he left quietly. When Genevan authorities became angry at Arminius's defense of French humanist Peter Ramus, Arminius left for Basel. He was offered a doctorate there but turned it down on the grounds that his youth (he was only 24 or 25) would bring dishonor to the title.

It was his study of the Epistle to the Romans as an Amsterdam minister that set Jacob Arminius firmly against Calvinism. Faith, he believed, was the cause of election: "It is an eternal and gracious decree of God in Christ, by which he determines to justify and adopt believers, and to endow them with eternal life but to condemn unbelievers, and impenitent persons."

Though he was accused of Pelagianism (an overemphasis on free will) and other heresies, his critics brought no proof of the charges.

"That teacher obtains my highest approbation who ascribes as much as possible to divine grace," he assured them, "provided he so pleads the cause of grace, as not to inflict

an injury on the justice of God, and not to take away the free will of that which is evil."

In 1606, while professor of theology at Leiden, Arminius delivered an address titled "On Reconciling Religious Dissensions among Christians":

"Religious dissension is the worst kind of disagreement," he wrote, "for it strikes the very altar itself. It engulfs everyone; each must take sides or else make a third party of himself."

Still, he continued to be disturbed by the determinism of Calvinism, and he called for a national synod to resolve the conflicts and to look critically at two crucial Calvinist documents, the Belgic Confession and the Heidelberg Catechism. The synod finally met but not until nine years after Arminius died (in good standing with the Dutch Reformed Church), and eight years after the Remonstrance was issued, which developed and articulated the key themes of what is today called Arminian theology: Christ died for all (not just the elect) and individuals can resist grace and even lose salvation. Arminianism since has influenced key figures in church history, such as John Wesley, the founder of Methodism.

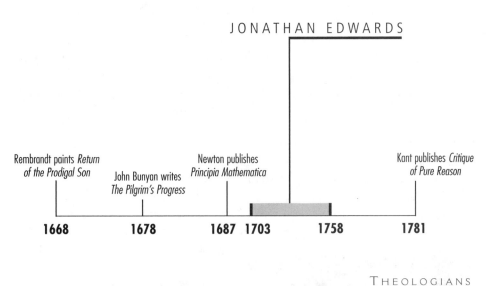

JONATHAN EDWARDS

| Rembrandt paints *Return of the Prodigal Son* | John Bunyan writes *The Pilgrim's Progress* | Newton publishes *Principia Mathematica* | | | Kant publishes *Critique of Pure Reason* |

| 1668 | 1678 | 1687 | 1703 | 1758 | 1781 |

Jonathan Edwards

AMERICA'S GREATEST THEOLOGIAN

> "[I wish] to lie low before God, as in the dust; that I might be nothing, and that God might be all, that I might become as a little child."

At age 14, Jonathan Edwards, already a student at Yale, read philosopher John Locke with more delight "than the most greedy miser finds when gathering up handfuls of silver and gold, from some newly discovered treasure."

He also was a young man with profound spiritual sensitivities. At age 17, after a period of distress, he said holiness was revealed to him as a ravishing, divine beauty. His heart panted "to lie low before God, as in the dust; that I might be nothing, and that God might be all, that I might become as a little child."

This combination of intellect and piety characterized Edward's whole life.

Dispassionate revivalist

Edwards was born in East Windsor, Connecticut, and he received his master's degree from Yale in 1722. He apprenticed for his grandfather, Solomon Stoddard, for two years before he became, in 1729, the sole preacher of the Northampton, Massachusetts, parish.

In the meantime, when he was 20, he had met Sarah Pierrepont. Their wedding followed four years of often agonizing courtship for the gawky and intense Edwards, but in the end, their marriage proved deeply satisfying to both. Edwards described it as an "uncommon union," and in a sermon on Genesis 2:21–25, he said, "When Adam rose from his deep sleep, God brought woman to him from near his heart." They eventually had 11 children.

In 1734 Edwards's preaching on justification by faith sparked a different sort of devotion: a spiritual revival broke out in his parish. In December there were six sudden conversions. By spring there were about thirty a week.

It was not due to theatrics. One observer wrote, "He scarcely gestured or even moved, and he made no attempt by the elegance of his style or the beauty of his pictures to gratify the taste and fascinate the imagination." Instead he convinced "with overwhelming weight of argument and with such intenseness of feeling."

Edwards kept a careful written account of his observations and noted them in *A Faithful Narrative of the Surprising Work of God* (1737), and his most effective sermons were published as *Justification by Faith* (1738), which were widely read in America and England. These works helped fuel the Great Awakening a few years later (1739–1741), during which thousands were moved by the preaching of Britain's George Whitefield. Whitefield had read Edwards's book and made it a point to visit him when he came to America. Edwards invited Whitefield to preach at his church and reported, "The congregation was extraordinarily melted ... almost the whole assembly being in tears for a great part of the time." The "whole assembly" included Edwards himself.

During the Great Awakening, Edwards contributed perhaps the most famous sermon in American history, "Sinners in the Hands of an Angry God." Unfortunately it has since cast Edwards as an emotional and judgmental revivalist, when in fact he preached it as dispassionately as any of his sermons.

In spite of his dispassionate style, Edwards insisted that true religion is rooted in the affections, not in reason. He defended the emotional outbursts of the Great Awakening, especially in *Treatise on Religious Affections* (1746), a masterpiece of psychological and spiritual discernment, and in *Some Thoughts Concerning the Present Revival of Religion in New England* (in which he included an account of his wife's spiritual awakening).

And in a day when psalm-singing was almost the only music to be heard in congregational churches, Edwards encouraged the singing of new Christian hymns, notably those of Isaac Watts.

Newton and the Bible

Edwards regarded personal conversion as critical, so he insisted that only persons who had made a profession of faith, which included a description of their conversion experience, could receive Communion. This reversed the policy of his grandfather and alienated his congregation, which ousted him in 1750.

For the next few years, he was a missionary pastor to Native Americans in Stockbridge, Massachusetts, and wrote, among other theological treatises, *Freedom of the Will* (1754), a brilliant defense of divine sovereignty. In it he argued that we are free to do whatever we want, but we will never want to do God's will without a vision of his divine nature imparted by the Spirit. Fascinated by Newtonian physics and enlightened by Scripture, Edwards believed that God's providence was literally the binding force of atoms—that the universe would collapse and disappear unless God sustained its existence from one moment to the next. Scripture affirmed his view that Christ is "upholding all things by his word of power" (Heb. 1:3 RSV). Such were the fruits of his lifelong habit of rising at 4:00 a.m. and studying 13 hours a day.

The College of New Jersey (later Princeton) called him as president in 1758. But soon after his arrival, Edwards died of the new smallpox vaccination. He was 55.

He left no small legacy: Edwards is considered (some would say with Reinhold Niebuhr) America's greatest theologian.

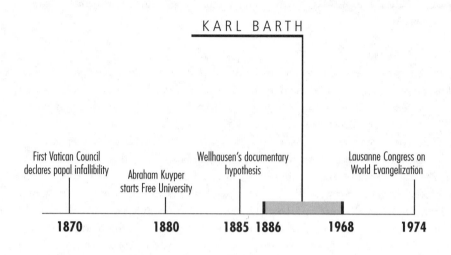

KARL BARTH

First Vatican Council declares papal infallibility	Abraham Kuyper starts Free University	Wellhausen's documentary hypothesis		Lausanne Congress on World Evangelization
1870	1880	1885 1886	1968	1974

THEOLOGIANS

Karl Barth

COURAGEOUS THEOLOGIAN

> *"Faith is awe in the presence of the divine incognito; it is the love of God that is aware of the qualitative difference between God and man and God and the world."*

"The gospel is not a truth among other truths. Rather, it sets a question mark against all truths." Karl Barth not only said this, he spent his life setting question marks, in the name of Christ, against all manner of "truths." In the process, he did nothing less than alter the course of modern theology.

Shocking liberalism

He started out life conventionally enough: he was born in Basel, Switzerland, the son of Fritz Barth (pronounced "bart"), a professor of New Testament and early church history at Bern, and Anna Sartorius. He studied at some of the best universities: Bern, Berlin, Tübingen, and Marburg. At Berlin he sat under the famous liberals of the day (like historian Adolph von Harnack), most of whom taught an optimistic Christianity that focused not so much on Jesus Christ and the Cross as the fatherhood of God and the brotherhood of man.

After serving a Geneva curacy from 1909 to 1911, Barth was appointed to a working-class parish in Switzerland, and in 1913 he married Nell Hoffman, a talented violinist (they eventually had one daughter and four sons).

As he pastored, he noted with alarm that Germany was becoming increasingly militaristic and that his former professors were supportive of this. Barth, dismayed with the moral weakness of liberal theology, plunged into a study of the Bible, especially Paul's Epistle to the Romans. He also visited Moravian preacher Christoph Frederick Blumhardt and came away with an overwhelming conviction about the victorious reality of Christ's resurrection—which deeply influenced his theology.

Out of this emerged his *Commentary on the Epistle to the Romans* (1919). He sounded themes that had been muted in liberal theology. Liberal theology had domesticated God into the patron saint of human institutions and values. Instead, Barth wrote of the "crisis," that is, God's judgment under which all the world stood; he pounded on the theme of God's absolute sovereignty, of his complete freedom in initiating his revelation in Jesus Christ.

He spoke dialectically, in paradox, to shock readers into seeing the radicalness of the gospel: "Faith is awe in the presence of the divine incognito; it is the love of God that is aware of the qualitative difference between God and man and God and the world."

The first of six heavily revised editions followed in 1922. It rocked the theological community. Barth later wrote, "As I look back upon my course, I seem to myself as one who, ascending the dark staircase of a church tower and trying to steady himself, reached for the banister, but got hold of the bell rope instead. To his horror he had then to listen to what the great bell had sounded over him and not over him alone." Liberal theologians gasped in horror and attacked Barth furiously. But Barth had given that form of liberalism a mortal wound.

His theology came to be known as "dialectical theology," or "the theology of crisis"; it initiated a trend toward neo-orthodoxy in Protestant theology.

In 1921 Barth was appointed professor of Reformed theology at the University of Göttingen, and later to chairs at Münster (1925) and Bonn (1930). He published works critiquing nineteenth-century Protestant theology and produced a celebrated study of Anselm.

In 1931 he began the first book of his massive *Church Dogmatics*. It grew year by year out of his class lectures; though incomplete, it eventually filled four volumes in 12 parts, printed with 500 to 700 pages each. Many pastors in the 1930s, '40s, and '50s, desperate for an antidote to liberalism, eagerly awaited the publication of each book.

Fascist idolatry

Barth fought not just with liberals but allies who challenged some of his extreme conclusions. When Emil Brunner proposed that God revealed himself not just in the Bible but in nature as well (though not in a saving way), Barth replied in 1934 with an article titled, "No! An Answer to Emil Brunner." Barth believed that such a "natural theology" was the root of the religious syncretism and anti-Semitism of the "German Christians"—

those who supported Hitler's national socialism.

By this time, Barth was immersed in the German church struggle. He was a founder of the so-called Confessing Church, which reacted vigorously against the ideology of "blood and soil" and the Nazis' attempt to create a "German Christian" church. The 1934 Barmen Declaration, largely written by Barth, pitted the revelation of Jesus Christ against the "truth" of Hitler and national socialism:

"Jesus Christ ... is the one Word of God.... We reject the false doctrine, as though the Church could and would have to acknowledge as a source of its proclamation, apart from and beside this one Word of God, still other events and powers, figures and truths, as God's revelation."

When Barth refused to take the oath of unconditional allegiance to the Führer, he was fired. He was offered the chair of theology in his native Basel, however, and from there he continued to champion the causes of the Confessing Church, the Jews, and oppressed people everywhere.

Pastor Karl

After the war, Barth engaged in controversies regarding baptism (though a Reformed theologian, he rejected infant baptism), hermeneutics, and the demythologizing program of Rudolf Bultmann (which denied the historical nature of Scripture, instead believing it a myth whose meaning could heal spiritual anxiety).

Barth also made regular visits to the prison in Basel, and his sermons to the prisoners, *Deliverance to the Captives*, reveal his unique combination of evangelical passion and social concern that characterized all his life.

When asked in 1962 (on his one visit to America) how he would summarize the essence of the millions of words he had published, he replied, "Jesus loves me this I know, for the Bible tells me so."

Though Barth made it possible for theologians again to take the Bible seriously, American evangelicals have been skeptical of Barth because he refused to consider the written Word "infallible" (he believed only Jesus was). Others gave up on Barth's theology because it overemphasized God's transcendance (to the point that some former Barthians began championing the "death of God"). Nonetheless, he remains the most important theologian of the twentieth century.

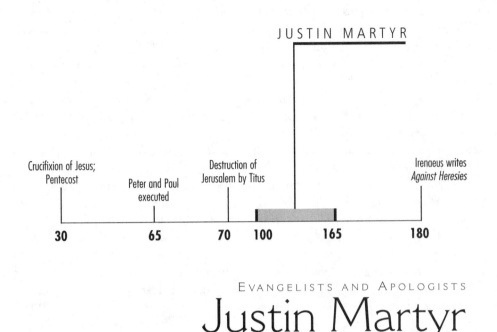

JUSTIN MARTYR

Crucifixion of Jesus; Pentecost	Peter and Paul executed	Destruction of Jerusalem by Titus		Irenaeus writes *Against Heresies*
30	65	70	100 165	180

EVANGELISTS AND APOLOGISTS

Justin Martyr

DEFENDER OF THE "TRUE PHILOSOPHY"

"I fell in love with the prophets and these men who had loved Christ; I reflected on all their words and found that this philosophy alone was true and profitable."

When Justin was arrested for his faith in Rome, the prefect asked him to denounce his faith by making a sacrifice to the gods. Justin replied, "No one who is rightly minded turns from true belief to false."

It was in one sense an easy answer for Justin because he had spent most of his adult life discerning the true from the false.

Fire in the soul

Justin was born in the Roman city of Flavia Neapolis (ancient Shechem in Samaria). Raised by pagan parents, he sought to find life's meaning in the philosophies of his day. This only brought a series of disappointments.

His first teacher was a Stoic who "knew nothing of God and did not even think knowledge of him to be necessary." There followed a Peripatetic (itinerant philosopher), who seemed most interested in getting his fees. Then came a Pythagorean, but his required course of music, astronomy, and geometry seemed far too slow. Finally, Platonism, though intellectually demanding, proved unfulfilling for Justin's hungry heart.

At last, about A.D. 130, after a conversation with an old man, his life was transformed: "A fire was suddenly kindled in my soul. I fell in love with the prophets and these men who had loved Christ; I reflected on all their words and found that this philosophy alone was true and profitable. That is how and why I became a philosopher. And I wish that everyone felt the same way that I do."

Justin continued to wear his philosopher's cloak, seeking to reconcile faith and reason. His teaching ministry took him first to Ephesus (c. 132), where he held a disputation with Trypho, a Jew, about the true interpretation of Scripture. *The Dialogue with Trypho* teaches three main points: the Old Covenant is passing away to make place for the New; the Logos is the God of the Old Testament; and the Gentiles are the new Israel.

Later Justin moved to Rome, founded a Christian school, and wrote two bold apologies (i.e., defenses—from the Greek *apologia*). Justin's *First Apology*, addressed to Emperor Antoninus Pius, was published in 155 and attempted to explain the faith. Christianity was not a threat to the state, he asserted, and should be treated as a legal religion. He wrote "on behalf of men of every nation who are unjustly hated and reviled."

Justin argued that Christians are, in fact, the emperor's "best helpers and allies in securing good order, convinced as we are that no wicked man ... can be hidden from God, and that everyone goes to eternal punishment or salvation in accordance with the character of his actions." He further showed that Christianity is superior to paganism, that Christ is prophecy fulfilled, and that paganism is actually a poor imitation of the true religion.

A picture of worship

However, this apology has gained the most attention for modern readers because in it Justin records detailed descriptions of early Christian worship (to show unbelievers that Christianity was not subversive). The most famous passage is this:

> On the day called Sunday there is a gathering together in the same place of all who live in a given city or rural district. The memoirs of the apostles or the writings of the prophets are read, as long as time permits. Then when the reader ceases, the president in a discourse admonishes and urges the imitation of these good things. Next we all rise together and send up prayers.
>
> When we cease from our prayer, bread is presented and wine and water. The president in the same manner sends up prayers and thanksgivings, according to his ability, and the people sing out their assent, saying the 'Amen.' A distribution and participation of the elements for which thanks have been given is made to each person, and to those who are not present they are sent by the deacons.
>
> Those who have means and are willing, each according to his own choice, gives what he wills, and what is collected is deposited with the president. He provides for the orphans and widows, those who are in need on account of sickness or some other

cause, those who are in bonds, strangers who are sojourning, and in a word he becomes the protector of all who are in need.

Justin's *Second Apology* was written soon after Marcus Aurelius became emperor in 161. In these writings, Justin tried to show that the Christian faith alone was truly rational. He taught that the Logos (Word) became incarnate to teach humanity truth and to redeem people from the power of the demons.

Four years later, Justin and his disciples were arrested for their faith. When the prefect threatened them with death, Justin said, "If we are punished for the sake of our Lord Jesus Christ, we hope to be saved." They were taken out and beheaded. Since he gave his life for the "true philosophy," Justin has been surnamed Martyr.

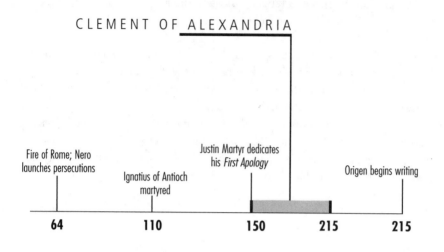

CLEMENT OF ALEXANDRIA

Fire of Rome; Nero
launches persecutions

Ignatius of Antioch
martyred

Justin Martyr dedicates
his *First Apology*

Origen begins writing

64   110   150   215   215

EVANGELISTS AND APOLOGISTS

Clement of Alexandria

THEOLOGIAN FOR THE INTELLIGENTSIA

> *"Let us remove the ignorance and darkness that spreads like a mist over our sight, and let us get a vision of the true God."*

New Age thought is really not all that new, nor is the twentieth century the first time Christians have been forced to respond to this strain of religious teaching. One early form of New Age type thinking was Gnosticism, which flourished in the second and third centuries, and one of the most effective Christian responders was Clement of Alexandria.

The "new philosophy"

He was born Titus Flavius Clemens, most likely to pagan parents in Athens. As an adult, he sought out truth from a number of teachers in Greece, lower Italy, Syria, Palestine, and finally Alexandria, a city of perhaps one million inhabitants. There he sat under Pantaenus, who taught Christianity in light of the scientific teachings of the day.

In about 190, Clement opened his own "school," which was

more like a cycle of conferences drawn out over years. He taught a "new philosophy" that addressed the cultural and philosophical concerns of the day. The "philosophy" was not all that new—Christianity—but Clement's teaching of it was. He wrote three books to expound his views.

His *Exhortation to the Greeks* was an introductory philosophical work for the unbaptized, in which he attempted to show the reasonableness of the Christian faith. "Away then, away with our forgetfulness of the truth!" he exhorted. "Let us remove the ignorance and darkness that spreads like a mist over our sight, and let us get a vision of the true God."

In *Instructor*, he outlined the specific duties and ethics taught by the "Instructor" (i.e., the Logos, or Christ): "Our superintendence in instruction and discipline is the office of the Word [Logos, in Greek], from whom we learn frugality and humility, and all that pertains to love of freedom, love of man, and love of excellence."

His *Miscellanies* is a multicolored patchwork of teachings in advanced philosophy, ethics, and disciplined instruction for "Christian Gnostics" to lead them into esoteric knowledge (*gnosis*): "The man of understanding and discernment is, then, a Gnostic. And his business is not abstinence from what is evil ... or the doing of good out of fear ... nor any more is he to do so from hope of promised recompense ... but only the doing of good out of love, and for the sake of its own excellence is the Gnostic's choice."

If this sounds mystical, it is. Clement sought to reach the literati of his day, and Gnosticism was the rage. He sought to present the Christian faith in terms these people could recognize.

The problem of wealth

Clement didn't spend all his time on pagans but also sought to help the church. One of history's most famous sermons is Clement's. In it he tried to address a recurring problem in church history, but one which Christians were facing for the first time in his day: in light of Jesus' parable of the rich young ruler, what should rich Christians do with their wealth? Clement took an approach that has been debated but usually followed ever since.

Clement puts the issue this way: "Since possessions of one kind are within the soul, and those of another kind outside it, and these latter appear to be good if the soul uses them well, but if they are badly used—which of the two is it that he [Jesus] asks us to renounce?"

He answers, "The Lord admits the use of outward things, bidding us put away, not the means of living, but the things that use these badly. And these are ... the infirmities and passions of the soul."

In other words, it's our attitude toward possessions (i.e., greed), not the possessions themselves, that are the problem.

Clement also advocated using the visual arts in worship at a time when some early Christians were reluctant to employ painting or drawing, fearing attention to their work might constitute idolatry. Clement concluded that Christians are not to depict pagan gods, nor sword or bow, nor wine cups, nor reminders of sexual immorality.

Instead, "Let our emblem be a dove, or a fish, or a ship running before the wind, or a musician's lyre, or a ship's anchor. And if there be a fisherman, he will remind us of an apostle, and little children being drawn up out of the water."

In addition, one of the earliest Christian hymns is that appended to Clement's *Instructor*, "Hymn of the Savior Christ." Its earliest rendering in English verse (in 1846) appears in many hymnals today as "Shepherd of Tender Youth." Three stanzas translated from the original Greek bring a vivid picture of the praise-life of the Alexandrian church:

Bridle-bit of untamed colts,
Wing of birds that do not go astray,
Sure Tiller of ships,
Shepherd of the King's lambs!
Gather your children
Who live in simplicity.
Let them sing in holiness.
Let them celebrate with sincerity,
With a mouth that knows no evil,
The Christ who guides his children!

His ministry, both in and outside the Alexandrian church, was cut abruptly short in 202, when persecution broke out during the reign of Emperor Septimius Severus. Clement was compelled to flee the city. He settled in Cappadocia, and by 215 had died.

But his influence did not end when his life did. He was, according to tradition, the teacher of Origen, a theologian of immense influence in the next generation. His mystical theology may have also influenced Psuedo-Dionysius, who was the theologian who shaped medieval mysticism. And in the 1700s, John Wesley drew on Clement's depiction of the true Gnostic for help in describing Christian perfection.

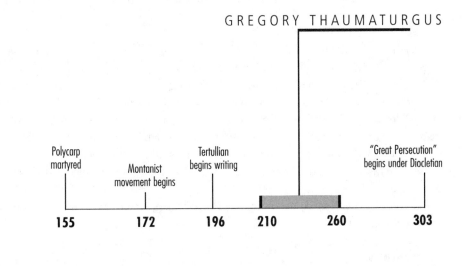

GREGORY THAUMATURGUS

Polycarp martyred	Montanist movement begins	Tertullian begins writing			"Great Persecution" begins under Diocletian
155	172	196	210	260	303

EVANGELISTS AND APOLOGISTS

Gregory Thaumaturgus
"THE WONDER WORKER"

> "Gregory was a great and conspicuous lamp, illuminating the church of God."
> — Basil the Great

Parents today sometimes worry that their children will go off to college and return as converts to some strange, new religion. That's exactly what happened 1,700 years ago to Gregory of Pontus (named Theodore at his birth), only the strange, new religion was Christianity.

Born into an affluent pagan family in Neocaesarea (in modern Turkey), Gregory studied law and the traditional Greek and Roman classics. Then he and his brother were sent for further study to Caesarea in Palestine, where they enrolled in the school of the great Christian thinker Origen. Gregory came to learn pagan philosophy; his teacher converted him (and his brother, Athenodorus) to Christianity.

When Gregory returned home, he found a Christian community of 17 people waiting for him. Soon afterward, Gregory was elected bishop. Although his training was in speculative theology, Gregory's pastoral work was concerned with practical applications of the faith. His skills were such that some of his flock soon attributed miracles to him—hence his nickname "The Wonder Worker."

One legend tells how two brothers quarreled over possession of a lake and asked Gregory to arbitrate between them; Gregory is said to have divided the lake into two bodies of water, giving one to each brother. In another legend, he moved an entire mountain.

"Gregory was a great and conspicuous lamp, illuminating the church of God," wrote Basil. "He possessed, from the co-operation of the Spirit, a formidable power against the demons, that he turned the course of rivers by giving them orders in the name of Christ; and that his predictions of the future made him the equal of other prophets."

By both his friends and his enemies, Basil concludes, Gregory was regarded "as another Moses."

Legends or no, Gregory's leadership must have been great, because during his ministry, most of the city of Pontus converted to Christianity.

The help of Mary

Doctrinal conflicts required him to participate in several church councils that condemned false teaching. Though much more of a practical pastor than a theological writer, Gregory's writings are strong defenses of Trinitarian doctrine. According to Eastern tradition, his principal work, *The Exposition of Faith*, was given to him in a vision of John the Evangelist with the intercession of the Virgin Mary—the first recorded Marian apparition.

But despite his pastoral care of the community, many deserted during the persecution ordered by Emperor Decius in 250. Gregory himself fled into the surrounding mountains with many from his flock. In another of the legends, his enemies pursued Gregory and his deacon to one of their hiding places, but when they arrived, the Christians had been turned into trees.

When the persecution ceased, Gregory returned to Neocaesarea, only to have his flock further decimated by a plague. Then Goths sacked his beloved home city. By his death, his congregation is said to have dwindled down to 17—the same number as when he became bishop.

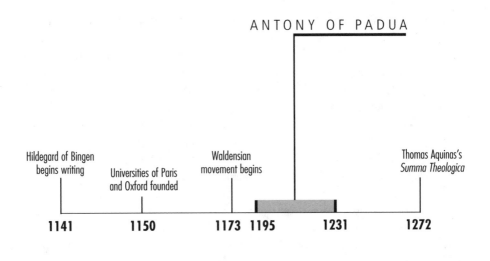

ANTONY OF PADUA

Hildegard of Bingen begins writing	Universities of Paris and Oxford founded	Waldensian movement begins		Thomas Aquinas's *Summa Theologica*
1141	1150	1173 1195	1231	1272

EVANGELISTS AND APOLOGISTS

Antony of Padua
"THE HAMMER OF HERETICS"

> "It pleases me that you teach sacred theology to the brothers, as long as—in the words of the Rule—you 'do not extinguish the Spirit of prayer and devotion' with study of this kind."
> —Francis of Assisi

Antony's mentor, Francis of Assisi, had a deep suspicion of scholarship, but he quickly recognized that his new disciple had a brilliant mind and that it would be a shame to waste such a talent.

"Brother Francis wishes health to Brother Antony, my bishop," he wrote. "It pleases me that you teach sacred theology to the brothers, as long as—in the words of the Rule—you 'do not extinguish the Spirit of prayer and devotion' with study of this kind."

With this blessing, Antony went on to a life of teaching and to preaching, becoming the most popular and effective preacher of his day.

Dying to be killed

Born in Lisbon, Portugal, and baptized Fernando, he joined an

Augustinian monastery at age 15.

In about 1220, some relics arrived in town: the bodies of Franciscan friars martyred in Morocco, whom Antony had known by name. Antony was electrified by the prospect of dying for Christ himself, and he hurried to the Franciscan friary in town.

"If I may go to Morocco and imitate these brothers," he pleaded, "I will gladly join you."

He was released from his Augustinian order and took the name Antony when he joined the Franciscans. Within months, he was sailing for Morocco to join the martyrs in glorious death. However, he became deathly ill with malaria en route and was forced to return to Europe. On the trip home, a violent storm arose, and Antony's ship was blown all the way to Sicily, just in time to join another group of Franciscan friars heading to Assisi to hear Francis speak.

For the next year, Antony lived a simple life of quiet prayer and work at a Franciscan hermitage. He cleaned, gardened, set tables, washed dishes. In 1222 he attended an ordination service, where the scheduled preacher failed to show. Antony was ordered to speak, and though slow and unassured at first, by the end of his sermon, everyone in attendance was surprised at his power and brilliance. It wasn't long, with Francis's permission, before he was teaching other Franciscans.

Preacher to the poor

For the next few years, Antony held various administrative posts, but he was always on the road, preaching and teaching. He was phenomenally popular, sometimes attracting crowds of up to 30,000. When he approached a town he was about to preach in, the shops closed and the markets suspended business.

In his messages, he often attacked the rich for their oppression of the poor, and he lambasted the moneylenders for charging exorbitant interest. He also spoke pointedly to church leaders if he knew they were not defending the poor.

Antony's second favorite topic was heresy. So successful was he at converting heretics in Southern France and Northern Italy, hotbeds for the dualistic Cathari, he was called "The Hammer of the Heretics." He backed up his arguments with an astonishing knowledge of Scripture.

"He is truly the Ark of the Covenant and the treasury of Holy Scripture," said Pope Gregory, who added that if all the Bibles of the world were lost, Antony could surely rewrite them.

Miracle worker

Part of Antony's draw has been attributed to miracle-working. Medieval legends abound: in one, he preaches to fish, who hold their heads above water to listen to him. In another, he preaches so eloquently, "that all who were assembled ... although they spoke different languages, clearly and distinctly heard and understood every one of his words as if he had spoken in each of their languages."

In 1230 Antony settled in Padua. The city was soon so overwhelmed with the crowds that came to hear him that the citizens ran out of accommodation and food.

Nevertheless, Antony's preaching reportedly had a tremendous effect: debtors were freed from prison, relationships were mended, and everyone vowed to live a better life.

The furious pace of Antony's life eventually took its toll, however. At only 36 years old, he died. Within six months of his death, Antony was canonized.

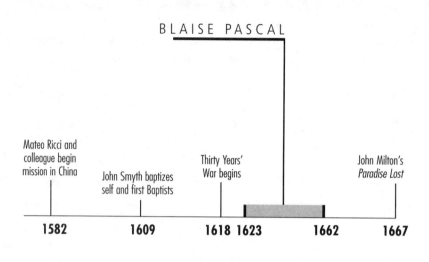

BLAISE PASCAL

Mateo Ricci and colleague begin mission in China

John Smyth baptizes self and first Baptists

Thirty Years' War begins

John Milton's Paradise Lost

| 1582 | 1609 | 1618 1623 | 1662 | 1667 |

EVANGELISTS AND APOLOGISTS

Blaise Pascal

SCIENTIFIC AND SPIRITUAL PRODIGY

> *"The heart has its reasons, which reason does not know at all."*

"Who needs God? Man can make it on his own." So claimed Reason, the philosophy that captured the imagination of seventeenth-century France. Its champions, Voltaire and Descartes, among others, tried to fashion a worldview ruled completely by reason.

French mathematician and physicist Blaise Pascal, though raised in the heyday of Enlightenment thought, found reason inadequate: "Reason's last step is the recognition that there are an infinite number of things which are beyond it." He concluded, "The heart has its reasons, which reason does not know at all"— a statement that soon became the chief critique of rationalism and the starting point for a defense of the Christian faith that still influences people today.

Scientific prodigy

Pascal's mother died when he was 3, and his father moved the family from Clermont-Ferrand, France, to Paris, where he homeschooled Blaise and his sister. By age 10, Pascal was doing original experiments in mathematics and physical science. To help his father, who was a tax collector, he invented the first calculating device (some call it the first "computer").

With this last invention, he had made a name for himself (at age 19!) and began his richly diverse scientific career. He tested the theories of Galileo and Torricelli (who discovered the principles of the barometer), culminating in his famous law of hydraulics, which states that pressure on the surface of a fluid is transmitted equally to every point in a fluid. He added important papers on the vacuum, on the weight and density of air, and the arithmetic triangle. He developed the theory of probability, which is still used today. He invented the syringe, the hydraulic lift, and is credited with inventing the wristwatch and mapping out the first bus route in Paris. It is said Pascal was embarrassed by his multiple talents.

"Night of fire"

All the while, Pascal was exploring the spiritual world, which was undergoing a revolution across Europe. While pietism flourished in Germany, and Wesleyan holiness spread through England, Catholic France was feeling the effects of Jansenism—a form of Augustinianism that taught predestination and divine grace, rather than good works, as vital for salvation.

In 1646 Pascal came in contact with Jansenism and introduced it to his sister, Jacqueline, who eventually entered the convent of Port-Royal, a center of Jansenism. Pascal, however, continued to struggle spiritually: he wrestled with the dichotomy between the world and God.

Then on November 23, 1654, Pascal experienced a "definitive conversion" during a vision of the crucifixion:

"From about half-past ten in the evening until about half-past twelve ... FIRE ... God of Abraham, the God of Isaac, the God of Jacob, and not of the philosophers and savants. Certitude. Certitude. Feeling. Joy. Peace."

He recorded the experience (called the "Mémorial") on a piece of parchment, which he carried with him the rest of his life, sewed inside his coat. He began a life-long association with Port-Royal—though he, unlike his sister, never became a "solitaire."

Passion for Christ

His greatest works are not only masterpieces of French prose but sterling defenses of the Christian faith.

Les Provinciales, 18 essays regarded as brilliant irony and satire, attacked the Jesuits and defended Jansenists' demand for a return to morality and Augustine's belief in divine grace. The Catholic church placed Les Provinciales on the Index, condemning it but failing to quell the controversy it stirred.

Pensées, a collection of Pascal's "thoughts" he intended to present as a Christian apology, was published after his death. In it, he portrayed humankind as suspended between wretchedness and happiness, and helpless without God. People try to avoid the abyss by engaging in distractions. Pascal denounced the idea that reason and science alone can lead a person to God. Only by experiencing Christ can people know God.

Belief comes through the "heart," which for Pascal was not merely feelings and sentiment but the intuition that understands without having to use reason. And God's grace makes it happen: "Do not be surprised at the sight of simple people who believe without argument. God makes them love him and hate themselves. He inclines their hearts to believe. We shall never believe with a vigorous and unquestioning faith unless God touches our hearts; and we shall believe as soon as he does so."

In the *Pensées*, Pascal also presents his famous argument for faith: the wager. Since reason cannot give one absolute certainty, he argued, every person must risk belief in something. When it comes to the Christian faith, he said, a wise person will gamble on it because, "If you win, you win everything; if you lose, you lose nothing."

Voltaire and other scholars denounced Pascal as a cheerless fanatic. Cheerless or not, he did live most of his life with a frail body, and his many illnesses finally took their toll at age 39.

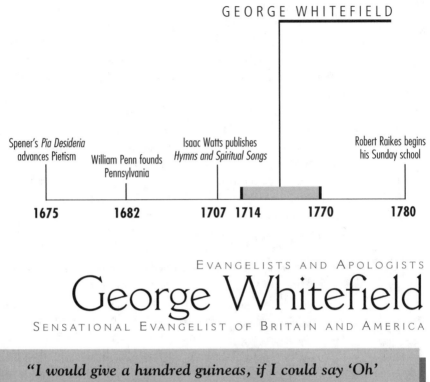

GEORGE WHITEFIELD

Spener's *Pia Desideria* advances Pietism

William Penn founds Pennsylvania

Isaac Watts publishes *Hymns and Spiritual Songs*

Robert Raikes begins his Sunday school

| 1675 | 1682 | 1707 | 1714 | 1770 | 1780 |

EVANGELISTS AND APOLOGISTS

George Whitefield

SENSATIONAL EVANGELIST OF BRITAIN AND AMERICA

> *"I would give a hundred guineas, if I could say 'Oh' like Mr. Whitefield."*
>
> — Actor David Garrick

Largely forgotten today, George Whitefield was probably the most famous religious figure of the eighteenth century. Newspapers called him the "marvel of the age." Whitefield was a preacher capable of commanding thousands on two continents through the sheer power of his oratory. In his lifetime, he preached at least 18,000 times to perhaps 10 million hearers.

Born thespian

As a boy in Gloucester, England, he read plays insatiably and often skipped school to practice for his schoolboy performances. Later in life, he repudiated the theater, but the methods he imbibed as a young man emerged in his preaching.

He put himself through Pembroke College, Oxford, by waiting on the wealthier students. While there, he fell in with a group of pious "methodists"—who called themselves "the Holy Club"—led by the Wesley brothers, John and Charles. Under their influence, he experienced a "new birth" and decided to become a missionary to the new Georgia colony on the other side of the Atlantic Ocean.

When the voyage was delayed, Whitefield was ordained a deacon in the Anglican church and began preaching around London. He was surprised to discover that wherever he spoke, crowds materialized and hung on every word.

These were no ordinary sermons. He portrayed the lives of biblical characters with a realism no one had seen before. He cried, he danced, he screamed. Among the enthralled was David Garrick, then the most famous actor in Britain. "I would give a hundred guineas," he said, "if I could say 'Oh' like Mr. Whitefield."

Once, when preaching on eternity, he suddenly stopped his message, looked around, and exclaimed, "Hark! Methinks I hear [the saints] chanting their everlasting hallelujahs, and spending an eternal day in echoing forth triumphant songs of joy. And do you not long, my brethren, to join this heavenly choir?"

Whitefield eventually made it to Georgia but stayed for only three months. When he returned to London, he found many churches closed to his unconventional methods. He then experimented with outdoor, extemporaneous preaching, where no document or wooden pulpit stood between him and his audience.

Spellbound crowds

In 1739, Whitefield set out for a preaching tour of the American colonies. Whitefield selected Philadelphia—the most cosmopolitan city in the New World—as his first American stop. But even the largest churches could not hold the 8,000 who came to see him, so he took them outdoors. Every stop along Whitefield's trip was marked by record audiences, often exceeding the population of the towns in which he preached. Whitefield was often surprised at how crowds "so scattered abroad, can be gathered at so short a warning."

The crowds were also aggressive in spirit. As one account tells it, crowds "elbowed, shoved, and trampled over themselves to hear of 'divine things' from the famed Whitefield."

Once Whitefield started speaking, however, the frenzied mobs were spellbound. "Even in London," Whitefield remarked, "I never observed so profound a silence."

Though mentored by the Wesleys, Whitefield set his own theological course: he was a convinced Calvinist. His main theme was the necessity of the "new birth," by which he meant a conversion experience. He never pleaded with people to convert, but only announced, and dramatized, his message.

Jonathan Edwards's wife, Sarah, remarked, "He makes less of the doctrines than our American preachers generally do and aims more at affecting the heart. He is a born orator. A prejudiced person, I know, might say that this is all theatrical artifice and display, but not so will anyone think who has seen and known him."

Whitefield also made the slave community a part of his revivals, though he was far from an abolitionist. Nonetheless, he increasingly sought out audiences of slaves and wrote on their behalf. The response was so great that some historians date it as the genesis of African-American Christianity.

Everywhere Whitefield preached, he collected support for an orphanage he had founded in Georgia during his brief stay there in 1738, though the orphanage left him deep in debt for most of his life.

The spiritual revival he ignited, the Great Awakening, became one of the most formative events in American history. His last sermon on this tour was given at Boston Commons before 23,000 people, likely the largest gathering in American history to that point.

"Scenes of uncontrollable distress"

Whitefield next set his sights on Scotland, to which he would make 14 visits in his life. His most dramatic visit was his second, when he visited the small town of Cambuslang, which was already undergoing a revival. His evening service attracted thousands and continued until 2:00 in the morning. "There were scenes of uncontrollable distress, like a field of battle. All night in the fields, might be heard the voice of prayer and praise." Whitefield concluded, "It far outdid all that I ever saw in America."

On Saturday, Whitefield, in concert with area pastors, preached to an estimated 20,000 people in services that stretched well into the night. The following morning, more than 1,700 communicants streamed alongside long Communion tables set up in tents. Everywhere in the town, he recalled, "you might have heard persons praying to and praising God."

Cultural hero

With every trip across the Atlantic, he became more popular. Indeed, much of the early controversy that surrounded Whitefield's revivals disappeared (critics complained of the excess enthusiasm of both preacher and crowds), and former foes warmed to a mellowed Whitefield.

Before his tours of the colonies were complete, virtually every man, woman, and child had heard the "Grand Itinerant" at least once. So pervasive was Whitefield's impact in America that he can justly be styled America's first cultural hero. Indeed, before Whitefield, it is doubtful any name, other than royalty, was known equally from Boston to Charleston.

Whitefield's lifelong successes in the pulpit were not matched in his private family life. Like many itinerants of his day, Whitefield was suspicious of marriage and feared a wife would become a rival to the pulpit. When he finally married an older widow, Elizabeth James, the union never seemed to flower into a deeply intimate, sharing relationship.

In 1770, the 55-year-old continued his preaching tour in the colonies as if he were still a young itinerant, insisting, "I would rather wear out than rust out." He ignored the danger signs, in particular asthmatic "colds" that brought "great difficulty" in breathing. His last sermon took place in the fields, atop a large barrel.

"He was speaking of the inefficiency of works to merit salvation," one listener recounted for the press, "and suddenly cried out in a tone of thunder, 'Works! works! A man gets to heaven by works! I would as soon think of climbing to the moon on a rope of sand.'"

The following morning he died.

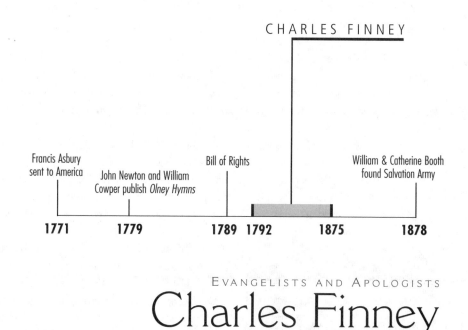

CHARLES FINNEY

Francis Asbury sent to America

John Newton and William Cowper publish *Olney Hymns*

Bill of Rights

William & Catherine Booth found Salvation Army

1771 1779 1789 1792 1875 1878

EVANGELISTS AND APOLOGISTS

Charles Finney

FATHER OF AMERICAN REVIVALISM

"I have a retainer from the Lord Jesus Christ to plead his cause, and cannot plead yours."

The 29-year-old lawyer Charles Grandison Finney had decided he must settle the question of his soul's salvation. So on October 10, 1821, he headed out into the woods near his Adams, New York, home to find God. "I will give my heart to God, or I never will come down from there," he said. After several hours, he returned to his office, where he experienced such forceful emotion that he questioned those who could not testify to a similar encounter.

"The Holy Spirit ... seemed to go through me, body and soul," he later wrote. "I could feel the impression, like a wave of electricity, going through and through me. Indeed it seemed to come in waves of liquid love, for I could not express it in any other way."

The next morning, Finney returned to his law office to meet with a client whose case he was about to argue. "I have a retainer from the Lord Jesus Christ to plead his cause," he told the man, "and cannot plead yours."

And so began the new career of the man who would become the leading revivalist in the nineteenth century.

Inside the burned-over district

Born in Connecticut, Finney was raised in Oneida County, New York. After a couple years teaching in New Jersey, he returned to New York to help his mother, who had become seriously ill. Meanwhile, he began studying law and became an apprentice to a judge in Adams.

After his conversion, Finney prepared for ministry in the Presbyterian church and was ordained in 1824. Hired by the Female Missionary Society of the Western District, he began his missionary labors in the frontier communities of upper New York. A rigid Calvinism dominated the theological landscape, but Finney urged his listeners to accept Christ openly and publicly. His style differed too; his messages were more like a lawyer's argument than a pastor's sermon.

At Evans Mills, he was troubled that the congregations continuously said they were "pleased" with his sermons. He set about to make his message less pleasing and more productive. At the end of his sermon, which stressed the need for conversion, he took a bold step: "You who have made up your minds to become Christians, and will give your pledge to make your peace with God immediately, should rise up."

The entire congregation, having never heard such a challenge, remained in their seats.

"You have taken your stand," he said. "You have rejected Christ and his gospel." The congregation was dismissed, and many left angry.

The next evening, Finney preached on wickedness, his voice like "a fire ... a hammer ... [and] a sword." But he offered no chance to respond. The next night, the entire town turned out, including a man so angry with Finney that he brought a gun and intending to kill the evangelist. But that night, Finney again offered congregants a chance to publicly declare their faith. The church erupted—dozens stood up to give their pledge, while others fell down, groaned, and bellowed. The evangelist continued to speak for several nights, visiting the new converts at their homes and on the streets.

He rode from town to town over what was known as the "burned-over district," a reference to the fact that the area had experienced so much religious enthusiasm that it was thought to have burned out. Newspapers, revivalists, and clergy took notice of the increasingly rowdy meetings—meetings unlike those of reserved Calvinists.

Identifying Finney's revivals with those a few decades earlier in places like Cane Ridge,

Kentucky, many were ecstatic about prospects for "awakening" in the northeast. But others were opposed to the "plain and pointed preacher." The Old School Presbyterians resented Finney's modifications to Calvinist theology. Traditional Calvinists taught that a person would only come to believe the gospel if God had elected them to salvation. Finney stated that unbelief was a "will not," instead of a "cannot," and could be remedied if a person willed to become a Christian.

Such rigid Calvinism, he said, "had not been born again, was insufficient, and altogether an abomination to God."

The revivalistic Congregationalists, led by Lyman Beecher, feared that Finney was opening the door to fanaticism by allowing too much expression of human emotion. Unitarians opposed Finney for using scare tactics to gain converts. Across the board, many thought that his habitual use of the words *you* and *hell* "let down the dignity of the pulpit."

"New Measures"

During this time, Finney developed what came to be known as "New Measures." He allowed women to pray in mixed public meetings. He adopted the Methodists' "anxious bench": he put a pew at the front of the church, where those who felt a special urgency about their salvation could sit. He prayed in colloquial, common, and "vulgar" language. Most of these New Measures were actually many decades old, but Finney popularized them and was attacked for doing so.

In July 1827, the New Lebanon Convention was held to examine these practices, as well as some false reports of excesses. Vote after vote ended in stalemate. When a last attempt was made at a resolution condemning questionable revivalistic practices, Finney countered by proposing a condemnation to "lukewarmness in religion." Neither proposal passed.

The zenith of Finney's evangelistic career was reached at Rochester, New York, where he preached 98 sermons between September 10, 1830, and March 6, 1831. Shopkeepers closed their businesses, posting notices urging people to attend Finney's meetings. Reportedly, the population of the town increased by two-thirds during the revival, but crime dropped by two-thirds over the same period.

From Rochester, he began an almost continuous revival in New York City as minister of the Second Free Presbyterian Church. He soon became disenchanted with Presbyterianism, however (due largely to his growing belief that people could, with God, perfect themselves). In 1834, he moved into the huge Broadway Tabernacle his followers had built for him.

He stayed there for only a year, leaving to pastor Oberlin Congregation Church and teach theology at Oberlin College. In 1851, he was appointed president, which gave him a new forum to advocate social reforms he championed, especially abolition of slavery.

Finney produced a variety of books and articles. His *Lectures on Revivals of Religion* (1835), a manual on how to lead revivals, inspired thousands of preachers to more consciously manage (critics said "manipulate") their revival meetings. His *Lectures on Systematic Theology* (1846) teach his special brand of "arminianized Calvinism."

Finney is called the "father of modern revivalism" by some historians, and he paved the way for later mass-evangelists like Dwight L. Moody, Billy Sunday, and Billy Graham.

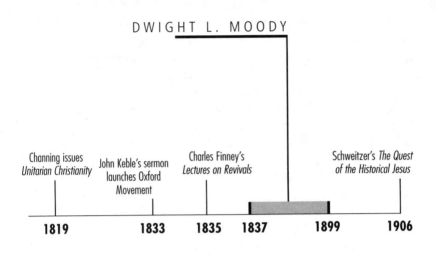

DWIGHT L. MOODY

| Channing issues Unitarian Christianity | John Keble's sermon launches Oxford Movement | Charles Finney's Lectures on Revivals | | Schweitzer's *The Quest of the Historical Jesus* |

1819   **1833**   **1835**   **1837**   **1899**   **1906**

EVANGELISTS AND APOLOGISTS

Dwight L. Moody

REVIVALIST WITH A COMMON TOUCH

> *"If this world is going to be reached, I am convinced that it must be done by men and women of average talent."*

With his boundless physical energy, natural shrewdness, self-confidence, and eternal optimism, Dwight Lyman Moody could have become a Gilded Age industrial giant like John D. Rockefeller or Jay Gould. Instead, he became one of the great evangelists of the nineteenth century.

Pony rides to the YMCA

He was born in Northfield, Massachusetts, to a Unitarian bricklayer's family. His father died when Moody was 4, leaving nine children for his mother, Betsey, to raise. His mother never encouraged Dwight to read the Bible, and he only acquired the equivalent of a fifth-grade education.

He struck out on his own at age 17 and sold shoes in his uncle's Boston store. He also attended YMCA and Sunday school classes, where he became a Christian at age 18. Shortly after that, he moved to Chicago, where he sold shoes and worked toward his goal of amassing a fortune of $100,000.

It slowly dawned on Moody that, in light of his new faith, his life should not be spent on amassing wealth as much as on helping the poor. In 1858 he established a mission Sunday school at North Market Hall in a slum of Chicago. It soon blossomed into a church (from which, six years later, was formed the Illinois Street Independent Church, precursor to the now famous Moody Memorial Church). By 1861 he had left his business to concentrate on social and evangelistic work. He drew the children of the German and Scandinavian immigrant underclass to his mission with candy and pony rides, and he drew the adults through evening prayer meetings and English classes. He was convinced, "If you can really make a man believe you love him, you have won him."

There he met and later married one of the Sunday school teachers, Emma C. Revell, with whom he had three children.

As president of the Chicago YMCA for four years, he championed evangelistic causes such as distributing tracts all over the city, and he held daily noon prayer meetings. During the Civil War, he refused to fight, saying, "In this respect I am a Quaker," but he worked through the YMCA and the United States Christian Commission to evangelize the Union troops. He relentlessly sought and received financial support for all his projects from rich Christian businessmen, such as Cyrus McCormick and John Wanamaker. In all this, he tried to mix effective social work with evangelism.

The Great Chicago Fire in October 1871 destroyed Moody's mission church, his home, and the YMCA. He traveled to New York to raise funds to rebuild the church and the YMCA, but while walking down Wall Street, he felt what he described as "a presence and power" as he had never known before, so much that he cried aloud, "Hold Lord, it is enough!" He returned to Chicago with a new vision: preaching the Kingdom of God, not social work, would change the world. He now devoted his immense energies solely to the "evangelization of the world in this generation."

Innovative evangelism

Moody believed music would be a valuable tool in his evangelistic campaigns, so when, in 1870, he heard Ira Sankey sing at a YMCA convention, he convinced Sankey to give up a well-paying government career to join him on the sawdust trail.

In the summer of 1873, Moody and Sankey were invited to the British Isles by evangelical Anglicans William Pennefather and Cuthbert Bainbridge, but both sponsors died before Moody and Sankey arrived. Without official endorsement, Moody and Sankey held campaigns in York, Sunderland, and Jarrow to minimal crowds. In Newcastle, their evangelistic efforts began to reap converts, and from then on their popularity escalated. After preaching for two years in England, Scotland, and Ireland, Moody returned to America as an internationally famous revivalist. Of his fame, Moody admitted, "I know perfectly well that, wherever I go and preach, there are many better preachers ... than I am; all that I can say about it is that the Lord uses me."

Immediately, calls for crusades poured in. During these crusades, Moody pioneered many techniques of evangelism: a house-to-house canvass of residents prior to a crusade; an ecumenical approach enlisting cooperation from all local churches and evangelical lay leaders regardless of denominational affiliations; philanthropic support by the business community; the rental of a large, central building; the showcasing of a gospel soloist; and the use of an inquiry room for those wanting to repent.

Alternating between Europe and America, Moody and Sankey held numerous evangelistic campaigns before more than 100 million people. At their 1883 Cambridge, England, meetings, seven leading university students, the famous "Cambridge Seven," committed themselves to become missionaries in China (under Hudson Taylor).

He used every opportunity to preach. When the managers of the 1893 World's Exhibition in Chicago decided to keep the Fair open on Sundays, many Christian leaders called for a boycott. Not Moody. He said, "Let us open so many preaching places and present the gospel so attractively that people will want to come and hear it." On one single day, over 130,000 people attended evangelistic meetings coordinated by Moody.

Training God's army

Through his revival work, he saw the need for an army of Bible-trained lay people to continue the work of inner-city evangelism. "If this world is going to be reached," he said, "I am convinced that it must be done by men and women of average talent. After all, there are comparatively few people in this world who have great talents." In 1879 he established Northfield Seminary for girls, followed two years later by Mount Hermon School for boys.

In 1880 Moody invited adults and college-age youth to the first of many summer Bible conferences at his home in Northfield. These conferences helped nurture dispensationalism and fundamentalism, both of which were just emerging. At one conference, the Student Volunteer Movement was founded by 100 collegians who pledged to work in foreign missions after their college education.

Finally, in 1886, Moody started the Bible-Work Institute of the Chicago Evangelization Society (renamed Moody Bible Institute shortly before his death), one of the first in the Bible school movement. From this work, he launched yet another work, the Colportage Association (later Moody Press), an organization using horse-drawn "Gospel wagons" from which students sold low-cost religious books and tracts throughout the nation.

Despite a tireless schedule (he preached six sermons a day just a month before he died), he loved to spend time with his children and grandchildren at their Northfield, Massachusetts farm, where he died.

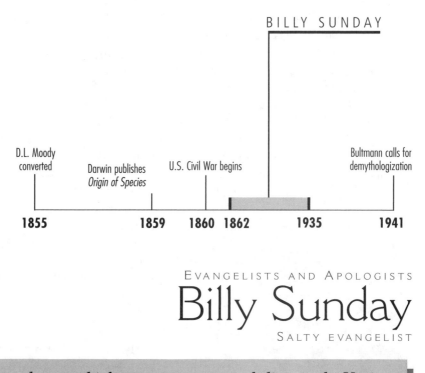

BILLY SUNDAY

D.L. Moody
converted

Darwin publishes
Origin of Species

U.S. Civil War begins

Bultmann calls for
demythologization

1855   1859   1860   1862   1935   1941

EVANGELISTS AND APOLOGISTS

Billy Sunday

SALTY EVANGELIST

"Nowadays we think we are too smart to believe in the Virgin birth of Jesus and too well educated to believe in the Resurrection. That's why people are going to the devil in multitudes."

"Center fielder Billy Sunday made a three-base hit at Farwell Hall last night. There is no other way to express the success of his first appearance as an evangelist in Chicago." So reported the local press about Sunday's first public appearance as a preacher in the late 1880s. "His audience was made up of about 500 men who didn't know much about his talents as a preacher but could remember his galloping to second base with his cap in hand."

This was just the beginning for Sunday. Until Billy Graham, no American evangelist preached to so many millions, or saw as many conversions—an estimated 300,000.

From baseball to the Y

"I never saw my father," Sunday began his autobiography, for his father had died of pneumonia in the Civil War five weeks after Sunday's birth. In fact, his early childhood in an Iowa log

73

cabin was enveloped by death—ten deaths before he reached the age of 10. His mother was so impoverished, she sent her children away to the Soldier's Orphans Home. Sunday survived only with the support of his brother and his love of sports, especially baseball.

His professional baseball career began with the Chicago White Stockings in 1883 (he struck out his first 13 at bats); he moved to the Pittsburgh Pirates, and in 1890, to the Philadelphia Athletics, where he was batting .261 and had stolen 84 bases when he quit.

Ever since his conversion to Christianity at the Pacific Garden Mission in Chicago in 1886, he had felt an increasingly strong call to preach. The YMCA finally convinced him to leave baseball to preach at their services (which meant a two-thirds cut in pay). He moved on to work with two other traveling evangelists, then was invited to conduct a revival in Garner, Iowa. From then on he was never without an invitation to preach, at first holding campaigns in midwestern towns and then, after World War I, preaching in Boston, New York, and other major cities.

Much of his success was due to his wife, Helen Amelia Thompson. She organized the campaigns and did much of the advance work. She even tried to better Billy's vocabulary in her letters to him, deliberately including words he would have to look up.

Prancing and cavorting

Sunday's preaching style was as unorthodox as the day allowed. His vocabulary was so rough (e.g., "I don't believe your own bastard theory of evolution, either; I believe it's pure jackass nonsense"), Christian leaders cringed, and they often publicly criticized him. But Sunday didn't care: "I want to preach the gospel so plainly," he said, "that men can come from the factories and not have to bring a dictionary."

Sunday was master of the one-liner, which he would use to clinch his practical, illustration-filled sermons. One of his most famous: "Going to church doesn't make you a Christian any more than going to a garage makes you an automobile."

He used his whole body in his sermons (and other nearby objects, such as his chair, which he would sometimes fling around while preaching). As one newspaper wrote, "Sunday was a whirling dervish that pranced and cavorted and strode and bounded and pounded all over his platform and left them thrilled and bewildered as they have never been before."

He concluded his sermons by inviting people to "walk the sawdust trail" to the front of the tabernacle to indicate their decision for Christ.

Unusual for American evangelists, Sunday also addressed social issues of the day. He supported women's suffrage, called for an end to child labor, and included blacks in his revivals, even when he toured the deep South. This made him enemies, as did his support of Roman Catholics (whom he considered fellow Christians) and Jews. On one of the hottest topics of the day, evolution, he walked a tightrope: he had no sympathy for evolution, but neither did he warm up to Genesis literalists.

However he was never a friend of liberals: "Nowadays we think we are too smart to believe in the Virgin birth of Jesus and too well educated to believe in the Resurrection. That's why people are going to the devil in multitudes."

And he firmly stood against card playing, movie going, and Roaring '20s fashions. "It's a damnable insult some of the rigs a lot of fool women are wearing up and down our streets," he said. His favorite vice was "Mr. Booze." In fact, his preaching was instrumental in getting Prohibition passed. "To know what the devil will do, find out what the saloon is doing," he said repeatedly. "If ever there was a jubilee in hell it was when lager beer was invented."

After World War I (which he raised millions of dollars to support), Sunday's influence decreased. Radio, movies, and other entertainments drew masses away from the preacher, though he never lacked for speaking engagements.

"I'm against sin," he once said. "I'll kick it as long as I have a foot. I'll fight it as long as I have a fist. I'll butt it as long as I have a head. I'll bite it as long as I've got a tooth. And when I'm old and fistless and footless and toothless, I'll gum it till I go home to Glory and it goes home to perdition."

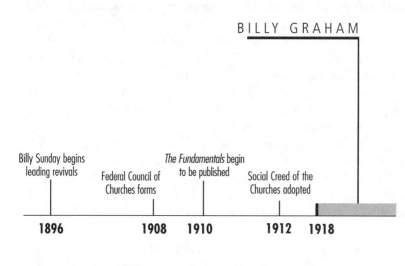

BILLY GRAHAM

Billy Sunday begins
leading revivals

Federal Council of
Churches forms

The Fundamentals begin
to be published

Social Creed of the
Churches adopted

| 1896 | 1908 | 1910 | 1912 | 1918 |

EVANGELISTS AND APOLOGISTS

Billy Graham

EVANGELIST TO MILLIONS

> *"When God gets ready to shake America, he may not take the Ph.D. and the D.D. God may choose a country boy … and I pray that he would!"*

The litany of accomplishments is familiar. Billy Graham has preached the gospel of Christ in person to more than 80 million people and to countless millions more over the airwaves and in films. Nearly 3 million have responded to the invitation he offers at the end of his sermons. When America needs a chaplain or pastor to help inaugurate or bury a president or to bring comfort in times of terrible tragedy, it turns, more often than not, to him.

For virtually every year since the 1950s, he has been a fixture on lists of the ten most admired people in America or the world. Thus, it is hardly surprising that a *Ladies Home Journal* survey once ranked the famed evangelist second only to God in the category "achievements in religion."

Into the spotlight

Born near Charlotte, North Carolina, in 1918, Billy Graham

first attended Bob Jones College, but he found both the climate and Dr. Bob's strict rule intolerable. He then followed a friend to Florida Bible Institute, where he began preaching and changed his denominational affiliation from Associate Reformed Presbyterian to Southern Baptist. To round out his intensive but academically narrow education, he moved north to Wheaton College, where he met and married Ruth Bell, the daughter of a medical missionary, and undertook his first and only stint as a local pastor.

In 1945 Graham became the field representative of a dynamic evangelistic movement known as Youth for Christ International. In this role, he toured the United States and much of Great Britain and Europe, teaching local church leaders how to organize youth rallies. He also forged friendships with scores of Christian leaders who would later join his organization or provide critical assistance to his crusades when he visited their cities throughout the world.

Graham gained further exposure and stature through nationally publicized crusades in Los Angeles, Boston, Washington, and other major cities from 1949 to 1952, and through his *Hour of Decision* radio program, begun in 1950. Stunningly successful months-long revivals in London (1954) and New York (1957), triumphant tours of the Continent and the Far East, the founding of *Christianity Today* magazine (1956), the launching of nationwide television broadcasts on ABC (1957), and a public friendship with President Dwight Eisenhower and Vice-President Richard Nixon firmly established him as the acknowledged standard-bearer for evangelical Christianity.

Friendly fire

As Graham's prestige and influence grew, particularly among "mainline" (non-evangelical) Christians, he drew criticism from fundamentalists who felt his cooperation with churches affiliated with the National and World Council of Churches signaled a compromise with the corrupting forces of modernism. Bob Jones accused him of peddling a "discount type of religion" and "sacrificing the cause of evangelism on the altar of temporary convenience." The enduring break with hard-line fundamentalism came in 1957, when, after accepting an invitation from the Protestant Council of New York to hold a crusade in Madison Square Garden, Graham announced, "I intend to go anywhere, sponsored by anybody, to preach the gospel of Christ, if there are no strings attached to my message. ... The one badge of Christian discipleship is not orthodoxy but love. Christians are not limited to any church. The only question is: are you committed to Christ?"

The New York Crusade marked another significant development in Graham's ministry. At a time when sit-ins and boycotts were stirring racial tensions in the South, Graham invited Dr. Martin Luther King, Jr., to discuss the racial situation with him and his colleagues and to lead the Garden congregation in prayer. The implication was unmistakable: Graham was letting both whites and blacks know that he was willing to be identified with the civil rights movement and its foremost leader, and King was telling blacks that Billy Graham was their ally. Graham would never feel comfortable with King's confrontational tactics; still, his voice was important in declaring that a Christian racist was an oxymoron.

During the decade that spanned the presidencies of Lyndon Johnson and Richard Nixon, to whom he had close and frequent access, Graham often drew fire from critics who felt he ought to be bolder in supporting the civil rights movement and, later, in opposing the war in Vietnam. The normally complimentary *Charlotte Observer* noted in 1971 that even some of Graham's fellow Southern Baptists felt he was "too close to the powerful and too fond of the things of the world, [and] have likened him to the prophets of old who told the kings of Israel what they wanted to hear."

The evangelist enjoyed his association with presidents and the prestige it conferred on his ministry. At the same time, presidents and other political luminaries clearly regarded their friendship with Graham as a valuable political asset. During his re-election campaign, for example, Nixon instructed his chief of staff, H.R. Haldeman, to call Graham about once every two weeks, "so that he doesn't feel that we are not interested in the support of his group in those key states where they can be helpful." After the Watergate scandal, Graham drew back a bit and began to warn against the temptations and pitfalls that lie in wait for religious leaders who enter the political arena.

When the movement known as the Religious Right surfaced in the late 1970s, he declined to participate in it, warning fellow Christian leaders to "be wary of exercising political influence" lest they lose their spiritual impact.

Global vision

As Graham came to sense the breadth of his influence, he grew ever more determined not only to help evangelicalism become increasingly dynamic and self-confident, but also to shape the direction of contemporary Christianity. That determination manifested itself in several major international conferences sponsored or largely underwritten by the Billy Graham Evangelistic Association (BGEA).

In particular, the 1966 World Congress on Evangelism in Berlin, attended by 1,200 evangelical leaders from 104 nations, and the 1974 International Congress on World Evangelization in Lausanne, Switzerland, attended by 2,400 delegates from 150 countries, helped evangelicals to see themselves as a worldwide Christian force, alongside Vatican II and the World Council of Churches, an international movement capable of accomplishing more than its constituents had dreamed possible.

Few, if any, developments in Billy Graham's ministry have been more surprising or controversial than his success in penetrating the Iron Curtain. Beginning in 1978, virtually every Soviet-controlled country progressively gave him privileges that no other churchman, including the most prominent and politically docile native religious leaders, had ever received. Graham used these visits to preach, to encourage Christian believers, and to explain to Communist leaders that their restriction of religious freedom was counterproductive, hampering diplomatic relations with America.

Graham's proudest achievements may be two BGEA-sponsored conferences in Amsterdam in 1983 and 1986, with a third scheduled for the year 2000. These gatherings, attended by a total of 13,000 on-the-job itinerant evangelists from 174 countries, provided basic instruction in such matters as sermon composition, fundraising, and effective use of films and videotapes. As a sign of Billy Graham's change-embracing spirit, approximately 500 attendees at the 1986 meeting were women, and Pentecostals outnumbered non-Pentecostals. Subsequent smaller gatherings throughout the world have afforded similar training to additional thousands of evangelists.

Indeed, it is plausible that the answer to the oft-asked question, "Who will be the next Billy Graham?" is no single man or woman, but this mighty army of anonymous individuals whose spirits have been thrilled by Billy Graham's example, their hands and minds prepared with his organization's assistance, and their hearts set on fire by his ringing exhortation at the Amsterdam meetings: "Do the work of an evangelist!"

Age and Parkinson's Disease have taken their toll, but they have not quenched Billy Graham's spirit. "My mind tells me I ought to get out there and go," he said, as he was beginning to feel the effects of his disease, "but I just can't do it. But I'll preach until there is no breath left in my body. I was called by God, and until God tells me to retire, I cannot. Whatever strength I have, whatever time God lets me have, is going to be dedicated to doing the work of an evangelist, as long as I live."

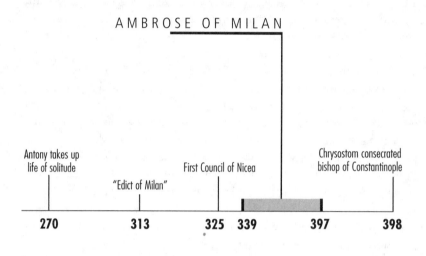

AMBROSE OF MILAN

Antony takes up life of solitude	"Edict of Milan"	First Council of Nicea		Chrysostom consecrated bishop of Constantinople
270	313	325	339	397	398

Ambrose of Milan

MOST TALENTED BISHOP OF THE EARLY CHURCH

> **"When we are speaking about truth and life and redemption, we are speaking about Christ."**

"When we speak of wisdom, we are speaking about Christ. When we speak about virtue, we are speaking about Christ. When we speak about justice, we are speaking about Christ. When we are speaking about truth and life and redemption, we are speaking about Christ." So wrote Ambrose, bishop of Milan, biblical exegete, political theorist, master of Latin eloquence, musician, and teacher; in all these roles, he was speaking about Christ.

Arrested career

The first Latin church father from a Christian family, Ambrose was also born into power, part of the Roman family of Aurelius. The pope and church dignitaries visited his parent's home when he was a child, and he was a governor in Italy's northern provinces before the age of 30. As he was sent, the prefect gave him a word of prophetic advice: "Go, conduct yourself not as a judge, but as a bishop."

Indeed, even as governor he had ecclesiastical problems to deal with. Orthodox Christians and Arians were practically at war at the time. Ambrose was no friend of the Arians, but he was so well regarded that both sides supported him. When the bishop of Milan (an Arian) died, Ambrose attended the meeting to elect a replacement, hoping that his presence would preempt violence between the parties. Much to his surprise, both sides shouted their wish for him to be their replacement.

Ambrose really didn't want to be an ecclesiastical leader; he was doing quite well as a political one. And he hadn't even been baptized yet! But the people wrote to Emperor Valentian, asking for his seal on their verdict. Ambrose was placed under arrest until he agreed to serve.

If the Arians had hoped to gain favor by supporting Ambrose as bishop, their hopes were soon dashed. The new bishop was as orthodox as could be, and he soon took the Arians to task. He refused to surrender a church for use by Arians, and he wrote several works against them, including On the Faith, The Mystery of the Lord's Incarnation, and On the Holy Spirit.

Having been trained in rhetoric and law and having studied Greek, Ambrose became known for his knowledge of the latest Greek writings, both Christian and pagan. In addition to Philo, Origen, and Basil of Caesarea, he even quoted Neoplatonist Plotinus in his sermons. He was widely regarded as an excellent preacher.

In many of those sermons, Ambrose expounded upon the virtues of asceticism. He was so persuasive that noble families sometimes forbade their daughters to attend his sermons, fearing they'd trade their marriageable status for a life of austere virginity.

One piece of his pastoral advice is still universally known: "When you are at Rome, live in the Roman style; when you are elsewhere, live as they live elsewhere."

Ambrose also introduced congregational singing, and he was accused of "bewitching" Milan by introducing Eastern melodies into the hymns he wrote. Because of his influence, hymn singing became an important part of the Western liturgy.

The emperor repents

Ambrose's most lasting contribution, though, was in the area of church-state relations. He wrestled with three emperors—and won each time. His relationship with Theodosius, the first emperor to try to make Rome a Christian state, is the most well-known example.

In 390, local authorities imprisoned a charioteer of Thessalonica for homosexuality. Unfortunately, the charioteer was one of the city's favorites, and riots broke out when the governor refused to release him. The governor and a few others were killed in the melee, and the charioteer was freed.

Fuming, Theodosius exacted revenge. He announced another chariot race, but after the crowds arrived, the gates were locked and the townspeople were massacred by the emperor's soldiers. Within three hours, 7,000 were dead.

Ambrose was horrified. He wrote an angry letter to Theodosius demanding his repentance. "I exhort, I beg, I entreat, I admonish you, because it is grief to me that the perishing of so many innocent is no grief to you," he wrote. "And now I call on you to repent." He forbade the emperor to attend worship until he prostrated himself at the altar.

Theodosius obeyed, marking the first time church triumphed over state.

In that event, Ambrose introduced the medieval concept of a Christian emperor as dutiful "son of the church serving under orders from Christ." For the next thousand years, secular and religious rulers struggled to determine who was sovereign in various spheres of life.

Though there is some question about the historicity of Theodosius's famous statement, "I know no bishop worthy of the name, except Ambrose," the emperor continued to hold the bishop in high regard and died in his arms.

"I confess I loved him, and felt the sorrow of his death in the abyss of my heart," Ambrose eulogized.

Two years later, Ambrose himself fell gravely ill. The worries of the country were expressed by one writer: "When Ambrose dies, we shall see the ruin of Italy." On Easter eve, 397, the man who had been bishop of Milan for more than 23 years finally succumbed.

Only one name is more associated with Ambrose than Theodosius's, and only one student outshined this teacher: Augustine. The skeptical professor of rhetoric had gone to Milan in 384 to hear the bishop's famous allegorical preaching. By the time he left four years later, he had been baptized by Ambrose and given a philosophical basis he would use to transform Christian theology.

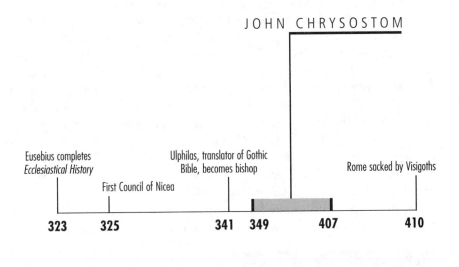

JOHN CHRYSOSTOM

Eusebius completes
Ecclesiastical History

First Council of Nicea

Ulphilas, translator of Gothic
Bible, becomes bishop

Rome sacked by Visigoths

323   **325**   **341**   **349**   **407**   **410**

PASTORS AND PREACHERS

John Chrysostom

EARLY CHURCH'S GREATEST PREACHER

"Preaching improves me. When I begin to speak, weariness disappears; when I begin to teach, fatigue too disappears."

"It is foolishness and a public madness to fill the cupboards with clothing," John of Antioch exhorted the congregation, "and allow men who are created in God's image and likeness to stand naked and trembling with the cold so that they can hardly hold themselves upright."

Eloquent and uncompromising preaching was typical of John and earned him the name history would remember him by: Chrysostomos—"golden mouth." But his preaching, though considered the best in the early church, was what got him into trouble and led to his untimely death.

Affair of the statues

John was raised in Antioch, a leading intellectual center of late antiquity, by his widowed mother, Anthusa, a pious Christian woman. His tutor was Libanius, the famous pagan rhetorician who had been a professor in both Athens and Constantinople.

After his education, like many devout men of his day, the spidery John (he was short, thin, and long-limbed) entered monastic seclusion. But his ascetic rigors were so strenuous, they damaged his health (the effects would last his whole life), and he was forced to return to public life. He quickly went from lector to deacon to priest at the church in Antioch.

During this time, he penned *On the Priesthood*, a justification for his own delay in entering the priesthood but also a mature look at the perils and possibilities of ministry: "I do not know whether anyone has ever succeeded in not enjoying praise," he wrote in one passage. "And if he enjoys it, he naturally wants to receive it. And if he wants to receive it, he cannot help being pained and distraught at losing it."

It was in Antioch where Chrysostom's preaching began to be noticed, especially after what has been called the "Affair of the Statues."

In the spring of 388, a rebellion erupted in Antioch over the announcement of increased taxes. Statues of the emperor and his family were desecrated. Imperial officials

responded by punishing city leaders, killing some; Archbishop Flavian rushed to the capital in Constantinople, some 800 miles away, to beg the emperor for clemency.

In Flavian's absence, John preached to the terrified city: "Improve yourselves now truly, not as when during one of the numerous earthquakes or in famine or drought or in similar visitations you leave off your sinning for three or four days and then begin the old life again." When eight weeks later, Flavian returned with the good news of the emperor's pardon, John's reputation soared.

From then on, he was in demand as a preacher. He preached through many books of the Bible, though he had his favorites: "I like all the saints," he said, "but St. Paul the most of all—that vessel of election, the trumpet of heaven." In his sermons, he denounced abortion, prostitution, gluttony, the theater, and swearing. About the love of horse racing, he complained, "My sermons are applauded merely from custom, then everyone runs off to [horse racing] again and gives much more applause to the jockeys, showing indeed unrestrained passion for them! There they put their heads together with great attention, and say with mutual rivalry, 'This horse did not run well, this one stumbled,' and one holds to this jockey and another to that. No one thinks any more of my sermons, nor of the holy and awesome mysteries that are accomplished here."

His large bald head, deeply set eyes, and sunken cheeks reminded people of Elisha the prophet. Though his sermons (which lasted between 30 minutes and two hours) were well attended, he sometimes became discouraged: "My work is like that of a man who is trying to clean a piece of ground into which a muddy stream is constantly flowing."

At the same time, he said, "Preaching improves me. When I begin to speak, weariness disappears; when I begin to teach, fatigue too disappears."

Kidnapped to Constantinople

In early 398, John was seized by soldiers and transported to the capital, where he was forcibly consecrated as archbishop of Constantinople. His kidnapping was arranged by a government official who wanted to adorn the church in the capital city with the best orator in Christianity. Rather than rebelling against the injustice, John accepted it as God's providence.

And rather than soften his words for his new and prestigious audience—which now included many from the imperial household—John continued themes he preached in Antioch. He railed against abuses of wealth and power. Even his lifestyle itself was a scandal: he lived an ascetic life, used his considerable household budget to care for the poor, and built hospitals.

He continued preaching against the great public sins. In a sermon against the theater, for example, he said, "Long after the theater is closed and everyone is gone away, those images [of "shameful women" actresses] still float before your soul, their words, their conduct, their glances, their walk, their positions, their excitation, their unchaste limbs.... And there within you she kindles the Babylonian furnace in which the peace of your home, the purity of your heart, the happiness of your marriage will be burnt up!"

His lack of tact and political skill made him too many enemies—in the imperial family and among fellow bishops. For reasons too complex to elaborate, Theophilus, the archbishop of Alexandria, was able to call a council outside of Constantinople and, trumping up charges of heresy, had John deposed from office. John was sent into exile by Empress Eudoxia and Emperor Arcadius.

John was transported across the plains of Asia Minor in the heat of summer, and almost immediately his health began to fail him. He was visited by loyal followers, and wrote letters of encouragement to others: "When you see the church scattered, suffering the most terrible trials, her most illustrious members persecuted and flogged, her leader carried away into exile, don't only consider these events, but also the things that have resulted: the rewards, the recompense, the awards for the athlete who wins in the games and the prizes won in the contest."

On the eastern shore of the Black Sea, at the edges of the empire, his body gave out and he died.

Thirty-four years later, after John's chief enemies had died, his relics were brought back in triumph to the capital. Emperor Theodosius II, son of Arcadius and Eudoxia, publicly asked forgiveness for the sins of his parents.

He was later given the title of "Doctor of the Church" because of the value of his writings (600 sermons and 200 letters survive). Along with Basil the Great, Gregory of Nazianzus, and Athanasius, he is considered one of the greatest of the early Eastern church fathers.

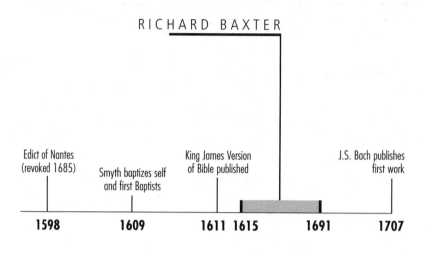

RICHARD BAXTER

Edict of Nantes (revoked 1685)	Smyth baptizes self and first Baptists	King James Version of Bible published		J.S. Bach publishes first work
1598	1609	1611 1615	1691	1707

PASTORS AND PREACHERS

Richard Baxter
MODERATE IN AN AGE OF EXTREMES

> *"I preached . . . as a dying man to dying men."*

Richard Baxter never received a higher commission than that of parish pastor to loom workers in Kidderminster. Still, he was the most prominent English churchman of the 1600s. He was a peacemaker who sought unity among Protestants, and yet he was a highly independent thinker—and at the center of every major controversy in England during his lifetime.

Nonconformist who sought unity
Born in Rowton to parents who undervalued education, Baxter was largely self-taught. He eventually studied at a free school, then at royal court, where he became disgusted at what he saw as frivolity. He left to study divinity, and at age 23, he was ordained into the Church of England.

Within the Anglican church, Baxter found common ground with the Puritans, a growing faction who opposed the church's episcopacy—and was itself breaking into factions.

Baxter, for his part, did his best to avoid the disputes between Anglicans, Presbyterians, Congregationalists, and other denominations, even convincing local ministers to cooperate in some pastoral matters. "In necessary things, unity; in doubtful things, liberty; in all things, charity," he was fond of saying.

The interest in cooperation was not due to a lack of conviction. On the contrary, Baxter was opinionated in his theology, which was not quite Separatist and not quite Conformist. Among his more than 200 works are long, controversial discourses on doctrine. Still, he believed society was a large family under a loving father, and in his theology, he tried to cut between the extremes. He eventually registered himself as "a mere Nonconformist" ("Nonconformist" was a technical term meaning "not Anglican"), breaking with the Church of England mainly because of the lack of power it gave parish clergy.

Persecuted moderate

Baxter also found himself as a peacemaker during the English Civil Wars. He believed in monarchy, but a limited one. He served as a chaplain for the parliamentary army, but then helped to bring about the restoration of the king. Yet as a moderate, Baxter found himself the target of both extremes.

He was still irritated with the episcopacy in 1660, when he was offered the bishopric of Hereford, so he declined it. As a result, he was barred from ecclesiastical office and not permitted to return to Kidderminster, nor was he allowed to preach. Between 1662 and 1688 (when James II was overthrown), he was persecuted and was imprisoned for 18 months, and he was forced to sell two extensive libraries.

Still, he continued to preach: "I preached as never sure to preach again," he wrote, "and as a dying man to dying men."

Baxter became even better known for his prolific writing. His devotional classic *The Saints' Everlasting Rest* was one of the most widely read books of the century. When asked what deviations should be permitted from the Anglican *Book of Common Prayer*, he created an entirely new one, called *Reformed Liturgy*, in two weeks. His *Christian Directory* contains over one million words. His autobiography and his pastoral guide, *The Reformed Pastor*, are still widely read today.

"The Gospel dieth not when I die: the church dieth not: the praises of God die not: the world dieth not: and perhaps it shall grow better," he wrote near the end of his life. "It may be that some of the seed that I have sown shall spring up to some benefit of the dark unpeaceable world when I am dead."

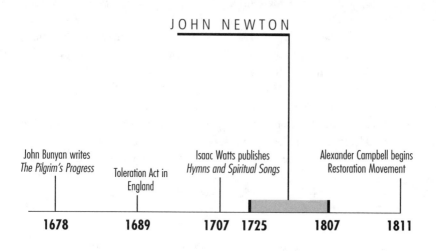

JOHN NEWTON

John Bunyan writes
The Pilgrim's Progress

Toleration Act in
England

Isaac Watts publishes
Hymns and Spiritual Songs

Alexander Campbell begins
Restoration Movement

1678   **1689**   **1707 1725**   **1807**   **1811**

PASTORS AND PREACHERS

John Newton

REFORMED SLAVE TRADER

"Amazing grace, how sweet the sound, that saved a wretch like me."

It is probably the most famous hymn in history:

Amazing grace, how sweet the sound,
that saved a wretch like me.
I once was lost, but now am found,
Was blind but now I see.

Though some today wonder if the word *wretch* is hyperbole or a bit of dramatic license, John Newton, the song's author, clearly did not.

Slave trader

Newton was nurtured by a Christian mother who taught him the Bible at an early age, but he was raised in his father's image after she died of tuberculosis when Newton was 7. At age 11, Newton went on his first of six sea-voyages with the merchant navy captain.

Newton lost his first job, in a merchant's office, because of "unsettled behavior and impatience of restraint"—a pattern that would persist for years. He spent his later teen years at sea before he was press-ganged aboard the H.M.S. Harwich in 1744. Newton rebelled against the discipline of the Royal Navy and deserted. He was caught, put in irons, and flogged. He eventually convinced his superiors to discharge him to a slaver ship. Espousing freethinking principles, he remained arrogant and insubordinate, and he lived with moral abandon: "I sinned with a high hand," he later wrote, "and I made it my study to tempt and seduce others."

He took up employment with a slave-trader named Clow, who owned a plantation of lemon trees on an island off of west Africa. But he was treated cruelly by Clow and the slaver's African mistress; soon Newton's clothes turned to rags, and Newton was forced to beg for food to allay his hunger.

The sluggish sailor was transferred to the service of the captain of the Greyhound, a Liverpool ship, in 1747, and on its homeward journey, the ship was overtaken by an enormous storm. Newton had been reading Thomas a Kempis's *The Imitation of Christ*, and was struck by a line about the "uncertain continuance of life." He also recalled the passage in Proverbs, "Because I have called and ye have refused, ... I also will laugh at your calamity." He converted during the storm, though he admitted later, "I cannot consider myself to have been a believer, in the full sense of the word."

Newton then served as a mate and then as captain of a number of slave ships, hoping as a Christian to restrain the worst excesses of the slave trade, "promoting the life of God in the soul" of both his crew and his African cargo.

Amazing hymnal

After leaving the sea for an office job in 1755, Newton held Bible studies in his Liverpool home. Influenced by both the Wesleys and George Whitefield, he adopted mild Calvinist views and became increasingly disgusted with the slave trade and his role in it. He quit, was ordained into the Anglican ministry, and in 1764 took a parish in Olney in Buckinghamshire.

Three years after Newton arrived, poet William Cowper moved to Olney. Cowper, a skilled poet who experienced bouts of depression, became a lay helper in the small congregation.

In 1769, Newton began a Thursday evening prayer service. For almost every week's service, he wrote a hymn to be sung to a familiar tune. Newton challenged Cowper also to write hymns for these meetings, which he did until falling seriously ill in 1773. Newton later combined 280 of his own hymns with 68 of Cowper's in what was to become the popular Olney Hymns. Among the well-known hymns in it are "Amazing Grace," "Glorious Things of Thee Are Spoken," "How Sweet the Name of Jesus Sounds," "O for a Closer Walk with God," and "There Is a Fountain Filled with Blood."

In 1787 Newton wrote *Thoughts Upon the African Slave Trade* to help William

Wilberforce's campaign to end the practice—"a business at which my heart now shudders," he wrote. Recollection of that chapter in his life never left him, and in his old age, when it was suggested that the increasingly feeble Newton retire, he replied, "I cannot stop. What? Shall the old African blasphemer stop while he can speak?"

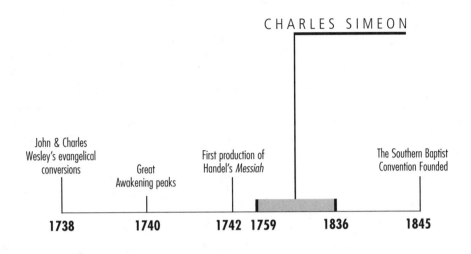

CHARLES SIMEON

John & Charles Wesley's evangelical conversions	Great Awakening peaks	First production of Handel's *Messiah*			The Southern Baptist Convention Founded
1738	**1740**	**1742**	**1759**	**1836**	**1845**

PASTORS AND PREACHERS

Charles Simeon

EVANGELICAL MENTOR AND MODEL

"On the Wednesday of Holy Week began a hope of mercy. On the Thursday, that hope increased. On . . . Easter Day . . . I awoke with these words upon my heart and lips: Jesus Christ is risen today, halleluja, halleluja!"

Though he became a model for modern figures like John Stott, Charles Simeon started his life in Cambridge as anything but a model.

In 1779, the young Simeon, from an aristocratic family, came to Kings College, Cambridge, to study, and he was told that he must attend chapel on Easter Day to receive Communion. Simeon's main interests to this point had been horses, games, and fashion. He considered that "Satan himself was as fit to attend [the sacrament] as I." Still, he sought hard to see how he might sort out his conscience. He began to read the Scriptures and various devotional books.

As he read about propitiatory sacrifice in the Old Testament, he thought, "What, may I transfer all my guilt to another? Has God provided an offering for me, that I may lie my sins on his head?" He immediately laid his sins "upon the sacred head of Jesus."

On the Wednesday of Holy Week, he wrote, he "began a hope of mercy. On the Thursday, that hope increased. On the Friday and Saturday, it became more strong. And on the Sunday morning, Easter Day, April 4, I woke early with these words upon my heart and lips: Jesus Christ is Risen Today, Halleluja, Halleluja!"

Simeon went on to be ordained, and after a short stint at St. Edwards, Cambridge, at age 23, he was appointed vicar of Holy Trinity Church. The parish had wanted another minister, and this fact—combined with Simeon's evangelical preaching—quickly alienated them. They locked their rented pews against him, and those who came to hear Simeon were forced to stand in the aisles.

When Simeon moved to put benches in the aisles, the church wardens threw them out. He battled with discouragement and at one point wrote out his resignation.

"When I was an object of much contempt and derision in the university," he later wrote, "I strolled forth one day, buffeted and afflicted, with my little Testament in my hand.... The first text which caught my eye was this: 'They found a man of Cyrene, Simon by name; him they compelled to bear his cross.'"

"Conversation parties"

Slowly the pews began to open up and fill, not primarily with townspeople but with students. Then Simeon did what was unthinkable at the time: he introduced an evening service. He invited students to his home on Sundays and Friday evening for "conversation parties" to teach them how to preach. By the time he died, it is estimated that one-third of all the Anglican ministers in the country had sat under his teaching at one time or another.

Simeon, an untiring activist, also helped found evangelistic organizations like the London Jews Society, the Religious Tract Society, and the British & Foreign Bible Society. He was also one of the founders of the Church Missionary Society, and he inspired dozens of young men from his church to take the gospel to the far corners of the world.

In 1817, with money inherited through a brother's death, he created what became known as the Simeon Trust to purchase rights to appoint evangelical clergy to the parishes. He remained a bachelor his whole life, and his entire ministry was at Holy Trinity Church, Cambridge—even today a focal point of evangelicalism in England.

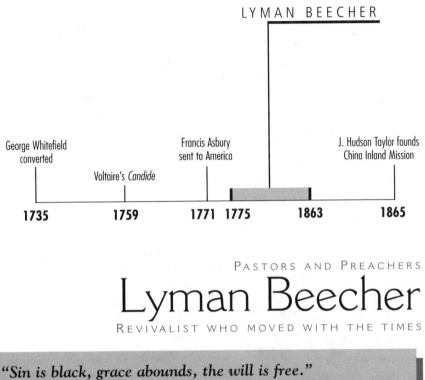

LYMAN BEECHER

George Whitefield converted

Voltaire's *Candide*

Francis Asbury sent to America

J. Hudson Taylor founds China Inland Mission

| 1735 | 1759 | 1771 | 1775 | 1863 | 1865 |

PASTORS AND PREACHERS

Lyman Beecher

REVIVALIST WHO MOVED WITH THE TIMES

"Sin is black, grace abounds, the will is free."
— one biographer's summary of
Lyman Beecher's Theology

During Lyman Beecher's sophomore year at Yale, school president Timothy Dwight launched a preaching campaign against the school's pervading religious skepticism. After a debate titled "Is the Bible the Word of God?" Beecher noted, "all infidelity skulked and hid its head." When Dwight preached, "The harvest is past, the summer is ended, and we are not saved," Beecher felt as if "a whole avalanche rolled down" upon him, and he went home, "weeping every step."

This personal transformation foreshadowed changes that were taking place in American Christianity, many of which he became a part.

Pragmatic preaching

A native of Connecticut, Beecher was licensed as a Congregational clergyman—though his first pastorate was a

Presbyterian church in East Hampton, Long Island. The young preacher was initially frustrated: "My preaching seems not to move," he complained. "I speak against a rock." But when he preached "The Remedy for Dueling," on the occasion of the Aaron Burr-Alexander Hamilton duel of 1806, a small revival broke out.

In 1810, he began pastoring a Congregationalist church in Litchfield, Connecticut, where his reputation as a revivalist and social reformer grew. He jealously defended the church's right to establishment (the state of Connecticut financed Congregationalism), but when Congregationalism was disestablished, he changed his mind: "It cut the churches loose from dependence on state support. It threw them wholly on their own resources and on God."

At his next church, Hanover Street Church, Boston, the great issue was unitarianism, which prevailed in the city. The revivalist quickly went to work with a strenuous campaign for orthodoxy.

Early on, Beecher's passion for saving souls drove his theology in a more pragmatic

direction. He appealed to one seeker's intellect, to another's emotions. His sermons had a rationalistic bent and were peppered with words and phrases like "common sense," "honorable" repentance, meeting "all objections"—while he strutted around and waved his arms (a style his children would affectionately imitate in play). He was considered the archetypal Yankee—canny, waggish, relentless in logical argument, sinewy, and ungraceful.

Champion of free-will

In 1832 Beecher began concurrent terms as pastor of Second Presbyterian Church and Lane Seminary, both in Cincinnati, Ohio. As the abolitionist movement heated up in the city, Beecher discovered how voluntary groups could powerfully work toward healing social ills.

This, in turn, prompted him to reevaluate his Calvinist doctrine of sin and to put a greater emphasis on free will. His Calvinism was increasingly shaped by Arminians like Charles Finney, and what has been called New School theology, summarized by one Beecher biographer: "Sin is black, grace abounds, the will is free."

In the Calvinist-imbued Congregationalism of the time, this didn't sit well, and Beecher was charged with heresy, but he was eventually acquitted.

Beecher's greatest legacy may be the family he produced. He was said to be the "father of more brains than any man in America," for among his children were Harriet Beecher Stowe, author of *Uncle Tom's Cabin*, and Henry Ward Beecher, the most famous American preacher of his day.

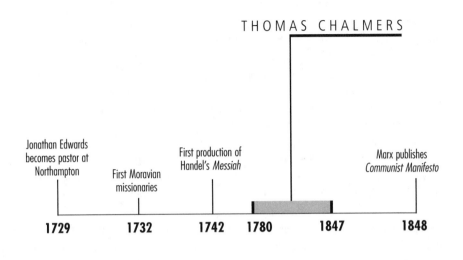

THOMAS CHALMERS

Jonathan Edwards becomes pastor at Northampton	First Moravian missionaries	First production of Handel's *Messiah*			Marx publishes *Communist Manifesto*
1729	1732	1742	1780	1847	1848

PASTORS AND PREACHERS

Thomas Chalmers

UNRELENTING ADVOCATE FOR THE POOR

> *"What is the most effectual method of making Christianity so to bear upon a population as that it shall reach every door and be brought into contact with all families?"*

William Wilberforce, the famous abolitionist, said, "All the world is wild" about him. And one bishop applied Dante's words to him: "The holy wrestler, gentle to his own and to his enemies terrible."

They were speaking of Thomas Chalmers, a man of extraordinary energy and passion whose life—at least after his conversion—took on a laser-like focus to answer the question he himself once posed rhetorically: "What is the most effectual method of making Christianity so to bear upon a population as that it shall reach every door and be brought into contact with all families?"

Parish system

Chalmers was born in Anstruther, Scotland, on the Fife coast and educated in local schools and then, beginning at age 12, at the University of St. Andrews (he was the second youngest student). In 1802, he became minister at Kilmany, where he took more interest in national intellectual life than his parish: in an 1805 pamphlet he wrote that a minister should be able to complete all his duties in two days and spend the rest of his "uninterrupted leisure" in whatever manner he wished.

But failure to establish literary fame or academic appointment, combined with a bout with tuberculosis, pushed Chalmers into spiritual crisis and then a conversion. He then began associating with evangelicals and became zealous for missions, home visitation, and relief of the poor.

His reputation as a preacher also grew. At age 35, he was invited to become the minister at a wealthy Glasgow parish, where his eloquence thrust him into the national spotlight. What ignited his passion in Glasgow—ravaged by the grime, squalor, and exploitation of the industrial revolution—was meeting the needs of his poor parishioners.

At his next parish, St. John's, the poorest parish in Glasgow, he was given free rein to try his schemes to make the parish the hub of spiritual care, education, and help for the poor. He wanted everyone to have a church (1) near enough, (2) at seat rents low enough, and (3) with a district small enough to be thoroughly cared for.

He divided the parish of 10,000 into manageable areas and appointed deacons and elders to visit families; he rejected government aid and encouraged self-help and communal sharing as the ways to help the poor. Chalmers was sharply criticized as unrealistic and many argued that he ultimately harmed the poor, but Chalmers claimed his experiment was a success.

Lack of support

In 1823, he left parish ministry for the chair of moral philosophy at St. Andrews University. He became increasingly troubled by the individualistic self-interest promoted by economists and politicians. He believed the only remedy for the evils of industrialization—and its attendant poverty, rootlessness, illiteracy, and threat of revolution—was a parish system, where the lives of the struggling poor could be ministered to effectively.

Furthermore, Chalmers believed a parish system could only work if administered by a well-endowed national church. In 1834, he began campaigning vigorously for a parish system in which no parish was larger than 2,000 inhabitants, in which Christian discipline and cooperation would be revived through evangelical preaching, and in which Scotland would become a "godly commonwealth."

"Disruption"

Though Chalmers founded over 200 churches, the British government refused to endow them. Chalmers's relationship with both the British and Scottish governments soured even more when the courts, against a large church lobby, agreed to continue to let patrons of churches (whether they were members of the Church of Scotland or not) to appoint ministers to local parishes (even against the wishes of the parish).

This was too much for Chalmers, who led a third of the clergy and people into the Free Church of Scotland (FCS) in 1843 (this event is commonly called "the

Disruption"). In a few years, the FCS erected over 800 churches and 500 schools to become the second largest church in the land.

Chalmers, however, became discouraged with the inability of the FCS to reverse the misery and growing irreligion in cities, and he spent his final years trying to organize urban missions. He argued that these were far more important than even the interests of the Free Church.

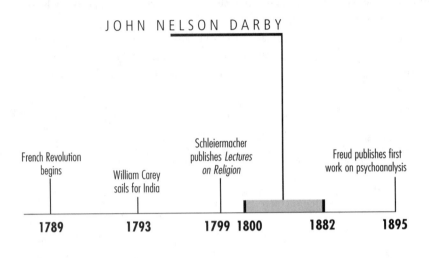

JOHN NELSON DARBY

French Revolution begins	William Carey sails for India	Schleiermacher publishes *Lectures on Religion*		Freud publishes first work on psychoanalysis
1789	1793	1799	1800	1882	1895

John Nelson Darby

FATHER OF DISPENSATIONALISM

> **"The Christian is directed to turn away from evil and turn to the Scriptures."**

"The church is in ruins," wrote John Darby, then a successful Anglican priest in Ireland. Echoing the lamentations of Protestant reformers three centuries earlier, he believed that the Church of England had lost any notion of salvation by grace and that it had forsaken biblical ideas of what church should be. For Darby it was time to start afresh with a new church and prepare for Jesus' imminent Second Coming. What resulted from Darby's departure was a new way of viewing the church and history that still pervades much of evangelical Christian thought.

Ever-changing vocation

Born in London into a prominent Anglo-Irish family, Darby received the best education possible. He attended London's Westminster School until his parents moved to an ancestral castle in Ireland. He graduated from Dublin's Trinity College as a

Classical Gold Medalist and continued his studies in law, being admitted to the Irish Chancery Bar in 1822.

But Darby's law career was to be short-lived. Within four years, largely due to his desire to help poor Irish Catholics, he was made a priest as a curate of the Church of Ireland. "I owed myself entirely to [God]," he explained of his career switch. "I longed for complete devotedness to the work of God."

He was assigned to a parish in the mountainous regions south of Dublin, and he quickly became an excellent pastor; rarely would he return to his cottage from pastoral visits before midnight. Still, as he read his Bible, he became frustrated with how "established" the church had become. The formalized Anglican church, so associated with the State, was lifeless beyond repair.

"It is positively stated (2 Tim. 3) that the church would fail and become as bad as heathenism," he wrote. "The Christian is directed to turn away from evil and turn to the Scriptures, and Christ (Rev. 2 and 3) is revealed as judging the state of the churches."

And so Darby resigned his position a mere two years and three months after receiving it. He joined a group of similarly disillusioned Christians who called themselves simply "Brethren." Committed to operate by strict biblical methods, the group had no professional ministers. Rejecting denominationalism, they believed the Holy Spirit would lead worship, so they focused their meetings on simple Communion services, served by a different individual each week.

Though officially no more a leader than anyone else in the group (now called the Plymouth Brethren because of their gathering in that city), Darby quickly became its most prominent voice. His pamphlet *The Nature and Unity of the Church of Christ* (1828), which described their beliefs and practices, quickly spread throughout the West. The former priest traveled to churches in Western Europe, North America, Australia, and New Zealand condemning denominationalism and calling believers to his new ecclesiology.

The end of the world

Believers came, drawn not only to Darby's view of the church but also to his view of history, especially the end of it. Premillennialism, the belief that the world will get worse until Christ returns to set up a visible, thousand-year reign of peace, had fallen out of favor for 1,500 years. Some occasional premillennalist movements had appeared over the centuries, but usually ended in disappointment after predicting Jesus' imminent return.

Darby, on the other hand, developed a new premillennialism, which he called "dispensationalism" after the division of history into eras or dispensations. Though later dispensationalists quibbled over the number and names of these periods, most agreed with Darby that there were seven, like the seven days of creation. Darby listed the ages as: Paradise, Noah, Abraham, Israel, Gentiles, the Spirit, and the Millennium.

Darby saw history as a "progressive revelation," and his system sought to explain the stages in God's redemptive plan for the universe. There was nothing especially radical about dividing history into periods. What separated Darby's dispensationalism was his novel method of biblical interpretation, which consisted of a strict literalism, the absolute separation of Israel and the church into two distinct peoples of God, and the separation of the rapture (the "catching away" of the church) from Christ's Second Coming. At the rapture, he said, Christ will come for his saints; and at the Second Coming, he will come with his saints.

Harsh critic

Though Darby's teachings became increasingly popular (and became more popular still after his death when C.I. Scofield published Darby's ideas in the annotated *Scofield Reference Bible* in 1909), Darby's return to England brought a split to the Plymouth Brethren. Riled at a member's differences on issues of prophecy and church order, Darby excommunicated him even after the man admitted and repudiated his error. Darby demanded that public refutation of those beliefs be the basis of admitting people to the Lord's Table. When the Bethesda church refused to comply with the demand, Darby refused to receive any of its members.

Eventually, Darby's followers created a tight group of churches known as Exclusive Brethren (also called Darbyites), while the others, maintaining a more congregational church government with less stringent membership standards, were called Open Brethren.

Historians have criticized Darby's tendency to treat opponents harshly: "His criticisms of what he considered error were forceful and enlightening yet at times extreme, perhaps closing otherwise open doors," says one, noting that Darby condemned Dwight Moody (they disagreed on freedom of will), who made efforts to befriend his British colleague.

Though Darby may have burned his bridges, his message gained a larger and larger following. Today his dispensational premillennialism is the view of many modern fundamentalists and conservative evangelicals.

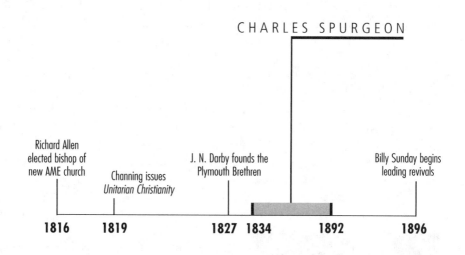

CHARLES SPURGEON

Richard Allen elected bishop of new AME church

Channing issues Unitarian Christianity

J. N. Darby founds the Plymouth Brethren

Billy Sunday begins leading revivals

1816   1819   1827 1834   1892   1896

PASTORS AND PREACHERS

Charles Spurgeon

FINEST NINETEENTH-CENTURY PREACHER

> "I am perhaps vulgar, but it is not intentional, save that I must and will make people listen."

When Charles Spurgeon died in January 1892, London went into mourning. Nearly 60,000 people came to pay homage during the three days his body lay in state at the Metropolitan Tabernacle. Some 100,000 lined the streets as a funeral parade two miles long followed his hearse from the Tabernacle to the cemetery. Flags flew at half-staff and shops and pubs were closed.

All this for a Victorian minister—who also happened to be the most extraordinary preacher of his day.

Calvinist Baptist

Spurgeon was born in Kelvedon, Essex, to a family of clerics. His father and grandfather were Nonconformist ministers (meaning they weren't Anglicans), and Spurgeon's earliest memories were of looking at the pictures in *Pilgrim's Progress* and *Foxe's Book of Martyrs*.

101

His formal education was limited, even by nineteenth-century standards: he attended local schools for a few years but never earned a university degree. He lived in Cambridge for a time, where he combined the roles of scholar and teaching assistant and was briefly tutored in Greek. Though he eschewed formal education, all his life he valued learning and books—especially those by Puritan divines—and his personal library eventually exceeded 12,000 volumes.

At age 15, Spurgeon broke with family tradition by becoming a Baptist. He attributed this conversion to a sermon heard by "chance"—when a snowstorm blew him away from his destination into a Primitive Methodist chapel. The experience forced Spurgeon to re-evaluate his idea on, among other things, infant baptism. Within four months he was baptized and joined a Baptist church.

His theology, however, remained more or less Calvinist, though he liked to think of himself as a "mere Christian." "I am never ashamed to avow myself a Calvinist," he once said. "I do not hesitate to take the name of Baptist, but if I am asked what is my creed, I reply, 'It is Jesus Christ.'"

Preaching sensation

Still a teen, Spurgeon began preaching in rural Cambridgeshire. He quickly filled the pews in his first pastorate in the village of Waterbeach. He had a boyish appearance that contrasted sharply with the maturity of his sermons. He had a good memory and always spoke extemporaneously from an outline.

His energy and oratorical skills and harmonious voice earned him such a reputation that within a year and a half, he was invited to preach in London, at the historic New Park Street Chapel. The congregation of 232 was so impressed, it voted for him to preach an additional six months. He moved to the city and never left.

As word spread of his abilities, he was invited to preach throughout London and the nation. No chapel seemed large enough to hold those who wanted to hear the "the preaching sensation of London." He preached to tens of thousands in London's greatest halls—Exeter, Surry Gardens, Agricultural. In 1861 his congregation, which kept extending his call, moved to the new Metropolitan Tabernacle, which seated 5,600.

At the center of controversy

Spurgeon did not go unnoticed in the secular press. On the one hand, his sermons were published in the Monday edition of the *London Times*, and even the *New York Times*. On the other hand, he was severely criticized by more traditional Protestants. His dramatic flair—he would pace the platform, acting out biblical stories, and fill his sermons with sentimental tales of dying children, grieving parents, and repentant harlots—offended many, and he was called "the Exeter Hall demagogue" and "the pulpit buffoon."

Spurgeon replied, "I am perhaps vulgar, but it is not intentional, save that I must and will make people listen. My firm conviction is that we have had enough polite preachers."

Not only his style, but his convictions created controversy as well. He never flinched from strong preaching: in a sermon on Acts 26:28, he said, "Almost persuaded to be a Christian is like the man who was almost pardoned, but he was hanged; like the man who was almost rescued, but he was burned in the house. A man that is almost saved is damned."

On certain subjects, he was incapable of moderation: Rome, ritualism, hypocrisy, and modernism—the last of which became the center of a controversy that would mark his last years in ministry.

The "Down-Grade Controversy," as it came to be known, was started in 1887 when Spurgeon began publicly claiming that some of his fellow Baptist ministers were "down grading" the faith. This was the late-nineteenth century, when Darwinism and critical biblical scholarship were compelling many Christians to re-evaluate their understanding of the Bible. Spurgeon believed the issue was not one of interpretation but of the essentials of the faith. He proclaimed in his monthly, *The Sword and the Trowel*, "Our warfare is with men who are giving up the atoning sacrifice, denying the inspiration of Holy Scripture, and casting slurs upon justification by faith."

The controversy took its toll on the denomination (which censured Spurgeon) and upon Spurgeon, whose already delicate health deteriorated even more during the year-long affair (he suffered from, among other things, recurring depressions and gout).

Spurgeon's contributions were larger than his pulpit, however. He established alms houses and an orphanage, and his Pastor's College, opened in 1855, continues to this day. He preached his last sermon in June 1891 and died six months later.

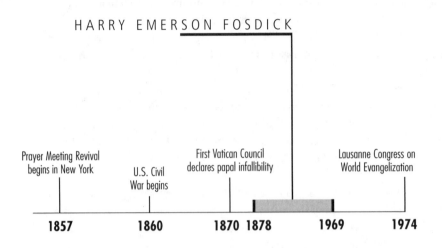

HARRY EMERSON FOSDICK

| Prayer Meeting Revival begins in New York | U.S. Civil War begins | First Vatican Council declares papal infallibility | | Lausanne Congress on World Evangelization |

| **1857** | **1860** | **1870 1878** | **1969** | **1974** |

PASTORS AND PREACHERS

Harry Emerson Fosdick

LIBERALISM'S POPULARIZER

> *"I believe in the personal God revealed in Christ, in his omnipresent activity and endless resources to achieve his purposes for us and for all men."*

Though "born again" at age 7, Harry Emerson Fosdick early on decided he wanted nothing to do with the born-again movement known as fundamentalism, just then coming into adolescence. Fosdick also rejected Calvinism, which he believed produced "a God who is a devil," and instead relied on his own personal spiritual experiences. The Lord was to be found in living experience, he argued, not at the end of some creed.

Fosdick, on the way to becoming the most celebrated preacher of his day, took some psychological and theological tumbles; yet he remained true to his early instincts, and as such, he mirrored the larger movements taking place in American Christianity. He became, as one biographer put it, "the most influential interpreter of religion to his generation."

Theological rebel

In his high school and college years, Fosdick was already developing a reputation as "the Jesse James of the theological world" (later in life he boasted that he had never repeated the Apostles' Creed). At Colgate University, under the tutelage of liberal William Newton Clarke, he studied the divide between religious experiences and the intellectual and cultural forms in which they were expressed: "We must distinguish between abiding experiences and changing categories," he wrote. From there he went on to New York's Union Theological Seminary.

In 1903 he was ordained at the Madison Avenue Baptist Church, and in 1911, he joined the Union faculty while accepting the pastorate at First Baptist Church in Montclair, New Jersey. His preaching reputation grew, but it was his writing that drew him to the nation's attention to him. Six early devotional books (among others, *The Meaning of Faith* and *The Meaning of Prayer*) sold in the millions.

He rejected a pessimistic Christianity that wallowed in sin or forecast doom for the planet. In spite of his experiences ministering in inner-city ghettos and French trenches (which he visited during World War I), he remained confident about the future: "I believe in the personal God revealed in Christ, in his omnipresent activity and endless resources to achieve his purposes for us and for all men."

Challenging the fundamentalists

From 1918 to 1925, Fosdick, though a Baptist, served as minister of First Presbyterian Church in New York, where his eloquence earned him a reputation among liberals and conservatives alike. The pressure built as fundamentalists worried aloud about Fosdick's brand of Christianity. Fundamentalist intellectual J. Gresham Machen asked, "The question is not whether Mr. Fosdick is winning men, but whether the thing to which he is winning them is Christianity."

In a May 1922 sermon, "Shall the Fundamentalists Win?" Fosdick replied by repudiating the core beliefs of the fundamentalist faith: belief in the virgin birth was unnecessary; the inerrancy of Scripture, untenable; and the doctrine of the Second Coming, absurd. Though he ended on a note of reconciliation, in the sermon he castigated fundamentalists as "bitterly intolerant."

Baptist oil baron John D. Rockefeller, the wealthiest man in the nation, loved it and paid for some 130,000 copies to be printed and distributed to every Protestant minister in the United States. What had been up to this time a series of skirmishes between fundamentalists and liberals now exploded into war.

Presbyterian William Jennings Bryan sought to expose Fosdick's "utter agnosticism" to the New York Presbytery and the General Assembly and have him dismissed from First Presbyterian. Debate raged across the nation, with prominent periodicals taking sides. Fosdick tried to be conciliatory, but he refused to budge theologically or become a Presbyterian to retain his pulpit. By 1924 he felt compelled to resign.

Pulpit psychologist

In May of the following year, he became pastor of Park Avenue Baptist Church in New York, and then moved on to newly built (thanks to Rockefeller money) Riverside Church, a modern Gothic cathedral seating over 2,300. For the last 16 years of his active ministry, and for the following 28 of his retirement, it was Fosdick's church home, where he practiced his liberal values (for example, offering worship in a variety of styles, from Quaker style to high church) and speaking out on key issues of the day (he was a champion of civil liberties, for instance, and invited blacks to preach from his pulpit).

Fosdick was no diehard liberal, and in 1935, he shocked his progressive colleagues with a sermon, "The Church Must Go Beyond Modernism." Incorporating the emerging neo-orthodox themes of Karl Barth and Reinhold Niebhur, he criticized liberalism's habit of changing beliefs to accommodate culture, of softening the reality of God and downplaying the themes of personal and social sin.

Since 1927 Fosdick's sermons had been broadcast from Boston to Chicago on the "National Vespers Hour," and more than 2 million listeners tuned in. For the most part, he concentrated on practical and experiential Christianity, defining preaching as "personal counseling on a group scale."

The personal emphasis didn't end in the pulpit—he did a great deal of counseling of individuals, and his *On Being a Real Person*, influenced by Freud, Jung, and his own personal experiences (he'd had a nervous breakdown in seminary), was a pioneering book in the newly emerging field of pastoral counseling.

As one historian put it, Fosdick's life was "the biopsy of an epoch." His ministry spanned two world wars and, in retirement, reached to Vietnam. In his 50 books, thousands of sermons, articles, and lectures, he walked hand-in-hand with American liberal Christianity as it made its way through the tumult of the first six decades of the twentieth century.

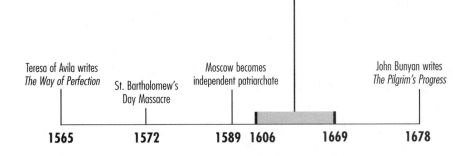

REMBRANDT HARMENSZ VAN RIJN

Teresa of Avila writes *The Way of Perfection*	St. Bartholomew's Day Massacre	Moscow becomes independent patriarchate			John Bunyan writes *The Pilgrim's Progress*
1565	1572	1589 1606	1669		1678

MUSICIANS, ARTISTS, AND WRITERS

Rembrandt Harmensz Van Rijn

DUTCH PAINTER OF THE SOUL

"[He paints with] the greatest and most natural emotion."
— a description of Rembrandt's style

The Dutch artists of Rembrandt's day gained respect painting landscapes, still lifes, and scenes glorifying ordinary life. But these subjects never held much interest for Rembrandt, who was captivated by the moving Bible stories his mother used to read to him. His contemporaries painted from the Bible, too, but not with the passion of Rembrandt, who remains famous for capturing the characters' emotions and involving his viewers in the stories.

Sorrows of an artist

At age 14, Rembrandt, the son of a wealthy miller, left the University of Leyden to study painting under an inconsequential painter of hell scenes. Three years later, however, he left the town he had lived in since birth to study art in Amsterdam, where he would live for the rest of his life.

In Amsterdam he developed both his affinity for depicting dramatic personal reactions and for chiaroscuro (painting in light and dark). In most of his paintings, light emerges from darkness, creating a timeless, emotional movement that draws the viewer into the scene.

By the late 1620s, he was already a renowned artist. "The Leyden miller's son is much praised, but before his time," wrote one critic, and a year later, the secretary of the Prince of Orange wrote an enthusiastic report commending Rembrandt's "penetration" into the essence of his subjects.

In 1634 Rembrandt married the wealthy and beautiful Saskia van Uylenburgh, who during the rest of her life was his inspiration. It was a time of professional triumph, as portrait commissions poured in and his paintings were highly praised. But though Rembrandt and Saskia's marriage was a happy one, it was also full of sorrow. Three children were born and died before a son, Titus, survived infancy. But the pregnancy was too difficult for Saskia, and she died the following year.

Rembrandt was also plagued by financial difficulties. He had a penchant for extravagant living, and when he purchased an expensive house in 1639, it placed him deep in debt.

Rembrandt acknowledged this extravagance by painting himself as the Prodigal Son, squandering money in the taverns with his wife, whom he depicted as a prostitute. In fact, Rembrandt often featured himself in his Bible paintings. In *The Raising of the Cross*, he even kept himself in his modern clothes to emphasize his personal involvement in the crucifixion. He believed the personalities in the Bible were like those of his Amsterdam acquaintances, so he painted these characters as he would his friends, with "the greatest and most natural emotion."

Then, on top of sorrow and a growing debt, came scandal. Rembrandt's servant, Hendrickje Stoffels, was summoned to appear before the Reformed church council. The official transcripts record that there, visibly pregnant, she "confesses to fornication with Rembrandt the painter, is gravely punished for it, admonished to penitence, and excluded from the Lord's Supper." Rembrandt himself was not censured, but his commissions, for which he could still command a good price, had dwindled in number.

In 1656 Rembrandt was forced to file for bankruptcy. He lost his house, his art collection, and soon after, his pride. He was forbidden from selling his own works and had to work for a firm set up by his servant Hendrickje and his son Titus. In 1663 Hendrickje died, and in 1668 Rembrandt's son Titus died.

The following year, Rembrandt died, leaving behind only one daughter, 650 paintings, 280 etchings, and 1,400 drawings. Among his last works is his one of his most famous, *The Return of the Prodigal Son*, which depicts the opulent and sinful sinner returning home to the presence of his father.

JOHANN SEBASTIAN BACH

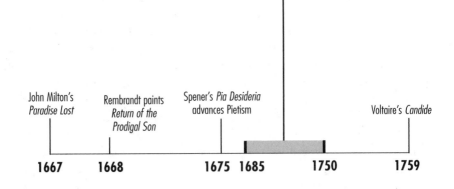

John Milton's *Paradise Lost*	Rembrandt paints *Return of the Prodigal Son*	Spener's *Pia Desideria* advances Pietism			Voltaire's *Candide*
1667	1668	1675	1685	1750	1759

MUSICIANS, ARTISTS, AND WRITERS

Johann Sebastian Bach

"THE FIFTH EVANGELIST"

> **"At a reverent performance of music, God is always at hand with his gracious presence."**

When he was 48, Johann Sebastian Bach acquired a copy of Luther's three-volume translation of the Bible. He pored over it as if it were a long-lost treasure. He underlined passages, corrected errors in the text and commentary, inserted missing words, and made notes in the margins. Near 1 Chronicles 25 (a listing of Davidic musicians) he wrote, "This chapter is the true foundation of all God-pleasing music." At 2 Chronicles 5:13 (which speaks of temple musicians praising God), he noted, "At a reverent performance of music, God is always at hand with his gracious presence."

As one scholar put it, Bach the musician was indeed "a Christian who lived with the Bible." Besides being the baroque era's greatest organist and composer, and one of the most productive geniuses in the history of Western music, Bach was also a theologian who just happened to work with a keyboard.

Early genius

He was born and schooled in Eisenach, Thuringia (at the same school Luther had attended), part of a family that in seven generations produced 53 prominent musicians. Johann Sebastian received his first musical instruction from his father, Johann Ambrosius, a town musician. By age 10 Bach was orphaned, and he went to live and study with his elder brother, Johann Christoph, an organist in Ohrdruf.

By age 15 Bach was ready to establish himself in the musical world, and he immediately showed immense talent in a variety of areas. He become a soprano (women weren't permitted to sing in church) in the choir of Lüneburg's Church of Saint Michael. Three years later, he was a violinist in the chamber orchestra of Prince Johann Ernst of Weimar. After a few months, he moved to Arnstadt to become a church organist.

In October 1705, Bach was invited to study for one month with the renowned Danish-born German organist and composer Dietrich Buxtehude. Bach was so enamored with his teacher, he stretched the visit to two months. When he returned to his church, he was severely criticized for breach of contract and, in the ensuing weeks, for his new organ flourishes and harmonies that accompanied congregational singing. But he was already too highly respected to be dismissed.

In 1707 he married a second cousin, Maria Barbara Bach, and went to Mülhausen to become organist in the Church of Saint Blasius. After various moves and prominent jobs, he finally settled down in Leipzig in 1723, where he remained for the rest of his life.

Maria died in 1720, and the next year he married Anna Magdalena Wilcken, an accomplished singer. She bore him 13 children, in addition to the seven he'd had by Maria, and helped copy his music for performers.

Bitter setting, brilliant work

Bach's stay in Leipzig, as musical director and choirmaster of Saint Thomas's church and school, wasn't always happy. He squabbled continually with the town council, and neither the council nor the populace appreciated his musical genius. They said he was a stuffy old man who clung stubbornly to obsolete forms of music. Consequently, they paid him a miserable salary, and when he died even contrived to defraud his widow of her meager inheritance.

Ironically, in this setting Bach wrote his most enduring music. For a time he wrote a cantata each week (today, a composer who writes a cantata a year is highly praised), 202 of which survive. Most conclude with a chorale based on a simple Lutheran hymn, and the music is at all times closely bound to biblical texts. Among these works are the *Ascension Cantata* and the *Christmas Oratorio*.

In Leipzig he also composed his epic *Mass in B Minor*, *The Passion of St. John* and *The Passion of St. Matthew*—all for use as worship services. The latter piece has sometimes been called "the supreme cultural achievement of all Western civilization," and even the radical skeptic Friedrich Nietzsche (1844–1900) admitted upon hearing it, "One who has completely forgotten Christianity truly hears it here as gospel."

Bach revival

After Bach's death, people seemed glad to wipe their ears of his music. He was remembered less as a composer than as an organist and harpsichordist. Some of his music was sold, and some was reportedly used to wrap garbage. For the next 80 years his music was neglected by the public, although a few musicians (Mozart and Beethoven, for example) admired it. Not until 1829, when German composer Felix Mendelssohn arranged a performance of *The Passion of St. Matthew*, did a larger audience appreciate Bach the composer.

In terms of pure music, Bach has become known as one who could combine the rhythm of French dances, the gracefulness of Italian song, and the intricacy of German counterpoint—all in one composition. In addition, Bach could write musical equivalents of verbal ideas, such as undulating a melody to represent the sea.

But music was never just music to Bach. Nearly three-fourths of his 1,000 compositions were written for use in worship. Between his musical genius, his devotion to Christ, and the effect of his music, he has come to be known in many circles as "the Fifth Evangelist."

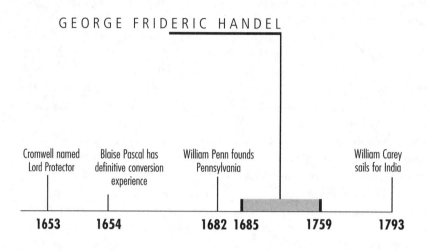

GEORGE FRIDERIC HANDEL

Cromwell named Lord Protector	Blaise Pascal has definitive conversion experience	William Penn founds Pennsylvania		William Carey sails for India
1653	1654	1682 1685	1759	1793

MUSICIANS, ARTISTS, AND WRITERS

George Frideric Handel

COMPOSER OF *MESSIAH*

> "He [Handel] would frequently declare the pleasure he felt in setting the Scriptures to music, and how contemplating the many sublime passages in the Psalms had contributed to his edification."
>
> — *Sir John Hawkins*

By 1741 George Frideric Handel was a failure. Bankrupted, in great physical pain, and the victim of plots to sabotage his career, the once-great opera composer scheduled a "farewell" appearance in London in April. To the London elite, it looked like this "German nincompoop," as he was once called, was through. That summer, however, he composed *Messiah*, which not only brought him back into the spotlight, but is still deemed by some to be "an epitome of Christian faith."

Opposition begins

Unlike Handel's fellow countryman and contemporary Johann Bach (the two were born the same year but never met), Handel never had a musical family. George's father was a practical "surgeon-barber" who discouraged his son's musical career at every turn. His son was to be a lawyer. Indeed, George studied law until 1703, even though his father (who finally allowed his son to take music lessons at age 9) died when he was 11. By age 12, Handel was substituting for his organ teacher and had written his first composition.

After musical studies in Germany and Italy, Handel moved to England, where he stayed for the rest of his life and became a composer for the Chapel Royal. His greatest passion was for the opera—an ill-timed passion, for the form was quickly falling out of fashion in England. The most popular work was the 1728 *Beggar's Opera*, which satirized the form itself. Still, Handel continued to pen operas into the 1740s, losing more and more money.

Handel's friends expressed concern that the concert hall was nearly empty. Never mind, he joked, an empty venue would mean great acoustics.

He didn't joke for long. In 1737 Handel's opera company went bankrupt, and he suffered what seems to be a mild stroke. But to make matters worse, his latest musical fascination—the oratorio (a composition for orchestra and voices telling a sacred story without costumes, scenery, or dramatic action)—was his most controversial yet. His first oratorio (actually, the first of its kind in English), *Esther*, was met with outrage by the church. A Bible story was being told by "common mummers," and even worse, the words of God were being spoken in the theater!

"What are we coming to when the will of Satan is imposed upon us in this fashion?" cried one minister. The bishop of London apparently agreed and prohibited the oratorio from being performed. When Handel proceeded anyway, and the royal family attended, it was met with success—but the church was still angry.

In 1739 advertisements for *Israel in Egypt* were torn down by devout Christians, who also disrupted its performances. All of this angered the devoutly Lutheran Handel. As his friend Sir John Hawkins commented, "Throughout his life, [he] manifested a deep sense of religion. In conversation he would frequently declare the pleasure he felt in setting the Scriptures to music, and how contemplating the many sublime passages in the Psalms had contributed to his edification."

Though irritated—and Handel was often irritated, earning a reputation for prolific cursing in five languages—he dismissed the Puritans' concerns. "I have read my Bible very well," he said, "and will choose for myself." In fact, Handel maintained that he knew the Bible as well as any bishop. Financially, however, it did him little good. Once the composer for royalty, he was now threatened with debtor's prison.

Delivered by *Messiah*

Deeply depressed, Handel was visited by his friend Charles Jennens. The wealthy, devout Anglican had written a libretto about the life of Christ and the work of redemption, with the text completely taken from the Bible. A fussy perfectionist, Jennens had written it to challenge the deists who denied the divinity of Jesus. Would Handel compose the music for it? he asked. Handel answered that he would, and estimated its completion in a year.

Soon thereafter, a group of Dublin charities approached Handel to compose a work for a benefit performance. The money raised would help free men from debtor's prison, and Handel would receive a generous commission. Now with a text and a motivation, Handel began composing *Messiah* on August 22, 1741. Within six days, Part One was finished. In nine more, Part Two. Six more and Part Three was done. It took him only an additional two days to finish the orchestration. Handel composed like a man obsessed. He rarely left his room and rarely touched his meals. But in 24 days he had composed 260 pages—an immense physical feat.

When he finished writing what would become known as the Hallelujah Chorus, he said, "I did think I did see all Heaven before me, and the great God himself."

Though the performance of the piece again caused controversy (Jonathan Swift, author of *Gulliver's Travels* and then the dean of Saint Patrick's Cathedral, was outraged and initially refused to allow his musicians to participate), the premiere on April 13, 1742, at the Fishamble Street Musick Hall was a sensation. An overcapacity crowd of 700 people attended, raising 400 pounds to release 142 men from prison. (The demand for tickets was so great that men were asked not to wear their swords and women asked not to wear hoops in their skirts, allowing 100 extra people into the audience. Such hoops immediately fell out of fashion for concerts.)

Still it took nearly a year for *Messiah* to be invited to London. Religious controversy surrounded it there, too, and Handel compromised a bit by dropping the "blasphemous" title from handbills. It was instead called "A New Sacred Oratorio." But the controversy wasn't strong enough to keep away the king, who stood instantly at the opening notes of the Hallelujah Chorus—(though some historians have suggested it was because he was partially deaf and mistook it for the national anthem) a tradition ever since.

Though it had met rave reviews in Dublin ("the most finished piece of music"), it was not very popular in London after its premiere. By 1745 Handel was again playing to empty houses and nearing poverty. Not until his oratorio *Judas Maccabeus*, which was misunderstood by the English as a veiled nationalistic anthem, did Handel (and with him *Messiah*) reach the pinnacle of his career.

Until his death, Handel conducted 30 performances of *Messiah* (none at Christmastime, for Handel deemed it a Lenten piece), only one of which was in a church, Bristol Cathedral. In that audience sat John Wesley. "I doubt if that congregation was ever so serious at a sermon as they were during this performance," he remarked.

Handel died on the day before Easter 1759, hoping to "meet his good God, his sweet Lord and Savior, on the day of his Resurrection." A close friend remarked, "He died as he lived—a good Christian, with a true sense of his duty to God and to man, and in perfect charity with all the world."

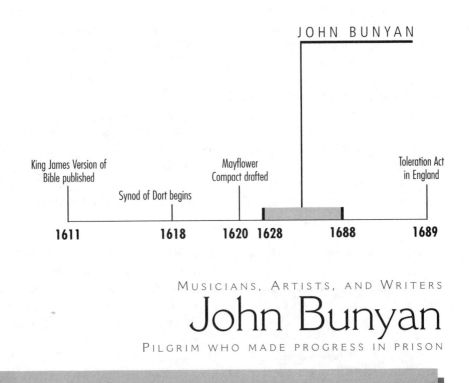

JOHN BUNYAN

King James Version of
Bible published

Synod of Dort begins

Mayflower
Compact drafted

Toleration Act
in England

1611   1618   1620   1628   1688   1689

MUSICIANS, ARTISTS, AND WRITERS

John Bunyan

PILGRIM WHO MADE PROGRESS IN PRISON

> *"I saw a man clothed with rags ... a book in his hand and a great burden upon his back."*

Successful English writers were, in John Bunyan's day, nearly synonymous with wealth. Men like Richard Baxter and John Milton could afford to write because they didn't need to earn a living. But Bunyan, a traveling tinker like his father, was nearly penniless before becoming England's most famous author. His wife was also destitute, bringing only two Puritan books as a dowry.

"We came together as poor as poor might be," Bunyan wrote, "not having so much household-stuff as a dish or spoon betwixt us both."

What allowed Bunyan to become the bestselling author of one of the most beloved books in the English language was when things actually got worse: an imprisonment of 12 years.

Early temptations

Born in Elstow, Bedfordshire, Bunyan married at age 21. Those books his wife brought to the marriage began a process of conversion. Gradually, he gave up recreations like dancing, bell ringing, and sports; he began attending church and fought off temptations. "One morning as I did lie in bed," he wrote in his autobiography, "I was, as at other times, most fiercely assaulted with this temptation, to sell and part with Christ; the wicked suggestion still running in my mind, Sell him, sell him, sell him, sell him, sell him, as fast as a man could speak."

Bunyan was drawn to the Christian fellowship he saw among "three or four poor women sitting at a door ... talking abut the things of God." He was also befriended by John Gifford, minister at a Separatist church in Bedford.

The tinker joined the church and within four years was drawing crowds "from all parts" as a lay minister. "I went myself in chains to preach to them in chains," he said, "and carried that fire in my own conscience that I persuaded them to beware of."

Prison: a mixed blessing

Bunyan's rise as a popular preacher coincided with the Restoration of Charles II.

The freedom of worship Separatists had enjoyed for 20 years was quickly ended; those not conforming with the Church of England would be arrested. By January 1661, Bunyan sat imprisoned in the county jail.

The worst punishment, for Bunyan, was being separated from his second wife (his first had died in 1658) and four children. "The parting ... hath oft been to me in this place as the pulling the flesh from my bones," he wrote. He tried to support his family making "many hundred gross of long tagg'd [shoe] laces" while imprisoned, but he mainly depended on "the charity of good people" for their well-being.

Bunyan could have freed himself by promising not to preach but refused. He told local magistrates he would rather remain in prison until moss grew on his eyelids than fail to do what God commanded.

Still, the imprisonment wasn't as bad as some have imagined. He was permitted visitors, spent some nights at home, and even traveled once to London. The jailer allowed him occasionally to preach to "unlawful assemblies" gathered in secret. More importantly, the imprisonment gave him the incentive and opportunity to write. He penned at least nine books between 1660 and 1672 (he wrote three others—two against Quakers and the other an expository work—before his arrest).

Profitable Mediations, Christian Behavior (a manual on good relationships), and *The Holy City* (an interpretation of Revelation) were followed by *Grace Abounding to the*

Chief of Sinners, considered the greatest Puritan autobiography. But from 1667 to 1672, Bunyan probably spent most of his time on his greatest legacy, *The Pilgrim's Progress*.

Pilgrim's success

Charles II eventually relented in 1672, issuing the Declaration of Indulgence. Bunyan was freed, licensed as a Congregational minister, and called to be pastor of the Bedford church. When persecution was renewed, Bunyan was again imprisoned for six months. After his second release, *Pilgrim's Progress* was published.

"I saw a man clothed with rags ... a book in his hand and a great burden upon his back." So begins the allegorical tale that describes Bunyan's own conversion process. Pilgrim, like Bunyan, is a tinker. He wanders from the City of Destruction to the Celestial City, a pilgrimage made difficult by the burden of sin (an anvil on his back), the Slough of Despond, Vanity Fair, and other such allegorical waystations.

The book was instantly popular with every social class. His first editor, Charles Doe, noted that 100,000 copies were already in print by 1692. Samuel Taylor Coleridge called it, "the best *Summa Theologicae Evangelicae* ever produced by a writer not miraculously inspired." Every English household that owned a Bible also owned the famous allegory. Eventually, it became the bestselling book (apart from the Bible) in publishing history.

The book brought Bunyan great fame, and though he continued to pastor the Bedford church, he also regularly preached in London. He continued to write. *The Life and Death of Mr. Badman* (1680) has been called the first English novel (since it is less of an allegory than *Pilgrim's Progress*), and was followed by another allegory, *The Holy War*. He also published several doctrinal and controversial works, a book of verse, and a children's book.

By age 59 Bunyan was one of England's most famous writers. He carried out his pastoring duties and was nicknamed "Bishop Bunyan." In August 1688, he rode through heavy rain to reconcile a father and son, became ill, and died.

HARRIET BEECHER STOWE

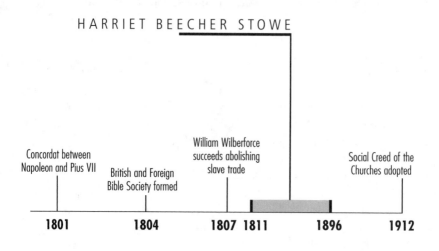

| 1801 | 1804 | 1807 1811 | 1896 | 1912 |

Concordat between Napoleon and Pius VII — 1801

British and Foreign Bible Society formed — 1804

William Wilberforce succeeds abolishing slave trade — 1807

Social Creed of the Churches adopted

MUSICIANS, ARTISTS, AND WRITERS

Harriet Beecher Stowe

AUTHOR OF *UNCLE TOM'S CABIN*

> "[Uncle Tom's Cabin is] perhaps the most influential novel ever published, a verbal earthquake, an ink-and-paper tidal wave."
>
> — one of Harriet Beecher Stowe's critics

When President Lincoln met Harriet Beecher Stowe in 1863, he is reported to have said, "So you're the little woman who wrote the book that made this great war!"

Uncle Tom's Cabin may not have caused the Civil War, but it shook both North and South. It declared the profound value of a human soul and made emancipation inevitable. Susan Bradford wrote, after her state of Florida seceded, "If Mrs. Harriet Beecher Stowe had died before she wrote *Uncle Tom's Cabin*, this would never have happened.... Isn't it strange how much harm a pack of lies can do?"

Absurdity of slavery

Harriet was the seventh of 12 children of Lyman Beecher, Congregationalist minister, noted revivalist and reformer. When

118

Harriet's mother lay dying, Lyman repeatedly spoke words to her that the family embraced as their life text, often repeating it to one another: "... Ye are come unto Mount Sion, and unto the city of the living God, the heavenly Jerusalem, and to an innumerable company of angels, to the general assembly and church of the firstborn, ... and to the spirits of just men made perfect, and to Jesus the mediator of the new covenant, and to the blood of sprinkling, that speaketh better things than that of Abel." The noble thought embedded in these words would energize the unanswerable argument *Uncle Tom's Cabin* proclaimed: if a slave can come to Mount Sion and to Jesus and to the company of saints in the New Jerusalem, how can you set him up on an auction block and trade him from one white man to another?

In 1832 her father moved the family to the frontier city of Cincinnati, where he became president of Lane Seminary, soon a center for abolitionists. At 25 Harriet married Calvin Ellis Stowe, professor of biblical literature at Lane.

Writing and mothering

During her child-rearing years, she read to her seven children two hours each evening and, for a time, ran a small school in her home. She described herself as "a little bit of a woman, just as thin and dry as a pinch of snuff; never very much to look at in my best days and very much used-up by now, a mere drudge with few ideas beyond babies and housekeeping."

But a mere drudge she was not. She found time to write, partially to bolster the meager family income. An early literary success at age 32 (for a collection of short stories) encouraged her, but she still worried about the conflict between writing and mothering. Despite privation and anxiety, due largely to her husband's precarious health, she wrote continually and in 1843 published *The Mayflower; or, Sketches of Scenes and Characters Among the Descendants of the Pilgrims*. Her husband urged her on, predicting she could mold "the mind of the West for the coming generation." That she did with the publication of *Uncle Tom's Cabin or Life Among the Lowly* at age 40.

She had lived for 18 years in Cincinnati, separated only by the Ohio River from a slave-holding community in Kentucky; she gained firsthand knowledge of fugitive slaves and about life in the South from friends and through her contact with the "Underground Railroad" there. The secret network was started in defiance of the "Fugitive Slave Acts" (severe measures passed the year before that mandated the return of runaway slaves without trial) to help escaped slaves reach safety in the North or in Canada. Stowe herself helped some slaves escape.

But Stowe still brooded over how she could further respond. Then, during a church Communion service, the scene of the triumphant death of Tom flashed before her. She soon formed the story that preceded Tom's death.

Million copy bestseller

In 1850 her husband became professor at Bowdoin College and moved his family to Brunswick, Maine. In Brunswick, Stowe wrote the story of *Uncle Tom's Cabin* for serial publication in the *National Era*, an antislavery paper of Washington, D.C., in 1851 and 1852 in 40 installments, each with a cliffhanger ending. Her name became anathema in the South. But elsewhere the book had an unparalleled popularity; it was translated into at least 23 languages. When it appeared in book form, it sold 1,000,000 copies before the Civil War. The dramatic adaptation of *Uncle Tom's Cabin* played to capacity audiences. Stowe reinforced her story with *The Key to Uncle Tom's Cabin* (1853), in which she accumulated a large number of documents and testimonies against slavery.

Its publication also inspired a reaction from the South: critical reviews and the publication of some 30 anti-abolitionist Uncle Tom novels within three years.

By literary standards, the novel's situations are contrived, the dialogue unreal, and the slaves romanticized. Still, Stowe communicated the absurdity of slavery through Tom's triumph over the brutal evil of Simon Legree.

"'How would ye like to be tied to a tree, and have a slow fire lit up around ye?' asked Legree. 'Wouldn't that be pleasant, eh, Tom?'

"'Mas'r,' said Tom, 'I know ye can do dreadful things, but'—he stretched himself upward and clasped his hands—'but after ye've killed the body, there ain't no more ye can do. And oh! there's all eternity to come after that!'"

Until her death in July 1896, Stowe averaged nearly a book a year, but *Uncle Tom's Cabin* was her legacy. Even one of her harshest critics acknowledged that it was "perhaps the most influential novel ever published, a verbal earthquake, an ink-and-paper tidal wave."

She thereafter led the life of a woman of letters, writing novels, of which *The Minister's Wooing* (1859) is best known, and many studies of social life in both fiction and essay. Stowe published also a small volume of religious poems and toward the end of her career gave some public readings from her writings.

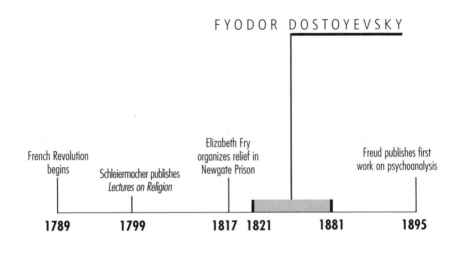

FYODOR DOSTOYEVSKY

| French Revolution begins | Schleiermacher publishes *Lectures on Religion* | Elizabeth Fry organizes relief in Newgate Prison | | Freud publishes first work on psychoanalysis |

1789   **1799**   **1817 1821**   **1881**   **1895**

MUSICIANS, ARTISTS, AND WRITERS

Fyodor Dostoyevsky

RUSSIAN NOVELIST OF SPIRITUAL DEPTH

> *"If someone proved to me that Christ is outside the truth and that in reality the truth were outside of Christ, then I should prefer to remain with Christ rather than with the truth."*

The sentence of death had been read, last rites offered. Fyodor Dostoyevksy, 29, watched as fellow prisoners were tied to a stake, readied to be shot.

Then a messenger burst upon this scene, saying the Tsar had decided to spare their lives (as it turned out, the mock execution had been part of his punishment). When the pardon was announced, two of the prisoners went permanently insane; another went on to write *Crime and Punishment* and *The Brothers Karamozov*—two of the greatest novels in Western literature.

The experience was perhaps the most dramatic but not the only crisis of Dostoyevsky's mercurial life. Though a devout Christian, he was never a good one; though a brilliant writer, his works remain technically unpolished. And yet, his insights into the human heart—perhaps because his own heart was so troubled—remain some of the most profound in literature.

121

Brutalized by chance

Dostoyevksy's father, a lecherous and cruel man (he was eventually murdered by his serfs), had marked out for him a career as a military engineer. But Dostoyevsky longed to take up the pen, and after completing his degree in 1843, he resigned his commission to commence his writing career.

His first novel, *Poor Folk*, won praise from Russian critics, who hailed him as the great new Russian talent. After the mock execution, Dostoyevsky was sent to a Siberian labor camp for four years for his involvement in "revolutionary activities." After his release, he wrote *The House of the Dead*, based on his brutal camp experiences. The novel initiated the Russian tradition of prison camp literature.

It was while in prison that Dostoyevsky suffered his first attacks of epilepsy, a condition that plagued him his whole life and that he described in his writings.

In the 1860s, Dostoyevsky edited (with his brother, Mikhail) two influential journals. In these journals, and in his 1864 *Notes from the Underground*, he increasingly distanced himself from utopian radicals (socialists and communists) who sought to abolish serfdom and corruption in the Tsarist government—in fact, the whole hierarchical nature of society—and usher in a better society.

In spite of his literary success, Dostoyevsky managed to bring his life to ruin. He had become addicted to gambling, and had lost all his own money and all that friends had loaned him. He fervently believed in a will to win: "In game of chance," he once wrote, "if one has perfect control of one's will ... one cannot fail to overcome the brutality of chance."

Chance was brutal to Dostoyevsky, and in order to stave off his creditors, he signed an unjust contract with a conniving publisher who sought to exploit Dostoyevsky's situation and lack of discipline: Dostoyevsky was to finish a novel by a certain date, and if he failed, the publisher would retain all the rights to all of Dostoyevsky's published work.

Dostoyevsky characteristically delayed until it seemed too late. Less than a month remained when finally he employed an 18-year old stenographer, Anna Smitkina. After dictating to her day and night for three weeks, he delivered the manuscript, titled *The Gambler*, to his publisher and was saved. It was the discipline and encouragement of Anna that had made the difference, and Dostoyevsky knew it.

His first marriage (which had ended with his wife's death) had been an emotional see-saw: "We were unhappy together ... but we could not cease to love one another," he wrote. "The more unhappy we were, the more we became attached to each other." His subsequent marriage to Anna proved to be a stabilizing force in his life, and only after marrying her did he produce his greatest works.

Troubled Christian

In his later novels, Christian themes emerge more explicitly, though they are never the only ones.

Crime and Punishment (which he was most of the way through when he wrote *The Gambler*) is about the commandment, "Thou shalt not kill." With rich psychological insight, Dostoyevsky tells the story of Raskolnikov, who murders a greedy old woman and is brought to ruin by the weight of his conscience.

In *The Idiot* (1868–69) Dostoyevsky presents a man of Christlike goodness in a world of thorny reality. In *The Possessed* (1872) he critiqued liberalism's skepticism, mockery of traditional values, and neglect of the family.

The Brothers Karamozov (1879–80) was his last and arguably greatest novel. Theological and philosophical themes emerge as he describes the lives of four brothers. The two most memorable are Alyosha, a Christ figure who desperately wants to put Christian love into practice, and Ivan, who angrily defends agnosticism.

In the chapter "Rebellion," Ivan indicts God the Father for creating a world in which children suffer. In "The Grand Inquisitor," Ivan tells the story of Christ's return to earth during the Spanish Inquisition. The Inquisitor arrests Christ as "the worst of heretics," because, the Inquisitor explains, the church has rejected Christ, trading away its freedom in Christ for "miracle, mystery, and authority."

Dostoyevsky, the Russian Orthodox believer, made room for a most scathing critique of Christianity. Yet at the same time he affirms it in the character of Alyosha, who believes passionately in Christlike love. In answer to the question "What is Hell?" one of the characters replies, "It is the suffering of being unable to love."

This internal war between the believer and the skeptic waged within Dostoyevsky's soul his entire life, both theologically and morally. One of Tolstoy's friends said, "I cannot consider Dostoyevsky either a good or happy man. He was wicked, envious, vicious, and spent the whole of his life in emotions and irritations.... In Switzerland he treated his servant, in my presence, so abominably that the offended servant cried out, 'I too am a human being!'" The writer Turgeniev once called him "the most evil Christian I have ever met in my life."

In addition, his social and political views were often extreme. He believed that western Europe was about to collapse, and that Russia and the Russian Orthodox Church ("Christ lives in the Orthodox Church alone," he once said) would create the kingdom of God on earth.

His faith, however, seemed deeply devout, if somewhat perplexing in its expression: "If someone proved to me that Christ is outside the truth," he wrote, "and that in reality the truth were outside of Christ, then I should prefer to remain with Christ rather than with the truth."

In spite of the paradoxes of his life, genius shines through his work, and no other novelist has ever presented characters with such depth and ideas so vital.

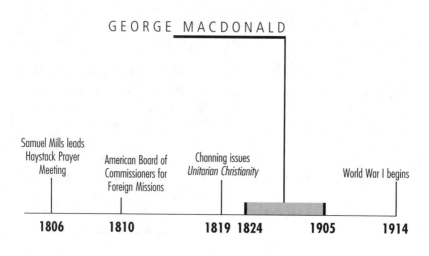

GEORGE MACDONALD

Samuel Mills leads Haystack Prayer Meeting	American Board of Commissioners for Foreign Missions	Channing issues *Unitarian Christianity*		World War I begins
1806	1810	1819 1824	1905	1914

MUSICIANS, ARTISTS, AND WRITERS

George MacDonald

FABLED VICTORIAN WRITER

> *"With his divine alchemy, he [God] turns not only water into wine, but common things into radiant mysteries, yea, every meal into a Eucharist, and the jaws of death into an outgoing gate."*

While he reserved a place in his theology for hell (though not an eternal one), George MacDonald was more fascinated with God's triumphant love: "I believe that no man is ever condemned for any sin except one—that he will not leave his sins and come out of them, and be the child of him who is his Father."

This poet, preacher, and writer of fairy tales was taken with the quote, "Our life is no dream; but it ought to become one, and perhaps will." His vision of the mystery that surrounds us and the fantastic world awaiting us enthralled readers in both Victorian England and post-Civil War America.

Transatlantic fame

After being raised in Huntley, Aberdeenshire, by devout Calvinist parents, he attended King's College in Aberdeen. At Highbury Theological College, he received his divinity degree, and in 1850 he became a pastor of a Congregational church in Arundel. Early the following year, he married Louisa Powell, with whom he enjoyed a long and happy marriage.

The Scotsman was forced to resign his pulpit in 1853 because he liked to dabble in "German theology," meaning the new higher critical approach to biblical studies emerging from that country. He never took another church but spent the rest of his life lecturing, preaching, and especially writing.

Between 1851 and 1897, he wrote over 50 books in all manner of genre: novels, plays, essays, sermons, poems, and fairy tales. And then there were his two fantasies for adults, *Phantastes* (1858) and *Lilith* (1895), which defy categorization. During these years, Lewis Carroll became a good friend and gave him the first manuscript of *Alice in Wonderland* to read to his children. Other British literary luminaries—like John Ruskin, Charles Kingsley, Lord Tennyson, and Matthew Arnold—were among his associates and admirers.

When McDonald visited the United States in 1872 for a lecture tour, the likes of Ralph Waldo Emerson, Henry Wadsworth Longfellow, John Greenleaf Whittier, Oliver Wendell Holmes, and Mark Twain paid him homage. After his stay in New York City, one large Fifth Avenue church offered him the almost unheard of salary of $20,000 a year to become its pastor. MacDonald thought the idea preposterous.

His success did not exempt him from more-than-ordinary suffering. Poverty plagued him so much that his family occasionally faced literal starvation. His own lungs were diseased, and tuberculosis killed two brothers and two half-sisters. It also ravaged his children, four of whom died before him. He himself had a stroke at age 74 and lapsed into virtual silence for the last seven years of his life.

Still, MacDonald believed suffering was finally redemptive: "All pains, indeed, and all sorrows, all demons, yea, and all sins themselves, under the suffering care of the highest minister, are but the ministers of truth and righteousness."

Inspiring writers

MacDonald eventually became an Anglican, but he never had much patience with high theology or liturgy—he said it often stood in the way of people encountering Christ personally. Furthermore, it wasn't just the church but all of creation that revealed God: "With his divine alchemy, he [God] turns not only water into wine, but common things into radiant mysteries, yea, every meal into a Eucharist, and the jaws of death into an outgoing gate."

MacDonald's popularity has faded with time, though he retains a small, loyal following, and his *The Fairy and the Goblin* (1872) and *The Fairy and Curdie* 1883) are still read by children. But in his day, he inspired not a few of the 20th century's favorite writers, like G.K. Chesterton, J.R.R. Tolkien, Madeleine L'Engle, and C.S. Lewis, to name four. "I have never concealed the fact that I regarded him as my master," wrote Lewis; "indeed I fancy I have never written a book in which I did not quote from him."

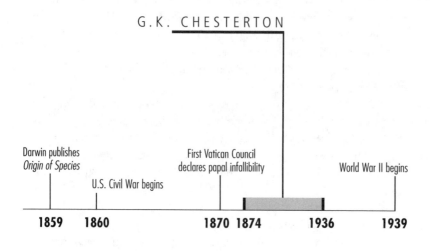

G.K. CHESTERTON

Darwin publishes
Origin of Species

U.S. Civil War begins

First Vatican Council
declares papal infallibility

World War II begins

1859   1860   1870 1874   1936   1939

MUSICIANS, ARTISTS, AND WRITERS
G.K. Chesterton
"ENORMOUS" ESSAYIST, POET, WRITER

> *"What can one be but frivolous about serious things? Without frivolity they are simply too tremendous."*

The life of Gilbert Keith Chesterton, like all lives, should not be summarized in a single word. Still, one asserts itself everywhere in his biographies: *enormous*. "He was close to 400 pounds," noted one chauffeur, in whose car door Chesterton was once stuck, "but he'd never give it away." Chesterton took his dilemma, like every other subject imaginable, with humor. He said he would have tried to exit the car sideways, but "I have no sideways."

Chesterton's gargantuan frame held within it a gargantuan mind, and for this, more than his obesity, is he called enormous. Noted one critic, "Chesterton is recognized by essayists as the greatest of essayists; by poets as a magnificent poet; by humorists as a humorist of tremendous versatility; by philosophers as a profound philosopher; by controversialists as a deadly but lovable master of controversy; by political economists as a man of deep political insights; by novelists as a most able novelist; and by theologians as one who saw, sometimes, far deeper than they are able to see into theological truths."

The absent-minded commentator

"I regret that I have no gloomy and savage father to offer to the public gaze as the true cause of all my tragic heritage," Chesterton wrote of his beginnings, "and that I cannot do my duty as a true modern, by cursing everybody who made me whatever I am." Born and educated in London, Chesterton first wanted to be an artist. In fact, he produced paintings and illustrations throughout his writing career. But growing up, he was mainly considered an absent-minded dunce. He once wandered around the playground during class, explaining he thought it was Saturday. His teachers believed him. His absent-mindedness continued throughout his life, even after he was hailed as one of the greatest geniuses of his day. He once telegraphed his wife: "Am at Market Harborough. Where ought I to be?" She responded, "Home."

But the mindless genius loved a great paradox and was considered a master of the form: "Anything worth doing is worth doing badly."

"About what else than serious subjects can one possibly make jokes?"

"The word *orthodoxy* no longer means being right; it practically means being wrong."

"Vice demands virgins."

"What can one be but frivolous about serious things? Without frivolity they are simply too tremendous."

These were not mere plays on words—Chesterton saw the nonsense of paradox as a "supreme assertion of truth": "Critics were almost entirely complimentary to what they were pleased to call my brilliant paradoxes," he admitted, "until they discovered that I really meant what I said."

These, and other epigrams fill Chesterton's 70 books, hundreds of newspaper columns, and countless other writings, including those in his own magazine, *G.K.'s Weekly*. He is, however, considered "a master without a masterpiece," since there is no crowning achievement in his social criticism, literary criticism, theological treatises, or novels.

Though many of his works are now forgotten, they have left a legacy on the world. Mahatma Gandhi was inspired by one of his essays in London's *Illustrated News* to nationalize India with a distinctly non-Western ambience. George Orwell borrowed the date 1984 from one of Chesterton's novels. Chesterton's apologetic works were key in the conversion of C.S. Lewis, and his playful style was adopted by that writer. Poet T.S. Eliot remarked that he "did more than any man in his time ... to maintain the existence of the [Christian] minority in the modern world."

And he did it all with joviality, even in such apologetic works as *Orthodoxy* (1908), historical theory in *The Everlasting Man* (1925), and theological biography in *St. Thomas Aquinas* (1933). Any subject may seem as "dull as ditchwater," he wrote, but added, "naturalists with microscopes have told me that ditchwater teems with quiet fun."

Drawn to Rome

Born and raised in the Church of England, Chesterton was long fascinated with

Roman Catholicism. Upon questioning a Yorkshire priest with "some rather sordid social questions of vice and crime," he was surprised to discover the clergyman's profound understanding of evil. He then fictionalized the priest in his best-known works, the Father Brown detective mysteries (1911–1935).

In 1922 Chesterton left Canterbury for Rome. Catholicism, he asserted, was the only church that "dared to go down with me into the depths of myself." He would have converted earlier, he told the hordes of shocked Protestants, but was "much too frightened of that tremendous Reality on the altar."

His conversion was followed by a few books on denominational topics, including some jabs at Puritanism and the Reformation. "But on the whole," one evangelical Protestant scholar is quick to add, "there has not been a more articulate champion of classic Christianity, virtue, and decency."

Shortly after writing his autobiography, Chesterton fell ill and died. Authors from T.S. Eliot (who penned his obituary) to H.G. Wells, a longtime friend and debating opponent, expressed their grief. After the funeral, Pope Pius XI declared the rotund writer Defender of the Faith—a title as true for Protestants as it is for Catholics.

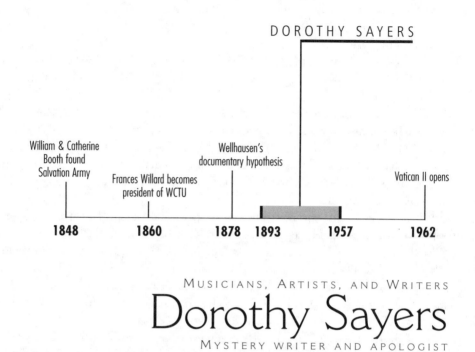

DOROTHY SAYERS

William & Catherine Booth found Salvation Army

Frances Willard becomes president of WCTU

Wellhausen's documentary hypothesis

Vatican II opens

1848   1860   1878   1893   1957   1962

MUSICIANS, ARTISTS, AND WRITERS

Dorothy Sayers

MYSTERY WRITER AND APOLOGIST

> *"Man is never truly himself except when he is actively creating something."*

She was summarizing a story others had criticized as dull: "So that is the outline of the official story—the talk of the time when God was the underdog and got beaten, when he submitted to the conditions he had laid down and became a man like the men he had made, and the men he had made broke him and killed him."

As if she hadn't already made the point, Dorothy Sayers continued: "This is the dogma we find so dull—this terrifying drama of which God is the victim and hero."

You can almost hear the pause after the period; then she concludes, "If this is dull, then what, in Heaven's name, is worthy to be called exciting?"

Sayers never found Christianity, nor life itself, dull. This type of passionate argument, usually accompanied by pointed humor, was typical for Sayers, as was passionate living. It seemed no matter what she put her hand to, it became a success; we can be thankful that Christian apologetics was one of her many passions.

Author of mysteries

She was born at Oxford, the only child of the Rev. Henry Sayers. She won a scholarship to Somerville College, Oxford, and in 1915 graduated with first class honors in modern languages.

The routine and isolation of academia hardly appealed to her, so she joined Blackwell's, the Oxford publishers, and then became a copywriter at Bensons, a London advertising firm. She struck gold right way, being largely responsible for a successful national campaign for Colman's mustard; she held the public's interest in the product by telling stories about the members of the imaginary Mustard Club (like Lord Bacon and Cookham, and Lady Hearty).

While at Bensons, *Whose Body?*, the first of her world-famous "Lord Peter Wimsey" detective novels, was published. Wimsey, with his signature monocle and "foppish" air, worked with his friend Inspector Parker of Scotland Yard to solve cases usually involving relatives or close friends. Sayers became known for using the techniques of fine novels in the popular genre of detective writing (at least one scholar has compared her fiction writing to that of Jane Austen). All told, Sayers published 12 detective novels between 1923 and 1937, several of which have become international classics.

And this all happened in an era before the writing of mysteries was considered a woman's domain. Sayers, however, did it because, frankly, she was broke and she found the genre fascinating—not because she was trying to prove anything: "It is ridiculous to take on a man's job in order to be able to say that 'a woman had done it—yah!'" she once wrote. "The only decent reason for tackling a job is that it is your job, and you want to do it."

The religious writer

Unfortunately, her private life was not always as successful as her public one. She fell in love with a young intellectual, who rejected her when she refused to sleep with him. On the rebound, she became sexually involved with a car salesman and got pregnant. The birth and upbringing of the boy (by a relative at first) remained a secret until 1975. Two years after her son's birth, she married the divorced Oswald Antony Fleming, who eventually adopted the boy.

Ironically, it was after a moral failure that her life as a religious writer blossomed. In 1937 she was asked to write a play for the Canterbury Festival. This play, *The Zeal of Thy House*, was followed by a series of BBC radio plays titled *The Man Born to Be King*. Then followed a series of essays and books on specifically Christian themes, including *Begin Here*, *The Mind of the Maker*, and *Creed or Chaos?*, which quickly established her as one of the foremost Christian apologists of her generation.

She wrote in terms that were at once uncompromising, learned, and humorous. Concerning the problem of evil, one of the thorniest theological dilemmas, for example, she refused to get swallowed up in vague abstractions:

"'Why doesn't God smite this dictator dead?' is a question a little remote from us," says one of the characters in *The Man Born to Be King*. "Why, madam, did he not strike you dumb and imbecile before you uttered that baseless and unkind slander the day before yesterday? Or me, before I behaved with such cruel lack of consideration to that well-meaning friend? And why, sir, did he not cause your hand to rot off at the wrist before you signed your name to that dirty little bit of financial trickery?"

Though she ardently defended the church, she was not blind to its shortcomings nor afraid to poke fun at it when it became merely moralistic or institutional: "The Church's approach to an intelligent carpenter," she wrote in *Creed or Chaos?*, "is usually confined to exhorting him not to be drunk and disorderly in his leisure hours, and to come to church on Sundays. What the Church should be telling him is this: that the very first demand that his religion makes upon him is that he should make good tables."

Mesmerized with Dante

"Man is never truly himself except when he is actively creating something," she once wrote, and all her life she was driven to create. At age 51, she picked up Dante's *Divine Comedy* for the first time, and she became mesmerized: "I bolted my meals, neglected my sleep, work, and correspondence, drove my friends crazy ...," she wrote "until I had panted my way through the Three Realms of the Dead from top to bottom and from bottom to top."

What she discovered, she said, was that Dante "was not grim and austere, but sweet and companionable ... an affable archangel ... [and] that he was a very great comic writer—which is quite the last thing one would ever have inferred from the things people say in their books."

She decided that one of her last efforts would be a fresh translation of Dante to help more readers delight in his great work. Her translation was immediately criticized by scholars who felt Sayers was dabbling in areas beyond her expertise, but the translation remains in print and is, according to one 1992 biography, "the most influential and popular translation on the market."

In her lifetime, she counted among her friends T.S. Eliot, Charles Williams, and C.S. Lewis, and after her death, she still holds the devotion of millions of mystery fans, as well as Christians who want the faith explained with energy, reason, and a twinkle in the eye.

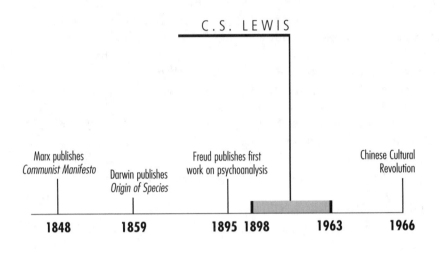

C.S. LEWIS

Marx publishes Communist Manifesto	Darwin publishes Origin of Species	Freud publishes first work on psychoanalysis		Chinese Cultural Revolution
1848	1859	1895 1898	1963	1966

MUSICIANS, ARTISTS, AND WRITERS

C.S. Lewis

SCHOLAR, AUTHOR, AND APOLOGIST

> "The intellectual life is not the only road to God, nor the safest, but we find it to be a road, and it may be the appointed road for us. Of course, it will be so only so long as we keep the impulse pure and disinterested."

"I'm tall, fat, rather bald, red-faced, double-chinned, black-haired, have a deep voice, and wear glasses for reading," Clive Staples Lewis wrote to a young admirer in 1954. If the famous author had been prone to notice clothing, he might have added that his trousers were usually in dire need of pressing, his jackets threadbare and blemished by snags and food spots, and his shoes scuffed and worn at the heels.

But "Jack," as C.S. Lewis's friends knew him, was not bothered by fashion. He was meticulous about the precise use of words, the quality of evidence presented in arguments, and meter in verse. And it is for his books and ideas that the Oxford scholar is remembered as one of the greatest Christian writers of the twentieth century.

Raised in a library

Lewis was born into a bookish family of Protestants in Belfast, Ireland. Eclectic in their reading tastes, they purchased and read "endless" books. "There were books in the study, books in the dining room, books in the cloakroom, books (two deep) in the great book-case on the landing, books in a bedroom, books piled as high as my shoulder in the cistern attic, books of all kinds," Lewis remembered, and none were off-limits to him. On rainy days—and there were many in northern Ireland—he pulled volumes off the shelves and entered into worlds created by authors such as Conan Doyle, E. Nesbit, Mark Twain, and Henry Wadsworth Longfellow.

After his only brother, Warren, was sent off to English boarding school in 1905, Jack became somewhat reclusive. He spent more time in books and an imaginary world of "dressed animals" and "knights in armor." But he did more than read books, he wrote and illustrated his own stories as well.

His mother's death from cancer in 1908 made him even more withdrawn. Mrs. Lewis's death came just three months before Jack's tenth birthday, and the young man was hurt deeply by her passing. Not only did he lose a mother, his father never fully recovered from her death. Both boys felt estranged from their father, and home life was never warm and satisfying again.

The death of Mrs. Lewis convinced young Jack that the God he encountered in the Bible his mother gave him was, if not cruel, at least a vague abstraction. By 1911 or 1912, with the additional influence of a spiritually unorthodox boarding school matron, Lewis rejected Christianity and became an avowed atheist.

A lifetime at Oxford

Lewis entered Oxford in 1917 as a student and never really left. Despite an interruption to fight in World War I (in which he was wounded by a bursting shell), he always maintained his home and friends in Oxford. His attachment to Oxford was so strong that when he taught at Cambridge from 1955 to 1963 he commuted back to Oxford on weekends so he could be close to familiar places and beloved friends.

In 1919 Lewis published his first book, a cycle of lyrics titled *Spirits in Bondage*, which he wrote under the pseudonym Clive Hamilton. In 1924 he became a philosophy tutor at University College, and was the following year elected a Fellow of Magdalen College, where he tutored in English language and literature. His second volume of poetry, *Dymer*, was also published pseudonymously.

Spiritual Awakening

As Lewis continued to read, he especially enjoyed Christian author George MacDonald. One volume, *Phantastes*, powerfully challenged his atheism. "What it actually did to me," wrote Lewis, "was to convert, even to baptize ... my imagination." G.K. Chesterton's books worked much the same way, especially *The Everlasting Man*, which raised serious questions about the young intellectual's materialism.

While MacDonald and Chesterton were stirring Lewis's thoughts, close friend Owen

Barfield pounced on the logic of Lewis's atheism. Barfield had converted from atheism to theism, then finally Christianity, and frequently badgered Lewis about his materialism. So did Nevill Coghill, a brilliant fellow student and lifelong friend who to Lewis's amazement, was "a Christian and a thoroughgoing supernaturalist."

Soon after joining the English faculty at Magdalen College, Lewis met two more Christians, Hugo Dyson and J.R.R. Tolkien. These men became close friends of Lewis. He admired their brilliance and their logic. Soon Lewis recognized that most of his friends, like his favorite authors—MacDonald, Chesterton, Johnson, Spenser, and Milton—held to this Christianity.

In 1929 these roads met, and C.S. Lewis surrendered, admitting "God was God, and knelt and prayed." Within two years the reluctant convert also moved from theism to Christianity and joined the Church of England.

Almost immediately, Lewis set out in a new direction, most demonstrably in his writing. Earlier efforts to become a poet were laid to rest. The new Christian devoted his talent and energy to writing prose that reflected his recently found faith. Within two years of his conversion, Lewis published *The Pilgrim's Regress: An Allegorical Apology for Christianity, Reason and Romanticism* (1933). This little volume opened a 30-year stream of books on Christian apologetics and discipleship that became a lifelong avocation.

Lewis's 25 Christian books sold millions of copies, including *The Screwtape Letters* (1942), *Mere Christianity* (1952), the *Chronicles of Narnia* (1950–56), *The Great Divorce* (1946), and the *Abolition of Man* (1943), which *Encyclopedia Britannica* included in its collection of *Great Books of the World*. But though his books gained him worldwide fame, Lewis was always first a scholar. He continued to write literary history and criticism, such as *The Allegory of Love* (1936), considered a classic in its field, and *English Literature in the Sixteenth Century* (1954).

In spite of his intellectual accomplishments, he refused to be arrogant: "The intellectual life is not the only road to God, nor the safest, but we find it to be a road, and it may be the appointed road for us. Of course, it will be so only so long as we keep the impulse pure and disinterested."

Fame and fortune

Preaching sermons, giving talks, and expressing his theological views over the radio throughout the United Kingdom bolstered Lewis's reputation and increased his book sales. With these new circumstances came other changes—not the least being a marked upswing in annual income.

Throughout the 1920s Lewis had been getting by on little money. During his student years his father provided an allowance, and Jack supplemented that in various ways. Nevertheless, money was always scarce. And when the young academician took on the responsibility for a friend's family, finances were always tight even with the regular tutorial stipend.

Now, with money no longer an issue, Lewis refused to upgrade his standard of living, and instead established a charitable fund for his royalty earnings. He supported numerous impoverished families, underwrote education fees for orphans and poor seminarians, and put monies into scores of charities and church ministries.

During the last decade of his earthly pilgrimage, Lewis's world was invaded by an American woman and her two children. In 1952 Joy Davidman Gresham, who had become a Christian through reading *The Great Divorce* and *The Screwtape Letters*, visited her spiritual mentor in England. Soon thereafter her husband abandoned her for another woman, and she moved to London with her two adolescent boys, David and Douglas.

Gresham gradually fell into financial trouble. Her acquaintance with Lewis led to his underwriting the boarding school education of David and Douglas. From charity and common literary interests grew a deep friendship, and eventually love. They were married in 1956.

Joy was 16 years Lewis's junior, but that did not prevent a happy marriage. A savage case of cancer, however, cut their marriage short less than four years after the wedding. She was so ill even before the wedding that he called it a "deathbed marriage."

Still, Joy brought Lewis happiness. As he wrote to one friend soon after their marriage, "It's funny having at 59 the sort of happiness most men have in their twenties ... 'Thou hast kept the good wine till now.'" A writer in her own right, her influence on what Jack considered his best book, *Till We Have Faces* (1956), was so profound that he told one close friend she was actually its co-author.

Thus her death, like the death of his mother, dealt Lewis a severe blow. In his *A Grief Observed*, he expressed his grief, anger, and doubts that ensued for the next few years.

Attacks from friends

The esteemed professor not only married late in life, he married an American who was at once Jewish, divorced, a former Communist, and personally abrasive. In brief, the marriage did not set well with most of Lewis's friends and acquaintances.

Lewis was hurt by the disapproval of friends and colleagues, but it was by no means a new experience for him. Although he enjoyed the conviviality of weekly get-togethers with fellow Inklings (intellectuals and writers who met regularly to exchange ideas), and the prodigious successes of his books, Lewis was frequently under attack for his decidedly Christian lifestyle. Even close Christian friends like Owen Barfield and J.R.R. Tolkien openly disapproved of Lewis's evangelistic speaking and writing.

In fact, Lewis's "Christian" books caused so much disapproval that he was more than once passed over for a professorship at Oxford, with the honors going to men of lesser reputation. It was Magdalene College at Cambridge University that finally honored Lewis with a chair in 1955 and thereby recognized his original and important contributions to English literary history and criticism.

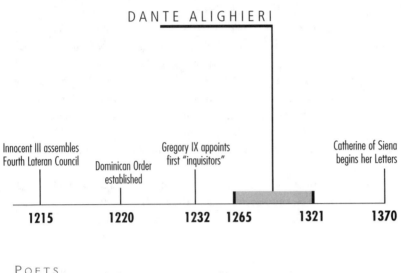

DANTE ALIGHIERI

| Innocent III assembles Fourth Lateran Council | Dominican Order established | Gregory IX appoints first "inquisitors" | | Catherine of Siena begins her Letters |

| 1215 | 1220 | 1232 | 1265 | 1321 | 1370 |

POETS

Dante Alighieri
WORLDLY CREATOR OF DIVINE VERSE

> "O conscience, upright and stainless, how bitter a sting to thee is a little fault!"

By his early fifties, Dante had been exiled from his hometown, wrestled with the top authorities of the church, and taken up arms against his fellow countrymen. He had made plenty of enemies, and he was not pleased. So he did with his enemies what many have wished to do: he sent them all, even the pope, to hell—literally, that is. But his damnatory writing was no screed; it was the finest poem of the Middle Ages, a summation of classical and medieval beliefs so profound that its critics labeled it "divine": *The Divine Comedy*.

Papal power plays

Dante was born into a Florentine family of low aristocracy. They likely had some status but not much wealth. More importantly, they were supporters of the pope. All of Dante's life was shaped by the long conflict between the champions of papal power (the Guelfs) and those who supported German imperial control of Italy (the Ghibellines). One side would rise to power and severely punish the other, only to be overthrown a few years later. The see-saw had continued for over a century, but during Dante's early years the Guelfs (to which his family belonged) had secured ascendancy. He witnessed the acme of Florentine democracy and fought in the front ranks for the Guelf cavalry.

All participants in public life had to belong to a guild, so Dante joined the union of physicians and apothecaries. Soon, he was elected as a prior (chief magistrate) of the city. When the republic was again ripped apart by political turmoil, Dante chose the wrong side. His opponents gained control, and the poet-philosopher was charged (falsely) of hostility to the church, fraud, and corrupt practices; he was fined and barred from holding office ever again. When he refused to pay the fine, he was sentenced to death by burning. Dante fled the city.

Exile

Dante left behind a wife and children, and plunged again into his writing. He had penned his first book in Florence: a mix of blank verse and poetic prose called *La Vita Nuova* ("the new life"). It tells the story of his love for Beatrice, a woman he'd met briefly when they were both 9 years old—and whom he had loved ever since, even after her death and his marriage.

In exile he also wrote a defense of the ideal Italian language: the vernacular. The clerical Latin, he wrote, would be eclipsed by the urban Italian vernacular. History would prove him right.

In 1308 Henry of Luxembourg became the Holy Roman Emperor (supported by French pope Clement V), and Dante, believing him to be the renovator of Christendom, wrote his famous work *De Monarchia*. He acknowledged "that the Roman government is in [some ways] subject to the Roman pontificate, for in some ways our mortal happiness is ordered for the sake of immortal happiness," but generally, the emperor is supreme in temporal matters over the authority of the pope. An earthly monarch is necessary for creating a universal peace, and his authority comes directly from God, not through the pope. Unfortunately for Dante, Henry's monarchy never really got off the ground.

The felicitous comedy

After wandering from town to town, the exiled Dante finally settled in Ravenna in about 1317, where he set about completing his masterpiece, *La Commedia*, begun a decade earlier. In essence, it is an epic poem chronicling an allegorical journey through the afterlife, divided into three parts: *Inferno*, *Purgatorio*, and *Paradiso*. The purpose, Dante wrote, was to convert a corrupt society to righteousness, "to remove those living in this life from a state of misery and lead them to a state of felicity."

In *Inferno*, Dante is guided by the Roman poet Virgil through the nine concentric circles of hell ("Abandon all hope, ye who enter here"), where they meet various sinners from history, myth, and Dante's enemies list. Purgatory is a nine-tiered mountain where Dante must confront his own shortcomings and seek redemption ("O conscience, upright and stainless, how bitter a sting to thee is a little fault!"). Before he reaches Paradise, Virgil is replaced by Dante's long-lost Beatrice and Bernard of Clairvaux, and together they meet Dante's heroes as they journey through the nine concentric circles of heaven ("Like the lark that soars in the air, first singing, then silent, content with the last sweetness that satiates it, such seems to me that image, the imprint of Eternal Pleasure"). Dante finished the epic poem just before his death, and it was almost immediately recognized as brilliant. His epitaph begins: "Dante the theologian, skilled in every branch of knowledge that philosophy may cherish in her illustrious bosom."

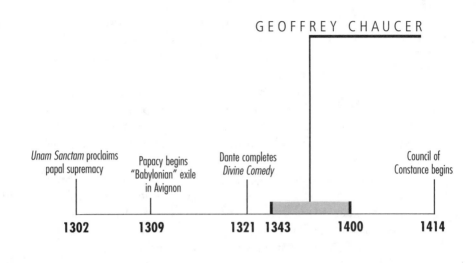

GEOFFREY CHAUCER

Unam Sanctam proclaims papal supremacy	Papacy begins "Babylonian" exile in Avignon	Dante completes Divine Comedy		Council of Constance begins
1302	**1309**	**1321**	**1343**	**1400**	**1414**

POETS

Geoffrey Chaucer

MEDIEVAL ENGLAND'S GREATEST STORYTELLER

> *"Now I beg all those that listen to this little treatise [Canterbury Tales], or read it, that if there be anything in it that pleases them, they thank our Lord Jesus Christ for it, from whom proceeds all understanding and goodness."*

Geoffrey Chaucer's first major poem, *Book of the Duchess*, was a well-received elegy for Blanche, the late wife of his patron John of Gaunt (who was also patron of Bible translator John Wycliffe). It was a gentle poem of courtly love and established Chaucer's reputation as a love poet who examined both the earthly and the eternal aspects of the subject.

Yet Chaucer was no mushy milquetoast; he had a few rough edges. He was once fined for beating a Franciscan friar and was charged with either sexual assault or abduction (the charge is unclear), though the case was dismissed.

This combination—sublimity and brutal realism—characterized not only Chaucer's life but his greatest literary contribution, *The Canterbury Tales*.

Political poet

Geoffrey's father, John, was an important London vintner (wine merchant) and a deputy to the king's butler, so Geoffrey received the best education of his day. He was well read, fluent in French and competent in Latin and Italian. By his early teens, he was already serving in the royal household; by his mid-teens, he was a member of the king's army in France. Unfortunately, a key siege in which Chaucer took part failed, and the future poet was captured and imprisoned. After being ransomed (the king paid 16 pounds for his release), Chaucer returned to court. Over the next few years, he was promoted from attendant of the king's chamber to squire and charged with providing the king with entertainments—especially poetry.

Chaucer's career continued upward, and eventually he became quite wealthy. Then a series of mishaps ensued. When his wife, Philippa, died in about 1387, he lost her annuity; when King Richard II and John of Gaunt were usurped, Chaucer was dismissed. He was sued for debts, then sued again. Then King Richard's usurpers gained control of Parliament and began executing many of Chaucer's close friends.

During this tumultuous time, Chaucer created much of his most famous poetry. He began his early work on *The Canterbury Tales* and penned *Troilus and Criseyde*, a humorous but tragic love narrative set against the Trojan War. Some scholars have named it the first English novel, and praise it even above *Canterbury Tales*.

At the time, however, *Troilus and Criseyde* had at least one major critic: Richard's wife, Queen Anne. She took issue with the poem's implication that women were less faithful than men in romance. Chaucer noted her critique and set about writing the *Legend of Good Women*, in which the women aren't really good, they're just betrayed by evil men. Chaucer left the work unfinished because, according to his disciple Lydgate, it was too taxing to come up with many good women in history.

Soon enough, Richard II, then only 23 years old, regained his throne. His supporters were rewarded, and Chaucer was no exception. Richard appointed him clerk of the royal works, including Westminster Palace and the Tower of London. But he was, at best, mediocre at his job, and it proved hazardous to his health. He was repeatedly robbed and once beaten. Two years after his lofty appointment, he was demoted to subforester of the king's park in North Peterton, Somerset.

Tales from the road

Again his demotion was fortuitous for future generations, for he devoted more time to his *Canterbury Tales*, which he'd begun several years earlier. The earthy, realistic *Tales* introduces readers to two dozen pilgrims making their way to the shrine of Thomas Becket in Canterbury, Kent. To amuse themselves, they engage in a storytelling contest. Chaucer portrays his pilgrims with vividness and detail, and religious themes color almost every page. Though a work of fiction, *Canterbury Tales* has helped historians peek into late-1300s English life, and it has helped to combat the notion that the medieval church was a monolith of religious attitudes.

The collection of stories brings together people from many vocations: knight, miller, reeve, cook, lawyer, shipman, prioress, monk, priest, physician, clerk, merchant, and so on. Among the more memorable characters are the Wife of Bath, one of literature's most endearing religious rebels and surely a protofeminist; the pardoner, a hawker of indulgences and charlatan; and the parson, a model priest (who may have been based on John Wycliffe) who says to his fellow travelers that his goal is

> to guide your way one further stage
> Upon that perfect, glorious pilgrimage
> Called the celestial, to Jerusalem.

The book was to have two tales from each pilgrim on the way to the cathedral and another two on the return trip. But Chaucer quit writing far before that goal was reached. It is not known when exactly he stopped, but the end of his tales includes a "Retraction," where Chaucer himself takes the stage and, nearing the end of his life, apologizes for his "translations and [writings] of worldly vanities."

In October 1400, Geoffrey Chaucer died. He was buried in Westminster Abbey, a high honor for a commoner, and became the first of those entombed in what is now called Poets' Corner.

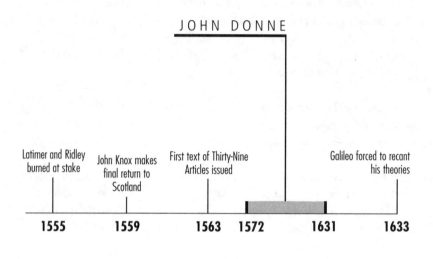

JOHN DONNE

| Latimer and Ridley burned at stake | John Knox makes final return to Scotland | First text of Thirty-Nine Articles issued | | Galileo forced to recant his theories |

| 1555 | 1559 | 1563 | 1572 | 1631 | 1633 |

POETS

John Donne

POET OF GOD'S LOVE

"Death, be not proud, though some have called thee Mighty and dreadful, for thou art not so."

"Lo," preached the newly ordained minister, quoting the Book of Lamentations at the funeral of his wife, "I am the man that hath seen affliction."

Indeed, from the death of his father to his own, John Donne witnessed much affliction. The Black Plague was repeatedly sweeping through London—three waves during his 10-year tenure as dean of St. Paul's Cathedral—killing tens of thousands with each recurrence. For months Donne thought himself a sure victim of the disease. Throughout his life, he withstood financial ruin, the destruction of his family, religious persecution, and other plagues. Yet, he became one of England's greatest love poets, and one of the greatest preachers of the 1600s.

Erotic early days

Donne was born to an old Roman Catholic family when anti-

Catholicism was running high in England. At age 2, his grand-uncle was hanged for being a priest, and his father died of more natural causes when he was 4. His younger brother Henry died in prison, having been arrested for sheltering a priest. Donne himself, a noteworthy student at both Oxford and Cambridge, was refused a degree at both schools because of his faith.

Donne's youthful response to these calamities was to reject his Catholicism. But neither did he accept the Protestantism of his family's persecutors. Instead, he walked the line between cynical rebellion and honest truthseeker, listing the pitfalls of various denominations and sects in his first book of poetry, *Satires*. At the same time, he lived a brazenly sexual life, writing some of the most erotic English poetry ever written.

Sometime during this period, Donne converted to the Church of England, and in 1596 sailed as a gentleman-adventurer on a naval expedition against Spain. When he returned, he was appointed the private secretary to the Lord Keeper of the Great Seal, sat in Queen Elizabeth's last Parliament, made connections, and continued his lustful ways. Then England's greatest love poet fell in love.

Her name was Anne More—the niece (by marriage) of the wife of his boss. As she was only 17 (Donne was then nearly 30), they married in secret. Her father was furious and had Donne immediately thrown into jail and removed from his post. Imprisoned, he wrote a characteristic pun, "John Donne, Anne Donne, Undone."

Though Donne was quickly released, the two lived in poverty for the next 13 years. Adding to the poverty, Anne bore 12 children (five of whom died in childhood). Donne, plagued also by headaches, intestinal cramps, and gout, fell into a deep depression. His longest work of that period was an essay endorsing and contemplating suicide: "Whensoever any affliction assails me, methinks I have the keys of my prison in mine own hand and no remedy presents itself so soon to my heart as mine own sword."

Lover of God

During this time, he also began studying religion more closely. One of two anti-Catholic works he published, *Pseudo-Martyr*, earned him the favor of King James I because it argued Catholics could pledge allegiance to the king without renouncing their faith.

The object of his poetry now became God, and he employed the same degree of ardor and amorousness as ever. He reasoned, "God is love." He took a page from Solomon, whom he observed "was amorous, and excessive in the love of women: when he turned to God, he departed not utterly from his old phrase and language, but ... conveys all his loving approaches and applications to God."

Thus, even some of his "Holy Sonnets" had amorous overtones:

> Batter my heart, three-person'd God; for you
> As yet but knock, breathe, shine, and seek to mend;
> That I may rise, and stand, o'erthrow me, and bend
> Your force to break, blow, burn, and make me new ...
> Take me to you, imprison me, for I

Except you enthrall me, never shall be free,
Nor ever chaste, except you ravish me.

Friends encouraged Donne, deemed by some critics to be a pornographer, to become a priest in the Church of England. Donne repeatedly refused, lamenting that "some irregularities of my life have been so visible to some men." But when King James refused to employ him anywhere but the church, Donne relented. He was granted a doctorate of divinity from Cambridge and took his first parish job in 1616.

The following year, Anne died. Grief-stricken, Donne pledged never to marry again and threw himself at his work. It seems to have done wonders for his vocation. By 1621 he was dean of St. Paul's Cathedral and the foremost preacher of his day. One hundred sixty of his sermons still survive.

In 1623 Donne fell seriously ill and believed he was dying of the plague. Unable to read but able to write, he penned his famous *Devotions upon Emergent Occasions*. In it, he records hearing church bells tolling a declaration of death, which he mistook to be an announcement of his own demise. When he realized they were for another, he penned one of literature's most famous lines: "No man is an island, entire of himself; ... therefore never send to know for whom the bell tolls; it tolls for thee."

Eight years later, the bell did toll for Donne, who died of stomach cancer about a month after preaching his famous "Death's Duel" sermon. Though he has occasionally been accused of an obsession with death (a claim backed up by his 54 songs and sonnets, 32 of which center on the topic), his poetry, sermons, and other writings clearly show his affinity for what lay beyond the tolling bells:

Death, be not proud, though some have called thee
Mighty and dreadful, for thou art not so ...
One short sleep past, we wake eternally,
And death shall be no more; Death, thou shalt die.

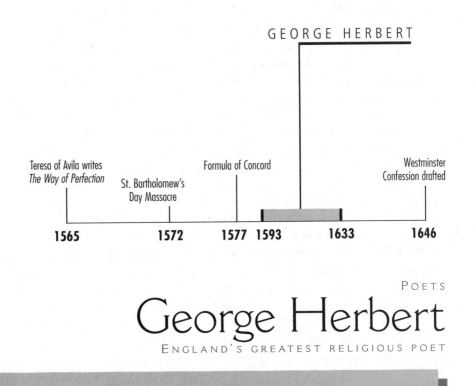

GEORGE HERBERT

Teresa of Avila writes
The Way of Perfection

St. Bartholomew's
Day Massacre

Formula of Concord

Westminster
Confession drafted

| 1565 | 1572 | 1577 | 1593 | 1633 | 1646 |

POETS

George Herbert
ENGLAND'S GREATEST RELIGIOUS POET

"A verse may find him who a sermon flies."

It was the New Year's celebration, and Magdalen Newport Herbert had received two sonnets from her son, George. These were quite unlike those of William Shakespeare, who had published his *Sonnets* the year earlier. They were far more akin to the work of John Donne, who had dedicated his *Holy Sonnets* to Magdalen, his patron. They referred not to his mother's kindness, her beauty, or any other characteristic, nor did they mention the occasion for the sonnet, New Year's Day. Instead, George wrote that the love of God is a fitter subject for verse than the love of woman. It foreshadowed the aesthetic and vocational bent of a man who was to become one of England's finest metaphysical poets.

"Holy Mr. Herbert"

Herbert's was a distinguished, noble Welsh family (his brother, Edward, became the father of English deism), but his father died when George was only 3 years old. His mother was left to raise ten children. She homeschooled George's siblings and then enrolled George in Westminister School, where he studied Latin, Greek, and Hebrew. From there he attended Trinity College in Cambridge, and in 1620, he became the university's "public orator," a position he described as "the finest place in the university." Since one of the main duties of the office was to express the sentiments of the university, it was considered a launching point to high office.

Herbert's career continued to climb, as did his prestige—Sir Francis Bacon dedicated his *Translation of Certain Psalmes* to him, and he was elected to Parliament—but then came a series of tragedies: King James died, as did many of Herbert's sponsors; Bacon died; his mother died (Donne delivered the funeral sermon); the plague broke out.

After getting married in 1629 (to his stepfather's cousin, Jane Danvers), he gave up his secular ambitions and prepared to enter holy orders. When his friends expressed shock at his taking a job so "beneath" him, Herbert brushed them off:

"It hath been formerly judged that the domestic servants of the King of Heaven should be the noblest families on earth. And though the iniquity of the late times have made clergymen meanly valued ... I will labor to make it honorable, by consecrating all my learning, and all my poor abilities, to advance the glory of that God that gave them."

Herbert moved to the rural countryside and became rector at Bremerton near Salisbury. He rebuilt the church with his own money, visited the poor, consoled the sick and dying, reconciled neighbors. He became known as "Holy Mr. Herbert." He served for only three years, however, dying of tuberculosis in 1633.

On his deathbed, Herbert sent a "little book of poems" to his friend Nicholas Ferrar, founder of a religious community nearby. "If he can think it may turn to the advantage of any dejected poor soul," he wrote in his instructions, "let it be made public; if not, let him burn it, for I and it are the least of God's mercies."

Pictures of spiritual conflict

The book, published later that year with the title *The Temple: Sacred Poems and Private Ejaculations*, contains some of the most memorable poetry in the English language. Several poems contained in the book are now used as hymns, such as "The God of Love my Shepherd Is," "Teach Me, My God and King," and "Let All the World in Every Corner Sing."

Herbert described his poetry as "a picture of the many spiritual conflicts that have passed between God and my soul, before I could subject mine to the will of Jesus, my Master, in whose service I have now found perfect freedom." Among his poems is "The Windows":

Lord, how can man preach thy eternal word?
    He is a brittle crazy glass;
Yet in thy temple thou dost him afford
    This glorious and transcendent place,
    To be a window, through thy grace.

But when thou dost anneal in glass thy story,
  Making thy life to shine within
The holy preachers, then the light and glory
  More reverend grows, and more doth win;
  Which else shows waterish, bleak, and thin.

Doctrine and life, colors and light, in one
  When they combine and mingle, bring
A strong regard and awe, but speech alone
  Doth vanish like a flaring thing
  And in the ear, not conscience, ring.

Herbert is also famous for his prose work, A *Priest to the Temple, or the Country Parson*, published posthumously in 1652. In it he outlines "the form and character of a true pastor, that I may have a mark to aim at: which also I will set as high as I can, since he shoots higher that threatens the moon, than he that aims at a tree." The key to being a good pastor, Herbert argues, is to be a good person. He was very concerned with the private personal life of the pastor, who was to serve as "all to his parish," as father, lawyer, doctor, counselor, and deputy of Christ.

Herbert believed poetry was in some ways a type of preaching: "A verse may find him who a sermon flies." For the same reason, he was also fond of proverbs, and many of those he used in his sermons survive today: "Whose house is of glass must not throw stones at another." "The eye is bigger than the belly." "His bark is worse than his bite." "Half the world knows not how the other half lives."

Though he was a genius in composing both poetry and proverbs, he believed something else was central: "By these [proverbs] and other means the Parson procures attention," he wrote, "but the character of his sermon is holiness; he is not witty, or learned or eloquent, but holy."

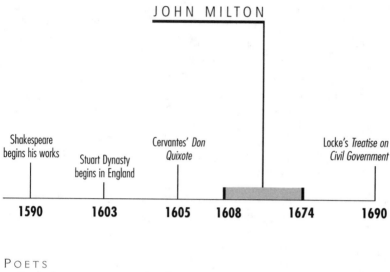

JOHN MILTON

Shakespeare begins his works		Cervantes' *Don Quixote*			Locke's *Treatise on Civil Government*	
	Stuart Dynasty begins in England					
1590	**1603**	**1605**	**1608**	**1674**	**1690**	

POETS

John Milton

PURITAN AUTHOR OF *PARADISE LOST*

> *"Who kills a man kills a reasonable creature, ... but he who destroys a good book kills reason itself."*

As a young man, John Milton wrote a friend: "Do you ask what I am meditating? By the help of Heaven, an immortality of fame." Not many can actually achieve such a goal, but Milton did. Next to William Shakespeare, he is regarded by many as the greatest English poet and the author of the language's finest epic poem.

First forays

Describing his childhood, Milton wrote, "I was born in London, of a good family, my father a very honorable man"—a man who was disinherited by his Roman Catholic family because he converted to Protestantism. Like his father, Milton became a talented musician, with a "delicate tunable voice and great skill." By age 9, he was writing verse and polishing his Latin and Greek under private tutors, and by the time he left for Cambridge at age 17, he had also begun learning French, Italian, and Hebrew.

He was hardworking and successful: an early biographer said he "was a very hard scholar at the University, and performed all his exercises there with very good applause." But he was also contentious, and as a contemporary put it, Milton "was esteemed to be a virtuous and sober person, yet not to be ignorant of his own parts." He was called "the lady of Christ's" (he was a member of Christ's College, Cambridge)—a tribute to his good looks and sarcasm about his austere life, a life Milton later described as "aloof from vice, and approved by all the good."

Milton left the university in July 1632 with bachelor's and master's degrees. He settled down, with his aging parents, at the family estate in Horton. He now gave himself to attempt "things unattempted yet in prose or rhyme." Of his six years at Horton, he said, "On my father's estate I enjoyed an interval of uninterrupted leisure, which I devoted to the perusal of Greek and Latin authors." At Horton he wrote the poems "L'Allegro," "Il Penseroso," "Comus," "Lycidas," and some sonnets. Though he thought of them as preliminary exercises, they still rank high in English poetry.

In 1637, as he approached his thirtieth year, solitude and obscurity began to irk Milton, so he set out on a continental tour—Paris, Florence (where "I found and visited the famous Galileo, grown old, a prisoner of the Inquisition"), Rome, and Naples. When he heard that civil war was brewing in England, he abandoned further travel: "I thought it disgraceful, while my fellow citizens fought for liberty at home, to be travelling for pleasure abroad."

Propagandist years

The poet settled in London, resumed his studies, and began to swim in "the troubled sea of noises and hoarse dispute" as a writer of pamphlets. His first pamphlet, published in 1641, was the opening volley of 20 years of political warfare. He attacked the corruptions of state and church while upholding the ideals of the Puritan party.

In the spring of 1642, the 33-year-old Milton married Mary Powell, the 17-year-old daughter of royalists. It was an unhappy marriage. Mary came from a large family and found Milton's quiet, bookish existence lonely. After a month, she returned to her family and remained there three years until she and her husband were reconciled.

His troubled marriage shocked Milton, and he set out to write *The Doctrine and Discipline of Divorce*, in which he argued that incompatibility—not just adultery—was grounds for divorce. The pamphlet was greeted by a storm of protest. When the government sought to prosecute him for having published without a license, Milton penned *Areopagitica*, which many consider the finest defense of freedom of the press ever written. "Who kills a man kills a reasonable creature," he wrote, "but he who destroys a good book kills reason itself."

In 1649, shortly after the execution of Charles I, he published *The Tenure of Kings and Magistrates*, becoming the first person to uphold the right of the people to execute a guilty sovereign. The following month, he was appointed secretary for foreign tongues, to correspond with foreign states and to write pamphlets defending the actions of the new government.

For years, Milton's eyesight had been suffering, and in 1652 complete blindness overcame him. Worse still, all his political ideals and hopes were crushed eight years later when the Commonwealth disintegrated and the monarchy was restored. In Milton's view, the event was spurred by the "epidemic madness and general defection of a misguided and abused multitude."

When Charles II landed in 1660, Milton was forced into hiding, was eventually arrested, and all copies of his Puritan pamphlets were burned. Only through the good offices of powerful friends at court did he escape prosecution.

Triumphant finish

By then Milton was blind, embittered, and hampered by insufficient finances. But he was free to again take up his grand poetic task. Few images in the history of literature are more poignant that of the blind Puritan dictating day after day his great epic, *Paradise Lost*, the theme of which is announced in the opening lines:

Of man's disobedience, and the fruit
Of that forbidden tree, whose mortal taste
Brought death into the world, and all our woe,
With loss of Eden.

He rose at four or five in the morning, listened to a chapter from the Hebrew Bible, ate breakfast, and then wrote until noon. After an hour walk and another hour playing the organ or viola, he worked until night. Then he would have a supper of "olives or some light thing," a pipe, and a glass of water.

In 1667, the work was complete, and the world received the book that would influence English thought and language nearly as much as the King James Version and the plays of Shakespeare.

Among other works published at the end of his life were *Paradise Regained*, the story of Jesus' temptation in the wilderness, and *Samson Agonistes*, the final triumph of the blinded Samson—in some ways the story of the blind Milton, finally triumphing at the end of his days.

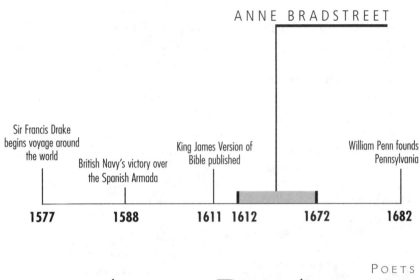

ANNE BRADSTREET

| Sir Francis Drake begins voyage around the world | British Navy's victory over the Spanish Armada | King James Version of Bible published | | William Penn founds Pennsylvania |

| 1577 | 1588 | 1611 | 1612 | 1672 | 1682 |

POETS

Anne Bradstreet

AMERICA'S FIRST POET

"I am obnoxious to each carping tongue
Who says my hand a needle better fits,
A Poet's pen all scorn I should thus wrong,
For such despite they cast on Female wits."

Almost all we know of Anne Bradstreet comes from her meditations and poems. As a poet, she combined the longings of the human heart with devout faith and piety, and she is recognized as a true Puritan and one of America's greatest poets.

Mayflower lineage

Bradstreet was born in a castle in Northampton, England, where her father was a steward for the Puritan earl of Lincoln. She enjoyed the advantages of privilege and wealth, once noting, "When I was about seven ... I had at one time eight tutors ... in languages, music, dancing."

At age 16, she married Simon Bradstreet, a recent graduate of Cambridge and also a steward at the earl's estate. Two years later, in 1630, she came to Massachusetts with a group of Puritans led by John Winthrop.

These sudden changes didn't suit her: "I changed my condition and was married, and came into this country, where I found a new world and new manners, at which my heart rose [in anger]," she later wrote her children. "But after I was convinced it was the way of God, I submitted to it and joined to the church at Boston."

She led the demanding but relatively comfortable life of a mother (eventually bearing eight children) and wife of a husband who traveled in the highest circles of Massachusetts society.

Between her domestic chores, she found time to write poetry. Her brother-in-law thought it so good, he managed to get a few of her poems printed in England, under the title *The Tenth Muse Lately Sprung up in America*.

Though she is today considered the first American poet, and though her poetry was admired by many contemporaries, she was criticized by some for writing poetry, as she once noted in a poem:

I am obnoxious to each carping tongue
Who says my hand a needle better fits,
A Poet's pen all scorn I should thus wrong,
For such despite they cast on Female wits.

Puritan passion

Still she composed poems: about nature, about marriage, about children, about faith—sometimes all at once. As one historian put it, her poetry shows "a Puritan could … combine sexual passion, love of children and good furniture, humor—that the female Puritan, in short, could be both a Puritan and a woman of great charm."

In "To My Dear and Loving Husband," she celebrates marital love while pointing to a love more eternal:

If ever two were one, then surely we.
If ever man were loved by wife, then thee.
If ever wife was happy in a man,
Compare with me, ye women, if you can.
I prize thy love more than whole mines of gold,
Of all the riches that the East doth hold.
My love is such that rivers cannot quench,
Nor ought but love from thee give recompense.

Thy love is such I can no way repay;
The heavens reward thee manifold I pray.
Then, while we live, in love let's so persever,
That when we live no more we may live ever.

One of her most poignant poems was written in 1665 upon the death of an infant grandchild:

Farewel dear babe, my heart's too much content,
Farewel sweet babe, the pleasure of mine eye,
Farewel fair flower that for a space was lent
Then ta'en away unto Eternity.
Blest babe why should I once bewail thy fate,
Or sigh the dayes so soon were terminate
Sith thou art setled in an Everlasting state.
By nature Trees do rot when they are grown.
And Plumbs and Apples throughly ripe do fall,
And Corn and grass are in their season mown,
And time brings down what is both strong and tall.
But plants new set to be eradicate,
And buds new blown, to have so short a date,
Is by his hand alone that guides nature and fate.

Her writings debunk the myth of the stodgy, prudish Puritan so long a part of the American psyche.

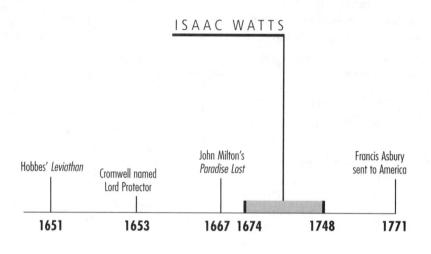

ISAAC WATTS

Hobbes' *Leviathan*	Cromwell named Lord Protector	John Milton's *Paradise Lost*			Francis Asbury sent to America
1651	1653	1667	1674	1748	1771

POETS

Isaac Watts

FATHER OF ENGLISH HYMNODY

> *"Joy to the world, the Lord is come / Let earth receive her King / Let every heart, prepare him room / And heaven and nature sing."*

In his later years, Isaac Watts once complained about hymn singing in church: "To see the dull indifference, the negligent and thoughtless air that sits upon the faces of a whole assembly, while the psalm is upon their lips, might even tempt a charitable observer to suspect the fervency of their inward religion."

He had been bemoaning such since his late teens. His father, tired of his complaints, challenged him to write something better. The following week, the adolescent Isaac presented his first hymn to the church, "Behold the Glories of the Lamb," which received an enthusiastic response. The career of the "Father of English Hymnody" had begun.

Head of a genius

At Isaac's birth in 1674, his father was in prison for his Nonconformist sympathies (that is, he would not embrace the established Church of England). His father was eventually freed (and fathered seven more children), but Isaac respected his courage and remembered his mother's tales of nursing her children on the jail steps.

Young Isaac showed genius early. He was learning Latin by age 4, Greek at 9, French (which he took up to converse with his refugee neighbors) at 11, and Hebrew at 13. Several wealthy townspeople offered to pay for his university education at Oxford or Cambridge, which would have led him into Anglican ministry. Isaac refused and at 16 went to London to study at a leading Nonconformist academy. Upon graduation, he spent five years as a private tutor.

In 1702 he became pastor of London's Mark Lane Independent (i.e. Congregational) Chapel, then one of the city's most influential independent churches. But the following year, he began suffering from psychiatric illness that would plague him for the rest of his life. He had to pass off more and more of his work to his assistant and eventually resigned in 1712.

His illness and unsightly appearance took its toll on his personal life. His five-foot, pale, skinny frame was topped by a disproportionately oversized head. Almost every portrait of him depicts him in a large gown with large folds—an apparent attempt by the artists to disguise his homeliness. This was probably the reason for Elizabeth Singer's rejection of his marriage proposal. As one biographer noted, "Though she loved the jewel, she could not admire the casket [case] which contained it."

Reaching the ordinary Christian

Though German Lutherans had been singing hymns for 100 years, John Calvin had urged his followers to sing only metrical psalms; English Protestants had followed Calvin's lead.

Watts's 1707 publication of *Hymns and Spiritual Songs* technically wasn't a collection of hymns or metrical psalms, but it was a collection of consequence. In fact, it contained what would become some of the most popular English hymns of all time, such as "When I Survey the Wondrous Cross."

Watts didn't reject metrical psalms; he simply wanted to see them more impassioned. "They ought to be translated in such a manner as we have reason to believe David would have composed them if he had lived in our day," he wrote. *Psalms of David Imitated in the Language of the New Testament* followed in 1719.

Many of his English colleagues couldn't recognize these translations. How could "Joy to the World" really be Psalm 98? Or "Jesus Shall Reign Where'er the Sun" be Psalm 72, or "O God Our Help in Ages Past" be Psalm 90?

Watts was unapologetic, arguing that he deliberately omitted several psalms and large parts of others, keeping portions "as might easily and naturally be accommodated to the various occasions of Christian life, or at least might afford us some beautiful allusions to Christian affairs." Furthermore, where the psalmist fought with personal enemies, Watts turned the biblical invective against spiritual adversaries: sin, Satan, and temptation. Finally, he said, "Where the flights of his faith and love are sublime, I have often sunk the expressions within the reach of an ordinary Christian."

Such looseness brought criticism. "Christian congregations have shut out divinely inspired psalms and taken in Watts's flights of fancy," protested one detractor. Others dubbed the new songs "Watts's whims."

But after church splits, pastor firings, and other arguments, Watts's paraphrases won out. "He was the first who taught the Dissenters to write and speak like other men, by showing them that elegance might consist with piety," wrote the famed lexicographer (and Watts's contemporary) Samuel Johnson.

More than a poet, however, Watts was also a scholar of wide reputation, especially in his later years. He wrote nearly 30 theological treatises; essays on psychology, astronomy, and philosophy; three volumes of sermons; the first children's hymnal; and a textbook on logic that served as a standard work on the subject for generations.

But his poetry remains his lasting legacy and earned him acclaim on both sides of the Atlantic. Benjamin Franklin published his hymnal, Cotton Mather maintained a long correspondence, and John Wesley acknowledged him as a genius—though Watts maintained that Charles Wesley's "Wrestling Jacob" was worth all of his own hymns.

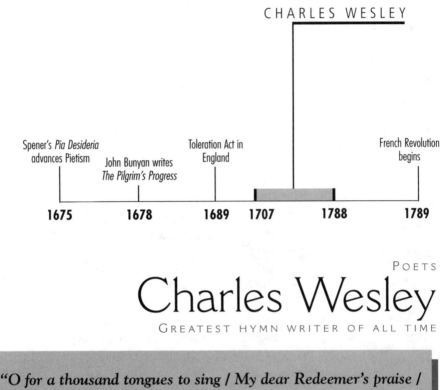

CHARLES WESLEY

Spener's *Pia Desideria* advances Pietism

John Bunyan writes *The Pilgrim's Progress*

Toleration Act in England

French Revolution begins

1675   1678   1689   1707   1788   1789

POETS

Charles Wesley

GREATEST HYMN WRITER OF ALL TIME

"O for a thousand tongues to sing / My dear Redeemer's praise / The glories of my God and King, / The triumphs of his grace!"

He was said to have averaged 10 poetic lines a day for 50 years. He wrote 8,989 hymns, 10 times the volume composed by the only other candidate (Isaac Watts) who could conceivably claim to be the world's greatest hymn writer. He composed some of the most memorable and lasting hymns of the church: "Hark! The Herald Angels Sing," "And Can It Be," "O for a Thousand Tongues to Sing," "Love Divine, All Loves Excelling," "Jesus, Lover of My Soul," "Christ the Lord Is Risen Today," "Soldiers of Christ, Arise," and "Rejoice! the Lord Is King!"

And yet he is often referred to as the "forgotten Wesley."

His brother John is considered the organizational genius behind the founding of Methodism. But without the hymns of Charles, the Methodist movement may have gone nowhere. As one historian put it, "The early Methodists were taught and led as much through [Charles's] hymns as through sermons and

[John] Wesley's pamphlets."

Language scholar

Charles Wesley was the eighteenth of Samuel and Susannah Wesley's nineteen children (only 10 lived to maturity). He was born prematurely in December 1707 and appeared dead. He lay silent, wrapped in wool, for weeks.

When older, Charles joined his siblings as each day his mother, Susannah, who knew Greek, Latin, and French, methodically taught them for six hours. Charles then spent 13 years at Westminster School, where the only language allowed in public was Latin. He added nine years at Oxford, where he received his master's degree. It was said that he could reel off the Latin poet Virgil by the half hour.

It was off to Oxford University next, and to counteract the spiritual tepidity of the school, Charles formed the Holy Club, and with two or three others celebrated Communion weekly and observed a strict regimen of spiritual study. Because of the

group's religious regimen, which later included early rising, Bible study, and prison ministry, members were called "methodists."

In 1735 Charles joined his brother John (they were now both ordained), to become a missionary in the colony of Georgia—John as chaplain of the rough outpost and Charles as secretary to Governor Oglethorpe.

Shot at, slandered, suffering sickness, shunned even by Oglethorpe, Charles could have echoed brother John's sentiments as they dejectedly returned to England the following year: "I went to America to convert the Indians, but, oh, who will convert me?"

It turned out to be the Moravians. After returning to England, Charles taught English to Moravian Peter Böhler, who prompted Charles to look at the state of his soul more deeply. During May 1738, Charles began reading Martin Luther's volume on Galatians while ill. He wrote in his diary, "I labored, waited, and prayed to feel 'who loved me, and gave himself for me.'" He shortly found himself convinced, and journaled, "I now found myself at peace with God, and rejoice in hope of loving Christ." Two days later he began writing a hymn celebrating his conversion.

Evangelistic preacher

At evangelist George Whitefield's instigation, John and Charles eventually submitted to "be more vile" and do the unthinkable: preach outside of church buildings. In his journal entries from 1739 to 1743, Charles computed the number of those to whom he had preached. Of only those crowds for whom he stated a figure, the total during these five years comes to 149,400.

From June 24 through July 8, 1738, Charles reported preaching twice to crowds of ten thousand at Moorfields, once called "that Coney Island of the eighteenth century." He preached to 20,000 at Kennington Common plus gave a sermon on justification before the University of Oxford.

On a trip to Wales in 1747, the adventurous evangelist, now 40 years old, met 20-year-old Sally Gwynne, whom he soon married. By all accounts, their marriage was a happy one.

Charles continued to travel and preach, sometimes creating tension with John, who complained that "I do not even know when and where you intend to go." His last nation-wide trip was in 1756. After that, his health led him gradually to withdraw from itinerant ministry. He spent the remainder of his life in Bristol and London, preaching at Methodist chapels.

Magnificent obsession

Throughout his adult life, Charles wrote verse, predominantly hymns for use in Methodist meetings. He produced 56 volumes of hymns in 53 years, producing in his lyrics what brother John called a "distinct and full account of scriptural Christianity."

The Methodists became known (and sometimes mocked) for their exuberant singing of Charles's hymns. A contemporary observer recorded, "The song of the Methodists is the most beautiful I ever heard.... They sing in a proper way, with devotion, serene mind and charm."

Charles Wesley quickly earned admiration for his ability to capture universal Christian experience in memorable verse. In the following century, Henry Ward Beecher declared, "I would rather have written that hymn of Wesley's, 'Jesus, Lover of My Soul,' than to have the fame of all the kings that ever sat on the earth." The compiler of the massive *Dictionary of Hymnology*, John Julian, concluded that "perhaps, taking quantity and quality into consideration, [Charles Wesley was] the greatest hymn-writer of all ages."

FANNY CROSBY

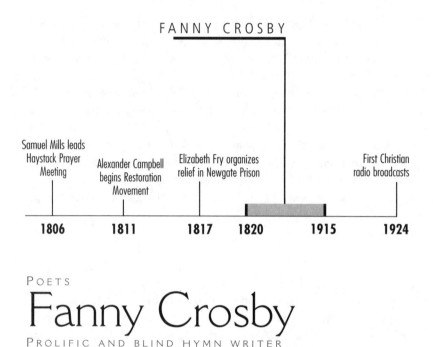

Samuel Mills leads Haystack Prayer Meeting	Alexander Campbell begins Restoration Movement	Elizabeth Fry organizes relief in Newgate Prison		First Christian radio broadcasts
1806	**1811**	**1817**	**1820** **1915**	**1924**

POETS

Fanny Crosby

PROLIFIC AND BLIND HYMN WRITER

> *"Oh, what a happy soul I am, / Although I cannot see! / I am resolved that in this world / Contented I will be."*

Francis Jane Crosby wrote more than 9,000 hymns, some of which are among the most popular in every Christian denomination. She wrote so many that she was forced to use pen names lest the hymnals be filled with her name above all others. And, for most people, the most remarkable thing about her was that she had done so in spite of her blindness.

"I think it is a great pity that the Master did not give you sight when he showered so many other gifts upon you," remarked one well-meaning preacher.

Fanny Crosby responded at once, as she had heard such comments before. "Do you know that if at birth I had been able to make one petition, it would have been that I was born blind?" said the poet, who had been able to see only for her first six weeks of life. "Because when I get to heaven, the first face that shall ever gladden my sight will be that of my Savior."

Blinded by a quack

Born in Putnam County, New York, Crosby became ill within two months. Unfortunately, the family doctor was away, and another man—pretending to be a certified doctor—treated her by prescribing hot mustard poultices to be applied to her eyes. Her illness eventually relented, but the treatment left her blind. When the doctor was revealed to be a quack, he disappeared. A few months later, Crosby's father died. Her mother was forced to find work as a maid to support the family, and Fanny was mostly raised by her Christian grandmother.

Her love of poetry began early—her first verse, written at age 8, echoed her lifelong refusal to feel sorry for herself:

Oh, what a happy soul I am,
Although I cannot see!
I am resolved that in this world
Contented I will be.

How many blessings I enjoy
That other people don't,
To weep and sigh because I'm blind
I cannot, and I won't!

While she enjoyed her poetry, she zealously memorized the Bible. Memorizing five chapters a week, even as a child she could recite the Pentateuch, the Gospels, Proverbs, the Song of Solomon, and many psalms chapter and verse.

Her mother's hard work paid off. Shortly before her fifteenth birthday, Crosby was sent to the recently founded New York Institute for the Blind, which would be her home for 23 years: 12 as a student, 11 as a teacher. She initially indulged in her own poetry and was called upon to pen verses for various occasions. In time the principal asked her to avoid such "distractions" in favor of her general instruction. "We have no right to be vain in the presence of the Owner and Creator of all things," he said.

It was the work of a traveling phrenologist (one who studies the shape and irregularities of the skull for insights into character and mental capacity) that changed the school's mind and again ignited her passion. Though his study is now the ridicule of science, the phrenologist's words were to prove prophetic: "Here is a poetess. Give her every possible encouragement. Read the best books to her and teach her the finest that is in poetry. You will hear from this young lady some day."

Poetry for presidents

It didn't take long. By age 23 Crosby was addressing Congress and making friendships with presidents. In fact, she knew all the chief executives of her lifetime, especially Grover Cleveland, who served as secretary for the Institute for the Blind before his election.

Another member of the institute, former pupil Alexander van Alstine, married Crosby in 1858. Considered one of New York's best organists, he wrote the music to many of Crosby's hymns. Crosby herself put music to only a few of hers, though she played harp, piano, guitar, and other instruments. More often, musicians came to her for lyrics. For example, one day musician William Doane dropped by her home for a surprise visit, begging her to put some words to a tune he had recently written and which he was to perform at an upcoming Sunday School convention. The only problem was that his train to the convention was leaving in 35 minutes. He sat at the piano and played the tune.

"Your music says, 'Safe in the Arms of Jesus,'" Crosby said, scribbling out the hymn's words immediately. "Read it on the train and hurry. You don't want to be late!" The hymn became one of Crosby's most famous.

Though she was under contract to submit three hymns a week to her publisher and often wrote six or seven a day (for a dollar or two each), many became incredibly popular. When Dwight Moody and Ira Sankey began to use them in their crusades, they received even more attention. Among them are "Blessed Assurance," "All the Way My Savior Leads Me," "To God Be the Glory," "Pass Me Not, O Gentle Savior," "Safe in the Arms of Jesus," "Rescue the Perishing," and "Jesus Keep Me Near the Cross."

She could write very complex hymns and compose music with a more classical structure (she could even improvise it), but she preferred to write simple, sentimental verses that could be used for evangelism. She continued to write her poetry up to her death, a month shy of her ninety-fifth birthday. "You will reach the river brink, some sweet day, bye and bye," was her last stanza.

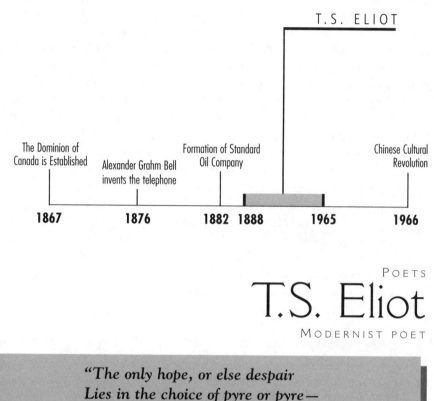

T.S. ELIOT

The Dominion of Canada is Established	Alexander Grahm Bell invents the telephone	Formation of Standard Oil Company		Chinese Cultural Revolution
1867	1876	1882	1888	1965	1966

T.S. Eliot
MODERNIST POET

> *"The only hope, or else despair*
> *Lies in the choice of pyre or pyre —*
> *To be redeemed from fire by fire."*

The man who wrote the most despairing poem of the twentieth century is today mostly remembered as the author of doggerel verse made popular in the hit musical *Cats*. Besides his poetry (the serious, the light, and the profoundly Christian), he produced literary criticism and drama so fine he was awarded the 1948 Nobel Prize for Literature and the British Order of Merit.

Brooding masterpiece

Thomas Stearns Eliot was born in St. Louis to a family descended from New England stock. There was no smoking or drinking in the Eliot household, and the literary-minded family—Tom, his brother, five sisters, and mother—would gather around his father, a wholesale grocer, as he read Dickens aloud. In fact, frail Tom spent much of his childhood curled up in a big leather armchair reading.

He was sent to New England to private schools and was accepted at Harvard University, where he studied under the likes of philosopher and poet George Santayana and completed his degree in three years. Though naturally shy, he gained a reputation as a dancer and party-goer, and when he decided he was too puny, he took boxing lessons.

Eliot won a traveling fellowship to Germany in 1914; he barely escaped getting caught by the war and made his way to Britain. It turned out to be a long stay. He never returned to take his oral examination, which was all that stood between him and a Harvard Ph.D.

After a year at Oxford University, then a stint at teaching history, Latin, French, German, arithmetic, drawing, and swimming in English schools, he became a banker with Lloyds of London. Later he became an editor with Faber and Faber (where he eventually became known as a prolific writer of blurbs for book jackets).

Meanwhile he brooded over the crumbling of European civilization.

His first masterpiece, the first "modernist" poem in English, was "The Love Song of J. Alfred Prufrock," a portrait of an aging man reviewing a life frittered away between timid hopes and lost opportunities:

> For I have known them all already, known them all
> Have known the evenings, mornings, afternoons
> I have measured out my life with coffee spoons....

With the publication of "The Waste Land" in 1922, he came to international attention. The poem begins,

> April is the cruelest month, breeding
> Lilacs out of the dead land, mixing
> Memory and desire, stirring
> Dull roots with spring rain.

It expresses the disillusionment and disgust after World War I, portraying a fearful world pursuing barren lusts, yearning desperately for any sign of redemption. It is considered by many to be the most influential poem of the twentieth century.

Redeemed from fire

Eliot's despair, however, was short-lived. After reading agnostic Bertrand Russell's essay "A Free Man's Worship," essentially an argument that man must worship man, Eliot decided its reasoning was shallow. He moved in the opposite direction and in 1927 was confirmed in the Church of England. The same year, he also gave up his American citizenship and became a British subject.

His faith became more widely known with the publication of "Ash Wednesday" in 1930, a poem showing the difficult search for truth ("Where shall the word be found, where will the word / Resound? Not here, there is not enough silence") and the discovery of a faith that will last, expressed in the repeated phrase, "Because I do not hope to turn again." Though criticized sharply by the literati for his turn to Christianity, he continued to express his faith in his poetry.

Eliot believed his finest achievement was writing the broadly religious poem "Four Quartets" (1943). It deals with the themes of incarnation, time and eternity, spiritual insight and revelation, culminating in an allusion to Pentecost:

The dove descending breaks the air
With flame of incandescent terror
Of which the tongues declare
The one discharge from sin and error.
The only hope, or else despair
Lies in the choice of pyre or pyre—
To be redeemed from fire by fire.

In *The Idea of a Christian Society* (1939), as well as other works, Eliot argued that the humanist attempt to form a non-Christian, "rational" civilization was doomed. "The experiment will fail," he wrote, "but we must be very patient in awaiting its collapse; meanwhile redeeming the time: so that the Faith may be preserved alive through the dark ages before us; to renew and rebuild civilization, and save the world from suicide."

He didn't believe society should be ruled by the church, only by Christian principles, with Christians being "the conscious mind and the conscience of the nation."

Eliot turned to writing plays in the 1930s and '40s because he believed drama attracts people who unconsciously seek a religion. The year 1935 saw the premiere of *Murder in the Cathedral*, a play based on the martyrdom of Thomas Becket, in which Eliot reiterates that faith can live only if the faithful are ready to die for it. It was followed by *The Family Reunion* (1939) and *The Cocktail Party* (1949), his greatest theatrical success. In his plays, he managed to handle complex moral and religious themes while entertaining audiences with farcical plots and keen social satire.

Verse to the postman

More personally, Eliot's first marriage was a disaster: his wife became increasingly unstable until she had to spend her last days in a mental institution. He then shared a flat with writer-critic John Hayward (who was almost completely paralyzed) until he married again in 1957.

Eliot enjoyed children, was a fan of Sherlock Holmes detective stories, addressed letters in verse ("Postman, propel thy feet / And take this note to greet / The Mrs. Hutchinson / Who lives on Charlotte Street..."), and made up rhymes about cats, which turned into his *Old Possum's Book of Practical Cats* (1939). He was an Anglican of Anglo-Catholic persuasion and served for a time as church warden at his local parish.

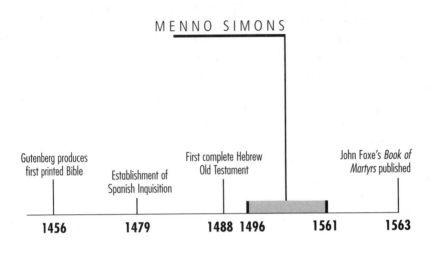

MENNO SIMONS

Gutenberg produces first printed Bible	Establishment of Spanish Inquisition	First complete Hebrew Old Testament		John Foxe's *Book of Martyrs* published
1456	**1479**	**1488 1496**	**1561**	**1563**

DENOMINATIONAL FOUNDERS

Menno Simons

ANABAPTIST PEACEMAKER

> *"If the Head had to suffer such torture, anguish, misery, and pain, how shall his servants, children, and members expect peace and freedom as to their flesh?"*

"The error of the cursed sect of the Anabaptists ... would doubtless be and remain extirpated, were it not that a former priest Menno Symons ... has misled many simple and innocent people," complained a letter to the regent of the Netherlands in 1541. "To seize and apprehend this man we have offered a large sum of money, but until now with no success. Therefore we have entertained the thought of offering and promising pardon and mercy to a few who have been misled ... if they would bring about the imprisonment of the said Menno Symons."

Holy Roman Emperor Charles V joined in the hunt, offering 100 gold guilders for Menno's arrest. One Dutch man was broken on the wheel and executed merely for allowing Menno to stay with him. But the former priest, a pacifist armed with ideas but no weapons, was never caught. Instead, he led the Anabaptists out of their radical, violent, millennialist fantasies into a moderate, devotional, pacifist movement. Neither the first nor the most original interpreter of the radical Reformation's Anabaptism, he was such an outstanding leader that the movement today is known by his name: Mennonites.

Eucharist crisis

Little is known about Menno's early life until his ordination as a priest at age 28. Though educated in a monastic school and trained for ministry, he had never even touched the Scriptures. "I feared if I should read them they would mislead me," he later wrote. "Behold! Such a stupid preacher was I for nearly two years."

After those two years, he had a crisis of faith. The bread and wine he dispensed at each Mass did not seem to transubstantiate into Christ's body and blood as Roman Catholic doctrine taught. He figured such thoughts had been suggested by the Devil, and prayed for God to ward them off. "Yet, I could not be freed from this thought," he wrote. "Finally, I got the idea to examine the New Testament diligently. I had not gone very far when I discovered that we were deceived, and my conscience, troubled on account of the aforementioned bread, was quickly relieved."

Believing the Bible to be authoritative, Menno developed the reputation as an "evangelical" preacher. "Everyone sought and desired me," he recounted. "It was said that I preached the Word of God and was a good fellow." But to Menno, it was a lie; his life was still empty and full of "diversions" like gambling and drinking.

Three years later, an otherwise unknown Leeuwarden Anabaptist was beheaded, sending Menno into another spiritual crisis. "It sounded very strange to me to hear of a second baptism," he wrote. "I examined the Scriptures diligently and pondered them earnestly but could find no report of infant baptism." Again, he wrote, "I realized that we were deceived." But his life changed little: "I spoke much concerning the Word of the Lord, without spirituality or love, as all hypocrites do."

Eventually, he was hit with a final crisis. Three hundred violent Anabaptists, dreaming of the imminent end of the world and attempting to escape persecution, captured a nearby town—and were savagely killed by the authorities. Among the dead was Menno's brother, Peter.

"I saw that these zealous children, although in error, willingly gave their lives and their estates for their doctrine and faith.... But I myself continued in my comfortable life and acknowledged abominations simply in order that I might enjoy comfort and escape the cross of Christ."

The realization led to an emotional, tearful cry to God for forgiveness. For nine months thereafter he essentially preached Anabaptist doctrine from his Catholic pulpit, until he finally left the church and (a year later) fully cast his lot with the radical Reformers.

Mellowing the fanatics

At the time, however, Anabaptists were unloved by all. Even Protestant Reformers like Martin Luther and John Calvin opposed them as "fanatics," "scatterbrains," and "asses"—just as bad as the papists. Those feelings weren't helped in 1535 when a despotic Anabaptist leader took over the town of Münster, ruling as a cruel theocratic dictator until Catholic and Protestant troops overran the city in bloody battle.

Menno was as worried about the violent Anabaptists as anyone and had even tried to stem their fanaticism as a priest. Sympathetic, he knew they had zeal without knowledge. But once he left the Catholic church, he met a group of peaceful Anabaptists who strongly opposed Münsterite thinking. He joined them and was ordained.

For the rest of his life, Menno (and, later, his wife and his children) lived in constant danger as heretics. He traveled throughout the Netherlands and Germany, writing extensively and establishing a printing press to circulate Anabaptist teaching. He took the Bible extremely literally, sometimes even legalistically; though he defended the doctrine of the Trinity in a small book, he refused to use the term because it did not appear in Scripture.

His writings aren't the most articulate Anabaptist theological treatises, nor are they

the first. But they served to defend the faith against both Catholic and Protestant attacks and to distance the group from more zealous militants. In one of his first writings, *The Blasphemy of Jan van Leyden*, Menno opposed the unchristlike "proponents of the sword philosophy": "It is forbidden to us to fight with physical weapons.... This only would I learn of you whether you are baptized on the sword or on the Cross?"

The Christian's duty was to suffer, not fight, Menno believed. "If the Head had to suffer such torture, anguish, misery, and pain," he asked, "how shall his servants, children, and members expect peace and freedom as to their flesh?"

In his later years, he was occupied with other internal Mennonite struggles, mainly over shunning excommunicated church members. But in each of his writings (more than 40 survive), he began by quoting Paul's letter to the Corinthians: "No other foundation can any one lay than that which is laid, which is Jesus Christ." He finally laid his pen down at age 66, as he became ill on the twenty-fifth anniversary of his renunciation of the Catholic church. The next day, he died a natural death. Today nearly 900,000 Mennonites follow his teachings.

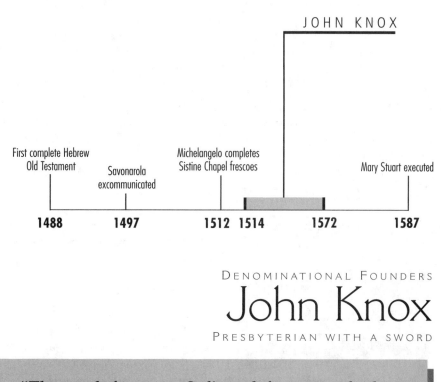

JOHN KNOX

First complete Hebrew Old Testament	Savonarola excommunicated	Michelangelo completes Sistine Chapel frescoes		Mary Stuart executed
1488	1497	1512	1514	1572	1587

DENOMINATIONAL FOUNDERS

John Knox

PRESBYTERIAN WITH A SWORD

> *"The sword of justice is God's, and if princes and rulers fail to use it, others may."*

He was a minister of the Christian gospel who advocated violent revolution. He was considered one of the most powerful preachers of his day, but only two of the hundreds of sermons he preached were ever published. He is a key figure in the formation of modern Scotland, yet there is only one monument erected to him in Scotland, and his grave lies beneath a parking lot.

John Knox was indeed a man of many paradoxes, a Hebrew Jeremiah set down on Scottish soil. In a relentless campaign of fiery oratory, he sought to destroy what he felt was idolatry and to purify Scotland's religion.

Taking up the cause

John Knox was born around 1514, at Haddington, a small town south of Edinburgh. Around 1529 he entered the University of St. Andrews and went on to study theology. He was ordained in 1536, but became a notary, then a tutor to the sons of local lairds (lower ranking Scottish nobility).

Dramatic events were unfolding in Scotland during Knox's youth. Many were angry with the Catholic church, which owned more than half the real estate and gathered an annual income of nearly 18 times that of the crown. Bishops and priests were often mere political appointments, and many never hid their immoral lives: the archbishop of St. Andrews, Cardinal Beaton, openly consorted with concubines and sired 10 children.

The constant sea traffic between Scotland and Europe allowed Lutheran literature to be smuggled into the country. Church authorities were alarmed by this "heresy" and tried to suppress it. Patrick Hamilton, an outspoken Protestant convert, was burned at the stake in 1528.

In the early 1540s, Knox came under the influence of converted reformers, and under the preaching of Thomas Guilliame, he joined them. Knox then became a bodyguard for the fiery Protestant preacher George Wishart, who was speaking throughout Scotland.

In 1546, however, Beaton had Wishart arrested, tried, strangled, and burned. In response, a party of 16 Protestant nobles stormed the castle, assassinated Beaton, and

mutilated his body. The castle was immediately put to siege by a fleet of French ships (Catholic France was an ally to Scotland). Though Knox was not privy to the murder, he did approve of it, and during a break in the siege, he joined the besieged party in the castle.

During a Protestant service one Sunday, preacher John Rough spoke on the election of ministers, and publicly asked Knox to undertake the office of preacher. When the congregation confirmed the call, Knox was shaken and reduced to tears. He declined at first, but eventually submitted to what he felt was a divine call.

It was a short-lived ministry. In 1547, after St. Andrews Castle had again been put under siege, it finally capitulated. Some of the occupants were imprisoned. Others, like Knox, were sent to the galleys as slaves.

Traveling preacher

Nineteen months passed before he and others were released. Knox spent the next five years in England, and his reputation for preaching quickly blossomed. But when Catholic Mary Tudor took the throne, Knox was forced to flee to France.

He made his way to Geneva, where he met John Calvin. The French reformer described Knox as a "brother ... laboring energetically for the faith." Knox for his part, was so impressed with Calvin's Geneva, he called it, "the most perfect school of Christ that was ever on earth since the days of the apostles."

Knox traveled on to Frankfurt am Main, where he joined other Protestant refugees—

and quickly became embroiled in controversy. The Protestants could not agree on an order of worship. Arguments became so heated that one group stormed out of a church one Sunday, refusing to worship in the same building as Knox.

Back in Scotland, Protestants were redoubling their efforts, and congregations were forming all over the country. A group that came to be called "The Lords of the Congregation" vowed to make Protestantism the religion of the land. In 1555, they invited Knox to return to Scotland to inspire the reforming task. Knox spent nine months preaching extensively and persuasively in Scotland before he was forced to return to Geneva.

Fiery blasts of the pen

Away from his homeland again, he published some of his most controversial tracts: In his *Admonition to England* he virulently attacked the leaders who allowed Catholicism back in England. In *The First Blast of the Trumpet Against the Monstrous Regiment of Women* he argued that a female ruler (like English Queen Mary Tudor) was "most odious in the presence of God" and that she was "a traitoress and rebel against God." In his *Appellations to the Nobility and Commonality of Scotland*, he extended to ordinary people the right—indeed the duty—to rebel against unjust rulers. As he told Queen Mary of Scotland later, "The sword of justice is God's, and if princes and rulers fail to use it, others may."

Knox returned to Scotland in 1559, and he again deployed his formidable preaching skills to increase Protestant militancy. Within days of his arrival, he preached a violent sermon at Perth against Catholic "idolatry," causing a riot. Altars were demolished, images smashed, and religious houses destroyed.

In June, Knox was elected the minister of the Edinburgh church, where he continued to exhort and inspire. In his sermons, Knox typically spent half an hour calmly exegeting a biblical passage. Then as he applied the text to the Scottish situation, he became "active and vigorous" and would violently pound the pulpit. Said one note taker, "he made me so to grew [quake] and tremble, that I could not hold pen to write."

The Lords of the Congregation militarily occupied more and more cities, so that finally, in the 1560 Treaty of Berwick, the English and French agreed to leave Scotland. (The English, now under Protestant Elizabeth I, had come to the aid of the Protestant Scots; the French were aiding the Catholic party). The future of Protestantism in Scotland was assured.

The Parliament ordered Knox and five colleagues to write a *Confession of Faith*, the *First Book of Discipline*, and *The Book of Common Order*—all of which cast the Protestant faith of Scotland in a distinctly Calvinist and Presbyterian mode.

Knox finished out his years as preacher of the Edinburgh church, helping shape the developing Protestantism in Scotland. During this time, he wrote his *History of the Reformation of Religion in Scotland*.

Though he remains a paradox to many, Knox was clearly a man of great courage: one man standing before Knox's open grave said, "Here lies a man who neither flattered nor feared any flesh." Knox's legacy is large: his spiritual progeny includes some 750,000 Presbyterians in Scotland, 3 million in the United States, and many millions more worldwide.

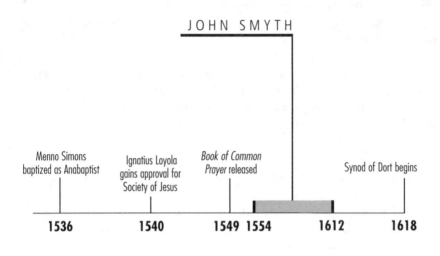

JOHN SMYTH

Menno Simons baptized as Anabaptist	Ignatius Loyola gains approval for Society of Jesus	Book of Common Prayer released		Synod of Dort begins
1536	1540	1549 1554	1612	1618

DENOMINATIONAL FOUNDERS

John Smyth

THE "SE-BAPTIST"

> "Baptism is not washing with water: but it is the baptism of the Spirit, the confession of the mouth, and the washing with water."

When he was exiled to Amsterdam from his native England, John Smyth gathered three dozen of his followers around him. The former Anglican preacher and Cambridge fellow recited a confession of faith; then he baptized himself.

The brazen act scandalized even those who, with Smyth, despised England's state church. Amsterdam Separatist Richard Bernard nicknamed him a "Se-Baptist" (self-baptizer). Though Smyth's followers preferred the term "Christians Baptized on Profession of Their Faith," the shorter, derogatory "se-baptist," later shortened again to "Baptist," stuck.

Not reformed enough

Though his early years are lost to history, Smyth was born in a time when the Reformation seemed to be grinding to a halt— Luther's death, the Counter-Reformation Council of Trent, and

England's break with Rome occurred a mere decade or so before his birth. Smyth studied for the Anglican priesthood at Christ's College, Cambridge, but found himself increasingly frustrated with the church—not only of Rome, but of Luther, Calvin, Zwingli, and especially his own Church of England. A mere six years after becoming a city preacher at Lincoln in 1600, he renounced Anglicanism altogether.

After a few years of practicing medicine, Smyth joined a group of like-minded Separatists who wanted to create a church of believers unbound by parochial or diocesan boundaries. Together they would "walk in all his [Christ's] ways, make known or to be made known among them ... whatever it might cost them."

What it cost them was their homeland. When James I ascended the throne in 1603, he began persecuting the Separatists. "I will make them conform themselves," he swore, "or I will have them out of the land."

Smyth's group of 50 or so fled to Amsterdam, which was known for its religious toleration and its already-sizable community of Separatist exiles. Still, Smyth did not see them as completely kindred spirits. He fought with them over the use of Scripture in worship (Smyth opposed using English translations), psalm singing, sermon reading, and the collection of offerings—all practices he condemned.

Smyth, who wanted to create a church like the one described in the Book of Acts, also fought against any attempts to create a hierarchy. Each congregation, not the congregation's officers, was the highest authority next to God, he wrote in his 1607 *Principles and Inferences Concerning the Visible Church*. The Bible, he believed, only allowed for bishops (also called elders) and deacons—and even they would be subject to the laity. The following year, he continued publishing his disagreements with the Separatists in *The Differences of the Churches of the Separation*.

Mennonite ending

Smyth's Amsterdam was also home to many Anabaptist Mennonites, who had for two generations practiced adult baptism based on a personal confession of faith. On this issue, Smyth finally broke with the Separatists. If the Church of England was, as he believed, "the Church of Antichrist," its baptism must be false. In fact, he wrote in *The Character of the Beast* (1609), the baptisms of all established churches were false. And the New Testament never even mentioned infant baptism—only the baptism of believing adults.

"Baptism is not washing with water," he wrote, "but it is the baptism of the Spirit, the confession of the mouth, and the washing with water: how then can any man without great folly wash with water which is the least and last of baptism?"

So, believing that there was no true church from which a valid baptism could be obtained, Smyth baptized himself. "There is good warrant for a man churching himself," he justified. "For two men singly are no church; so may two men put baptism upon themselves." He then baptized 36 others, including Thomas Helwys, who would later return to England and establish the first permanent Baptist church there.

The more Smyth conversed with the Mennonites, the more he liked them. And the more he became convinced that baptizing himself—like his ordination in the Anglican church and acceptance of Separatist teachings—had been a mistake. "We are inconstant in error," he wrote. Eventually, Smyth applied for membership with the Mennonites. Helwys, who agreed with Smyth on nearly every point but could not accept Mennonite teachings on Christ and ministerial succession, recommended to the church that Smyth, then in bad health, be excommunicated. In 1611 they agreed. Smyth continued to defend his membership with the Mennonites up to his death in 1616. But to this day, it is not as a Mennonite that he is remembered, but as the first Baptist.

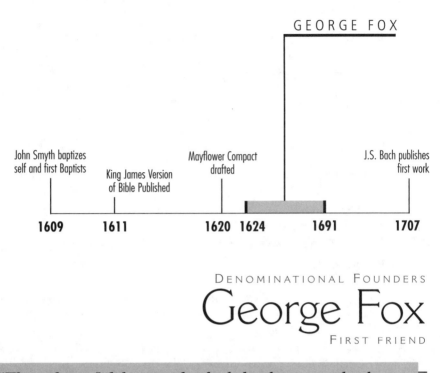

GEORGE FOX

| John Smyth baptizes self and first Baptists | King James Version of Bible Published | Mayflower Compact drafted | | J.S. Bach publishes first work |

1609   1611   1620 1624   1691   1707

DENOMINATIONAL FOUNDERS

George Fox

FIRST FRIEND

> *"These things I did not see by the help of man, nor by the letter ... but I saw them in the light of the Lord Jesus Christ, and by his immediate spirit and power, as did the holy men of God by whom the Holy Scriptures were written."*

Even as a child, George Fox knew he was somehow different. He was repelled when he watched older men "carry themselves lightly and wantonly towards each other" in pointless diversions and drunkenness. He vowed, "If ever I come to be a man, surely I shall not do so."

As a man, he went even further—founding a movement that helped others meet Christ and live lives worthy of their Lord.

The inner light

Fox was born in a small English village, the son of a weaver. He became a cobbler's apprentice, but, disgusted with the lax morals of his fellow apprentices, he quit and set off on a spiritual journey. He traveled all over England, attending religious meetings and seeking illumination. He immersed himself in the Bible and wrestled to discover truth.

He eventually came to the conclusion that all sects were wrong and that their worship was a disgrace. Pastors who worked for a salary were nothing but "journeymen." Hymns, sermons, sacraments, and creeds hindered—rather than helped—people to worship.

Instead, Fox looked to the "inner light" for inspiration. This inner light, he argued, was in everyone, though it might be very dim in some. It is not intellect nor natural reason nor morality, but a capacity to recognize and accept God. It also makes it possible for people to understand and believe the Bible. Therefore it is through the inner light, first and foremost, that people come to know God.

"These things I did not see by the help of man, nor by the letter," he concluded, "but I saw them in the light of the Lord Jesus Christ, and by his immediate spirit and power, as did the holy men of God by whom the Holy Scriptures were written."

Persecution and practice

He was hesitant to share these insights at first, but one day he said he felt called by the Spirit to speak out at a Baptist meeting. The promptings of the Spirit became increasingly frequent; in his journals he regularly writes, "At the command of God, I ..." and "I was moved to go...."

As he went forth, however, "with the word of life into the world, the world swelled and made a noise like the great raging waves of the sea." In many places, Fox was treated with contempt; he was physically thrown from meetings, beaten, stoned, and jailed. He spent a total of six years in prison—the first time, for interrupting a preacher who was saying that ultimate truth was found in the Bible. Other times it was for blasphemy or for conspiring against the government (i.e., for his pacifism).

Still, he gathered followers. They structured their worship so nothing could get in the way of the Spirit. The sacraments were rejected, and the service took place in silence, though any who felt called to speak or pray aloud could do so. People began calling them "quakers" because many would tremble as they were moved by the Spirit, but Fox preferred the term "friends."

To thwart individualism, Fox emphasized the importance of community and love. Decisions among the Friends were not made by majority vote but by consensus. If consensus wasn't reached, decisions were postponed until the group as a whole could discern the leading of the Spirit.

The Friends also refused to swear oaths or tithes or bow to their betters (they insisted on using the familiar "thou" instead of the respectful "you"). Like their founder, they were staunch pacifists.

Spreading the faith

Fox traveled abroad to spread his gospel of the inner light. In Scotland, he was accused of sedition. He went to Ireland, then to the Caribbean and North America;

he also made two visits to the Continent.

In both England and America, the Friends were severely persecuted for decades, but the movement continued to grow. The most famous convert in America was William Penn, founder of Pennsylvania.

The Quakers have never become large numerically (there are now a mere half-million worldwide), but they eventually earned the respect of the other Christian denominations.

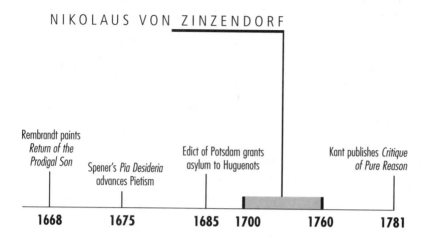

NIKOLAUS VON ZINZENDORF

Rembrandt paints *Return of the Prodigal Son*

Spener's *Pia Desideria* advances Pietism

Edict of Potsdam grants asylum to Huguenots

Kant publishes *Critique of Pure Reason*

| 1668 | 1675 | 1685 | 1700 | 1760 | 1781 |

DENOMINATIONAL FOUNDERS

Nikolaus von Zinzendorf

CHRIST-CENTERED MORAVIAN "BROTHER"

> *"There can be no Christianity without community."*

Nearly two centuries after Luther posted his 95 *Theses*, Protestantism had lost some of its soul. Institutions and dogma had, in many people's minds, choked the life out of the Reformation.

Lutheran minister P.J. Spener hoped to revive the church by promoting the "practice of piety," emphasizing prayer and Bible reading over dogma. It worked. Pietism spread quickly, reinvigorating Protestants throughout Europe—including underground Protestants in Moravia and Bohemia (modern Czechoslovakia).

The Catholic church cracked down on the dissidents, and many were forced to flee to Protestant areas of neighboring Germany. One group of families fled north to Saxony, where they settled on the lands belonging to a rich young ruler, Count Nikolaus Ludwig von Zinzendorf.

Rich young ruler

Born into Austrian nobility and raised by his grandmother,

Zinzendorf showed an early inclination toward theology and religious work. As the god-son of P.J. Spener, he was raised in a strong Pietist tradition. But as a count, he was expected to follow his late father's footsteps into government. He did as he was told and in October 1721 became the king's judicial counselor at Dresden.

After less than a year at court, he bought the estate of Berthelsdorf from his grand-mother, hoping to form a Christian community for oppressed religious minorities. Almost immediately a Moravian named Christian David showed up at his door and became his first tenant. Ten Moravian Protestants arrived before December and found-ed a settlement on the count's land. They named it Herrnhut—"the Lord's watch."

By May 1725, 90 Moravians were gathered at Herrnhut. Because of the spirited preaching at the Berthelsdorf parish church, the population of this "small city" had reached 300 by 1726.

The count was still a devout Lutheran and tried to keep the refugees within the parish church. His goal was to form *ecclesiolae in ecclesia*—"little churches within the church"—to act as a leaven, revitalizing and unifying churches into one communion. But with the diversity at Herrnhut, discord soon arose. When it did, Zinzendorf moved to Herrnhut with his family. He went from house to house counseling those who needed it and cre-ated a "Brotherly Agreement" of manorial rules. He also appointed watchmen, almoners, and other caretakers.

"There can be no Christianity without community," he said.

Getting serious

In July 1737 Zinzendorf accidentally discovered a copy of the constitution of the *Unitas Fratrum* (Unity of the Brethren) of the fifteenth-century Hussite movement in Bohemia and Moravia. He was amazed that the *Unitas Fratrum* was "a fully established church antedating Lutheranism itself." Even more amazing, the constitution was very similar to his newly adopted "Brotherly Agreement."

He raced back to Herrnhut to share his discovery, and at a powerful Communion service, the Moravians at Herrnhut vowed to restore the older church with Zinzendorf. The Berthelsdorf parish church would continue as a Lutheran parish, but became Herrnhut, a Unity of the Brethren congregation; they would later become known as the Moravian Church.

Like the Pietists, the Moravian Brethren believed that Christianity should be a "reli-gion of the heart"—which went against the grain of the growing acceptance of Enlightenment beliefs. They emphasized experience of faith and love over doctrine, and thus were more accepting of varying denominational differences. In fact, Zinzendorf may have been the first churchman to use the word "ecumenism." The Moravians also placed special importance on community: families' allegiances were superseded by "choirs"—groups delineated by age, sex, and marital status.

The real missions father

Visiting Copenhagen in 1731 to attend the coronation of King Christian VI,

Zinzendorf met a converted slave from the West Indies, Anthony Ulrich. The man was looking for someone to go back to his homeland to preach the gospel to black slaves, including his sister and brother. Zinzendorf raced back to Herrnhut to find men to go; two immediately volunteered, becoming the first Moravian missionaries—and the first Protestant missionaries of the modern era, antedating William Carey (often called "the father of modern missions") by 60-some years.

Within two decades, Zinzendorf sent missionaries around the globe: to Greenland, Lapland, Georgia, Surinam, Africa's Guinea Coast, South Africa, Amsterdam's Jewish quarter, Algeria, the native North Americans, Ceylon, Romania, and Constantinople. In short order, more than 70 missionaries from a community of fewer than 600 answered the call.

By the time Zinzendorf died in 1760 in Herrnhut, the Moravians had sent out at least 226 missionaries.

Zinzendorf's influence is felt much wider than in the Moravian Church. His

emphasis on the "religion of the heart" deeply influenced John Wesley. He is remembered today, as Karl Barth put it, as "perhaps the only genuine Christocentric of the modern age." Scholar George Forell put it more succinctly: Zinzendorf was "the noble Jesus freak."

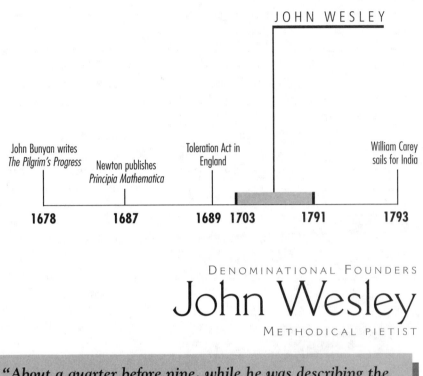

JOHN WESLEY

| John Bunyan writes *The Pilgrim's Progress* | Newton publishes *Principia Mathematica* | Toleration Act in England | | | William Carey sails for India |

| 1678 | 1687 | 1689 1703 | 1791 | 1793 |

DENOMINATIONAL FOUNDERS

John Wesley

METHODICAL PIETIST

> *"About a quarter before nine, while he was describing the change which God works in the heart through faith in Christ, I felt my heart strangely warmed."*

In late 1735, a ship made its way to the New World from England. On board was a young Anglican minister, John Wesley, who had been invited to serve as a pastor to British colonists in Savannah, Georgia. When the weather went sour, the ship found itself in serious trouble. Wesley, also chaplain of the vessel, feared for his life.

But he noticed that the group of German Moravians, who were on their way to preach to American Indians, were not afraid at all. In fact, throughout the storm, they sang calmly. When the trip ended, he asked the Moravian leader about his serenity, and the Moravian responded with a question: Did he, Wesley, have faith in Christ? Wesley said he did, but later reflected, "I fear they were vain words."

In fact, Wesley was confused by the experience, but his perplexity was to lead to a period of soul searching and finally to one of the most famous and consequential conversions in church history.

Religious upbringing

Wesley was born into a strong Anglican home: his father, Samuel, was priest, and his mother, Susanna, taught religion and morals faithfully to her 19 children.

Wesley attended Oxford, proved to be a fine scholar, and was soon ordained into the Anglican ministry. At Oxford, he joined a society (founded by his brother Charles) whose members took vows to lead holy lives, take Communion once a week, pray daily, and visit prisons regularly. In addition, they spent three hours every afternoon studying the Bible and other devotional material.

From this "holy club" (as fellow students mockingly called it), Wesley sailed to Georgia to pastor. His experience proved to be a failure. A woman he courted in Savannah married another man. When he tried to enforce the disciplines of the "holy club" on his church, the congregation rebelled. A bitter Wesley returned to England.

Heart strangely warmed

After speaking with another Moravian, Peter Boehler, Wesley concluded that he lacked saving faith. Though he continued to try to be good, he remained frustrated.

"I was indeed fighting continually, but not conquering.... I fell and rose, and fell again."

On May 24, 1783, he had an experience that changed everything. He described the event in his journal:

"In the evening, I went very unwillingly to a society in Aldersgate Street, where one was reading Luther's preface to the Epistle to the Romans. About a quarter before nine, while he was describing the change which God works in the heart through faith in Christ, I felt my heart strangely warmed. I felt I did trust in Christ, Christ alone for salvation, and an assurance was given me that he had taken away my sins, even mine, and saved me from the law of sin and death."

Meanwhile, another former member of the "holy club," George Whitefield, was having remarkable success as a preacher, especially in the industrial city of Bristol. Hundreds of working-class poor, oppressed by industrializing England and neglected by the church, were experiencing emotional conversions under his fiery preaching. So many were responding that Whitefield desperately needed help.

Wesley accepted Whitefield's plea hesitantly. He distrusted Whitefield's dramatic style; he questioned the propriety of Whitefield's outdoor preaching (a radical innovation for the day); he felt uncomfortable with the emotional reactions even his own preaching elicited. But the orderly Wesley soon warmed to the new method of ministry.

With his organizational skills, Wesley quickly became the new leader of the movement. But Whitefield was a firm Calvinist, whereas Wesley couldn't swallow the doctrine of predestination. Furthermore, Wesley argued (against Reformed doctrine) that Christians could enjoy entire sanctification in this life: loving God and their neighbors, meekness and lowliness of heart, abstaining from all appearance of evil, and doing all for the glory of God. In the end, the two preachers parted ways.

From "methodists" to Methodism

Wesley did not intend to found a new denomination, but historical circumstances and his organizational genius conspired against his desire to remain in the Church of England.

Wesley's followers first met in private home "societies." When these societies became too large for members to care for one another, Wesley organized "classes," each with 11 members and a leader. Classes met weekly to pray, read the Bible, discuss their spiritual lives, and to collect money for charity. Men and women met separately, but anyone could become a class leader.

The moral and spiritual fervor of the meetings is expressed in one of Wesley's most famous aphorisms: "Do all the good you can, by all the means you can, in all the ways you can, in all the places you can, at all the times you can, to all the people you can, as long as ever you can."

The movement grew rapidly, as did its critics, who called Wesley and his followers "methodists," a label they wore proudly. It got worse than name calling at times: methodists were frequently met with violence as paid ruffians broke up meetings and threatened Wesley's life.

Though Wesley scheduled his itinerant preaching so it wouldn't disrupt local Anglican services, the bishop of Bristol still objected. Wesley responded, "The world is my parish"—a phrase that later became a slogan of Methodist missionaries. Wesley, in fact, never slowed down, and during his ministry he traveled over 4,000 miles annually, preaching some 40,000 sermons in his lifetime.

A few Anglican priests, such as his hymn-writing brother Charles, joined these Methodists, but the bulk of the preaching burden rested on John. He was eventually forced to employ lay preachers, who were not allowed to serve Communion but merely served to complement the ordained ministry of the Church of England.

Wesley then organized his followers into a "connection," and a number of societies into a "circuit" under the leadership of a "superintendent." Periodic meetings of methodist clergy and lay preachers eventually evolved into the "annual conference," where those who were to serve each circuit were appointed, usually for three-year terms.

In 1787, Wesley was required to register his lay preachers as non-Anglicans. Meanwhile, on the other side of the Atlantic, the American Revolution isolated Yankee methodists from their Anglican connections. To support the American movement, Wesley independently ordained two lay preachers and appointed Thomas Coke as superintendent. With these and other actions, Methodism gradually moved out of the Church of England—though Wesley himself remained an Anglican until his death.

An indication of his organizational genius, we know exactly how many followers Wesley had when he died: 294 preachers, 71,668 British members, 19 missionaries (5 in mission stations), and 43,265 American members with 198 preachers. Today Methodists number about 30 million worldwide.

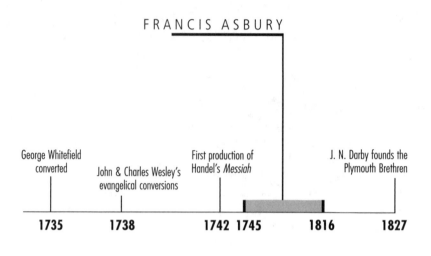

FRANCIS ASBURY

George Whitefield converted	John & Charles Wesley's evangelical conversions	First production of Handel's *Messiah*		J. N. Darby founds the Plymouth Brethren
1735	1738	1742 1745	1816	1827

DENOMINATIONAL FOUNDERS

Francis Asbury

METHODIST ON HORSEBACK

> "Under the rush of his [Asbury's] utterance, people sprang to their feet as if summoned to the judgment bar of God."
> — Biographer Ezra Tipple

Some today might call him a workaholic. Or maybe just utterly dedicated. English-born Francis Asbury certainly had the numbers: during his 45-year ministry in America, he traveled on horseback or in carriage an estimated 300,000 miles, delivering some 16,500 sermons. He was so well-known in America that letters addressed to "Bishop Asbury, United States of America" were delivered to him.

And the result of all this labor and fame? He put American Methodism on the denominational map.

Rapid ordination

Asbury was born into a working-class Anglican family; he dropped out of school before he was 12 to work as a blacksmith's apprentice. By the time he was 14, he had been "awakened" in the Christian faith.

He and his mother attended Methodist meetings, where soon he began to preach; he was appointed a full-time Methodist preacher by the time he was 21. In 1771, at a gathering of Methodist ministers, John Wesley asked, "Our brethren in America call aloud for help. Who are willing to go over and help them?" Asbury volunteered.

When in October 1771, Asbury landed in Philadelphia, there were only 600 Methodists in America. Within days, he hit the road preaching but pushed himself so hard that he fell ill that winter. This was the beginning of a pattern: over the next 45 years, he suffered from colds, coughs, fevers, severe headaches, ulcers, and eventually chronic rheumatism, which forced him off his horse and into a carriage. Yet he continued to preach.

During the Revolutionary War, Asbury remained politically neutral. To avoid signing an oath disclaiming his allegiance to England and to dodge the American draft, he went into hiding for several months. "I am considered by some as an enemy," he wrote, "liable to be seized by violence and abused." By war's end, he had retained his credibility with the victorious Americans and was able to continue his ministry among them.

After the war, John Wesley ordained Englishman Thomas Coke as Wesley's American superintendent. Coke, in turn, ordained Asbury at the famous Baltimore "Christmas Conference" of 1784, which gave birth to the American Methodist Episcopal Church. On Christmas Day, Asbury was ordained a deacon, the following day, an elder, and on December 27, a superintendent (against Wesley's advice, Asbury later used the term "bishop"). As Coke put it, "We were in great haste and did much business in a little time." Within six months, Coke returned to England, and thereafter, Asbury held the reins of American Methodism.

Organizational man

Organization was Asbury's gift. He created "districts" of churches, each of which would be served by circuit riders—preachers who traveled from church to church to preach and minister, especially in rural areas. In the late 1700s, 95 percent of Americans lived in places with fewer than 2,500 inhabitants, and thus most did not have access to church or clergy.

This is one reason Asbury pushed for missionary expansion into the Tennessee and Kentucky frontier—even though his and other preachers' lives were constantly threatened by illness and Indian attacks. According to biographer Ezra Tipple, Asbury's preaching was more zeal than art, and highly effective. Tipple wrote there were occasions when "under the rush of his utterance, people sprang to their feet as if summoned to the judgment bar of God."

Though a school dropout, Asbury launched five schools. He also promoted "Sunday schools," in which children were taught reading, writing, and arithmetic.

Asbury didn't limit his work to administration and preaching. Asbury hated slavery and petitioned George Washington to enact antislavery legislation. "My spirit was grieved at the conduct of some Methodists," wrote Asbury, "that hire slaves at public places to the highest bidder, to cut skin, and starve them."

Asbury pushed himself to the end. After preaching what was to be his last sermon, he was so weak he had to be carried to his carriage. By then, though, Methodism had grown under his leadership to 200,000 strong. His legacy continued with the 4,000 Methodist preachers he had ordained: by the Civil War, American Methodists numbered 1.5 million.

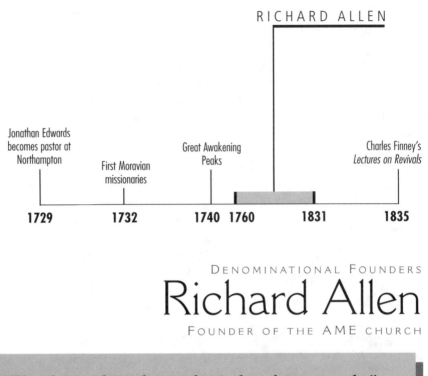

RICHARD ALLEN

Jonathan Edwards
becomes pastor at
Northampton

First Moravian
missionaries

Great Awakening
Peaks

Charles Finney's
Lectures on Revivals

1729   **1732**   **1740 1760**   **1831**   **1835**

DENOMINATIONAL FOUNDERS

Richard Allen

FOUNDER OF THE AME CHURCH

"The plain and simple gospel suits best for any people."

Richard Allen and his associate Absalom Jones were the leaders of the black Methodist community in Philadelphia in 1793 when a yellow fever epidemic broke out. Many people, black and white, were dying. Hundreds more fled the city. City officials approached Allen and asked if the black community could help serve as nurses to the suffering and help bury the dead.

Allen and Jones recognized the racism inherent in the request: asking black folks to do the risky, dirty work for whites. But they consented—partly from compassion and partly to show the white community, in one more way, the moral and spiritual equality of blacks.

Preaching in his sleep

Allen was born into slavery in Philadelphia in 1760. He was converted at age 17 and began preaching on his plantation and at local Methodist churches, preaching whenever he had the chance. "Sometimes, I would awake from my sleep preaching and praying," he later recalled. His owner, one of Allen's early converts, was so impressed with him that he allowed Allen to purchase his freedom.

In 1781, Allen began traveling the Methodist preaching circuits in Delaware and surrounding states. "My usual method was, when I would get bare of clothes, to stop travelling and go to work," he said. "My hands administered to my necessities." Increasingly, prominent Methodist leaders, like Francis Asbury, made sure Allen had places to preach. In 1786 the former slave returned to Philadelphia and joined St. George's Methodist Church. His leadership at prayer services attracted dozens of blacks into the church, and with them came increased racial tension.

By 1786 blacks made up about 10 percent of the Methodist church in the United States, and though whites and blacks often worshiped together, blacks enjoyed no real freedom or equality. Segregated seating was typical; the area reserved for blacks was usually called the "Negro Pew" or the "African Corner."

St. George's had no history of segregated seating, at least until the later 1780s. Then white leaders required black parishioners to use the chairs around the walls rather than the pews. During one service in 1787, a group of blacks sat in some new pews that, unbeknownst to them, had been reserved for whites. As these blacks knelt in prayer, a white trustee came over and grabbed Absalom Jones, Allen's associate, and began pulling on him, saying, "You must get up—you must not kneel here."

Jones asked him to wait until prayer was over, but the trustee retorted, "No, you must get up now, or I will call for aid and force you away." But the group finished praying before they got up and walked out.

Allen had for some time thought of establishing an independent black congregation, and this incident pushed him over the edge. Nonetheless, he had no desire to leave Methodism or the local Conference: "I was confident," he later wrote, "that there was no religious sect or denomination would suit the capacity of the colored people as well as the Methodist; for the plain and simple gospel suits best for any people." Still he recognized that blacks needed a place they could worship in freedom.

Though Methodist leaders resisted Allen and Jones, threatening them with expulsion from the Methodist Conference (while at the same time pleading for their help during the 1793 epidemic), Allen went ahead and, in 1794, purchased an old frame building, formerly a blacksmith's shop, and created the Bethel African Methodist Episcopal Church. Bishop Francis Asbury dedicated the building and, in 1799, ordained Allen as a deacon.

For the next 15 years, white Methodist leaders in Philadelphia tried to keep Allen's congregation and property under its jurisdiction. But on the first day of 1816, the Pennsylvania Supreme Court ruled that the church belonged to Allen and his associates.

A denomination quickly came together. In April, delegates from several black Methodist churches convened in Philadelphia and drew up an "Ecclesiastical Compact" that united them in the independent African Methodist Episcopal Church (AME). Allen was ordained an elder and then consecrated as bishop—the first black to hold such an office in America.

Blacks in Baltimore, Wilmington, Attleboro, and Salem followed Allen's example and established independent African Methodist churches. Allen oversaw the rapid growth of the AME's mother church in Philadelphia, which grew to 7,500 members in the 1820s. The denomination became by all accounts the most significant black institution in the nineteenth century, and today has over 6,000 churches and over 2 million members.

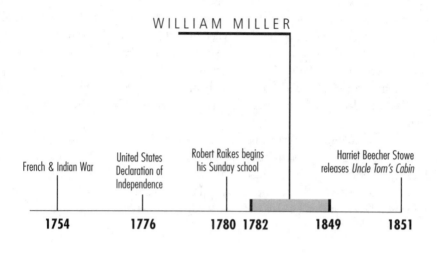

WILLIAM MILLER

French & Indian War | United States Declaration of Independence | Robert Raikes begins his Sunday school | Harriet Beecher Stowe releases *Uncle Tom's Cabin*

| 1754 | 1776 | 1780 1782 | 1849 | 1851 |

DENOMINATIONAL FOUNDERS

William Miller

MISTAKEN FOUNDER OF ADVENTISM

> *"We have passed what the world calls the last round of 1843.... Does your heart begin to quail? Or are you waiting for your blessed hope in the glorious appearing of Jesus Christ?"*

In recent years, we have almost come to expect the well-publicized reports from Bible-belt Texas and avant-garde California of a self-proclaimed prophet announcing the end of the world. He attracts a large following or triggers a near panic—and ends up wrong. The most famous case on American soil, however, took place in the northeastern United States just before the Civil War.

The prophet of doom was no bug-eyed fanatic. He was a square-jawed, honest, church-going farmer named William Miller.

A former captain in the War of 1812, Miller converted from Deism in 1816. Excited, he began to "search the Scriptures" for the truth. After two years he was convinced he understood them—especially Daniel 8:14: "Unto 2,300 days; then shall the sanctuary be cleansed."

The cleansing of the sanctuary, Miller believed, could only mean the purging of the earth by fire—in short, the end of the world.

By interpreting these prophetic days as years and beginning from the date of the prophecy (placed by James Ussher at 457 B.C.), Miller concluded that the end of the 2,300 "days" would fall in 1843: "I was thus brought to the solemn conclusion that in about 25 years from that time all the affairs of our present state would be wound up."

Marketing Miller

At first Miller was reluctant to reveal his secret. He had grown up in Low Hampton, New York, near the Vermont border. He married in 1803 and moved to Poultney, Vermont, where he farmed and served as a simple sheriff and justice of the peace. But in 1828, he felt an inward "call" to tell the world of his discovery. "I tried to excuse myself," he later wrote, "I told the Lord that I was not used to speaking ... that I was slow of speech and slow of tongue. But I could get no relief."

By 1831 he found the courage to share his discovery with neighbors and friends. When asked to discuss his views in a nearby church, he suddenly discovered that on this one subject he could be eloquent. Invitations multiplied, and Miller gained a bit of local notoriety. Though never ordained, his status was regularized in 1833 with a license to preach.

Then two events combined to give Miller a much larger audience. First, in 1838 he published his *Evidence from Scripture and History of the Second Coming of Christ, About the Year 1843*. Next he made an excursion to the large cities in New England for a series of lectures. At Exeter, New Hampshire, he met Joshua V. Himes, pastor of the Chardon Street Baptist Chapel in Boston. Himes sensed immediately the power in the message of the quiet, middle-aged farmer, and he joined Miller as his manager and publicity agent. Himes equipped Miller with a great chart displaying the millennial calculations in graphic form, purchased the biggest tent in the country for his meetings, and edited two journals—New York's *Midnight Cry* and Boston's *Signs of the Times*.

Miller the man was transformed overnight into the Millerite Movement. Himes and his associates recruited other evangelists and sent them on speaking tours; organized camp meetings; and published tracts, books, and pamphlets.

As the dreaded year approached, Miller's preaching drew larger crowds. In six months, he delivered more than 300 lectures with the constant theme: Are you ready to meet your Savior?

Mobs of angry citizens tried to break up some of the meetings. Miller himself was pelted with eggs and decaying vegetables. But the crowds grew larger and the number of converts mounted. More than 50,000 believed Miller, and as many as a million others were curious and expectant.

Setting a date

With excitement rising, people began to demand a definite day for the Lord's appearance. Miller was reluctant to be more specific, but in January 1843, he announced that this Hebrew year—March 21, 1843, to March 21, 1844—must see the end of time. But, he pleaded, if the estimate should prove slightly inaccurate, his followers should have faith that their deliverance would come soon, in God's appointed time.

As the year progressed, tension mounted, especially when a comet suddenly appeared in the heavens. There were huge meetings in New York and Philadelphia, but dates for future gatherings were announced with the proviso "if time continues."

Miller was ill through most of 1843, and his lieutenants, many far less cautious than the old soldier, carried on the fight. Their radicalism added to the weary prophet's pain.

The opening days of 1844 found Miller, then 62, at home resting from a strenuous speaking tour—85 lectures in eight weeks. But he believed firmly that the end was near. Aware of the scoffers, he thought it time to write "to second advent believers" a few words of encouragement:

> We have passed what the world calls the last round of 1843 ... Does your heart begin to quail? Or are you waiting for your blessed hope in the glorious appearing of Jesus Christ? Let me say to you in the language of the blessed Book of God, 'Although it tarry, wait for it; it will surely come, it will not tarry.' Never has my faith been stronger than at this very moment.

Then March 21, 1844, came—and nothing happened. After a month, Miller confessed his error and acknowledged his disappointment. But one of his followers pointed to other verses (Hab. 2:3, Lev. 25:9) and explained there must be a "tarrying time" of seven months and ten days.

So October 22, 1844, became the new day of Christ's return, and people were rallied again with the slogan: "The Tenth Day of the Seventh Month." Miller was finally converted to the new date. "I see a glory in the seventh month," he said. "Thank the Lord, O my soul! ... I am almost home." The excitement revived, and the number living on the edge of eternity seemed to be greater than ever.

When the second date came and went, just as the first one, most of Miller's followers were completely disillusioned. Many became bitter toward Miller, who lived until 1849, and died a discredited, almost forgotten man.

In spite of the "great disappointment," as it came to be called, some adventists remained steadfast. One small group in New England led by James White and his wife, Ellen Gould White, became the Seventh-Day Adventist Church we know today. Other adventists met in Albany in 1845 to form a conference that later splintered into three groups. One of these is today called Second Advent Christians. They believe Miller was wrong on the time, but this was a minor matter. He was right on the essential: Christ is coming soon.

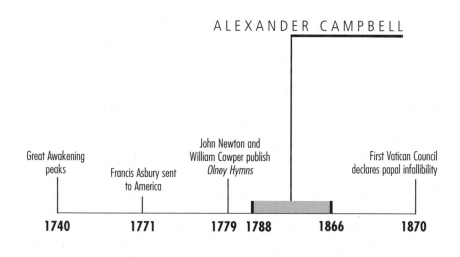

ALEXANDER CAMPBELL

| Great Awakening peaks | Francis Asbury sent to America | John Newton and William Cowper publish *Olney Hymns* | | First Vatican Council declares papal infallibility |

| 1740 | 1771 | 1779 | 1788 | 1866 | 1870 |

DENOMINATIONAL FOUNDERS

Alexander Campbell

CHRISTIAN

"The union of Christians with the apostles' testimony is all-sufficient and alone sufficient to the conversion of the world."

Separated by the Atlantic Ocean, Presbyterian preacher Thomas Campbell and his son Alexander simultaneously came to the same conclusion: the future was not with Presbyterianism.

Why these two Irish men concluded that, and what they did about it, created one of the most powerful movements in American religious history—and a uniquely American denomination.

Just Christians

The plan was for Thomas to sail to America first with his family to follow later. But the ship carrying Campbell's family was shipwrecked, and they had to spend a year in Scotland. There, 19-year-old Alexander answered the call to preach and began studying at the University of Glasgow. He quickly became disgusted with what he perceived to be theological pettiness in Presbyterianism. One Sunday he refused Communion, symbolically breaking with the faith of his father.

When Alexander finally arrived in Pennsylvania, though, he discovered his father had also seceded from the local presbytery! One reason: a perceived lack of scriptural support for infant baptism. Thomas had founded The Christian Association of Washington (County, Pennsylvania). "Where the Scriptures speak, we speak," declared Thomas, "where the Scriptures are silent, we are silent."

In 1811, Alexander began pastoring Bull Run Church, a group of Presbyterian refugees. The birth of his first child led him to reconsider his views on infant baptism. He decided that his own infant baptism was invalid, so he sought out a Baptist minister to immerse him as an adult believer. His church then joined the local Baptist association.

Alexander traveled on horseback through the Midwest and South, preaching a simple gospel stripped of "dogma" and "creeds." In 1823 he launched *The Christian Baptist*, a monthly that, wrote editor Campbell, "shall espouse the cause of no religious sect, excepting that ancient sect 'called Christians first at Antioch.'"

That purist spirit eventually drove a wedge between Campbell and the Baptists, but it created an affinity with Barton Stone and his followers, some 10,000 strong and known simply as "Christians." They too were championing a "restoration" of primitive Christianity. Stone's followers and Campbell's (some 12,000 known as "Disciples") merged in 1832 to form a loosely organized group of independent-minded churches committed to primitive Christianity—eventually called the Christian Church (Disciples of Christ).

The Bible alone

Campbell's evangelistic methods were varied, to say the least. A life-long debater, Campbell once sparred with popular atheist Robert Owen, delivering an address on the evidences of Christianity that lasted 12 hours! Later Campbell visited Owen and pleaded with him to accept the Christian faith; Owen wouldn't budge, though Campbell's appeal allegedly moved him to tears.

Perhaps Campbell's most important work was launching and editing *The Millennial Harbinger*. The journal defined and fueled the Restoration movement's spectacular growth, from about 22,000 in 1830, when the journal was launched, to over 200,000 in the year of Campbell's death.

In 1840 Campbell chartered Bethany College in Bethany, Virginia, to provide more education for ministers. He published a translation of the New Testament (1827), and wrote several books, including *The Christian System* (1839) and *Christian Baptism* (1854).

In *The Christian System*, he elaborated on the principles that drove him all his ministry. He was deeply disturbed by denominationalism: "In what moral desolation is the kingdom of Jesus Christ! Was there at any time, or is there now, in all the earth, a kingdom more convulsed by internal broils and dissensions than what is commonly called the church of Jesus Christ?"

He sought desperately to get back to a "simple evangelical Christianity," founded on the Bible and the Bible alone. Only this—not creeds or confessions or liturgy—could bring unity to Christians: "The testimony of the Apostles is the only and all-sufficient means of uniting Christians." And only in unity could Christians effectively evangelize: "The union of Christians with the apostle's testimony is all-sufficient and alone sufficient to the conversion of the world."

Campbell's emphasis on New Testament Christianity appealed powerfully to frontier Americans—and to many Christians since.

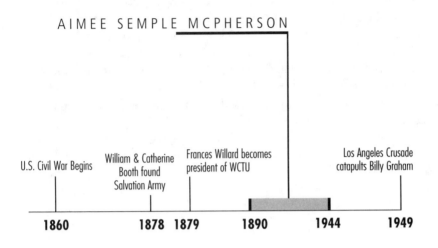

AIMEE SEMPLE MCPHERSON

U.S. Civil War Begins	William & Catherine Booth found Salvation Army	Frances Willard becomes president of WCTU	Los Angeles Crusade catapults Billy Graham

1860   **1878 1879**   **1890**   **1944**   **1949**

Aimee Semple McPherson
FOURSQUARE PHENOMENON

> *"Never did I hear such language from a human being. Without one moment's intermission, she would talk from an hour to an hour and a half, holding her audience spellbound."*
> — *a reporter's description*

In 1913 a 23-year-old Salvation Army daughter was rushed to the hospital with appendicitis, her life hanging in the balance. But for months the young woman had felt her spiritual life was also in peril. She'd had a deep, gnawing sense that God expected more of her.

As she later recounted, her condition deteriorated until a hospital attendant came to move her into a room set apart for the dying. She struggled to breathe as she heard a nurse say, "She's going."

Then she heard another voice: "Now will you go?" She understood it to mean she was to choose between going into eternity or going into ministry. She yielded to ministry. Instantly, she said, the pain was gone, her breathing eased, and she soon regained her strength.

Within a decade, the young woman would become an American phenomenon. Though hardly known today, during the 1920s her name appeared on the front page of America's leading newspapers three times a week. Today, as her International Church of the Foursquare Gospel carries on her legacy, historians consider her (along with Billy Sunday) the most significant revivalist in the early twentieth century.

Living in a gospel car

Aimee was born in October 1890, to James and Minnie Kennedy, a Methodist and a Salvation Army devotee respectively, in Ontario, Canada. As a teenager, Aimee was introduced to Pentecostalism through the preaching of Robert Semple, whom she eventually married. When he died two years later, she married young businessman Harold McPherson. For a few years, they shared a hand-to-mouth existence. They lived in a "gospel" car plastered with Bible verses and slogans (like "Where will you spend eternity?") and loaded with religious tracts. Slowly she began attracting crowds and the attention of the press.

Though Aimee and Harold quietly divorced, Aimee's ministry continued to expand. Using Hebrews 13:8 ("Jesus Christ, the same yesterday, and today, and forever") as her theme, she preached that the "full menu" of Bible Christianity was available for listeners' firsthand experience. Around the country, she spoke about the lavish feast Christ offered the faithful and summoned people with the words of a familiar gospel song: "Come and dine, the Master calleth, come and dine!"

From Los Angeles in 1919, McPherson launched a series of meetings that catapulted her to national fame. Within a year, America's largest auditoriums could not hold the crowds. She acquiesced to popular demand that she pray for the sick, and "stretcher days" became hallmarks of her campaigns.

Reporters marveled at her oratorical skills: "Never did I hear such language from a human being. Without one moment's intermission, she would talk from an hour to an hour and a half, holding her audience spellbound." Pastors from many denominations threw their support behind her city-wide campaigns. In 1922 her ministry took her to Australia, the first of a number of trips abroad.

On January 1, 1923, McPherson dedicated Angelus Temple, which held up to 5,300 worshipers. The ceremonies included hundreds of colorfully clad gypsies (who had named her their queen), a roster of prominent Protestant preachers, and thousands of adoring fans. A church-owned radio station was launched in 1924.

While she continued to preach "the four-square Gospel" (Jesus as the Only Savior, the Great Physician, the Baptizer with the Holy Spirit, and the Coming Bridegroom), she become a citizen of note in a burgeoning city. Angelus Temple floats won prizes in Rose Bowl parades, and the Temple itself became a tourist attraction. The comings and goings of "Sister" (as she was affectionately known) from the city's Union Station drew more people than visits of presidents and other dignitaries.

Well-advertised illustrated sermons offered the faithful who shunned nearby Hollywood entertainments a taste of theater. Parades, uniforms, award-winning bands, and catchy music attracted people of all ages. Ambitious programs to feed the hungry and respond to natural disasters gained goodwill.

People responded as well to her motherly qualities. During midnight forays into Denver's red light districts, she promised Denver's outcasts a bright future if they would be true to themselves. She embraced Winnipeg prostitutes with the assurance that she loved them and that there was hope for them in Christ. In San Francisco's Barbary Coast, she walked into a "dive," sat down at the piano, and got the crowd's attention by playing "Jesus, Lover of My Soul."

Kidnapped?

Her rising popularity was checked in May 1926. As McPherson later told it, she was kidnapped on Tuesday afternoon, May 26, and spirited away to a cabin where she was held prisoner. That evening, it was announced at Angelus Temple that Sister had gone for a swim, failed to return, and was presumed drowned. For the next few days, Los Angeles talked of little else. Thousands walked aimlessly on the Ocean Park Beach where Sister

had last been seen, and an elaborate memorial service was held for McPherson on June 20.

Three days later, McPherson reappeared in Douglas, Arizona, with a tale of having escaped from kidnappers. The crowds that had mourned her loss prepared a lavish welcome home. On Saturday, June 26, 150,000 lined the route from the train station to Angelus Temple, cheering and wishing Sister well.

Some law enforcement officials challenged her kidnapping story, but the Los Angeles district attorney acknowledged that he had no case against McPherson. When the focus finally shifted away from the "scandal" in January, Sister immediately set out on a national evangelistic tour. Her support base remained strong, but press coverage changed. The months of innuendo left a legacy of unanswered questions that took a toll on her popularity.

Yet her ministry continued. During the depression, the Angelus Temple's Commissary provided food, clothing, and other necessities to needy families—no questions asked. In the 1940s, McPherson began barnstorming again, and in September 1944, she addressed 10,000 people in the Oakland Auditorium. She died the next day of kidney failure and the effects of the mixture of prescription drugs she had been taking. McPherson's funeral took place on her fifty-fourth birthday, October 9, 1944.

Though her popularity had shrunk significantly since the 1920s, 50,000 people filed past her coffin. Her lasting legacy is the denomination she founded, the International Church of the Foursquare Gospel, with some 2 million members in nearly 30,000 churches worldwide.

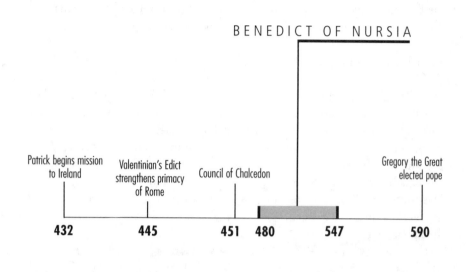

BENEDICT OF NURSIA

Patrick begins mission to Ireland	Valentinian's Edict strengthens primacy of Rome	Council of Chalcedon			Gregory the Great elected pope
432	445	451	480	547	590

Benedict of Nursia

FATHER OF WESTERN MONASTICISM

> *"The good of all concerned, however, may prompt us to a little strictness in order to amend faults and to safeguard love."*

The first monks who tried to live under Benedict's direction hated his regimen, so much so they plotted to kill their abbot. They put poison in a glass of wine and offered it to Benedict. Before he took it, he blessed it, as was the custom. According to the story told by Pope Gregory I (Benedict's biographer), when Benedict made the sign of the cross over the wine glass, it shattered, and the wine spilled to the floor.

Benedict, Gregory wrote, "perceived that the glass had in it the drink of death," called his monks together, said he forgave them, reminded them that he doubted from the beginning whether he was a suitable abbot for them, and concluded, "Go your ways, and seek some other father suitable to your own conditions, for I intend not now to stay any longer amongst you."

We don't know if Benedict was overly strict or if his first monks were simply obstinate. But years later, when Benedict wrote a rule of life for another group of monks, it turned out to be a model of monastic moderation and one reason monasticism blossomed in the West.

Compassionate discipline

Despite the fact that we have a full biography by Gregory, we know very little about Benedict. The biography mostly tells of signs and wonders performed by Benedict (miraculously mending a broken sieve, calling forth water from a rock, raising the dead, and so on). We can piece together, though, a sketch of his life.

Benedict was born as the Roman Empire was disintegrating, and during his youth, the Italian peninsula was the scene of constant war between barbarian tribes. The young Benedict moved from his birthplace (Nursia in Umbria) to Rome but soon abandoned the "eternal city" when he became disgusted with the paganism and immorality he saw there. He retired to a cave at Subiaco, some 30 miles east of Rome, where he lived as a hermit and endured severe privations.

He sought as little contact as possible with others. An admiring monk delivered Benedict his food from above the cave, dangling it by a rope with a bell attached to get Benedict's attention.

He also disciplined his flesh. According to Gregory, he was once nearly overcome with lust as he remembered a certain woman. Benedict stripped himself and ran naked into thorn bushes so that "all his flesh was pitifully torn: and so by the wounds of his body, he cured the wounds of his soul, in that he turned pleasure into pain, and by the outward burning of extreme smart, quenched that fire."

As his reputation for holiness—and perhaps performing miracles—spread, more and more monks tried to attach themselves to him. He reluctantly agreed to become abbot of a small monastery, but after the attempted murder, he moved back into solitude.

Again monks sought him out, and before long he had established 12 monasteries with 12 monks in each. But the envy of local clergy (one of whom, according to Gregory, tried to put the poison in a loaf of bread) so disturbed Benedict that he moved again, and with some disciples established another monastery, this time on the mountain above Cassino, about 80 miles south of Rome.

His fame continued to spread (even the king of the Goths, Totila, came to see him) as his reforms continued. Gregory says that when Benedict came across a local chapel devoted to the old Roman god Apollo, he "beat in pieces the idol, overthrew the altar, set fire to the woods," and made it into a Christian sanctuary.

Taking ideas from a number of earlier monastic writings (and likely from his own experience), Benedict wrote a Rule for his monks, one that is today praised for its balanced approach to monastic life. Besides the vows of poverty, chastity, and obedience, it stressed communal living, physical labor, common meals, and the avoidance of unnecessary conversation.

At the same time, Benedict made allowances for his monks—for differences of age, capabilities, dispositions, needs, and spiritual stature. There is a frank allowance for weaknesses and failure, as well as compassion for the physically weak. "In drawing up these regulations," he said, "we hope to set down nothing harsh, nothing burdensome."

But he was no libertine: "The good of all concerned, however, may prompt us to a little strictness in order to amend faults and to safeguard love."

It is this combination of compassion and discipline that made the Rule a model for many later monastic orders besides the Benedictine, and one reason why monasticism became such a viable life for so many over the next centuries, during which the institution literally shaped the future of Europe.

When Benedict died, he was buried next to his sister, Scholastica, traditionally regarded his twin and also a follower of the monastic way.

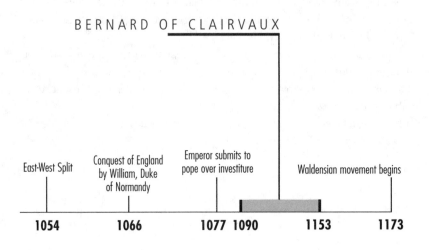

BERNARD OF CLAIRVAUX

East-West Split	Conquest of England by William, Duke of Normandy	Emperor submits to pope over investiture		Waldensian movement begins
1054	1066	1077 1090	1153	1173

Bernard of Clairvaux
MEDIEVAL REFORMER AND MYSTIC

> *"You wish me to tell you why and how God should be loved. My answer is that God himself is the reason he is to be loved."*

It's hard to know how to characterize Bernard of Clairvaux. On the one hand, he is called the "honey-tongued doctor" for his eloquent writings on the love of God. On the other hand, he rallied soldiers to kill Muslims. He wrote eloquently on humility; then again, he loved being close to the seat of power and was an adviser to five popes.

What is clear is this: 400 years after his death, he was still widely quoted by Catholics and Protestants, both of whom claimed his support. John Calvin considered him the major witness to truth between Gregory the Great and the 1500s. And today his writings still guide spiritual lives not only of the order he made famous, the Cistercians, but by men and women in all walks of life.

Austere leader

Bernard was born on the outskirts of Dijon in Burgundy to a

family of lower nobility. Both his parents were models of virtue, but it was his mother who exerted the most influence on him (some speculate only second to what Monica had done for Augustine of Hippo). Her death, in 1107, marked for Bernard the beginning of his "long path to complete conversion."

Bernard sought the counsel of the abbot of Citeaux, Stephen Harding, and decided to enter his struggling, small, new community called the Cistercians. The order had been established in 1098 to restore Benedictine monasticism to a more primitive and austere state. Bernard was so taken with the order, he persuaded not only his brothers but some 25 others to join him at Citeaux in 1112.

Here he began practicing lifelong ascetic disciplines (strict fasting, sleep deprivation, etc.), which severely impaired his health—he was plagued by anemia, migraines, gastritis, hypertension, and an atrophied sense of taste his whole life.

Within three years of joining the order, he was appointed abbot of the third Cistercian monastery, at Clairvaux. There Bernard showed little patience with monks who wanted him to relax his standards. Mocking other monasteries' eating habits, he wrote, "The cooks prepare everything with such skill and cunning that the four or five dishes already consumed are no hindrance to what is to follow, and the appetite is not checked by satiety."

At the same time, he showed his growing spiritual wisdom. Regarding the danger of spiritual pride, he said, "There are people who go clad in tunics and have nothing to do with furs, who nevertheless are lacking in humility. Surely humility in furs is better than pride in tunics."

Despite the objection of some monks, the monastery under his leadership prospered. By 1118 Clairvaux was able to found its first daughter house—the first of some 70 Cistercian monasteries Bernard founded (which in turn founded another 100 monasteries in Bernard's lifetime).

World monk

As the order grew, so did Bernard's influence and responsibilities. Though he longed to return to a life of solitude (he had been a hermit for a time), he was thrust into the world for many of his remaining years.

Bernard had warm relationships with other reforming orders of his day, like the Carthusians and the Premonstratensians. He also wrote the Rule for the new order known as the Knights Templar, an order of men who took monastic vows and swore to defend the Holy Land militarily.

When influential and controversial Paris theologian, Peter Abelard, wrote, "It is by doubting that we come to inquire and by inquiring that we reach truth," and suggested that Christ died not to pay a penalty but merely to demonstrate God's love, Bernard was scandalized. In 1139, he wrote a lengthy letter to the pope refuting Abelard. He called the Parisian a "son of perdition" who "disdains and scoffs" the death of Christ: "I was made a sinner by deriving my being from Adam; I am made just by being washed in the blood of Christ and not by Christ's 'words and example.'"

Because of Bernard's letter and political influence (Pope Innocent III owed his position, in part, to Bernard's public support), Abelard's teaching was condemned, and he was forced to retire to a monastery.

Bernard's informal political influence was further enhanced with the election of Pope Eugenius III, one of Bernard's former pupils. Bernard had a high view of the papacy, and he called the pope "the unique vicar of Christ who presides over not a single people but over all." At the same time, he warned Eugenius, "You have been entrusted with stewardship over the world, not given possession of it.... There is no poison more dangerous for you, no sword more deadly, than the passion to rule." All in all, he wielded such influence with Eugenius III that Eugenius once complained to Bernard, "They say that it is you who are pope and not I."

When Eugenius called for the Second Crusade, he enlisted Bernard as the crusade's chief promoter. Bernard traveled over Europe calling upon men to enlist in "the cause of Christ." In one sermon he pleaded, "I ask you and advise you not to want to put your own business before the business of Christ."

Because of bickering and ineffective leadership, though, the crusade was a disaster, ending in an embarrassing retreat, and Bernard's reputation suffered the last four years of his life. Still, just a little over 20 years after his death, he was esteemed enough to be canonized.

Mystic pen

What Bernard is remembered for today, more than his reforming zeal and crusade preaching, is his mystical writings. His best known work is *On Loving God*, in which he states his purpose at the beginning: "You wish me to tell you why and how God should be loved. My answer is that God himself is the reason he is to be loved."

His other great literary legacy is *Sermons on the Song of Songs*, 86 sermons on the spiritual life that, in fact, only tangentially touch on the biblical text. One passage in particular speaks aptly to Bernard's lifelong passion to know God (and, likely, the temptations that troubled him):

> There are some who long to know for the sole purpose of knowing, and that is shameful curiosity; others who long to know in order to become known, and that is shameful vanity.... There are others still who long for knowledge in order to sell its fruits for money or honors, and this is shameful profiteering; others again who long to know in order to be of service, and this is charity. Finally, there are those who long to know in order to benefit themselves, and this is prudence.

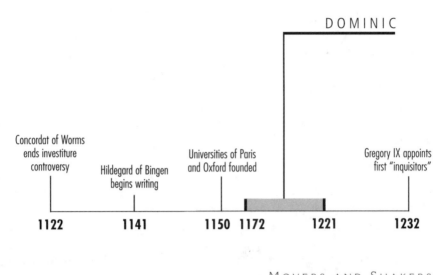

DOMINIC

Concordat of Worms
ends investiture
controversy

Hildegard of Bingen
begins writing

Universities of Paris
and Oxford founded

Gregory IX appoints
first "inquisitors"

1122   1141   1150 1172   1221   1232

MOVERS AND SHAKERS

Dominic

FOUNDER OF THE ORDER OF PREACHERS (DOMINICANS)

> *"The heretics are to be converted by an example of humility and other virtues far more readily than by any external display or verbal battles. So let us arm ourselves with devout prayers and set off showing signs of genuine humility and barefooted to combat Goliath."*

It was just a stopover, really. Just a place to spend the night on his way from Spain to Denmark. But Dominic was already becoming known for his friendliness, and he struck up a conversation with the innkeeper. As it turned out, his host was an Albigensian who believed that two supreme beings, Good and Evil, dominate spirit and matter respectively. Whatever concerned the body, be it eating, possessing worldly goods, or even marriage, is essentially evil, the innkeeper told Dominic.

The young prior was amazed at the age-old heresy and spent the night discussing the man's beliefs with him. By daylight the innkeeper was ready to return to orthodoxy. And Dominic had a new mission: the conversion of the Albigensians.

Filling the needy

Dominic, Domingo de Guzman in his native tongue, was from a noble family in Castile, Spain. At 14, as was typical for those who did so, he was sent to the University of Palencia, where he studied arts and theology. He was an excellent scholar, and his books—carefully annotated in his own hand—were his only prized possessions. If there was something he loved more than scholarship, however, it was caring for the needy. He once sold his books to help war refugees.

"I could not bear to prize dead skins when living skins were in starving and want," he said.

In his mid-twenties, Dominic was ordained a priest and served as a canon (a kind of traveling priest for parishes without one) for nine years. In 1199 he was elected subprior of his chapter, then succeeded the prior, Diego d'Azevedo, when he became bishop.

It was on a trip with Diego, to arrange a marriage of the prince of Castile to a Danish noblewoman, that Dominic met the Albigensians of southern France. Though the

Albigensians thought of Christ as an angel in a phantom body and believed his redemptive work was only in his teaching true doctrine, they had a profound knowledge of the New Testament and the prophetic parts of the Old Testament. But because they believed everything corporeal was evil, they could be tremendously austere. So Dominic was shocked to meet some papal legates whose job it was to evangelize the Albigensians by trying to impress them with horses, regalia, fancy robes and costumes, great food, and plush living quarters. If you're trying to reach the austere, Dominic reasoned, you have to use other means.

"The heretics are to be converted by an example of humility and other virtues far more readily than by any external display or verbal battles," he said. "So let us arm ourselves with devout prayers and set off showing signs of genuine humility and barefooted to combat Goliath."

The priest from a noble family opted to live a life of poverty. He began by removing his shoes, preaching and traveling barefoot. He refused to sleep on a bed in favor of the ground, and one Lent he lived completely on bread and water; he even went so far as to whip himself. As one biographer noted, "They may have been done for show, but the hard floor was real, the emptiness in his stomach was real, the lashes he received were real."

Though the response was not overwhelming, Dominic did make many converts. In 1206 he opened the first Dominican convent, a hostel for women converted from the heresy.

Two years later, history took a bad turn. The papal legate in charge of the preaching mission to the Albigensians was killed by those he was ministering to. Pope Innocent III called for a seven-year crusade against the heretics. Though he did not ally himself against the church, Dominic regretted the crusade's bloodshed. "Logic and persuasion, not force," was the call he reiterated throughout his life.

At the end of the unsuccessful crusade, Dominic went to Rome, presenting a plan for an Order of Preachers to the Fourth Lateran Council in 1215. At first, this was not possible, as the council had prohibited the formation of any new religious orders. But Dominic got around that by choosing the Rule of Augustine for his order, and in 1216 the official sanction came from Honorius III.

On his trip to seek authorization, he reportedly received a personal tour of the Vatican's treasures by the pope. "Peter can no longer say, 'Silver and gold have I none,'" said Innocent III, referring to Acts 3:6.

Dominic, now wholly dedicated to his life of poverty, replied, "No, and neither can he say, 'Rise and walk.'"

Legacy of intellect

Dominic's group was popularly known as the Dominicans or the Blackfriars (from the color of their cloaks), but officially as the Order of Preachers. This was an important designation, for it meant that priests, not just bishops, could preach, and it indicated the group's primary function.

From its inception, the life of the mind has played a central role in its work. Two of its most famous members were Albertus Magnus (1200–1280) and Thomas Aquinas (1225–1274). Upon returning to France, Dominic sent many followers to Paris, then the intellectual capital of the world. He sent others to Bologna, another university center, and he decided that each of his houses should form a school of theology.

With the sending out of his followers (others were sent to Spain and Rome), Dominic's chief work was done. Three times he was asked to become a bishop, but he steadfastly refused, believing he was called to other work. He spent his later years traveling barefoot through Europe, preaching and gaining converts. On one of these travels, he fell ill. He confessed his darkest sins (that, though he had always been chaste, he enjoyed talking with younger women more than older ones), and left his "inheritance" to his followers: "Have charity among you, hold to humility, possess voluntary poverty."

At age 51, Dominic died. A mere five years earlier, he had six followers. On his deathbed, he had thousands. But more important than the numbers, Dominic had created a new form of Christian life, with highly educated Christians whose job it was to preach the gospel.

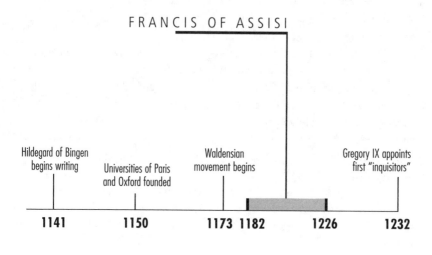

FRANCIS OF ASSISI

Hildegard of Bingen begins writing	Universities of Paris and Oxford founded	Waldensian movement begins		Gregory IX appoints first "inquisitors"	
1141	**1150**	**1173**	**1182**	**1226**	**1232**

Francis of Assisi

MYSTICAL FOUNDER OF THE FRANCISCANS

"Praised be You, my Lord, with all your creatures, especially Sir Brother Sun, who is the day and through whom You give us light."

It is difficult to think clearly about Francis of Assisi. The first thing that comes to mind is the gentle saint who preached to birds, tamed wolves, and padded about in flower-filled fields basking in the love of God. But it's also difficult to imagine how such a benign figure could turn thirteenth-century Europe upside down.

In fact, Francis was a complex figure, a man who contemporaries claimed lived out the Sermon on the Mount better than anyone else, except of course, the man who first preached it. If that's even close to the truth, it's a bit easier to see why he left such an impression on his age and every age since.

From hermit to itinerant

He was born in Assisi, Italy, as Giovanni Francesco Bernardone, son of a wealthy merchant. As a young man, Francis led a worldly, carefree life. An early biographer said, "He squandered his time terribly. Indeed, he outshone all his friends in trivialities." In 1202 he marched off to battle against the city of Perugia, full of a young man's dreams of military glory. But he was taken prisoner during the battle, and a year passed before his father could arrange ransom. That was followed by a year's convalescence in Assisi, a year in which Francis, now in his early twenties, was slowly transformed.

During his illness, he experienced dreams and visions. One day as he prayed in a dilapidated church in San Damiano, at the edge of Assisi, he heard Christ say three times from the crucifix: "Francis, go repair my house, which, as you can see, is falling completely to ruin." Francis understood that he was to repair the church he prayed in (though his followers later would see this as his call to reform the church), so he proceeded to sell off family goods to raise money for repairs.

When his father caught wind of this, he was furious. He dragged Francis before the local bishop to force his son into changing his unseemly behavior and to pay him back. In the course of the interview, Francis took off his clothes and laid them neatly in a pile before his father. "Up to today I called you 'father,'" he said to him, "but now I can say in all honesty, 'Our Father who art in heaven.'" He walked out of the cathedral to become a hermit—to "be alone in solitude and silence," a biographer noted, "to hear the secrets which God could reveal to him."

Other inspirations followed. One day in church he heard from the Gospel of Matthew, "Take no gold or silver or copper in your wallet, no bag for your journey, nor two tunics or sandals or a staff." He took it literally and began an itinerant life: he intended to live in utter simplicity and to preach a gospel that usually entailed strong injunctions to repent. "He denounced evil whenever he found it," wrote one early biographer, "and made no effort to palliate it; from him a life of sin met with outspoken rebuke, not support."

Francis was more rigorous than popular imagination allows. In winter, he sometimes hurled himself in a ditch full of ice and stayed there until every vestige of sinful temptation departed. To avoid lust, he fixed his gaze on the sky or ground whenever he spoke with a woman.

Though known for his infectious joy, Francis abhorred laughing or idle words. "Not only did he wish that he should not laugh, but that he should not even afford to others the slightest occasion for laughing."

By 1209 he had gathered a small band of "brothers" (12 men who wished to share in his life and ministry). He wrote a Rule and set off to Rome to gain the church's approval for his work. This became the First Order of Franciscans, and Francis was elected superior.

Women also were fascinated by Francis's message, and when Francis received a rich young women of Assisi named Clare, the Second Order of Franciscans was founded, also known as Poor Clares. (The Third Order of Franciscans, which Francis founded in 1221, is for those who lead their secular lives while trying to live by a modified Franciscan rule.)

Francis wandered all over Italy and at one point crossed the Mediterranean, visited a Crusader expedition in Egypt, crossed enemy lines, and attempted to convert the Muslim sultan. The sultan was unconvinced by the message but so impressed by the messenger that he afforded him safe passage back.

Embracing death

Soon his brothers (called friars, and growing rapidly in numbers) were making trips to France, Spain, Germany, England, Hungary, and Turkey, preaching the message of repentance, gospel simplicity, and radical obedience to Christ's teaching.

It was an era, like many, in which corruption infected ecclesiastical circles and indifference permeated the laity. But as one contemporary noted, as a result of the preaching of the Franciscan brothers and sisters, "persons of both sexes, rich and worldly, have renounced possessions and, for the love of Christ, turned their backs on the world." In short, Francis had begun a religious revival that spread over Europe.

With the order's growth came complications. The Rule that had served a small band was inadequate for the large organization the Franciscans were becoming. Francis himself sensed his own inadequacy to continue leading a large organization, so after penning a new Rule and his Testament (in a sense, last wishes), urging his brothers to retain the primitive standards used from the beginning, he resigned as head of the order.

In his last years, Francis popularized the living creche to highlight the poverty into which Christ was born. In 1224, on a mountaintop retreat, Francis had a mystical encounter that left him with bleeding wounds in his feet, hands, and side—the first recorded instance of stigmata.

As he entered his mid-forties, illness racked his body, finally taking his eyesight completely.

In his last years, he composed his famous *Canticle of Brother Sun*. From this poem Francis gets his deserved reputation as one who reveled in God's creation:

"Praised be You, my Lord, with all your creatures, especially Sir Brother Sun, Who is the day and through whom You give us light ..."

In the poem Francis also praised "Brother Wind" and "Brother Fire" and "Sister Mother Earth." What many forget is that near the end of the poem, he wrote this:

"Praised be You, my Lord, through our Sister Bodily Death, from whom no man can escape.

Woe to those who die in mortal sin.

Blessed are those whom death will find in Your most holy will ...."

Such was the death of Francis, whose life was so clearly committed to God's "holy will" that he was canonized within two years—exceedingly fast by Roman Catholic standards.

After Francis's death, the Franciscans continued to grow and—ironic for an order once told by their founder "to appropriate nothing for themselves, neither a house, nor a place, nor anything else"—soon became quite rich. A stunning basilica was built in Assisi, and Francis's relics were moved there in 1230.

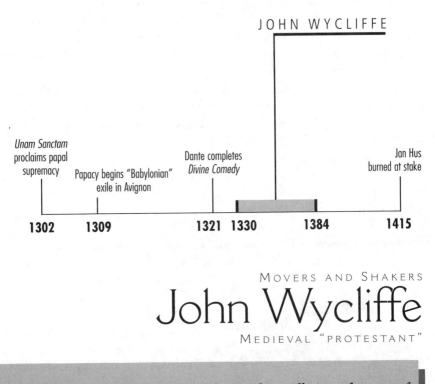

JOHN WYCLIFFE

Unam Sanctam proclaims papal supremacy

Papacy begins "Babylonian" exile in Avignon

Dante completes Divine Comedy

Jan Hus burned at stake

| 1302 | 1309 | 1321 | 1330 | 1384 | 1415 |

MOVERS AND SHAKERS

John Wycliffe

MEDIEVAL "PROTESTANT"

> "Trust wholly in Christ; rely altogether on his sufferings; beware of seeking to be justified in any other way than by his righteousness."

John Wycliffe left quite an impression on the church: 43 years after his death, officials dug up his body, burned his remains, and threw the ashes into the river Swift. Still, they couldn't get rid of him. Wycliffe's teachings, though suppressed, continued to spread. As a later chronicler observed, "Thus the brook hath conveyed his ashes into Avon; Avon into Severn; Severn into the narrow seas; and they into the main ocean. And thus the ashes of Wycliffe are the emblem of his doctrine which now is dispersed the world over."

"Master of errors"

Wycliffe had been born in the hinterlands, on a sheep farm 200 miles from London. He left for Oxford University in 1346, but because of periodic eruptions of the Black Death, he was not able to earn his doctorate until 1372. Nonetheless, by then he

211

was already considered Oxford's leading philosopher and theologian.

In 1374 he became rector of the parish in Lutterworth, but a year later he was disappointed to learn he was not granted a position at Lincoln nor the bishopric of Worcester—setbacks that some have seized upon as motives for his subsequent attacks on the papacy.

In the meantime, Rome had demanded financial support from England, a nation struggling to raise money to resist a possible French attack. Wycliffe advised his local lord, John of Gaunt, to tell Parliament not to comply. He argued that the church was already too wealthy and that Christ called his disciples to poverty, not wealth. If anyone should keep such taxes, it should be local English authorities.

Such opinions got Wycliffe into trouble, and he was brought to London to answer charges of heresy. The hearing had hardly gotten underway when recriminations on both sides filled the air. Soon they erupted into an open brawl, ending the meeting. Three months later, Pope Gregory XI issued five bulls (church edicts) against Wycliffe, in which Wycliffe was accused on 18 counts and was called "the master of errors."

At a subsequent hearing before the archbishop at Lambeth Palace, Wycliffe replied,

"I am ready to defend my convictions even unto death.... I have followed the Sacred Scriptures and the holy doctors." He went on to say that the pope and the church were second in authority to Scripture.

This didn't sit well with Rome, but because of Wycliffe's popularity in England and a subsequent split in the papacy (the Great Schism of 1378, when rival popes were elected), Wycliffe was put under "house arrest" and left to pastor his Lutterworth parish.

Disputing the church

He deepened his study of Scripture and wrote more about his conflicts with official church teaching. He wrote against the doctrine of transubstantiation: "The bread while becoming by virtue of Christ's words the body of Christ does not cease to be bread."

He challenged indulgences: "It is plain to me that our prelates in granting indulgences do commonly blaspheme the wisdom of God."

He repudiated the confessional: "Private confession ... was not ordered by Christ and was not used by the apostles."

He reiterated the biblical teaching on faith: "Trust wholly in Christ; rely altogether on his sufferings; beware of seeking to be justified in any other way than by his righteousness."

Believing that every Christian should have access to Scripture (only Latin translations were available at the time), he began translating the Bible into English, with the help of his good friend John Purvey.

The church bitterly opposed it: "By this translation, the Scriptures have become vulgar, and they are more available to lay, and even to women who can read, than they were to learned scholars, who have a high intelligence. So the pearl of the gospel is scattered and trodden underfoot by swine."

Wycliffe replied, "Englishmen learn Christ's law best in English. Moses heard God's law in his own tongue; so did Christ's apostles."

Wycliffe died before the translation was complete (and before authorities could convict him of heresy); his friend Purvey is considered responsible for the version of the "Wycliffe" Bible we have today. Though Wycliffe's followers (who came to be called "Lollards"—referring to the region of their original strength) were driven underground, they remained a persistent irritant to English Catholic authorities until the English Reformation made their views the norm.

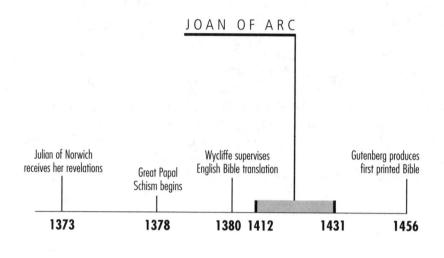

JOAN OF ARC

| Julian of Norwich receives her revelations | Great Papal Schism begins | Wycliffe supervises English Bible translation | | Gutenberg produces first printed Bible |

1373　　　　1378　　　1380 1412　　　1431　　　1456

Joan of Arc

TEENAGE WAR HERO WITH VISIONS

"If I were to say that God sent me, I shall be condemned, but God really did send me."

She has been called a saint, a heretic, and "a diamond among pebbles." But who was this illiterate French peasant girl, who in 15 months changed the history of western Europe and became, according to one historian, "the most widely known of all medieval women"?

Her voices

Joan's father was the most prosperous farmer in the small French village of Domremy. She spun wool and gathered the harvest, a typical life interrupted only by occasional encounters with soldiers from the Hundred Years' War (1337–1453), the lingering conflict between France and England. Once English soldiers burned the village church; two other times Joan herded the livestock to safety from their marauding invasions.

One summer when Joan was about 13, she was working in her

father's garden at noon. Suddenly she saw a bright light and heard a voice. The voice called her "Joan the Maid" and told her to live a virtuous life. Voices came more often and gave instructions: Joan was to save France and help the dauphin (France's rightful heir) be crowned. Joan questioned how she could possibly accomplish these astounding feats. The voices said God would be with her.

Joan later identified the voices as belonging to the archangel Michael and the saints Margaret of Antioch and Catherine of Alexandria. At any rate, Joan's voices impelled her to attempt unthinkable tasks; she would rather die than deny them.

With her cousin's help, Joan gained access to Robert de Baudricourt, the local lord. He flatly ordered, "Give her a good slapping and take her back to her father."

Joan would not relent, and nearly nine months later, she convinced her hearers that she was divinely chosen to help France. With knights at her side, she rode over 300 miles—across enemy territory, at night—to tell the dauphin, Charles, of her plans.

Charles was unsure whether to receive her, so when Joan entered the 70-foot-long hall, filled with dozens of courtiers, the dauphin was not on his throne. Instead, dressed like the others, he mingled with the crowd. Somehow, Joan walked directly to him.

"But I am not the dauphin," he protested when she addressed him.

"In God's name, gentle sire, you are," Joan responded.

Charles turned her over to churchmen from the University of Poitiers. Weeks of doubt and indecision followed while she was questioned, but finally her examiners found "only humility, purity, honesty, and simplicity." Soon she was helping 4,000 troops to relieve the besieged city of Orleans.

Though not the commander of the troops, she led troops in taking a number of forts that surrounded Orleans. During the battle for the fort of Les Tourelles, Joan was wounded (an arrow through the shoulder) but quickly returned to the fight, and her fortitude inspired many French commanders to maintain the attack until the English capitulated. The next day the English were seen retreating, but, because it was a Sunday, Joan refused to allow any pursuit. It didn't matter; Orleans was back in French hands.

In a few months, the town of Reims was recaptured, and the dauphin was officially crowned king of France (Reims was the traditional city for coronation). But Charles suddenly lost his nerve. Joan's insistent pleas to drive the English out of Paris went unheeded. On a sortie the next year, the 18-year-old soldier was captured by the English, who put her on ecclesiastical trial in Rouen.

Reverse decision

Joan was imprisoned for nearly five months, repeatedly questioned about her views, and finally charged on 70 counts of heresy. Authorities were troubled that she claimed for her pronouncements the authority of divine revelation, prophesied the future, endorsed her letters with the names of Jesus and Mary (thereby identifying herself with a novel and suspect cult called the Name of Jesus), professed to be assured of salvation, and wore men's clothing. She was finally convicted of being a schismatic (she said she felt accountable first to God and her saints rather than the church). When her sentence

was read—execution by the secular authorities—Joan quailed and declared she would do all that the church required of her. Her sentence was changed to life imprisonment.

Three days later, however, she was found wearing men's clothes again, and when asked about it, she said the voices of Catherine and Margaret had censured her for her "treason." She was handed over to secular authorities.

At 9 a.m. on May 30, 1431, 19-year-old Joan walked toward the market square. She knelt and prayed for her enemies, then mounted the prepared pyre. As the flames leapt upward, Joan asked for a cross to be held before her. Gazing upon it, her final word was "Jesus."

It would be 25 years before a church commission overturned the charges against her and declared her innocent. In 1920 Joan—remembered for her heroism and devotion far more than her military and political conquests—was canonized a saint by the Roman Catholic Church.

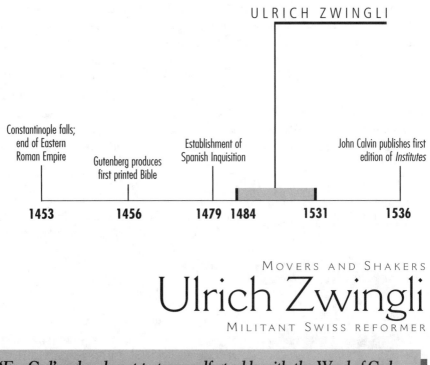

ULRICH ZWINGLI

Constantinople falls; end of Eastern Roman Empire	Gutenberg produces first printed Bible	Establishment of Spanish Inquisition			John Calvin publishes first edition of *Institutes*
1453	**1456**	**1479**	**1484**	**1531**	**1536**

MOVERS AND SHAKERS

Ulrich Zwingli

MILITANT SWISS REFORMER

"For God's sake, do not put yourself at odds with the Word of God. For truly it will persist as surely as the Rhine follows its course. One can perhaps dam it up for awhile, but it is impossible to stop it."

Ulrich Zwingli, the city chaplain, stood before the Zurich City Council in January 1523. The winds of reform had made their way over the Alps from Luther's Germany, and Zwingli was arguing 67 theses, beginning with "All who say that the gospel is invalid without the confirmation of the church err and slander God." Though 28 shy of Luther's *95 Theses*, published some six years earlier, Zwingli's arguments were more persuasive: authorities gave him permission to continue his preaching, which emphasized Christ first and the church second ("Christ is the only mediator between God and ourselves," said another of Zwingli's theses). The Reformation in Switzerland was now well on its way, and Zwingli would play the key role in the early years.

Anxious for his charge

Zwingli was born to a successful farmer in the Toggaburg Valley of the eastern lower Alps. Here Zwingli developed a deep love for his homeland. Later he translated one line of Psalm 23, "In the beautiful Alps, he tends me," and he used the Rhine River as an illustration of a key theme of his preaching: "For God's sake, do not put yourself at odds with the Word of God. For truly it will persist as surely as the Rhine follows its course. One can perhaps dam it up for awhile, but it is impossible to stop it."

But it took Zwingli years to discover the power of this Word. After graduating from the University of Basel in 1506, he became a parish priest in Glarus. From the beginning, he took his priestly duties seriously. He later wrote, "Though I was young, ecclesiastical duties inspired in me more fear than joy, because I knew, and remain convinced that I would give an account of the blood of the sheep which would perish as a consequence of my carelessness."

The feeling of responsibility for his charge (rather than, like Luther, a personal search for salvation) motivated Zwingli's increasing interest in the Bible. In an age when priests were often unfamiliar with the Scriptures, Zwingli became enamored with it, first after

purchasing a copy of Erasmus's New Testament Latin translation. He began teaching himself Greek, bought a copy of Erasmus's Greek New Testament, and started memorizing long passages. In 1519 he began preaching from the New Testament regularly.

Privately Zwingli also started challenging the customs of medieval Christendom he thought unbiblical. He had struggled with clerical celibacy for some time (and even admitted that as a young priest, he'd had an affair). In 1522 he secretly married. That same year, he broke the traditional Lenten fast (by eating sausages in public) and wrote against fasting.

By 1523 he was ready to take his ideas to a larger audience, and in January he did just that before the Zurich City Council at what is now called the First Disputation. The Second Disputation came in October, and with further approval from the council, more reforms were carried out: images of Jesus, Mary, and the saints were removed from the churches; the Bible was to have preeminence.

Arguments over Supper

Things moved rapidly after that. In 1524 he wedded his wife publicly, insisting that pastors had the right to marry. In 1525 he and others convinced the city to abolish the Mass, with its emphasis on the miracle of transubstantiation, and replace it with a simple service that included the Lord's Supper but only as a symbolic memorial.

As it turned out, it was the Lord's Supper that prevented the uniting of the German and Swiss reform movements. At a 1529 meeting at Marburg, called to unite the two movements, Luther and Zwingli met. Though they agreed on 14 points of doctrine, they stumbled on the fifteenth: the Lord's Supper. Against Zwingli's view, Luther insisted on Christ's literal presence. Zwingli balked. Luther said Zwingli was of the devil and that he was nothing but a wormy nut. Zwingli resented Luther's treating him "like an ass." It was evident no reconciliation was possible.

Zwingli died two years later in battle, defending Zurich against Catholic forces, and plans for spreading the Reformation into German Switzerland were ended. Still Zurich remained Protestant, and under the leadership of Heinrich Bullinger, Zwingli's successor, this unique branch of the Reformation continued to blossom.

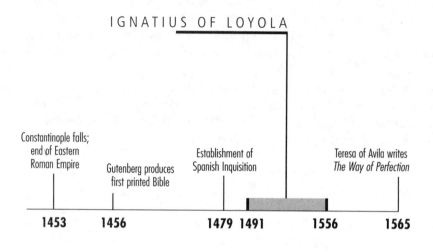

IGNATIUS OF LOYOLA

Constantinople falls; end of Eastern Roman Empire	Gutenberg produces first printed Bible	Establishment of Spanish Inquisition		Teresa of Avila writes *The Way of Perfection*
1453	1456	1479	1491	1556 1565

MOVERS AND SHAKERS

Ignatius of Loyola

FOUNDER OF THE SOCIETY OF JESUS (THE JESUITS)

> *"Without seeing any vision, he understood and knew many things, as well spiritual things as things of the faith."*
> — *Ignatius of Loyola, writing of himself*

"Soul of Christ, make me holy."

So says the first line of a prayer that Ignatius of Loyola recommends to those who take up his *Spiritual Exercises*, one of the most influential devotional books in the church's history—it's still being published, and followed, some 460 years after he first conceived it.

In fact, whatever Ignatius touched seemed to be set apart as something special: the order he founded, the Society of Jesus, became one of the most influential of Catholic orders.

Yet Ignatius' little prayer sums up not only his legacy but also his person.

Given to vanities

He was born Iñigo Lopez de Loyola, to a noble and wealthy Basque family, and sent to the Spanish court to become a page.

He embraced court life with enthusiasm, learning weapons, gambling, and courtly love—he was "a man given to the vanities of the world," he later wrote in his auto-biography, "whose chief delight consisted in martial exercises, with a great and vain desire to win renown."

In a battle with the French for the town of Pamplona, Spain, he was hit by a cannon ball the size of a fist. The five-foot-two-inch Iñigo was helped back to Loyola by French soldiers (who admired his courage). He underwent surgeries to reset his right knee and remove a protruding bone. For seven weeks he lay in bed recuperating.

During this time, he began reading spiritual books and accounts of the exploits of Dominic and Francis. In one book by a Cistercian monk, the spiritual life was conceived as one of holy chivalry; the idea fascinated Iñigo. During his convalescence he received spiritual visions, so that by the time he recuperated, he had resolved to live a life of austerity to do penance for his sins.

In February 1522, Iñigo bade farewell to his family and went to Montserrat, a pilgrimage site in northeastern Spain. He spent three days confessing his life sins, then hung his sword and dagger near the statue of the Virgin Mary to symbolize his break with his old life. He donned sack cloth and walked to Manresa, a town 30 miles from Barcelona, to pass the decisive months of his career (from March 1522 to mid-February 1523). He lived as a beggar, ate and drank sparingly, scourged himself, and for a time neither trimmed his tangled hair nor cut his nails. He attended Mass daily and spent seven hours a day in prayer, often in a cave outside Manresa.

While sitting one day by the Cardoner River, "the eyes of his understanding began to open," he later wrote, referring to himself in the third person, "and, without seeing any vision, he understood and knew many things, as well spiritual things as things of the faith." At Manresa, he sketched the fundamentals of his little book *Spiritual Exercises*.

After a pilgrimage to the Holy Land, he headed back to Europe: "After the pilgrim he learned that it was God's will that he should not stay in Jerusalem," he wrote, "he pondered in his heart what he should do and finally decided to study for a time in order to be able to help souls."

He chose to defer priesthood, which would have taken but a few years of study, for a more intense and lasting 12 years of education. Iñigo studied at Barcelona, then Alcala, where he acquired followers. But Iñigo soon fell under suspicion of heresy (as a non-ordained person encouraging others to reflect on their spiritual experiences, he was distrusted by the church hierarchy), was imprisoned and tried by the Spanish Inquisition—the first of many such encounters with the Inquisition. He was found innocent, left for Salamanca, where he was imprisoned (and acquitted) again. With this, he and his companions left Spain for study at Paris.

During his long stay in the French capital, where he changed his name to Ignatius, he won the coveted master of arts degree, gathered more companions (among them Francis Xavier, who became one of the order's greatest missionaries). In 1534 he and his little band bound themselves by vows of poverty, chastity, and obedience—though they had not yet decided to found a religious order.

Jesus incorporated

Then they made their way to Venice, and there, in 1537, Ignatius and most of his companions were ordained. For the next 18 months they ministered and prayed together. One companion later remembered about Ignatius, "When he did not weep three times during Mass, he considered himself deprived of consolation."

During this time Ignatius had one of his most decisive visions. While in prayer one day, he saw Christ with a cross on his shoulder, and beside him was God the Father, who said, "I wish you to take this man [meaning Ignatius] for your servant."

Jesus said to Ignatius, "My will is that you should serve us."

Ignatius was also told that his group was to be called "the company of Jesus," that they were to be like a company of fur traders yet focused on doing God's will.

In 1540 the small band gained the pope's approval and was named the Society of Jesus: they determined a method of decision making, vowed to obey the pope as the voice of Christ, and elected Ignatius as superior general. Thus began 15 years of administrative life in Rome for Ignatius.

The vision and disciplines of the "Jesuits," as they came to be called, caught the imagination of Europe. Soon Jesuits were found in Europe's major cities as well as in the new world: Gao, Mexico City, Quebec, Buenos Aires, and Bogota. They opened hospices for the dying, sought financial support for the poor, founded orphanages, and opened schools.

The *Constitutions of the Society of Jesus* was probably the most important work of Ignatius's later years. His followers abandoned some traditional forms of religious life (such as chanting the divine office, physical punishments, and penitential garb), in favor of greater adaptability and mobility. The Society was above all to be an order of apostles "ready to live in any part of the world where there was hope of God's greater glory and the good of souls."

His greatest legacy is his *Spiritual Exercises*, which has been in constant use for 460 years. The *Exercises* lead a person through four "weeks" (a flexible term) of meditations and prayers, guided by a spiritual director, generally during a retreat (though there are provisions for non-retreat direction).

Purifying one's soul is the object of the first week; greater knowledge and the love of Christ, the second; freeing the will to follow Christ, the third; and releasing the heart from worldly attachments, the fourth. The perfection of the soul, the imitation of Christ, and the soul's attachment to God are goals for the exercises that reflect the holy ambitions of Ignatius from his conversion.

Ignatius was canonized by Pope Gregory XV in 1622. In 1922 he was declared patron of all spiritual retreats by Pope Pius XI.

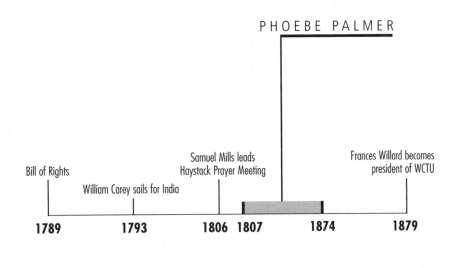

PHOEBE PALMER

Bill of Rights

William Carey sails for India

Samuel Mills leads
Haystack Prayer Meeting

Frances Willard becomes
president of WCTU

1789   1793   1806 1807   1874   1879

MOVERS AND SHAKERS

Phoebe Palmer

MOTHER OF THE HOLINESS MOVEMENT

"*Earnest prayers, long fasting, and burning tears may seem befitting, but cannot move the heart of infinite love to a greater willingness to save. God's time is now. The question is not, What have I been? or What do I expect to be? But, Am I now trusting in Jesus to save to the uttermost? If so, I am now saved from all sin.*"

For the century after John Wesley founded Methodism, *conversion* meant emotion, an intense religious experience lasting moments or days. It established one's salvation and was considered the absolute prerequisite of Christian perfection, or "entire sanctification."

For years that was Phoebe Worrall's problem. Born December 18, 1807, to zealous Methodists who conducted family worship twice a day, she had never felt *not* a Christian.

At age 11, she inscribed a poem on the flyleaf of her Bible:

This revelation—holy, just, and true—
Though oft I read, it seems forever new;
While light from heaven upon its pages rest,

I feel its power, and with it I am blessed.
Henceforth, I take thee as my future guide,
Let naught from thee my youthful heart divide.
And then, if late or early death be mine,
All will be well, since I, O Lord, am Thine!

But still she had not experienced the "powerful conversion" (as she put it) as had her Methodist friends and family.

Her first decade of marriage to Methodist physician Walter Palmer didn't help. Their marriage was strong, but their first two children died mere months after their births. Phoebe was convinced God was punishing her for not totally devoting herself to him: "Surely I needed it, or it would not have been given," she wrote. "Though painfully learned, yet I trust the lesson has been fully apprehended."

A year later, while her sister was visiting, Phoebe's spiritual crisis was resolved. She

didn't need "joyous emotion" to believe—belief itself was grounds for assurance. Reading Jesus' words that "the altar sanctifies the gift," she believed that God would make her holy if she "laid her all upon the altar." She divided John Wesley's perfectionism into a three-step process: consecrating oneself totally to God, believing God will sanctify what is consecrated, and telling others about it.

"I now see that the error of my religious life has been a desire for signs and wonders," she wrote. "Like Naaman, I have wanted some great thing, unwilling to rely unwaveringly on the still small voice of the Spirit, speaking through the naked Word."

Prayer meetings nationwide

Phoebe and her sister began women's prayer meetings each Tuesday afternoon—which, six years later, would include a male philosophy professor. Eventually, word of these successful prayer meetings inspired similar gatherings around the country, bringing Christians of many denominations together to pray. Phoebe soon found herself in the limelight—the most influential woman in the largest, fastest-growing religious group in America. At her instigation, missions began, camp meetings evangelized, and an estimated 25,000 Americans converted.

She herself would often preach, "Earnest prayers, long fasting, and burning tears may seem befitting, but cannot move the heart of infinite love to a greater willingness to save. God's time is now. The question is not, What have I been? or What do I expect to be? But, Am I now trusting in Jesus to save to the uttermost? If so, I am now saved from all sin."

Palmer was also deeply concerned about social ills. She was an ardent supporter of the temperance movement and one of the founding directors of America's first inner-city mission—New York's Five Points Mission.

A prominent religious woman in such an age was met with suspicion. Actually, she agreed with critics that it was not right for women to engage in "women preaching, technically so called." But, she added, "it is in the order of God that women may occasionally be brought out of the ordinary sphere of action and occupy in either church or state positions of high responsibility."

Such an example inspired other women, like the Salvation Army's Catherine Booth and the Women's Christian Temperance Union's Frances Willard.

Though she considered herself simply a "Bible Christian" who took Scripture with absolute seriousness, her theology is her legacy. Considered the link between Wesleyan revivalism and modern Pentecostalism, her "altar covenant" gave rise to denominations like The Church of the Nazarene, The Salvation Army, The Church of God, and The Pentecostal-Holiness Church.

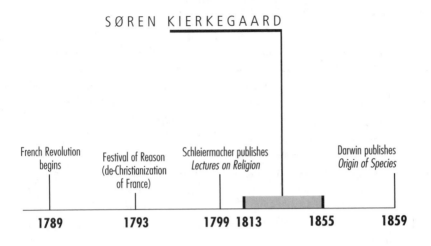

SØREN KIERKEGAARD

French Revolution begins	Festival of Reason (de-Christianization of France)	Schleiermacher publishes *Lectures on Religion*		Darwin publishes *Origin of Species*	
1789	1793	1799	1813	1855	1859

MOVERS AND SHAKERS

Søren Kierkegaard
CHRISTIAN EXISTENTIALIST

> *"Affliction is able to drown out every earthly voice ... but the voice of eternity within a man it cannot drown. When by the aid of affliction all irrelevant voices are brought to silence, it can be heard, this voice within."*

"My life is one great suffering, unknown and incomprehensible to all others." And it was out of this suffering that Søren Kierkegaard laid siege to the reigning European philosophy and the comfortable Christianity of his day.

Forsaking love

Kierkegaard was born in Copenhagen, into a strict Danish Lutheran home. He inherited a melancholy disposition from his father and suffered through an unhappy youth. His frail and slightly twisted frame made him an object of mockery throughout his life. Still, his father was sufficiently wealthy that Kierkegaard never had to hold down a job but was free to spend his life as a writer and philosopher.

He attended the University of Copenhagen to prepare for the

Lutheran ministry, but it took him ten years to earn his degree, and he never was ordained. It was philosophy, not theology, that captured his imagination.

And Regine Olsen captured his heart. They became engaged, but Kierkegaard had doubts and quickly broke off the engagement, though he admitted he was still deeply in love. He was weighed down by his unusual consciousness of the complexities of the human mind, which he would never be able to communicate to Regine. As he wrote in his diary: "I was a thousand years too old for her." Years later he compared that painful decision with Abraham's willingness to sacrifice Isaac, and some of his books were written "because of her."

Subjective truth

His first book, *Either/Or* (1843), was a brilliant, dialectical, and poetic discussion in which he sought to justify his break with Regine, and in which set forth a basic tenet of his philosophy: each individual must choose—consciously and responsibly—among the alternatives life presents.

He followed this up with other philosophical works: *Fear and Trembling* (1843), *Philosophical Fragments* (1844), *The Concept of Dread* (1844), and *Concluding Unscientific Postscript to the Philosophical Fragment* (1846).

His target was the "system" (as he mockingly put it) of G.W.F. Hegel, the great philosopher of idealism. He attacked Hegel's attempt to systematize all of reality; Hegel, he said, left out the most important element of human experience: existence itself. Kierkegaard felt that no philosophical system could explain the human condition. The experience of reality—the loss of a loved one, the feelings of guilt and dread—was what mattered, not the "idea" of it.

Hegel emphasized universals; Kierkegaard argued for decision and commitment. Hegel sought an objective theory of knowledge upon which everyone could agree; Kierkegaard believed in the subjectivity of truth—meaning that truth is understood and experienced individually.

Existence, he believed, is actual, painful, and more important than "essence" or "idea." The authentic person wrestles with fundamental questions that cannot be answered rationally. As Kierkegaard once wrote, "My life has been brought to an impasse, I loathe existence.... Where am I? What is this thing called the world? What does this word mean? Who is it that has lured me into the thing and now leaves me there? Who am I? How did I come into the world? Why was I not consulted, why not made acquainted with its manners and customs? ... How did I obtain an interest in it? Is it not a voluntary concern? And if I am to be compelled to take part in it, where is the director? Whither shall I turn with my complaint?"

The only way to live in this painful existence is through faith. But to Kierkegaard, faith is not a mental conviction about doctrine, nor positive religious feelings, but a passionate commitment to God in the face of uncertainty. Faith is a risk (the "leap of faith"), an adventure that requires the denial of oneself. To choose faith is what brings authentic human existence.

This is the "existentialism" that Kierkegaard is considered the founder of—though later existentialists had significantly different agendas than his.

Attack on Christendom

In his later writings—*Works of Love* (1847), *Christian Discourses* (1848), and *Training in Christianity* (1850)—he tried to clarify the true nature of Christianity.

The greatest enemy of Christianity, he argued, was "Christendom"—the cultured and respectable Christianity of his day. The tragedy of easy Christianity is that existence has ceased to be an adventure and a constant risk in the presence of God but has become a form of morality and a doctrinal system. Its purpose is to simplify the matter of becoming a Christian. This is just paganism, "cheap" Christianity, with neither cost nor pain, Kierkegaard argued. It is like war games, in which armies move and there is a great deal of noise, but there is no real risk or pain—and no real victory. Kierkegaard believed the church of his day was merely "playing at Christianity."

Kierkegaard became increasingly convinced that his calling was in "making Christianity difficult." He was to remind people of his day that to be truly Christian, one must become aware of the cost of faith and pay the price.

So he chastised: "We are what is called a 'Christian' nation—but in such a sense that not a single one of us is in the character of the Christianity of the New Testament."

And he mocked: "Most people believe that the Christian commandments (e.g., to love one's neighbor as oneself) are intentionally a little too severe, like putting the clock half an hour ahead to make sure of not being late in the morning."

He believed that only by making things difficult—by helping people become aware of the pain, guilt, and feelings of dread that accompany even the life of faith—could he help Christians hear God again: "Affliction is able to drown out every earthly voice ... but the voice of eternity within a man it cannot drown. When by the aid of affliction all irrelevant voices are brought to silence, it can be heard, this voice within."

Kierkegaard was not just a suffering prophet, though. He was a man of deep, almost mystical faith, and his acerbic pen could also compose lyrical prayers like these:

"Teach me, O God, not to torture myself, not to make a martyr out of myself through stifling reflection, but rather teach me to breathe deeply in faith."

And "Father in Heaven, when the thought of Thee wakes in our hearts, let it not awaken like a frightened bird that flies about in dismay, but like a child waking from its sleep with a heavenly smile."

Like his philosophy, then, he was himself paradoxical.

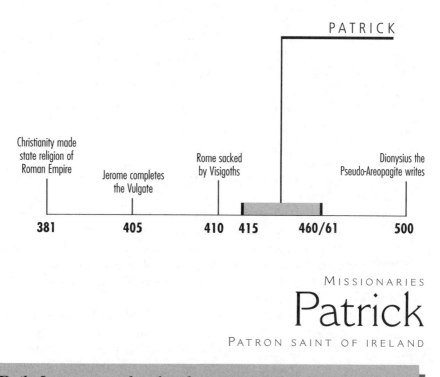

PATRICK

Christianity made state religion of Roman Empire		Rome sacked by Visigoths		Dionysius the Pseudo-Areopagite writes
	Jerome completes the Vulgate			
381	**405**	**410 415**	**460/61**	**500**

MISSIONARIES

Patrick

PATRON SAINT OF IRELAND

"Daily I expect murder, fraud or captivity, but I fear none of these things because of the promises of heaven. I have cast myself into the hands of God almighty who rules everywhere."

Patrick is remembered today as the saint who drove the snakes out of Ireland (not true), the teacher who used the shamrock to explain the Trinity (doubted), and the namesake of annual parades in New York and Boston. What is less well-known is that Patrick was a humble missionary (this saint regularly referred to himself as "a sinner") of enormous courage. When he evangelized Ireland, he set in motion a series of events that impacted all of Europe. It all started when he was carried off into slavery by Irish raiders.

Escape from sin and slavery

A 16-year-old Romanized Briton, Patrick was sold to a cruel warrior chief whose opponents' heads sat atop sharp poles around his palisade in Northern Ireland. While Patrick minded his master's pigs in the nearby hills, he lived like an animal himself, enduring long bouts of hunger, thirst, and isolation. A nominal

Christian to this point, he now turned to the Christian God of his fathers for comfort.

"I would pray constantly during the daylight hours," he later recalled. "The love of God and the fear of him surrounded me more and more. And faith grew. And the spirit roused so that in one day I would say as many as a hundred prayers, and at night only slightly less."

After six years of slavery, a mysterious, supernatural voice spoke to him: "Soon you will return to your homeland."

So Patrick fled and ran 200 miles to a southeastern harbor. There he boarded a ship of traders bound for Europe.

Return to the homelands

After a few years on the continent, Patrick returned to his family in England—only to be called back to Ireland as an evangelist.

"I seemed to hear the voice of the same men who lived beside the forest of Foclut ... and they cried out as with one voice, 'We appeal to you, holy servant boy, to come and walk among us.' I was deeply moved in heart and I could read no further, so I awoke."

Whether Patrick was the first missionary to Ireland or not, paganism was still dominant when he arrived. "I dwell among gentiles," he wrote, "in the midst of pagan barbarians, worshipers of idols, and of unclean things."

Patrick's mission faced the most opposition from the druids, who practiced magic, were skilled in secular learning (especially law and history), and advised Irish kings. Biographies of the saint are replete with stories of druids who "wished to kill holy Patrick."

"Daily I expect murder, fraud or captivity," Patrick wrote, "but I fear none of these things because of the promises of heaven. I have cast myself into the hands of God almighty who rules everywhere."

Patrick was as fully convinced as the Celts that the power of the druids was real, but he brought news of a stronger power. The famous *Lorica* (or "Patrick's Breastplate"), a prayer of protection, may not have been written by Patrick (at least in its current form), but it expresses perfectly Patrick's confidence in God to protect him from "every fierce merciless force that may come upon my body and soul."

There was probably a confrontation between Patrick and the druids, but scholars doubt it was as dramatic and magical as later stories recounted. One biographer from the late 600s, Muirchú, described Patrick challenging druids to contests at Tara, in which each party tried to outdo the other in working wonders before the audience. Patrick, the legend says, won, as God killed several of the druids and soldiers:

"The king summoned his council and said, 'It is better for me to believe than to die.' And he believed as did many others that day."

Yet to Patrick, the greatest enemy was one he had been intimately familiar with—slavery. He was, in fact, one of the earliest Christians to speak out strongly against the practice. Scholars agree he is the true author of a letter excommunicating a British tyrant, Coroticus, who had carried off some of Patrick's converts into slavery.

"Ravenous wolves have gulped down the Lord's own flock which was flourishing in Ireland," he wrote, "and the whole church cries out and laments for its sons and daughters." He called Coroticus's deed "wicked, so horrible, so unutterable," and told him to repent and to free the converts.

It remains unknown if he was successful in freeing Coroticus's slaves, but within his lifetime (or shortly thereafter), the entire Irish slave trade had ended.

Self doubt

Despite his success as a missionary, Patrick was self-conscious, especially about his educational background. "I still blush and fear more than anything to have my lack of learning brought out into the open," he wrote in his *Confession*. "For I am unable to explain my mind to learned people."

Nevertheless, he gave thanks to God, "who stirred up me, a fool, from the midst of those who are considered wise and learned in the practice of the law as well as persuasive in their speech and in every other way and ahead of these others, inspired me who is so despised by the world."

Over and over again, Patrick wrote that he was not worthy to be a bishop. He wasn't the only one with doubts. At one point, his ecclesiastical elders in Britain sent a deputation to investigate his mission. A number of concerns were brought up, including a rash moment of (unspecified) sin from his youth. His *Confession*, in fact, was written in response to this investigation.

If Patrick was not confident about his own shortcomings, he held a deep sense of God's intimate involvement in his life. "I have known God as my authority, for he knows all things even before they are done," he wrote. "He would frequently forewarn me of many things by his divine response."

"Flame of a splendid sun"

According to the Irish annals, Patrick died in 493, when he would have been in his seventies. But we do not know for sure when, where, or how he died. Monasteries at Armagh, Downpatrick, and Saul have all claimed his remains. His feast day is recorded as early as March 17, 797, with the annotation; "The flame of a splendid sun, the apostle of virginal Erin [Ireland], may Patrick with many thousands be the shelter of our wickedness."

It will always be difficult to separate fact from fiction in the stories of Patrick's biographers. It is historically clear, however, that Patrick was one of the first great missionaries who brought the gospel beyond the boundaries of Roman civilization. According to tradition, only Ireland's inaccessible south remained untouched by his work by the time he died.

Patrick also became the model for later Celtic Christians. He engaged in continuous prayer. He was enraptured by God and loved sacred Scripture. He also had a rich poetic imagination with the openness to hear God in dreams and visions and a love of nature. Hundreds of Celtic monks, in emulation of Patrick, left their homeland to spread the gospel to Scotland, England, and continental Europe.

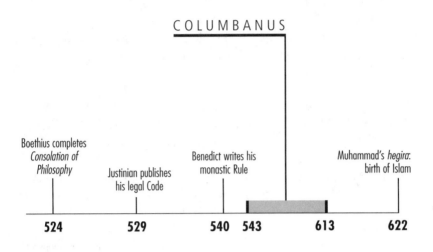

COLUMBANUS

| Boethius completes *Consolation of Philosophy* | Justinian publishes his legal Code | Benedict writes his monastic Rule | | Muhammad's *hegira*: birth of Islam |

524   **529**   **540**   **543**   **613**   **622**

MISSIONARIES

Columbanus

IRISH MISSIONARY TO EUROPE

> *"Away, O youth, away! Flee from corruption, into which, as you know, many have fallen."*
> — *an abbess's well-heeded advice to Columbanus*

The handsome and hot-headed Columbanus was one of Western Europe's most successful evangelists ever.

According to Columbanus's first biographer, writing a mere 28 years after his subject's death, "Columbanus's fine figure, his splendid color, and his noble manliness made him beloved by all." And therein lay the problem: "He aroused ... the lust of lascivious maidens, especially of those whose fine figure and superficial beauty are wont to enkindle mad desires in the minds of wretched men."

As a young man, he was afraid he was on the brink of giving in to such vain "lusts of the world," so he sought the guidance of a local female hermit.

"Away, O youth, away!" she advised. "Flee from corruption, into which, as you know, many have fallen." Columbanus left, shaken, to pack his things to take up the monastic life. When he told his mother he was leaving, she became so distraught, she blocked the doorway. But Columbanus was undeterred, "leaping over both threshold and mother."

Thus began his peripatetic life.

Asceticism with a smile

Columbanus continued his studies with Comgall of Bangor, whose monastery was famous for its asceticism. Not only did Columbanus thrive there, but he codified such asceticism into two rules for monasteries—one for individual monks, the other for communities. These rules could be extremely harsh: merely desiring to hit someone meant 40 days on bread and water. Actually hitting someone (and drawing blood) meant penance for three years. Even speaking ill of the rules meant exile from the community.

Yet Columbanus had another side, which some of his sermons and letters suggest. A letter to Pope Boniface IV is loaded with puns about the previous pope, Vigilus: "Be vigilant, I urge you, pope, be vigilant and again I say be vigilant, since perhaps he who was called Vigilant was not." In a letter to Gregory the Great, he made puns on Pope Leo's name: "A living dog is better than a dead Leo [lion]." Columbanus is also credited with a spirited "Boat Song" which was chanted by monks rowing up the "two-horned Rhine."

Even though he was witty, Columbanus was painfully serious about his faith. In his forties, he left Bangor to follow God's command, which was the same command given to Abraham: "Get thee out of thy country." With 12 companions, he left for Gaul, large parts of which had reverted to paganism (and the remaining Christians were likely nominal or Arian heretics). He founded three monasteries in rapid succession—Annegray, Luxeuil, and Fontaine—each one growing so quickly new ones had to be created.

Before he could build many more, he had a run-in with the polygamous king, Theuderic, and his mother, Brunhilde, and was thrown out of the country. It wasn't the only dispute in the hot-blooded monk's life. He feuded with popes, kings, bishops, and even his own followers. (After Gall, one of his most faithful disciples, became ill and could not travel, Columbanus forbade him to say Mass. The ban was not lifted until Columbanus was on his deathbed.)

Columbanus and his men roamed the continent, preaching in what would become France, Germany, and Switzerland. Finally, he traveled to northern Italy to convert the Lombards. There, in his seventies, he took part in the construction of Bobbio, the first Italo-Irish monastery, where he died November 23, 613. His legacy was extraordinary: he and his disciples founded at least 60—and possibly more than 100—monasteries throughout Europe.

CYRIL AND METHODIUS

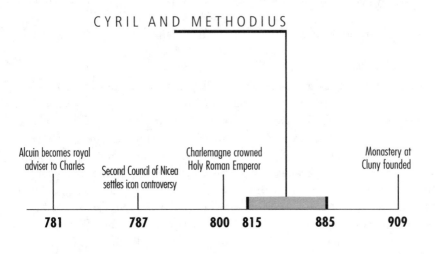

Alcuin becomes royal adviser to Charles	Second Council of Nicea settles icon controversy	Charlemagne crowned Holy Roman Emperor		Monastery at Cluny founded
781	**787**	**800 815**	**885**	**909**

Cyril and Methodius

APOSTLES TO THE SLAVS

> *"One cannot estimate the significance, for the future of Orthodoxy, of the Slavonic translations [of Cyril and Methodius]."*
> — *Orthodox apologist Timothy Ware*

When the Moravian Prince Ratislav requested that the Byzantine Emperor Michael III send missionaries to Moravia "to explain to us the Christian truths in our own language," it was the brothers Cyril and Methodius who were sent. They had already developed a reputation as keen thinkers and administrators. By the end of their lives, they were well on the way to becoming the most celebrated missionary team in Eastern Orthodox history.

The politics of liturgy

They were born "Constantine" and "Michael" to a high ranking officer in the Byzantine Army, and both studied at the Imperial School of Constantinople. They each carved out a successful career: Constantine (later Cyril) as professor of philosophy at the Imperial school; Michael, first as governor in Macedonia and then abbot of a monastery in Asia Minor (where he took the name Methodius).

In 863, when they started their work among the Slavs, they began using Slavonic in the liturgy. They translated the Bible into the language later known as Old Church Slavonic (or Old Bulgarian) and invented a Slavic alphabet based on Greek characters, which in its final Cyrillic form is still in use as the alphabet for a number of Slavic languages.

International politics soon swirled around their little mission. The German archbishop of Salzburg claimed that Cyril and Methodius had invaded his ecclesiastical territory. Jealous for the church in Rome, the archbishop insisted that Latin, not Slavonic, be used in the liturgy.

So in 868, the brothers found themselves in Rome explaining themselves to Pope Adrian II, who took their side and formally authorized the use of the Slavonic liturgy. Though Cyril died in Rome, Methodius was sent back to the Slavs as Adrian's legate and as archbishop of Sirmium, a province that included all of Moravia.

When power in Moravia fell into new hands, Methodius was abandoned by the government; he was accused of usurping the Catholic archbishops' authority and of the "scandalous use of the Slavonic language" in the liturgy. He was brutally treated and jailed, and only freed by the intervention of Pope John VIII.

Successful exile

Unfortunately, after Methodius' death, Pope Stephen V reversed John VIII's ruling and forbade the use of the Slavonic liturgy. Wiching, Methodius's successor, drove the disciples of Cyril and Methodius into exile.

The exile only facilitated the spread of their work. "One cannot estimate the significance, for the future of Orthodoxy, of the Slavonic translations," said Orthodox apologist Timothy Ware. The Slavonic liturgy and Bible made their way all over Eastern Europe and gave birth to the Bulgarian and Serbian Orthodox churches (which still use the Slavonic liturgy). Russia, which converted to Orthodoxy about a century after Methodius died, continues to use his Cyrillic alphabet to this day.

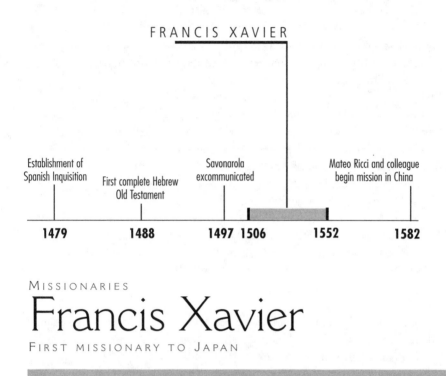

FRANCIS XAVIER

Establishment of Spanish Inquisition	First complete Hebrew Old Testament	Savonarola excommunicated		Mateo Ricci and colleague begin mission in China
1479	1488	1497 1506	1552	1582

MISSIONARIES

Francis Xavier

FIRST MISSIONARY TO JAPAN

> *"Be great in little things."*

Within five years of its founding, the Order of the Jesuits was already famous for religious zeal. Word of Jesuit preaching and care of the sick in central Italy had spread throughout the Continent, and Catholic princes everywhere wrote begging for as many Jesuits as the Order could spare. When Portugal's King John III asked for six Jesuits for colonies in the Orient, founder Ignatius Loyola replied that he could only send two.

At the last minute, however, one fell ill. His replacement, Francis Xavier, was given time only to mend his cassock before shipping out. Such was the beginning of one of the most wide-ranging and successful of missionary endeavors.

Occidental accident

The son of an aristocratic Spanish-Basque family, Xavier had been Loyola's roommate at the University of Paris, Europe's theological center. Gradually, the two had forged a friendship and a kinship in religious ideals, and with five others, they dedicated themselves to lives of poverty and celibacy in imitation of Christ. While Xavier traveled to Lisbon, Pope Paul III formally recognized his and Ignatius's followers as a religious order: the Society of Jesus, or Jesuits.

At the request of King John III, Xavier was sent to Goa, India, the center of Portuguese operations in the East. After a year's journey (during which he first earned his reputation for sea-sickness), Xavier spent five months preaching and ministering to the hospitalized. He walked the streets with a bell, inviting children to church. Once he had enough Portuguese children, he taught them the catechism and gave them instructions to share what they learned with their parents.

"Give me the children until they are 7 and anyone may have them afterwards," he said. Eventually the adults themselves, originally unreceptive to the missionary, were flocking to hear him preach.

But Xavier figured that if he was meant to evangelize the Portuguese, he could have stayed in Portugal. He boarded a ship again, bound for the pearl fisheries of India's southern peninsula. About 20,000 Indians in the area had been baptized a mere seven years earlier, mainly because Christianity was the religion of the powerful Portuguese. Xavier wanted to instruct and confirm these neophytes as well as evangelize.

However, India's caste system created another block to sincere conversion: many members of the lower castes sought conversion mostly as a means of social advancement. Higher castes saw the religion as subversive to the social order. Xavier and his followers were often persecuted, and Xavier himself was once shot with arrows. To make matters worse, reputedly Christian Portuguese soldiers were setting horrible examples for the new converts.

Complications

On his missionary travels (he definitely reached Sri Lanka, and some believe he may have been the first apostle to the Philippines), Xavier converted a Japanese man named Han-Sir. Japan had been reached only five years earlier by Europeans, and Xavier was astonished at Han-Sir's reports of Japan's sophisticated culture.

Hoping to reach "the best people yet discovered," as he called them, he sailed with Han-Sir, two other Japanese men, and two fellow Jesuits. As in India, he was well-received and thousands converted. Convinced that he had the beginnings of a flourishing church, Xavier returned to India for a brief respite.

News awaited him. The Jesuit order had decided to organize a new province including all the territories east of South Africa's Cape of Good Hope. Xavier himself was to be its head. What Xavier really wanted, however, was to continue evangelizing Japan.

In fact, he thought he could reach more Japanese if he could first reach China, because, as Xavier believed, the Japanese looked to China for wisdom: "What encourages us is that God has inspired this thought in us," Xavier wrote to the King of Portugal. "And we do not doubt that the power of God is infinitely superior to that of the king in China."

China, however, was closed to outsiders, and Xavier died of fever while trying to gain entrance to the country.

Catholicism's greatest missionary?

How many converts Xavier made is left to the educated guesswork of history. The numbers go as high as 1 million, but modern scholars peg the number around 30,000, while the Jesuits claim 700,000. And while some of Xavier's methods have been criticized (he forced converts to take Portuguese names and dress in Western clothes, approved the persecution of the Eastern Church, and used the Goa government as a missionary tool), he has also earned praise. He insisted that missionaries adapt to many of the customs, and most certainly the language, of the culture they wish to evangelize. And unlike later missionaries, Xavier supported an educated native clergy. Though for a time, it seemed his work in Japan was subsequently destroyed by persecution, Protestant missionaries three centuries later discovered 100,000 Christians in the Nagasaki area.

In 1622 the Roman Catholic church canonized Xavier—and in 1927 named him patron saint of all missions.

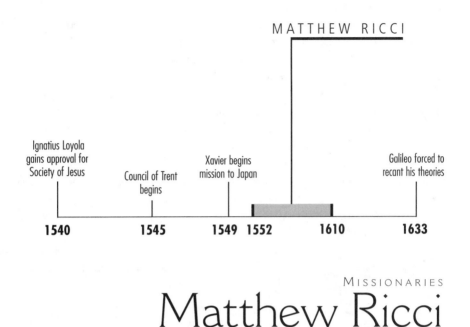

MATTHEW RICCI

Ignatius Loyola
gains approval for
Society of Jesus

Council of Trent
begins

Xavier begins
mission to Japan

Galileo forced to
recant his theories

| 1540 | 1545 | 1549 1552 | 1610 | 1633 |

MISSIONARIES

Matthew Ricci

CONTROVERSIAL EVANGELIST TO CHINA

> *"Those that adore Heaven instead of the Lord of Heaven are like a man who, desiring to pay the emperor homage, prostrates himself before the imperial palace at Peking and venerates its beauty."*

In 1579, a man named Valignano arrived at Macao, a Portuguese trading post on the coast of China. Looking toward the nearby mainland, the aspiring missionary was said to have cried out, "Rock, rock, oh when wilt thou open, rock?" Priests in Macao had told him not to hold his breath: the conversion of the Chinese, they argued, was completely impossible.

Within four years, though, a 30-year-old Italian Jesuit was living in the provincial capital and introducing Chinese to the Christian faith. His name was Matthew Ricci, and he was destined to become, along with Francis Xavier, one of the most successful missionaries to the Far East.

Moving to the Chinese capital

Ricci's father was an Italian aristocrat who sent his son to Rome to study law. Ricci instead joined the Society of Jesus (the

239

Jesuits), under whom he studied mathematics to prepare him for missionary work. He was sent, along with 13 others, to Goa in India, where he taught children who were to become the next generation's Christian leaders.

Ricci had bargained for more when he signed up with the Jesuits, and after four years, he asked for a transfer. He was reassigned to Macao.

When Chinese officials heard that Ricci had expertise in mathematics, astronomy, and geography, they invited him and his companion Ruggieri to settle in the provincial capital of Chaoch'ing in 1583. Little by little, Ricci moved closer to the imperial capital, Peking, and in 1600, he was invited by the emperor to dwell there.

The Chinese considered theirs the only true civilization, and Ricci accommodated them when he addressed them: "Li Ma-ton, your Majesty's servant, comes from the Far West, addresses himself to your majesty with respect.... Despite the distance [of my home-land], fame told me of the remarkable teaching and fine institutions with which the imperial court has endowed all its peoples."

He told the emperor that he only wanted to be "of some small use," and at first, that meant repairing clocks, two of which he'd given the emperor upon his arrival. Ricci's skill at this and mapmaking so impressed the emperor, more doors were opened for him, so that he was able to remain in the capital, with government protection, for ten years.

"It is a miracle of the omnipotent hand of the Most High," wrote Ricci, "The miracle appears all the greater in that not only do we dwell in Peking, but we enjoy here an incontestable authority."

Controversial evangelism

To translate Christianity into the Chinese idiom, Ricci had to innovate. For example, the Chinese did not have a word for "God," so Ricci at first used *T'ien Chu*, "Lord of Heaven." In one of his earliest catechisms, he wrote, "Those that adore Heaven instead of the Lord of Heaven are like a man who, desiring to pay the emperor homage, prostrates himself before the imperial palace at Peking and venerates its beauty."

Later he decided that *T'ien* ("heaven") alone already had theistic overtones to the Chinese. He also believed that terms like *Sheng*, often translated "holy," were used in a wide sense to describe anything held as venerable. Thus Ricci used it when referring to Confucius.

Furthermore, to give himself a hearing among the Chinese intelligentsia, most of whom were devotees of Confucianism, Ricci decided he needed to become a Confucian scholar.

And in order to honor local traditions, he permitted his converts to continue many ancient customs, like ancestor "worship." In China, society was founded on the cohesion of the family, and paying reverence to ancestors (burning incense to them) was a traditional rite that reinforced this family value. Ricci, after prolonged study, decided the practice was not worship, as some Christians charged, but merely an act of respect for those family members who had gone before.

Ricci's methods came under fire almost immediately, especially from competing orders, the Dominicans and Franciscans, who were jealous of Jesuit success. The affair become known as the Chinese Rites Controversy. Rome tended to take the side of the friars and tried to curtail Ricci's work. Peking, on the other hand, sided with the Jesuits, and the controversy raged for centuries without being resolved.

Ricci maintained his mission until he died. Though the number of his converts was relatively small, it included many influential Chinese scholars and families who played key roles in the future of Christianity in China.

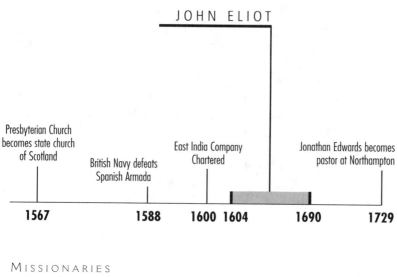

JOHN ELIOT

| Presbyterian Church becomes state church of Scotland | British Navy defeats Spanish Armada | East India Company Chartered | | Jonathan Edwards becomes pastor at Northampton | |

1567   **1588**   **1600 1604**   **1690**   **1729**

MISSIONARIES

John Eliot

APOSTLE TO NATIVE AMERICANS

> "When I came to this blessed family, I then saw, and never before, the power of godliness in its lively vigor and efficacy."

Historians customarily date the beginning of the modern missionary movement in 1792, with William Carey's voyage to India. But a full 150 years earlier, Puritan John Eliot was evangelizing Native Americans—though the long-range impact of his work was destroyed by colonists' fears.

Impressed with the vigor of godliness

Eliot was born to a wealthy family in Herfordshire, England. After graduating from Cambridge in 1622, he came under the influence of Puritan pastor Thomas Hooker, the man chiefly responsible for his conversion: "When I came to this blessed family," Eliot later wrote, "I then saw, and never before, the power of godliness in its lively vigor and efficacy."

In 1631, as Anglican leaders applied heat to Puritans, Eliot emigrated to Roxbury, Massachusetts. There he became pastor of a church composed of many of his English friends. The following year, he married Ann (Hannah) Mumford.

The main legacy of Eliot's early years was producing the first book published in America: the *Bay Psalm Book* (1640), which put the psalms in metrical verse.

Eliot was a quintessential Puritan: he was frugal, eating just one plain dish for dinner. He also rejected tobacco, wigs, and long hair for men. But he was unique in this: he cared deeply for the Indians who populated New England. At Roxbury, he began learning Algonkian and by 1647 was preaching in the native tongue. He began translating and in 1663 published the entire Algonkian Bible—the first Bible printed in America.

Unfortunately, he was a product of his age: he confused Christianity with English culture. He delayed many Indian baptisms "until they were come up unto civil cohabitation, government, and labor, which a fixed condition of life will put them upon." In other words, until they began living like Englishmen, "they were not so capable to be trusted with that treasure of Christ."

This meant, among other things, haircuts for the men, English clothing for all, and moving Indians into villages patterned after English towns. By 1674, there were 14 such towns with a total of 1,100 "praying Indians," as they were called.

Ministering to broken bands

The system gave some Indians the rudiments of the Christian faith and some training for the ministry. But it also isolated them, both from their own people (whose culture they were required to reject) and from their English sponsors (they were not even permitted to join Puritan churches).

During the bloody King Philip's War (1675–76) between Wampanoags and the English, the "praying Indians" were caught in the middle. Though they supported the English, the English colonists distrusted their loyalty, rounded them up, and confined them to concentration camps. The war not only destroyed the trust of the Indians, but also nearly all copies of Eliot's Algonkian Bible and all but four of the Indian villages.

Eliot refused to be discouraged, and he continued to minister to broken bands of Indians until his death. Villages of "praying Indians" continued into the early eighteenth century.

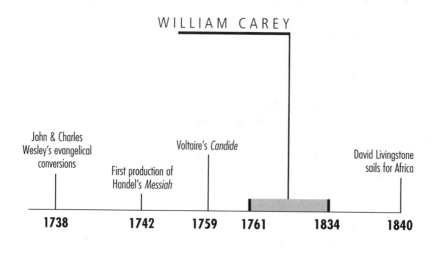

WILLIAM CAREY

John & Charles Wesley's evangelical conversions

First production of Handel's *Messiah*

Voltaire's *Candide*

David Livingstone sails for Africa

| 1738 | 1742 | 1759 | 1761 | 1834 | 1840 |

MISSIONARIES

William Carey

FATHER OF MODERN PROTESTANT MISSIONS

> "*Expect great things; attempt great things.*"

At a meeting of Baptist leaders in the late 1700s, a newly ordained minister stood to argue for value of overseas missions. He was abruptly interrupted by an older minister who said, "Young man, sit down! You are an enthusiast. When God pleases to convert the heathen, he'll do it without consulting you or me."

That such an attitude is inconceivable today is largely due to the subsequent efforts of that young man, William Carey.

Plodder

Carey was raised in the obscure, rural village of Paulerpury, in the middle of England. He apprenticed in a local cobbler's shop, where the nominal Anglican was converted. He enthusiastically took up the faith, and though little educated, the young convert borrowed a Greek grammar and proceeded to teach himself New Testament Greek.

When his master died, he took up shoemaking in nearby Hackleton, where he met and married Dorothy Plackett, who soon gave birth to a daughter. But the apprentice cobbler's life was hard—the child died at age 2—and his pay was insufficient. Carey's family sunk into poverty and stayed there even after he took over the business.

"I can plod," he wrote later, "I can persevere to any definite pursuit." All the while, he continued his language studies, adding Hebrew and Latin, and became a preacher with the Particular Baptists. He also continued pursuing his lifelong interest in international affairs, especially the religious life of other cultures.

Carey was impressed with early Moravian missionaries and was increasingly dismayed at his fellow Protestants' lack of missions interest. In response, he penned *An Enquiry into the Obligations of Christians to Use Means for the Conversion of the Heathens*. He argued that Jesus' Great Commission applied to all Christians of all times, and he castigated fellow believers of his day for ignoring it: "Multitudes sit at ease and give themselves no concern about the far greater part of their fellow sinners, who to this day, are lost in ignorance and idolatry."

Carey didn't stop there: in 1792 he organized a missionary society, and at its inaugural meeting preached a sermon with the call, "Expect great things from God; attempt great things for God!" Within a year, Carey, John Thomas (a former surgeon), and Carey's family (which now included three boys, and another child on the way) were on a ship headed for India.

Stranger in a strange land

Thomas and Carey had grossly underestimated what it would cost to live in India, and Carey's early years there were miserable. When Thomas deserted the enterprise, Carey was forced to move his family repeatedly as he sought employment that could sustain them. Illness racked the family, and loneliness and regret set it: "I am in a strange land," he wrote, "no Christian friend, a large family, and nothing to supply their wants." But he also retained hope: "Well, I have God, and his word is sure."

He learned Bengali with the help of a pundit, and in a few weeks began translating the Bible into Bengali and preaching to small gatherings.

When Carey himself contracted malaria, and then his 5-year-old Peter died of dysentery, it became too much for his wife, Dorothy, whose mental health deteriorated rapidly. She suffered delusions, accusing Carey of adultery and threatening him with a knife. She eventually had to be confined to a room and physically restrained.

"This is indeed the valley of the shadow of death to me," Carey wrote, though characteristically added, "But I rejoice that I am here notwithstanding; and God is here."

Gift of tongues

In October 1799, things finally turned. He was invited to locate in a Danish settlement in Serampore, near Calcutta. He was now under the protection of the Danes, who permitted him to preach legally (in the British-controlled areas of India, all of Carey's missionary work had been illegal).

Carey was joined by William Ward, a printer, and Joshua and Hanna Marshman, teachers. Mission finances increased considerably as Ward began securing government printing contracts, the Marshmans opened schools for children, and Carey began teaching at Fort William College in Calcutta.

In December 1800, after seven years of missionary labor, Carey baptized his first convert, Krishna Pal, and two months later, he published his first Bengali New Testament. With this and subsequent editions, Carey and his colleagues laid the foundation for the study of modern Bengali, which up to this time had been an "unsettled dialect."

Carey continued to expect great things; over the next 28 years, he and his pundits translated the entire Bible into India's major languages: Bengali, Oriya, Marathi, Hindi, Assamese, and Sanskrit and parts of 209 other languages and dialects.

He also sought social reform in India, including the abolition of infanticide, widow burning (*sati*), and assisted suicide. He and the Marshmans founded Serampore College in 1818, a divinity school for Indians, which today offers theological and liberal arts education for some 2,500 students.

By the time Carey died, he had spent 41 years in India without a furlough. His mission could count only some 700 converts in a nation of millions, but he had laid an impressive foundation of Bible translations, education, and social reform.

His greatest legacy was in the worldwide missionary movement of the nineteenth century that he inspired. Missionaries like Adoniram Judson, Hudson Taylor, and David Livingstone, among thousands of others, were impressed not only by Carey's example, but by his words "Expect great things; attempt great things." The history of nineteenth-century Protestant missions is in many ways an extended commentary on the phrase.

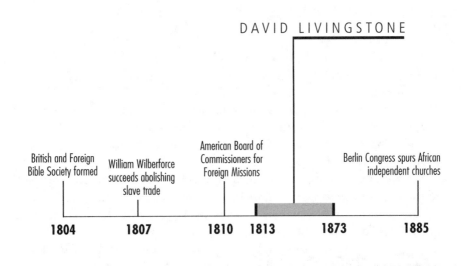

DAVID LIVINGSTONE

| British and Foreign Bible Society formed | William Wilberforce succeeds abolishing slave trade | American Board of Commissioners for Foreign Missions | | Berlin Congress spurs African independent churches |

| 1804 | 1807 | 1810 | 1813 | 1873 | 1885 |

MISSIONARIES

David Livingstone

MISSIONARY-EXPLORER OF AFRICA

"[I am] serving Christ when shooting a buffalo for my men or taking an observation, [even if some] will consider it not sufficiently or even at all missionary."

With four theatrical words, "Dr. Livingstone, I presume?"— words journalist Henry Morton Stanley rehearsed in advance—David Livingstone became immortal. Stanley stayed with Livingstone for five months and then went off to England to write his bestseller, *How I Found Livingstone.* Livingstone, in the meantime, got lost again—in a swamp literally up to his neck. Within a year and a half, he died in a mud hut, kneeling beside his cot in prayer.

The whole civilized world wept. They gave him a 21-gun salute and a hero's funeral among the saints in Westminster Abbey. "Brought by faithful hands over land and sea," his tombstone reads, "David Livingstone: missionary, traveler, philanthropist. For 30 years his life was spent in an unwearied effort to evangelize the native races, to explore the undiscovered secrets, and to abolish the slave trade." He was Mother

Teresa, Neil Armstrong, and Abraham Lincoln rolled into one.

Highway man

At age 25, after a childhood spent working 14 hours a day in a cotton mill, followed by learning in class and on his own, Livingstone was captivated by an appeal for medical missionaries to China. As he trained, however, the door to China was slammed shut by the Opium War. Within six months, he met Robert Moffat, a veteran missionary of southern Africa, who enchanted him with tales of his remote station, glowing in the morning sun with "the smoke of a thousand villages where no missionary had been before."

For ten years, Livingstone tried to be a conventional missionary in southern Africa. He opened a string of stations in "the regions beyond," where he settled down to station life, teaching school and superintending the garden. After four years of bachelor life, he married his "boss's" daughter, Mary Moffat.

From the beginning, Livingstone showed signs of restlessness. After his only convert decided to return to polygamy, Livingstone felt more called than ever to explore. During his first term in South Africa, Livingstone made some of the most prodigious—and most dangerous—explorations of the nineteenth century. His object was to open a "Missionary Road"—"God's Highway," he also called it—1,500 miles north into the interior to bring "Christianity and civilization" to unreached peoples.

Explorer for Christ

On these early journeys, Livingstone's interpersonal quirks were already apparent. He had the singular inability to get along with other Westerners. He fought with missionaries, fellow explorers, assistants, and (later) his brother Charles. He held grudges for years. He had the temperament of a book-reading loner, emotionally inarticulate except when he exploded with Scottish rage. He held little patience for the attitudes of missionaries with "miserably contracted minds" who had absorbed "the colonial mentality" regarding the natives. When Livingstone spoke out against racial intolerance, white Afrikaners tried to drive him out, burning his station and stealing his animals.

He also had problems with the London Missionary Society, who felt that his explorations were distracting him from his missionary work. Throughout his life, however, Livingstone always thought of himself as primarily a missionary, "not a dumpy sort of person with a Bible under his arms, [but someone] serving Christ when shooting a buffalo for my men or taking an observation, [even if some] will consider it not sufficiently or even at all missionary."

Though alienated from the whites, the natives loved his common touch, his rough paternalism, and his curiosity. They also thought he might protect them or supply them with guns. More than most Europeans, Livingstone talked to them with respect, Scottish laird to African chief. Some explorers took as many as 150 porters when they traveled; Livingstone traveled with 30 or fewer.

On an epic, three-year trip from the Atlantic Ocean to the Indian Ocean (reputedly the first by a European) Livingstone was introduced to the 1,700-mile-long Zambezi. The river was also home to Victoria Falls, Livingstone's most awe-inspiring discovery. The scene was "so lovely," he later wrote, that it "must have been gazed upon by angels in their flight."

Despite its beauty, the Zambezi was a river of human misery. It linked the Portuguese colonies of Angola and Mozambique, the main suppliers of slaves for Brazil, who in turn sold to Cuba and the United States. Though Livingstone was partially driven by a desire to create a British colony, his primary ambition was to expose the slave trade and cut it off at the source. The strongest weapon in this task, he believed, was Christian commercial civilization. He hoped to replace the "inefficient" slave economy with a capitalist economy: buying and selling goods instead of people.

The ill-fated Zambezi expedition

After a brief heroic return to England, Livingstone returned to Africa, this time to navigate 1,000 miles up the Zambezi in a brass-and-mahogany steamboat to establish a mission near Victoria Falls. The boat was state-of-the-art technology but proved too frail for the expedition. It leaked horribly after repeatedly running aground on sandbars.

Livingstone pushed his men beyond human endurance. When they reached a 30-foot waterfall, he waved his hand, as if to wish it away, and said, "That's not supposed to be there." His wife, who had just given birth to her sixth child, died in 1862 beside the river, only one of several lives claimed on the voyage. Two years later, the British government, which had no interest in "forcing steamers up cataracts," recalled Livingstone and his mission party.

A year later, he was on his way back to Africa again, this time leading an expedition sponsored by the Royal Geographical Society and wealthy friends. "I would not consent to go simply as a geographer," he emphasized, but as biographer Tim Jeal wrote, "It would be hard to judge whether the search for the Nile's source or his desire to expose the slave trade was his dominant motive." The source of the Nile was the great geographical puzzle of the day. But more important to Livingstone was the possibility of proving that the Bible was true by tracing the African roots of Judaism and Christianity.

For two years he simply disappeared, without a letter or scrap of information. He reported later that he had been so ill he could not even lift a pen, but he was able to read the Bible straight through four times. Livingstone's disappearance fascinated the public as much as Amelia Earhart's a few generations later.

When American journalist Henry Stanley found Livingstone, the news exploded in England and America. Papers carried special editions devoted to the famous meeting. In August 1872, in precarious health, Livingstone shook Stanley's hand and set out on his final journey.

When Livingstone had arrived in Africa in 1841, it was as exotic as outer space, called the "Dark Continent" and the "White Man's Graveyard." Although the Portuguese, Dutch, and English were pushing into the interior, African maps had blank unexplored areas—no roads, no countries, no landmarks. Livingstone helped redraw the maps, exploring what are now a dozen countries, including South Africa, Rwanda, Angola, and the Republic of the Congo (formerly Zaire). And he made the West aware of the continuing evil of African slavery, which led to its being eventually outlawed.

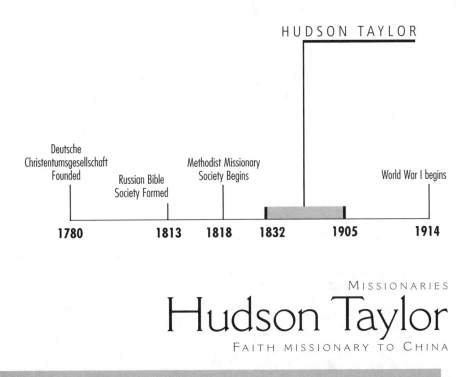

HUDSON TAYLOR

| Deutsche Christentumsgesellschaft Founded | Russian Bible Society Formed | Methodist Missionary Society Begins | | | World War I begins |

| 1780 | 1813 | 1818 | 1832 | 1905 | 1914 |

MISSIONARIES

Hudson Taylor
FAITH MISSIONARY TO CHINA

"China is not to be won for Christ by quiet, ease-loving men and women.... The stamp of men and women we need is such as will put Jesus, China, [and] souls first and foremost in everything and at every time—even life itself must be secondary."

In September 1853, a little three-masted clipper slipped quietly out of Liverpool harbor with Hudson Taylor, a gaunt and wild-eyed 21-year-old missionary, aboard. He was headed for a country that was just coming into the Christian West's consciousness; only a few dozen missionaries were stationed there. By the time Taylor died a half-century later, however, China was viewed as the most fertile and challenging of mission fields as thousands volunteered annually to serve there.

Radical missionary

Taylor was born to James and Amelia Taylor, a Methodist couple fascinated with the Far East who had prayed for their newborn, "Grant that he may work for you in China." Years later, a teenage Hudson experienced a spiritual birth during an intense time of prayer as he lay stretched, as he later put, "before Him with unspeakable awe and unspeakable joy." He spent the next years in frantic preparation, learning the rudiments of medicine, studying Mandarin, and immersing himself ever deeper into the Bible and prayer.

His ship arrived in Shanghai, one of five "treaty ports" China had opened to foreigners following its first Opium War with England. Almost immediately Taylor made a radical decision (as least for Protestant missionaries of the day): he decided to dress in Chinese clothes and grow a pigtail (as Chinese men did). His fellow Protestants were either incredulous or critical.

Taylor, for his part, was not happy with most missionaries he saw: he believed they were "worldly" and spent too much time with English businessmen and diplomats who needed their services as translators. Instead, Taylor wanted the Christian faith taken to the interior of China. So within months of arriving, and the native language still a challenge, Taylor, along with Joseph Edkins, set off for the interior, setting sail down the Huangpu River distributing Chinese Bibles and tracts.

When the Chinese Evangelization Society, which had sponsored Taylor, proved incapable of paying its missionaries in 1857, Taylor resigned and became an independent missionary; trusting God to meet his needs. The same year, he married Maria Dyer, daughter of missionaries stationed in China. He continued to pour himself into his work, and his small church in Ningpo grew to 21 members. But by 1861, he became seriously ill (probably with hepatitis) and was forced to return to England to recover.

In England, the restless Taylor continued translating the Bible into Chinese (a work he'd begun in China), studied to become a midwife, and recruited more missionaries. Troubled that people in England seemed to have little interest in China, he wrote *China: Its Spiritual Need and Claims*. In one passage, he scolded, "Can all the Christians in England sit still with folded arms while these multitudes [in China] are perishing—perishing for lack of knowledge—for lack of that knowledge which England possesses so richly?"

Taylor became convinced that a special organization was needed to evangelize the interior of China. He made plans to recruit 24 missionaries: two for each of the 11 unreached inland provinces and two for Mongolia. It was a visionary plan that would have left veteran recruiters breathless: it would increase the number of China missionaries by 25 percent.

Taylor himself was wracked with doubt: he worried about sending men and women unprotected into the interior; at the same time, he despaired for the millions of Chinese who were dying without the hope of the gospel. In 1865 he wrote in his diary, "For two or three months, intense conflict.... Thought I should lose my mind." A friend invited him to the south coast of England, to Brighton, for a break. And it was there, while walking along the beach, that Taylor's gloom lifted:

"There the Lord conquered my unbelief, and I surrendered myself to God for this service. I told him that all responsibility as to the issues and consequences must rest with him; that as his servant it was mine to obey and to follow him."

His new mission, which he called the China Inland Mission (CIM), had a number of distinctive features, including this: its missionaries would have no guaranteed salaries nor could they appeal for funds; they would simply trust God to supply their needs; furthermore, its missionaries would adopt Chinese dress and then press the gospel into the China interior.

Within a year of his breakthrough, Taylor, his wife and four children, and 16 young missionaries sailed from London to join five others already in China working under Taylor's direction.

Strains in the organization

Taylor continued to make enormous demands upon himself (he saw more than 200 patients daily when he first returned) and on CIM missionaries, some of whom balked. Lewis Nicol, who accused Taylor of tyranny, had to be dismissed. Some CIM missionaries, in the wake of this and other controversies, left to join other missions, but in 1876, with 52 missionaries, CIM constituted one-fifth of the missionary force in China.

Because there continued to be so many Chinese to reach, Taylor instituted another radical policy: he sent unmarried women into the interior, a move criticized by many veterans. But Taylor's boldness knew no bounds. In 1881, he asked God for another 70 missionaries by the close of 1884: he got 76. In late 1886, Taylor prayed for another 100 within a year: by November 1887, he announced 102 candidates had been accepted for service.

His leadership style and high ideals created enormous strains between the London and China councils of the CIM. London thought Taylor autocratic; Taylor said he was only doing what he thought was best for the work, and then demanded more commitment from others: "China is not to be won for Christ by quiet, ease-loving men and women," he wrote. "The stamp of men and women we need is such as will put Jesus, China, [and] souls first and foremost in everything and at every time—even life itself must be secondary."

Taylor's grueling work pace, both in China and abroad (to England, the United States, and Canada on speaking engagements and to recruit), was carried on despite Taylor's poor health and bouts with depression. In 1900 it became too much, and he had complete physical and mental breakdown. The personal cost of Taylor's vision was high on his family as well: his wife Maria died at age 33, and four of eight of their children died before they reached the age of 10. (Taylor eventually married Jennie Faulding, a CIM missionary.)

Between his work ethic and his absolute trust in God (despite never soliciting funds, his CIM grew and prospered), he inspired thousands to forsake the comforts of the West to bring the Christian message to the vast and unknown interior of China. Though mission work in China was interrupted by the communist takeover in 1949, the CIM continues to this day under the name Overseas Missionary Fellowship (International).

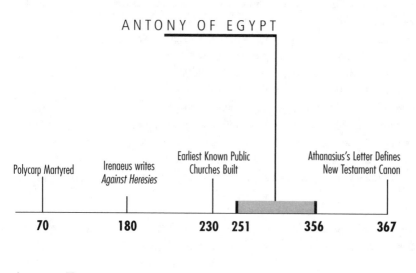

ANTONY OF EGYPT

Polycarp Martyred	Irenaeus writes *Against Heresies*	Earliest Known Public Churches Built		Athanasius's Letter Defines New Testament Canon	
70	**180**	**230**	**251**	**356**	**367**

INNER TRAVELERS

Antony of Egypt

GREATEST DESERT FATHER

> *"Wherever you find yourself, do not go forth from that place too quickly. Try to be patient and learn to stay in one place."*

Born into a wealthy family, Antony submitted to his parents and their expectations that he follow in their wealthy footsteps. They died when Antony was only about 20 years old, and he inherited every penny. But about that same time, Antony happened to hear a reading from the Gospel of Matthew, where Jesus tells a rich young man, "If you want to be perfect, go and sell everything you have and give the money to the poor." Antony believed he was that rich young man and immediately did exactly as Jesus instructed.

Fleeing to the desert

Everything we know about Antony comes from a hagiography (a favorable biography of a saintly person) written shortly after his death by the famous theologian Athanasius. According to him, Antony saw the Christian's task as both simple and formidable:

become a "lover of God" by resisting the Devil and yielding to Christ. Antony saw the world as a battlefield on which God's servants waged war against the Devil and his demons.

His journey into purity began by removing himself from the village. He took up strenuous spiritual exercises: sleepless nights spent in prayer, fasting every other day, and eating only bread and water. He discovered, Athanasius wrote, "the mind of the soul is strong when the pleasures of the body are weak."

Soon Antony left the village territories and sought refuge in nearby tombs where, according to Athanasius, devils and wild beasts assaulted him both physically and spiritually. Like an athlete in the arena, Antony endured repeated attacks until the demons were finally scattered by the presence of God. In the peace after the turmoil, Antony asked God why he had been left to do battle alone. God told him that, though he was present, he waited to see the saint fight.

From the tombs Antony fled again, this time seeking refuge in an abandoned Roman fort on a solitary desert mountain. There he shut himself up for 20 years, waging a silent, solitary battle. When he emerged, Antony had become a symbol of strength and wisdom for all of Egypt.

Ascetic superstar

Having built a foundation of solitude and ceaseless prayer, Antony was ready to share his secrets with others who sought to follow his way. Many were attracted to his wisdom, and these he encouraged to seek self-denial and the hermetic life. The *Apophthegmata*, a collection of sayings attributed to the desert fathers and mothers, tells this story of Antony's wisdom:

> A brother renounced the world and gave his goods to the poor, but he kept back a little for his personal expenses. He went to see Abba Antony. When he told him this, the old man said to him, "If you want to be a monk, go into the village, buy some meat, cover your naked body with it and come here like that." The brother did so, and the dogs and birds tore at his flesh. When he came back the old man asked him whether he had followed his advice. He showed him his wounded body, and Saint Antony said, "Those who renounce the world but want to keep something for themselves are torn in this way by the demons who make war on them."

Antony also came to the aid of the larger church. When Roman Emperor Diocletian began persecuting Egyptian Christians in 303, word reached the lonesome Antony in his desert cell. He and several other monks traveled to Alexandria and ministered to the persecuted. He was so respected that even the authorities left him alone to evangelize, console, and ease the suffering of the prisoners. In fact, under Maximin he offered himself as a martyr but was refused.

Only one other time did Antony leave his desert solitude. Near the end of Antony's life, Arius (a former deacon in Alexandria) began to spread his heresy that Christ was created, and thus not equal with God. Many Egyptian Christians were swayed by Arian teachings. Athanasius, leader of the church in Alexandria and defender of orthodoxy, called Antony to the Egyptian capital to champion the truth. After preaching, the monk fled the world a last time, returning to his quiet cell. When, at the age of 105, he knew he was near the end of his life, he took two companions with him into the desert to wait for his death. They were ordered to bury his body without a marker so no one could make his grave or relics an object of reverence.

Though Antony was not the first monk, his passion for purity blazed the way for a monastic spirituality. Athanasius's biography became a "best-seller" and inspired thousands to take up the monastic life, which developed into one of the most important institutions in Western history.

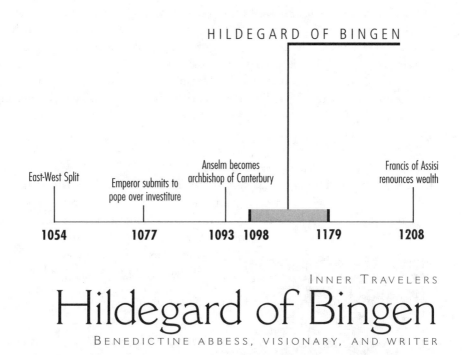

HILDEGARD OF BINGEN

| East-West Split | Emperor submits to pope over investiture | Anselm becomes archbishop of Canterbury | | | Francis of Assisi renounces wealth |
| 1054 | 1077 | 1093 | 1098 | 1179 | 1208 |

INNER TRAVELERS

Hildegard of Bingen

BENEDICTINE ABBESS, VISIONARY, AND WRITER

"A fiery light, flashing intensely, came from the open vault of heaven and poured through my whole brain. Like a flame that is hot without burning it kindled all my heart and all my breast.... Suddenly I could understand."

In one of the earliest manuscripts of Hildegard's works, an illustration shows the abbess seated, tablet in hand; above her head, fiery light streams down, penetrating her mind, bringing visions that illumined her life from childhood.

She believed that not only her visions but also her interpretation of them were from God, and so she announced them with vigor and authority. Though commonly called a mystic, she did not think of these as private illuminations but as prophetic words of God for the church.

Prophetic patterns

She was born to a noble family in Mainz, Germany, in the year that Urban II announced the First Crusade. Medieval Europe had undergone spiritual renewal the previous century, and spiritual enthusiasm hung in the air. Hildegard, the youngest of 10 children, was 8 years old when she was given by her parents as a tithe to God. They entrusted her to Jutta, an anchoress, to be her maid and apprentice. Even at that young age, Hildegard experienced visions of light, but she could not understand what they meant.

When other women joined Jutta and Hildegard, they formed a Benedictine convent, and when Jutta died in 1136, Hildegard became abbess and later moved the community near Bingen, by the Rhine river. For her last 43 years, she cared for these women.

A fiery light

Hildegard received a remarkable vision at age 42: "A fiery light, flashing intensely, came from the open vault of heaven and poured through my whole brain. Like a flame that is hot without burning, it kindled all my heart and all my breast.... Suddenly I could understand."

Hildegard's ministry exploded after that. In addition to recording her visions and their interpretations in books, Hildegard wrote works on medicine and natural science. She composed music and wrote plays.

The most controversial part of her ministry was her several preaching tours around the Rhineland, during which she rebuked church's leaders for spiritual abuses.

Scivias, her best-known work, contains 26 visions with their interpretations. Its name is an abbreviation for *Scito vias Domini*, "Know the ways of the Lord." In it she spoke with a prophet's voice, using the first person, speaking as it were for God.

"I spoke and wrote these things not by the invention of my heart or that of any other person," she said, "but as by the secret mysteries of God; I heard and received them in the heavenly places. And again I heard a voice from heaven saying to me, 'Cry out therefore, and write thus!'"

A unique voice

In spite of her harsh denunciations, Hildegard believed that her "new song must float like a feather on the breath of God." Still, though both Bernard of Clairvaux and Pope Eugenius III recognized her spiritual authenticity, she encountered fierce opposition from other church leaders.

During her last year, her superiors, unhappy with her opposition to local church policies, placed her community under interdict for six months. During that time she and her daughters were denied both the Eucharist and music.

Regardless, Hildegard pursued her ministry until she died: "By a just measure I mark out the ways of good and bad people, and weigh their wills according to what my eye sees of their desires."

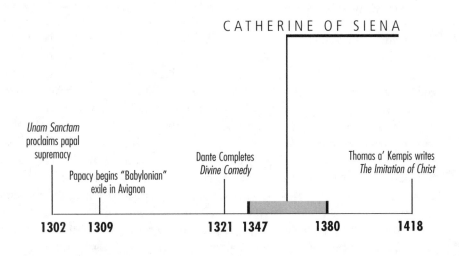

CATHERINE OF SIENA

Unam Sanctam
proclaims papal
supremacy

Papacy begins "Babylonian"
exile in Avignon

Dante Completes
Divine Comedy

Thomas a' Kempis writes
The Imitation of Christ

1302   1309   1321 1347   1380   1418

INNER TRAVELERS

Catherine of Siena

MYSTIC AND POLITICAL ACTIVIST

> "[You are] not to love Me for your own sake, or your neighbor for your own sake, but to love Me for Myself, yourself for Myself, your neighbor for Myself."
> — from a divine vision to Catherine of Siena

As a young girl, Catherine often went to a cave near her home in Siena to meditate, fast, and pray. At about age 7, she claimed to have seen a vision of Jesus with Peter, Paul, and John the evangelist; then she announced to her parents her determination to live a religious life. Convinced of her devotion, they gave her a small room in the basement of their home that acted as a hermitage.

This extraordinary girl blossomed into a no less extraordinary woman whose spiritual, moral, and political efforts had a lasting effect.

Mystical child

Caterina Benincasa's birth into a middle-class Sienese wool dyer's family caused scarcely a ripple; she was the twenty-third of 25 children. Another event that year, a flea full of the *bacillus*

Yersinia pestis entering the Italian port of Messina, brought a tidal wave of disease called the "Black Death." In just three years, 1348 to 1350, more than one-third of Europe died. Baby Catherine survived the onslaught and, in adulthood, saved many plague victims through her compassionate nursing.

After moving into her hermitage, she slept on a board, used a wooden log for a pillow, and meditated on her only spiritual token, a crucifix. She claimed to have received an invisible (for humility) stigmata by which she felt the wounds of Christ. At one time, her parents tried to persuade her to marry, but Catherine was steadfast and at age 15, she cut off her hair to thwart their designs.

Catherine was not satisfied living a contemplative life; she wanted to help the poor and sick. But she did not want to be an ordinary nun. Through the influence of her cousin, a Dominican priest and her first confessor, Catherine joined the Dominican Order of Penance (later known as the Dominican Third Order) in 1363. This "third way" was an organization of religious lay people who lived at home, wore distinctive dress, and directed their own activities in sacrificial service to the poor and sick.

From ages 16 to 19, Catherine continued living a secluded life at home and attracted many followers, who were drawn by her feisty personality and exemplary sanctity. During this time, she learned to read and became familiar with the church fathers, like Gregory the Great and Augustine, as well as popular preachers of the day. At the end of this three-year seclusion, Catherine experienced what she later described as "spiritual marriage" to Christ. In this vision, Jesus placed a ring on her finger, and her soul attained mystical union with God. She called this state an "inner cell in her soul" that sustained her all her life as she traveled and ministered.

Mysticism in action

Catherine began an active ministry to the poor, the sick, and the imprisoned of Siena. When a wave of the plague struck her hometown in 1374, most people fled, but she and her followers stayed to nurse the ill and bury the dead. She was said to be tireless by day and night, healing all of whom the physicians despaired; some even claimed she raised the dead.

When the crisis abated, she embarked on a letter-writing ministry to convert sinners and reform the church and society. Like many reformers of the day, she was disturbed by the rampant corruption of the church, and she believed the source of the problem was the so-called Babylonian Captivity. Because of early fourteenth-century political intrigue, the papacy had moved to Avignon, France. This scandalized people for two reasons: first, the papacy was divorced from the special sanctity of Rome. Second, the popes became increasingly captive to French politics and lifestyle, which were decadent and corrupt.

In a series of letters, Catherine exhorted the pope to address the problems of the church and charged him to return to Rome: "Respond to the Holy Spirit who is calling you! I tell you: Come! Come! Come! Don't wait for time because time isn't waiting for you."

One year later, in 1377, after Catherine had visited with him in Avignon, Gregory XI finally returned to Rome. It was the great moment of her public life.

In her 383 extant letters and *The Dialogue*, which she referred to as "my book" and which describes her mystical experiences, she expressed her driving motivation to love God. She wrote that God told her "not to love Me for your own sake, or your neighbor for your own sake, but to love Me for myself, yourself for Myself, your neighbor for Myself."

At the heart of Catherine's teaching was the image of a bleeding Christ, the Redeemer—ablaze with fiery charity, eager sacrifice, and unqualified forgiveness. And it was not the cross or nails that held Christ to the tree; those were not strong enough to hold the God-Man. It was love that held him there. She records God's words to her: "My son's nailed feet are a stair by which you can climb to his side, where you will see revealed his inmost heart. For when the soul has ... looked with her mind's eye into my son's opened heart, she begins to feel the love of her own heart in his consummate and unspeakable love."

Catherine died in Rome at the age of 33. In 1970 the Roman Catholic Church declared her a doctor of the church, an honor bestowed on only 31 others (and only one other woman).

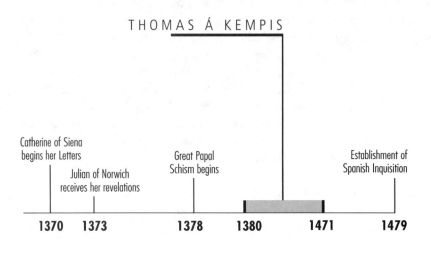

THOMAS Á KEMPIS

| Catherine of Siena begins her Letters | Julian of Norwich receives her revelations | Great Papal Schism begins | Establishment of Spanish Inquisition |

| 1370 | 1373 | 1378 | 1380 | 1471 | 1479 |

Thomas à Kempis

AUTHOR OF THE MOST POPULAR DEVOTIONAL CLASSIC

> *"We must imitate Christ's life and his ways if we are to be truly enlightened and set free from the darkness of our own hearts. Let it be the most important thing we do."*

Sir Thomas More, England's famous lord chancellor under Henry VIII (and subject of the film *A Man for All Seasons*) said it was one of the three books everybody ought to own. Ignatius of Loyola, founder of the Jesuits, read a chapter a day from it and regularly gave away copies as gifts. Methodist founder John Wesley said it was the best summary of the Christian life he had ever read.

They were talking about Thomas à Kempis's *The Imitation of Christ*, the devotional classic that has been translated into over 50 languages, in editions too numerous for scholars to keep track of (by 1779 there were already 1,800 editions).

Little is known of Thomas himself, and he is known for little else—although this one contribution to history seems to be enough.

Humility first

Called the "calamitous century," the fourteenth century into which Thomas Hemerken was born felt the shadow of the apocalypse. Constant wars and repeated bouts of the Black Plague drove population down. The Great Schism tore the church apart, seating one pope in Rome and another in Avignon. In rural areas, roving marauders knew no restraints, and peasant revolts kept urban centers reeling with confusion.

Early on Thomas gave himself to a Dutch Augustinian monastery associated with a group called The Brethren of the Common Life. There he became the prior's assistant, charged with instructing novices in the spiritual life. In that capacity, he wrote four booklets between 1420 and 1427; they were collected and named after the title of the first booklet: *The Imitation of Christ*.

In *The Imitation*, Thomas combines a painfully accurate analysis of the soul with a clear vision of the fullness of the divine life. He does not describe the spiritual life in a linear way, as if one step precedes another, but instead repeats and embellishes themes, like a symphonic composer.

In the first treatise, "Useful reminders for the spiritual life," Thomas lays out the primary requirement for the spiritually serious: "We must imitate Christ's life and his ways if we are to be truly enlightened and set free from the darkness of our own hearts. Let it be the most important thing we do, then, to reflect on the life of Jesus Christ."

The highest virtue, from which all other virtues stem, is humility. Thomas bids all to let go of the illusion of superiority. "If you want to learn something that will really help you, learn to see yourself as God sees you and not as you see yourself in the distorted mirror of your own self-importance," he writes. "This is the greatest and most useful lesson we can learn: to know ourselves for what we truly are, to admit freely our weaknesses and failings, and to hold a humble opinion of ourselves because of them."

Furthermore, humility leads us to embrace the path of suffering: "Plan as you like and arrange everything as best you can, yet you will always encounter some suffering whether you want to or not. Go wherever you will, you will always find the cross.... God wants you to learn to endure troubles without comfort, to submit yourself totally to him, and to become more humble through adversity."

Trust not yourself

Thomas goes on to tell his novices how to handle criticism, failures, sensual desires, and the difficulties of obedience—always with an eye to the paradoxes of the deeper Christian life. For example, in chapter 20 of the first book, he writes, "If you aim at a fervent spiritual life, then you too must turn your back on the crowds as Jesus did. The only man who can safely appear in public is the one who wishes he were at home. He alone can safely speak who prefers to be silent. Only he can safely govern who prefers to live in submission, and only he can safely command who prefers to obey."

The first two treatises are written as sermons or reflections. In the third treatise, "Of Inner Comfort," Jesus and the Disciple talk together about the spiritual life, and in the fourth treatise, "The Book on the Sacrament," Thomas discusses how the Eucharist can help the faithful draw nearer to Christ.

Throughout the book, Thomas's advice is consistent: Do not trust yourself, do not indulge yourself, do not put yourself forward; instead put your full trust in God and, out of love for God's will, yield to all the circumstances of life into which God places you.

The Imitation was published in Latin, French, German, Spanish, Italian, and English by the end of the fifteenth century, and it remains one of the most popular devotional guides to this day.

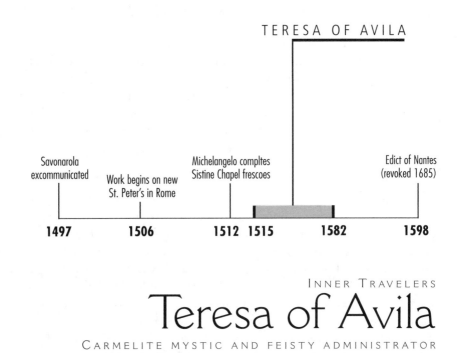

TERESA OF AVILA

Savonarola excommunicated	Work begins on new St. Peter's in Rome	Michelangelo compltes Sistine Chapel frescoes		Edict of Nantes (revoked 1685)
1497	**1506**	**1512 1515**	**1582**	**1598**

INNER TRAVELERS

Teresa of Avila

CARMELITE MYSTIC AND FEISTY ADMINISTRATOR

"Whoever has not begun the practice of prayer, I beg for the love of the Lord not to go without so great a good. There is nothing here to fear but only something to desire."

The first 40 years of Teresa's life gave no clue to the rich depth and productivity of the second half of her life. Born Teresa de Cepeda y Ahumada in central Spain, she spent her early years with her family, giving herself to the duties of extended family life. At age 21, against her father's wishes, she professed vows as a Carmelite at the Spanish Convent of the Incarnation in Avila.

Still, according to her own account, she waffled spiritually. The convent was known for its leniency, for example, permitting relationships with those outside the convent and allowing worldly possessions within. Teresa, enjoying the convent's indulgences, waned in her devotion. Then a serious, prolonged illness (and partial paralysis from an attempted cure) forced her to spend three years in relative quiet, during which time she read books on the spiritual life. When she recovered and returned to the convent she resumed what to her later seemed only a half-hearted spirituality. Of these years, she wrote in her *Autobiography*, "I voyaged on this tempestuous sea for almost 20 years with these fallings and risings."

Then one day while walking down a hallway in the convent, her glance fell on a statue of the wounded Christ, and the vision of his constant love throughout her inconstancy pierced her heart. Gently but powerfully, she said Jesus began to break down her defenses and reveal to her the cause of her spiritual exhaustion: her dalliance with the delights of sin.

She immediately broke with her past, undergoing a final conversion. After this, she began experiencing profound mystical raptures, though these soon passed. For the rest of her life, she gave herself completely to her spiritual growth and the renewal of the Carmelite monasteries.

A spiritual legacy

Teresa dreamed of establishing convents where young women could pursue deep lives of deep prayer and devotion. She once wrote, "Whoever has not begun the practice of prayer, I beg for the love of the Lord not to go without so great a good. There is nothing here to fear but only something to desire." Teresa spent days on end traveling the countryside establishing reformed (or "Discalced," meaning "unshod," that is, more simple) Carmelite convents. She convinced John of the Cross to join her in this work.

Her success as an administrator and reformer (she founded 14 monasteries) was due in part to her natural leadership gifts, her tenacity in the face of adversity (especially from older Carmelites who resented her reforms), and a keen sense of humor. Once when praying about her many trials and sufferings, she thought she heard God say, "But this is how I treat my friends." Teresa replied, "No wonder you have so few friends."

Yet it is her gift of spiritual direction, practiced personally with nuns and publicly in her writings, for which she is known today.

She was hesitant to put her insights to paper and had to be ordered by her superiors to do so. Thankfully for later generations, she obeyed: her three works, *Autobiography*, *Way of Perfection*, and *Interior Castle*, contain some of the most profound insights into the spiritual life ever written.

To take one example, considered by many her masterpiece: *Interior Castle* describes the soul as a "castle made entirely of diamond or of a very clear crystal, in which there are many rooms." Some are above, some below, some to the sides, "and in the very center and middle is the main dwelling place where the very secret exchanges between God and the soul take place." Teresa wanted to teach her readers how to enter this castle, that is, how to pray, so that they might commune more intimately with God.

For Teresa, prayer is the source of Christian life and the wellspring of all moral virtues. Prayer is not everything, but without prayer, nothing else is possible. By prayer does the soul enter the Castle, and by prayer does the soul continue the journey. Under this umbrella of prayer, God works, in mysterious, often unpredictable ways, and the soul works strongly. Without the soul's active compliance, God will not move (though human effort cannot do what God alone must do).

From the First Dwelling Place, where the soul begins to pray, to the Seventh Dwelling

Place, where the soul, united to God, finds both perfect peace and deepest suffering, the person builds on prayer and the progressive disengagement from the things of this world. But unlike her partner in reform, John of the Cross, Teresa's understanding of disengagement is not ascetic. On the contrary, for Teresa true suffering comes from being in the world and serving others. Spiritual progress is measured neither by self-imposed penance nor by the sweetest pleasures of mystical experiences but by growth in constant love for others and an increasing desire within for the will of God.

This love for her sisters and brothers and this union with the will of God compelled Teresa onward in constant efforts. To someone who encouraged her to rest, she once said, "Rest, indeed! I need no rest; what I need is crosses." In her last years, her health suffered, as did her reputation with church authorities, who sought to restrict her influence. On yet another mission of service, her body exhausted, Teresa died reciting verses from the Song of Songs.

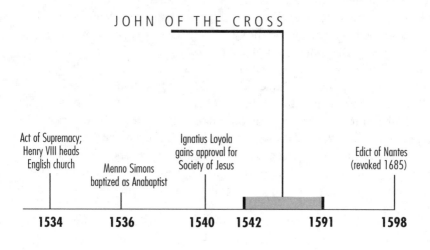

JOHN OF THE CROSS

Act of Supremacy; Henry VIII heads English church		Ignatius Loyola gains approval for Society of Jesus		Edict of Nantes (revoked 1685)
	Menno Simons baptized as Anabaptist			
1534	1536	1540	1542	1591	1598

INNER TRAVELERS

John of the Cross

SPANISH MYSTIC OF THE SOUL'S DARK NIGHT

> *"Turn not to the easiest, but to the most difficult ... not to the more, but to the less; not towards what is high and precious, but to what is low and despised; not towards desiring anything, but to desiring nothing."*

Spain's Siglo de Oro was indeed a "golden century," a time remembered for its artists, playwrights, novelists, poets, and explorers—the names Cervantes, Vega, and Cortez are but three of the most famous. One undersized, narrow-minded friar who spent most of his energy on reforming yet another religious order could easily be overlooked. But today John of the Cross, as he came to be called, is remembered as one of history's most influential spiritual guides.

Taking the harder road

Juan de Yepes, his name at birth, failed at a variety of trades before entering first the local Jesuit school and then the University of Salamanca, where he pursued holy orders. There he met Teresa of Avila, who persuaded him to join her to reform the

Carmelite order.

Believing that struggle and suffering, which such reform would likely entail, were necessary for spiritual growth, Juan entered the Carmelite Order in 1568 as Fray Juan de la Cruz, Friar John of the Cross. And a life of the cross it was, as John intended: "Turn not to the easiest, but to the most difficult ... not to the more, but to the less; not towards what is high and precious, but to what is low and despised; not towards desiring anything, but to desiring nothing."

John allowed himself no respite from suffering, but heaped it upon himself with long fasting and whippings. If that were not enough, he was also severely criticized and ignored when he exhorted his fellow friars to give up their comforts, freedoms, and pleasures.

Imprisonment and creativity

In 1577 church authorities, resentful of John, had him kidnapped, and he was imprisoned for nine months in a windowless six-by-ten-foot cell, with a ceiling so low he couldn't stand up. The stone cell was unheated in winter, unventilated in summer. Malnourished and flogged weekly, John was constantly ill.

Yet it was during this dark time that, by the light of a three-inch hole high in the wall, John wrote his two greatest poems, "Cantico Espiritual" (Spiritual Canticle, 1578) and "Noche Oscura del Alma" (Dark Night of the Soul). These two extraordinary pieces illumined both his own darkness and the mystery of his path, which many people since have followed.

After escaping, John spent eight months recuperating and writing *Ascent of Mt. Carmel,* the prose commentaries on his poetry that explained the mystic way.

Ascending to God

For John, the mystic path meant living with an all-consuming desire more fully to know and love God, abandoning everything that did not contribute to that communion. God illuminates the individual who, in consequence, has the desire and power to shed the illusions of this world. These illusions include the messages of the senses, which distort the reality of union with God.

In his poem "Dark Night," John extols the value of extinguishing everything but the desire for God:

One dark night, fired with love's urgent longings—ah, the sheer grace!—
I went out unseen, my house being now all stilled.

In darkness, and secure, by the secret ladder, disguised—ah, the sheer grace!—
in darkness and concealment, my house being now all stilled.

On that glad night, in secret, for no one saw me,
Nor did I look at anything, with no other light or guide than the one that burned in my heart

This guided me more surely than the light of noon
To where he was awaiting me—him I knew so well—there in a place where no one
appeared

O guiding night! O night more lovely than the dawn!
O night that has united the Lover with his beloved, transforming the beloved in her Lover.

Upon my flowering breast, which I kept wholly for him alone,
There he lay sleeping, and I caressing him there in a breeze from the fanning cedars.
When the breeze blew from the turret, as I parted his hair,
It wounded my neck with its gentle hand, suspending all my senses.
I abandoned and forgot myself, laying my face on my Beloved.
All things ceased; I went out from myself, leaving my cares forgotten among the lilies.

This first step in knowing God is called purification: the speaker slips away from the silenced house—the passionate flesh. The soul is then readied for the second stage, illumination, a blissful state characterized by a heightened awareness of the presence of God and an enjoyment of his gifts. Nevertheless, as delightful as God's gifts are, they are not God himself, and anything short of the fullness of God is not enough.

To go further on the way requires another purification, one of the spirit; this process is what is called the "Dark Night of the Soul," or the "wounded neck" and "suspended senses." The mystic feels an absolute loss of God, a sense that the sun has been completely obliterated. Desolation and despair are the usual emotions. Yet no matter how long the emptiness continues, the soul clings to God, for this "spiritual crucifixion" is necessary: one must learn to seek God for God's sake, not for the sake of the happiness God brings. Only then can one enjoy perfect union with God.

John spent another decade championing reform before retiring to a small village whose prior disliked John and who treated him shamefully (it seems John chose this particular village deliberately). He finally succumbed to a severe infection in his right foot.

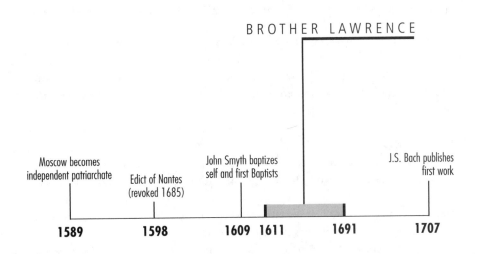

BROTHER LAWRENCE

Moscow becomes independent patriarchate	Edict of Nantes (revoked 1685)	John Smyth baptizes self and first Baptists			J.S. Bach publishes first work
1589	1598	1609	1611	1691	1707

INNER TRAVELERS

Brother Lawrence
PRACTITIONER OF GOD'S PRESENCE

"It is enough for me to pick up but a straw from the ground for the love of God."

In tumultuous seventeenth-century France, with its power struggles, debts, and perpetual unrest, lived several spiritual luminaries whose wisdom still guides people today. Francis de Sales, Blaise Pascal, Madame Guyon, and Francois Fenelon all pursued an inner path of devotion to Jesus that shed light on both their world and ours.

Of all the shining lights of that century, though, none speak with the simplicity and humble grace of one lay monk whose quiet presence resided in the heart of turbulent Paris. More than any other of his day, Brother Lawrence understood the holiness available within the common business of life.

Most of what is known about Brother Lawrence comes through the efforts of Abbe de Beaufort, the Cardinal de Noailles's envoy and investigator. By 1666 Brother Lawrence's unusual wisdom had caught the cardinal's attention, and Beaufort was directed to interview the lowly kitchen aide. Upon ascertaining that Beaufort's interest was genuine, and not politically motivated, Brother Lawrence granted four interviews, "conversations," in which he describes his way of life and how he came to it.

Besides these recorded thoughts, Lawrence's fellow monks found in his personal effects several pages of *Maxims*, the only organized written material Brother Lawrence left. These, the conversations (now entitled *The Practice of the Presence of God*) and 16 letters represent Lawrence's full teaching.

God is in the kitchen

He began life as Nicholas Herman, born to peasant parents in Lorraine, France. As a young man, his poverty forced him into joining the army, and thus he was guaranteed meals and a small stipend. During this period, Herman had an experience that set him on a unique spiritual journey; it wasn't, characteristically, a supernatural vision, but a supernatural clarity into a common sight.

In the deep of winter, Herman looked at a barren tree, stripped of leaves and fruit, waiting silently and patiently for the sure hope of summer abundance. Gazing at the tree, Herman grasped for the first time the extravagance of God's grace and the unfailing sovereignty of divine providence. Like the tree, he himself was seemingly dead, but God had life waiting for him, and the turn of seasons would bring fullness. At that moment, he said, that leafless tree "first flashed in upon my soul the fact of God," and a love for God that never after ceased to burn. Sometime later, an injury forced his retirement from the army, and after a stint as a footman, he sought a place where he could suffer for his failures. He thus entered the Discalced Carmelite monastery in Paris as Brother Lawrence.

He was assigned to the monastery kitchen where, amidst the tedious chores of cooking and cleaning at the constant bidding of his superiors, he developed his rule of spirituality and work. In his *Maxims*, Lawrence writes, "Men invent means and methods of coming at God's love, they learn rules and set up devices to remind them of that love, and it seems like a world of trouble to bring oneself into the consciousness of God's presence. Yet it might be so simple. Is it not quicker and easier just to do our common business wholly for the love of him?"

For Brother Lawrence, "common business," no matter how mundane or routine, was the medium of God's love. The issue was not the sacredness or worldly status of the task but the motivation behind it. "Nor is it needful that we should have great things to do.... We can do little things for God; I turn the cake that is frying on the pan for love of him, and that done, if there is nothing else to call me, I prostrate myself in worship before him, who has given me grace to work; afterwards I rise happier than a king. It is enough for me to pick up but a straw from the ground for the love of God."

Brother Lawrence retreated to a place in his heart where the love of God made every detail of his life of surpassing value. "I began to live as if there were no one save God and me in the world." Together, God and Brother Lawrence cooked meals, ran errands, scrubbed pots, and endured the scorn of the world.

He admitted that the path to this perfect union was not easy. He spent years disciplining his heart and mind to yield to God's presence. "As often as I could, I placed myself as a worshiper before him, fixing my mind upon his holy presence, recalling it when I found it wandering from him. This proved to be an exercise frequently painful, yet I persisted through all difficulties."

Only when he reconciled himself to the thought that this struggle and longing was his destiny did he find a new peace: his soul "had come to its own home and place of rest." There he spent the rest of his 80 years, dying in relative obscurity and pain and perfect joy.

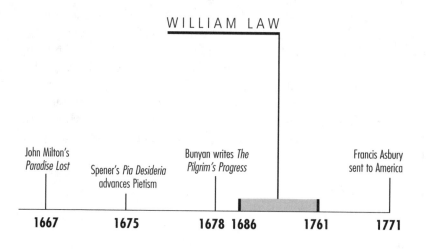

WILLIAM LAW

John Milton's Paradise Lost	Spener's *Pia Desideria* advances Pietism	Bunyan writes *The Pilgrim's Progress*		Francis Asbury sent to America
1667	**1675**	**1678 1686**	**1761**	**1771**

INNER TRAVELERS

William Law

CHAMPION OF THE SERIOUS, DEVOUT, AND HOLY LIFE

> "He therefore is a devout man who lives no longer to his own will, or the way and spirit of the world, but to the sole will of God, who considers God in everything, who serves God in everything, who makes all the parts of his common life parts of piety by doing everything in the name of God."

From a professional perspective, William Law's life seemed to be over when he was 28 years old. Son of a prosperous businessman, Law had received an excellent education at Cambridge and had a solid future as a scholar or clergyman ahead of him. Then Queen Anne died without an heir. On the ascension of the German George I to the English throne, Law refused to swear an oath of allegiance. As a "nonjuror," Law was forced to give up his fellowship and was denied further advancement in the Church of England or in any academic institution.

The outer structure of his life to his death 47 years later is easily told. For many years, he served as tutor to Edward Gibbons, father of the renowned historian. When Edward left home, Law retired to his family home where he devoted his life to writing. Celibate, rigorous, and solitary, Law honed his writing skills.

Rules for living

As a young adult preparing for university studies, Law had written a list of 18 rules to guide his living. They included the commitment to the will of God, the primacy of Scripture, the value of time, a distrust of the world, temperance in all things, humility and charity, prayer, and constant self-examination.

Clearly Law was not a product of his age. Catholic, Anglican, and Puritan factions warred within the English church. Morality and piety were correct in form but devoid of spiritual passion in many quarters. Many found "philosophical religion"—deism or rationalism—more to their liking. Law would have none of it. Regarding "philosophical religion," for example, he said, "There can be no such thing. Religion is the most plain, simple thing in the world. It is only, 'We love him, because he first loved us.' So far as you add philosophy to religion, just so far you spoil it."

Law's writings aimed at uncovering shallow devotion and stirring up readers to renewed moral vigor and holiness. Some writings were responses to published works; others were more broadly addressed, such as *The Absolute Unlawfulness of Stage Entertainment*. But most of his works were in the area of Christian spirituality, which he refused to relegate to a comfortable corner of life.

William Law's most widely known book, *A Serious Call to a Devout and Holy Life*, pulls together many of his thoughts in a lucid work addressed to the "average" Christian. It challenged Christians to wake up from their spiritual stupor and apply all their energy to the holy life: "He therefore is a devout man who lives no longer to his own will, or the way and spirit of the world, but to the sole will of God, who considers God in everything, who serves God in everything, who makes all the parts of his common life parts of piety by doing everything in the name of God."

Law used fictional characters to make his points. For example, "Julius," though he is "fearful of missing his prayers," is a "companion of the silliest people in their most silly pleasures," and for "Claudius ... every hour of the day is with him an hour of business, and though he eats and drinks very heartily, yet every meal seems to be in a hurry, and he would say grace if he had time." These portraits teach that every aspect of the Christian's life—relationships, business endeavors, family matters, leisure, dress—should be shaped by unwavering devotion.

"As a good Christian should consider every place as holy," he wrote, "so he should look upon every part of his life as a matter of holiness.... Everything that lives must all with one spirit live wholly to the praise and glory of this one God and Father of them all. This is the common business of all persons in this world."

In his later years, Law, influenced by German mysticism, produced *The Spirit of Prayer* and *The Spirit of Love*, which emphasized the indwelling of Christ in the soul. (This, however, alienated some, like John Wesley, who had up to this time eagerly followed his work.) The day before he died, he said, "Oh what hast thou done? Thou has awakened such a spark of divine love that quite devours me. Who would have thought that all my life should end in my dying a martyr to love!"

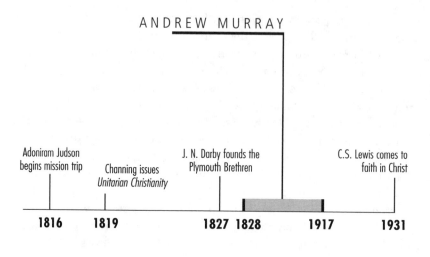

ANDREW MURRAY

| Adoniram Judson begins mission trip | Channing issues Unitarian Christianity | J. N. Darby founds the Plymouth Brethren | | C.S. Lewis comes to faith in Christ |

1816   **1819**   **1827 1828**   **1917**   **1931**

INNER TRAVELERS

Andrew Murray

LEADING STUDENT IN CHRIST'S SCHOOL OF PRAYER

> *"May not a single moment of my life be spent outside the light, love, and joy of God's presence."*

As a young man, Andrew Murray wanted to be a minister, but it was a career choice rather than an act of faith. Not until he had finished his general studies and begun his theological training, in the Netherlands, did he experience a conversion of heart. In a letter to his parents, Murray wrote, "Your son has been born again.... I have cast myself on Christ."

This "casting of the self" became Murray's life theme. Sixty years of ministry in the Dutch Reformed Church of South Africa, more than 200 books and tracts on Christian spirituality and ministry, extensive social work, and the founding of educational institutions—all these were outward signs of the inward grace that Murray experienced by continually casting himself on Christ.

"May not a single moment of my life be spent outside the light, love, and joy of God's presence," was his prayer. "And not a moment without the entire surrender of myself as a vessel for him to fill full of his Spirit and his love."

School of prayer

At age 21, Murray received his first appointment as the only minister in the Orange River Sovereignty, a 50,000-square-mile territory in remote South Africa. Constant travel to distant parishes and outreach to the unevangelized soon depleted his strength. A bout of illness so weakened him, he was forced to return to England for rest.

When he returned to South Africa, he took a position in Worcester, where he became involved with the newly opened Theological Seminary of Stellenbosch. His passion for Christian education prompted him to found a succession of institutions, such as the Bible and Prayer Union (which encouraged Bible study and prayer) and the Huguenot Seminary, where young women could prepare for educational work.

From Worcester, Murray accepted a more prestigious preaching position in Cape Town and then, seven years later, the pastorate of a church in Wellington, a more rural parish. Here Murray honed his preaching skills and led a holiness revival (historian Walter Hollenweger considers Murray a forerunner of Pentecostalism). Through his preaching and writing, Murray slowly became an international figure.

Murray wrote to interpret the Scriptures in such a way that Christians were free to believe and experience the grace of God. He believed that God had done everything necessary for people to live rich, productive, meaningful lives that participated in the life of God. The obstacles to such lives included half-hearted surrender to God, a lack of confidence in the anointing of the Spirit, and a deep-rooted skepticism about the power of prayer.

One of his most popular books, *With Christ in the School of Prayer*, takes New Testament teachings about prayer and illumines them in 31 "lessons" designed to help the reader move past shallow, ineffectual prayer into a fuller understanding of the work God has called them to do. According to Murray, the church does not realize that "God rules the world by the prayers of his saints, that prayer is the power by which Satan is conquered, that by prayer the church on earth has disposal of the powers of the heavenly world."

He strove to align his spiritual insights with his Reformed theology, but he was accused by Reformed critics of teaching free will and that God wills the redemption of all.

In the face of criticism, though, Murray insisted that the believer can expect to receive the fullness of the Spirit. As Murray put it, "I must be filled; it is absolutely necessary. I may be filled; God has made it blessedly possible. I would be filled; it is eminently desirable. I will be filled; it is so blessedly certain."

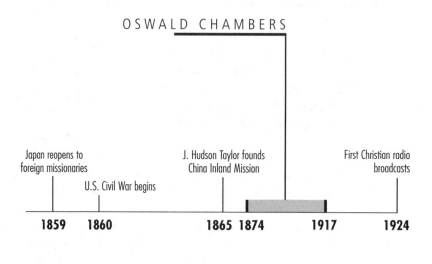

OSWALD CHAMBERS

Japan reopens to foreign missionaries	U.S. Civil War begins	J. Hudson Taylor founds China Inland Mission		First Christian radio broadcasts
1859	**1860**	**1865 1874**	**1917**	**1924**

INNER TRAVELERS

Oswald Chambers

PREACHER WHO GAVE HIS UTMOST

> *"The great word of Jesus to his disciples is abandon. When God has brought us into the relationship of disciples, we have to venture on his word; trust entirely to him and watch that when he brings us to the venture, we take it."*

"I feel I shall be buried for a time, hidden away in obscurity; then suddenly I shall flame out, do my work, and be gone." So wrote 22-year-old Oswald Chambers as he began his long preparation in a remote Scottish town before being thrust into the world as a preacher. He was partially right; after 15 years of public ministry, Chambers died suddenly at age 43. But he remains far from gone—his devotional *My Utmost for His Highest* (sermons published posthumously, like nearly 50 other devotionals bearing his name) remains one of the most popular devotional guides ever printed.

Portrait of an artist

Born as a Baptist preacher's son in Aberdeen, Scotland, Chambers converted under the preaching of Charles Spurgeon. In his twenties, he sought to portray the message of God's redemption in art, studying technique in London and Edinburgh.

Gradually Chambers began to believe God wanted him not to pursue the arts for God's sake, but God for the sake of his will alone. As he later wrote, "It takes me a long while to realize that God has no respect for anything I bring him. All he wants from me is unconditional surrender."

His decision led him to Dunoon College, a small, interdenominational theological school. It wasn't long before Chambers himself began to believe, like family members and his artist colleagues, he was foolish—or insane. During those "four years of hell on earth," Chambers continued his work but inside felt overcome by an acute vision of his own depravity and the powerlessness of his faith.

The experience brought Chambers to the brink of spiritual desperation. He threw himself completely on Jesus' promise that God would give his Spirit to those who ask. The struggle was instantly over. Chambers later described the restult: "Glory be to God, the last aching abyss of the human heart is filled to overflowing with the love of God."

A brief, shining light

Soon after his "spiritual emancipation," Chambers became much in demand as an itinerant speaker and teacher through the revivalistic League of Prayer.

Because Chambers believed that spiritual mediocrity was often the result of mental lethargy, he opened the Bible Training College with the League in 1911. When World War I interrupted academic life, Chambers enlisted as a chaplain to the armed forces. In October 1915, he proceeded to Zeitoun, Egypt, where he and his wife evangelized soldiers.

Whether speaking to soldiers or students, Chambers called his listeners to live aggressively for God. God's will, he said, can be found in any circumstance of life, so long as individuals are willing to have a personal relationship with Christ and completely abandon themselves to him. "The great word of Jesus to his disciples is *abandon*," he wrote. "When God has brought us into the relationship of disciples, we have to venture on his word; trust entirely to him and watch that when he brings us to the venture, we take it."

His utmost

A ruptured appendix and consequent complications cut Chambers's life short in late 1917. It seemed an unbelievably tragic end to a life of promise. But it wasn't the end. His wife, whose ambition to become secretary to England's prime minister prompted her to acquire an astonishing skill at shorthand, transcribed and published Chambers's lectures. She sent them in pamphlet form to many soldiers to whom Chambers had ministered, as well as to past students. Soon she gathered the material into book form and, in 1927, she first published *My Utmost for His Highest*.

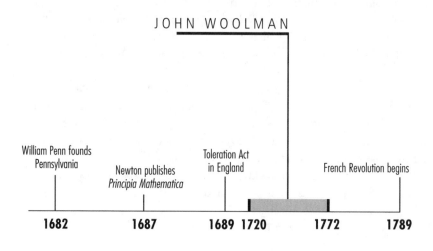

JOHN WOOLMAN

William Penn founds Pennsylvania

Newton publishes *Principia Mathematica*

Toleration Act in England

French Revolution begins

| 1682 | 1687 | 1689 | 1720 | 1772 | 1789 |

ACTIVISTS

John Woolman

QUAKER MYSTIC AND ABOLITIONIST

> "About the twenty-third year of my age, I had many fresh and heavenly openings, in respect to the care and providence of the Almighty over his creation in general, and over man as the most noble amongst those which are visible."

Two years before his death, John Woolman had a dream in which he heard an angel announce, "John Woolman is dead." When he awoke, he pondered what the dream meant. Then he said, "At length I felt divine power prepare my mouth that I could speak, and then I said, 'I am crucified with Christ, nevertheless I live yet not I, but Christ liveth in me.'"

He wrote in his journal, "I perceived ... that language 'John Woolman is dead' meant no more than the death of my own will."

Such dreams and spiritual insights were characteristic of Woolman, who is remembered today as one of America's first abolitionists and most profound mystics.

Woolman was born into a devout Quaker family who lived in a small New Jersey Quaker village. Spiritual experiences came early: "Before I was 7 years old," he later wrote in his journal, "I began to be acquainted with the operations of Divine Love."

At age 21, he was hired out to a merchant, and two years later, began having more spiritual experiences, which he called "openings": "About the twenty-third year of my age, I had many fresh and heavenly openings, in respect to the care and providence of the Almighty over his creation in general, and over man as the most noble amongst those which are visible."

This new appreciation was soon tested when his employer asked him to write up a bill of sale for a black female. Woolman objected, telling his employer he believed "slave keeping to be a practice inconsistent with the Christian religion." Since he also felt duty-bound to honor his master, he did as he was told. But his conscience remained uneasy, and the next time he was asked to write a slave bill of sale, he flatly refused.

Desiring independence, he took up tailoring. Because he felt called to public ministry, he deliberately chose a profession that wouldn't demand an inordinate amount of time. Within a few years, when his business began to prosper, he encouraged customers to go to competitors: "For though my natural inclination was towards merchandise," he wrote, "yet I believed Truth required me to live more free from outward cumbers."

By this time, around age 36 (when he began his journal, a document of his inner journey), he had married. He had also taken two important journeys through the American South, which convinced him more than ever that slavery was "a dark gloominess hanging over the Land," and had predicted "in future consequence will be grievous to posterity."

In 1754 and 1762 respectively, he published the first and second parts of *Some Considerations on the Keeping of Negroes*, in which he argued for the connection between Christianity and freedom. The idea that men and women are created equal in the image of God leads directly to "an idea of general brotherhood and a disposition easy to be touched with a feeling of each other's afflictions."

His concern about the "extreme oppression of many slaves" also translated into concern for Native Americans. He visited Indian villages on the Pennsylvania frontier and supported Moravian missionary attempts; he sought to curtail the sale of rum to the Indians and worked for a more just Indian land policy.

Woolman maintained a strict manner of life, traveling by foot whenever possible. He wore undyed garments (because he was told dyes were produced by slave labor) and generally abstained from the use of any product connected with the slave trade. Eventually he refused hospitality in homes of slaveholders because he recognized that the luxury the family enjoyed was due to slavery.

His views on slavery were not only unusual for whites in his day, but even unusual among his fellow Quakers. He is a large reason American Quakers abandoned slaveholding voluntarily within 25 years of his death. His method was moral persuasion backed up by consistent practice.

In 1758, for example, he preached a sermon against slavery in a rural community between Philadelphia and Baltimore. He was then taken to the home of Thomas Woodward for dinner. When Woolman determined that the "Negro servants" were actually slaves, he quietly slipped out of the house without saying a word. The owner's conscience was so troubled, the next morning he vowed to liberate his slaves.

In 1772 Woolman visited England to preach, and characteristically he traveled by steerage as a testimony against class distinction. The relatively wealthy and proud London Quakers were at first cool toward the rustic New Jersey preacher, but his sincerity and spiritual maturity eventually won them over. But within a few months of his arrival, he died, at age 52, and was buried in England.

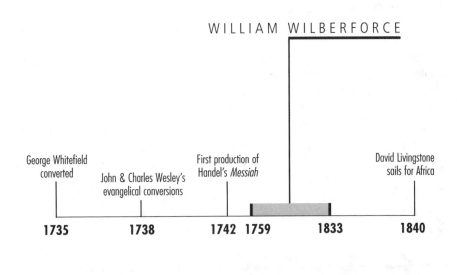

WILLIAM WILBERFORCE

| George Whitefield converted | John & Charles Wesley's evangelical conversions | First production of Handel's *Messiah* | | David Livingstone sails for Africa |

| 1735 | 1738 | 1742 1759 | 1833 | 1840 |

ACTIVISTS

William Wilberforce

ANTISLAVERY POLITICIAN

"So enormous, so dreadful, so irremediable did the [slave] trade's wickedness appear that my own mind was completely made up for abolition. Let the consequences be what they would: I from this time determined that I would never rest until I had effected its abolition."

In the late 1700s, when William Wilberforce was a teenager, English traders raided the African coast on the Gulf of Guinea, captured between 35,000 and 50,000 Africans a year, shipped them across the Atlantic, and sold them into slavery. It was a profitable business that many powerful people had become dependent upon. One publicist for the West Indies trade wrote, "The impossibility of doing without slaves in the West Indies will always prevent this traffic being dropped. The necessity, the absolute necessity, then, of carrying it on, must, since there is no other, be its excuse."

By the late 1700s, the economics of slavery were so entrenched that only a handful of people thought anything could be done about it. That handful included William Wilberforce.

Taking on a purpose

This would have surprised those who knew Wilberforce as a young man. He grew up surrounded by wealth. He was a native of Hull and educated at St. John's College at Cambridge. But he wasn't a serious student. He later reflected, "As much pains were taken to make me idle as were ever taken to make me studious." A neighbor at Cambridge added, "When he [Wilberforce] returned late in the evening to his rooms, he would summon me to join him.... He was so winning and amusing that I often sat up half the night with him, much to the detriment of my attendance at lectures the next day."

Yet Wilberforce had political ambitions and, with his connections, managed to win election to Parliament in 1780, where he formed a lasting friendship with William Pitt, the future prime minister. But he later admitted, "The first years in Parliament I did nothing—nothing to any purpose. My own distinction was my darling object."

But he began to reflect deeply on his life, which led to a period of intense sorrow. "I am sure that no human creature could suffer more than I did for some months," he later

wrote. His unnatural gloom lifted on Easter 1786, "amidst the general chorus with which all nature seems on such a morning to be swelling the song of praise and thanksgiving." He had experienced a spiritual rebirth.

He abstained from alcohol and practiced rigorous self-examination as befit, he believed, a "serious" Christian. He abhorred the socializing that went along with politicking. He worried about "the temptations at the table," the endless dinner parties, which he thought were full of vain and useless conversation: "[They] disqualify me for every useful purpose in life, waste my time, impair my health, fill my mind with thoughts of resistance before and self-condemnation afterwards."

He began to see his life's purpose: "My walk is a public one," he wrote in his diary. "My business is in the world, and I must mix in the assemblies of men or quit the post which Providence seems to have assigned me."

In particular, two causes caught his attention. First, under the influence of Thomas Clarkson, he became absorbed with the issue of slavery. Later he wrote, "So enormous, so dreadful, so irremediable did the trade's wickedness appear that my own mind was completely made up for abolition. Let the consequences be what they would: I from this time determined that I would never rest until I had effected its abolition."

Wilberforce was initially optimistic, even naively so. He expressed "no doubt" about his chances of quick success. As early as 1789, he and Clarkson managed to have 12 resolutions against the slave trade introduced—only to be outmaneuvered on fine legal points. The pathway to abolition was blocked by vested interests, parliamentary filibustering, entrenched bigotry, international politics, slave unrest, personal sickness, and political fear. Other bills introduced by Wilberforce were defeated in 1791, 1792, 1793, 1797, 1798, 1799, 1804, and 1805.

When it became clear that Wilberforce was not going to let the issue die, pro-slavery forces targeted him. He was vilified; opponents spoke of "the damnable doctrine of Wilberforce and his hypocritical allies." The opposition became so fierce, one friend feared that one day he would read about Wilberforce's being "carbonated [broiled] by Indian planters, barbecued by African merchants, and eaten by Guinea captains."

Prime minister of philanthropy

Slavery was only one cause that excited Wilberforce's passions. His second great calling was for the "reformation of manners," that is, morals. In early 1787, he conceived of a society that would work, as a royal proclamation put it, "for the encouragement of piety and virtue; and for the preventing of vice, profaneness, and immorality." It eventually become known as the Society for the Suppression of Vice.

In fact, Wilberforce—dubbed "the prime minister of a cabinet of philanthropists"—was at one time active in support of 69 philanthropic causes. He gave away one-quarter of his annual income to the poor. He fought on behalf of chimney sweeps, single mothers, Sunday schools, orphans, and juvenile delinquents. He helped found parachurch groups like the Society for Bettering the Cause of the Poor, the Church Missionary Society, the British and Foreign Bible Society, and the Antislavery Society.

In 1797, he settled at Clapham, where he became a prominent member of the "Clapham Sect," a group of devout Christians of influence in government and business. That same year he wrote *Practical View of the Prevailing Religious System of Professed Christians*—a scathing critique of comfortable Christianity that became a bestseller.

All this in spite of the fact that poor health plagued him his entire life, sometimes keeping him bedridden for weeks. During one such time in his late twenties, he wrote, "[I] am still a close prisoner, wholly unequal even to such a little business as I am now engaged in: add to which my eyes are so bad that I can scarce see how to direct my pen."

He survived this and other bouts of debilitating illness with the help of opium, a new drug at the time, the affects of which were still unknown. Wilberforce soon became addicted, though opium's hallucinatory powers terrified him, and the depressions it caused virtually crippled him at times.

When healthy, however, he was a persistent and effective politician, partly due to his natural charm and partly to his eloquence. His antislavery efforts finally bore fruit in 1807: Parliament abolished the slave trade in the British Empire. He then worked to ensure the slave trade laws were enforced and, finally, that slavery in the British Empire was abolished. Wilberforce's health prevented him from leading the last charge, though he heard three days before he died that the final passage of the emancipation bill was ensured in committee.

Though some historians argue that Thomas Clarkson and others were just as important in the antislavery fight, Wilberforce in any account played a key role in, as historian G.M. Trevelyan put it, "one of the turning events in the history of the world."

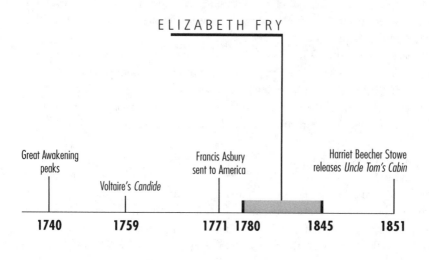

ELIZABETH FRY

Great Awakening peaks	Voltaire's *Candide*	Francis Asbury sent to America		Harriet Beecher Stowe releases *Uncle Tom's Cabin*	
1740	1759	1771	1780	1845	1851

ACTIVISTS

Elizabeth Fry

PRISON REFORMER

"... to form in them, as much as possible, those habits of sobriety, order, and industry, which may render them docile and peaceable while in prison, and respectable when they leave it."

In the early 1800s, English prisons were pits of indecency and brutality. The idea was to punish, not reform prisoners. Most people thought this was the way things should be or believed nothing could be done to change the entrenched system. Elizabeth Fry disagreed on both accounts and pushed for a number of prison reforms we still practice today.

Horrifying conditions

The daughter of an English banker, the 20-year-old Elizabeth married Joseph Fry, a wealthy tea dealer. Children came quickly, eventually numbering 11. When she had rededicated her life to Christ at age 18, she wanted to help the downtrodden. So as a young bride and mother, she gave medicine and clothes to the homeless and helped establish the Sisters of Devonshire Square, a nursing school. In 1813, at age 33, her attention turned to the female prisoners in London's Newgate prison. She began to visit the prison almost daily, and what she found there horrified her.

At Newgate, women awaiting trial for stealing apples were crammed into the same cell as women who had been convicted of murder or forgery (both capital crimes). Women ate, defecated, and slept in the same confined area. If an inmate had children, they accompanied her to prison and lived in the same inhumane conditions. For those without help from family, friends, or charities, the options were to beg and to steal food, or to starve to death. Many women begged for alcohol as well, languishing naked and drunk. The sight of children clinging to their mothers as they were dragged to the gallows was a scene replayed time and again.

Better life for inmates

Prison officials warned Fry of the risks she was taking in visiting prisons (exposure to violence and disease), but she waved the warnings aside. Besides comforting women, she taught them basic hygiene and to sew and quilt (so they might earn a living when they were released). She read the Bible to inmates and gave Bibles away. She intervened for women on death row, and if her pleas were unsuccessful, she accompanied women to the scaffold and comforted them in their last moments.

To expand her efforts, in 1816 she founded the Association for the Improvement of the Female Prisoners of Newgate "to provide for the clothing, instruction, and employment of the women; to introduce them to a knowledge of the Holy Scriptures, and to form in them, as much as possible, those habits of sobriety, order, and industry, which may render them docile and peaceable while in prison, and respectable when they leave it." Specific reforms she campaigned for included: separation of men and women prisoners, paid work for inmates, women guards for women prisoners, and the housing of criminals based on their crimes.

Beyond Newgate

To nineteenth-century observers, Fry's efforts produced a miracle: many of the reportedly wild and incorrigible inmates became, under her care, orderly, disciplined, and devout. Mayors and sheriffs from surrounding regions visited Newgate and began initiating reforms in their own prisons. In 1818 Fry gave testimony before the House of Commons on the state of English prisons, which contributed to the Prison Reform Act of 1823.

Fry's concern extended to women in half-way houses, where she introduced education, discipline, and Bible instruction. She helped establish a night shelter in London (1820) and formed societies to minister to vagrant families. She also promoted her prison reform ideas in France, Belgium, Holland, and Germany. Until her death in 1845 at age 65, she visited every convict ship that carried female prisoners to the British colonies.

Fry's ideas inspired subsequent generations to combine social work and gospel proclamation and reshaped how prisoners have been treated, ever since.

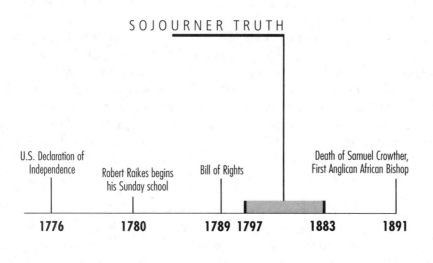

SOJOURNER TRUTH

U.S. Declaration of Independence	Robert Raikes begins his Sunday school	Bill of Rights		Death of Samuel Crowther, First Anglican African Bishop	
1776	**1780**	**1789**	**1797**	**1883**	**1891**

ACTIVISTS

Sojourner Truth

ABOLITIONIST AND WOMEN'S RIGHTS ADVOCATE

"The Lord has made me a sign unto this nation, an' I go round a'testifyin' an' showin' on 'em their sins agin my people."

At a gathering of prominent clergymen and abolitionists at the home of Harriet Beecher Stowe, author of *Uncle Tom's Cabin,* Stowe was informed that Sojourner Truth was downstairs and wanted to meet her.

"You's heerd o' me, I reckon?" the former slave asked Stowe when she came downstairs.

"Yes, I think I have. You go about lecturing, do you not?"

"Yes, honey, that's what I do. The Lord has made me a sign unto this nation, an' I go round a'testifyin' an' showin' on 'em their sins agin my people."

Fascinated by Truth's stories and demeanor, Stowe called down several of the more well-known ministers at the party. When asked if she preached from the Bible, Truth said no, because she couldn't read.

"When I preaches," she said, "I has just one text to preach

from, an' I always preaches from this one. My text is, 'When I found Jesus.' "

"Well, you couldn't have found a better one," said one of the ministers.

In fact, Truth preached on more themes than that—abolition and women's rights to name two—and became one of the most celebrated and controversial itinerants of her era.

Out of slavery

Born a slave named Isabella Baumfree in southeastern New York, the future abolitionist had several owners during her childhood—many of them cruel—before ending up the property of John Dumont at age 13. For 17 years, she worked for him and then escaped. She made her way to the home of Issac and Maria Van Wagener—whose home she said God showed her in a vision. The Quaker couple bought her from Dumont and then freed her.

A couple of years later, she had an experience that solidified her emerging faith. According to her dictated autobiography, one day "God revealed himself to her, with all the suddenness of a flash of lightning, showing her, 'in the twinkling of an eye, that he was all over,' that he pervaded the universe, 'and that there was no place where God was not.'"

"I jes' walked round an' round in a dream," the former slave later told Stowe. "Jesus loved me! I knowed it, I felt it."

During her early years, though, her faith was confused, and at one point she joined a cult whose leader eventually murdered one of the members; for another period, she followed the Millerites, who predicted Christ would return in 1843.

Wanting to make a fresh start, Isabella asked God for a new name. Again she had a vision—God renamed her Sojourner "because I was to travel up an' down the land, showin' the people their sins, an' bein' a sign unto them." She soon asked God for a second name, "'cause everybody else had two names; and the Lord gave me Truth, because I was to declare the truth to the people."

With this new mission, she left New York and traveled throughout New England, attending local prayer meetings and others she called on her own. In 1850 she published her autobiography, written with Olive Gilbert. It brought her fame, and with that fame came harassment. When she was once told the building she was to speak in would be burned if she preached, she replied, "Then I will speak to the ashes." Her quick wit and determination were only successful to a point. After being physically assaulted by one particularly vicious mob, she was forced to walk with a cane for the rest of her life.

It was against slavery that the former slave made her most virulent attacks. But she was also a woman, and once she met other female abolitionists, she became an avid supporter of women's rights as well. For many northerners, this was even more controversial than her abolitionist preaching. Some tried to stop her from speaking at a Women's Rights Convention in Akron, Ohio, in 1851—they feared it would weaken the abolitionist movement. But Truth spoke anyway, delivering her most famous speech:

> That man over there says that women need to be helped into carriages and lifted over ditches and to have the best place everywhere. Nobody

helps me any best place. And ain't I a woman? Look at me! Look at my arm. I have plowed, I have planted, and I have gathered into barns. And no man could head me. And ain't I a woman? I could work as much and eat as much as man—when I could get it—and bear the lash as well! And ain't I a woman? I have borne children and seen most of them sold into slavery, and when I cried out with a mother's grief, none but Jesus heard me. And ain't I a woman?

By the end of the Civil War, Truth had met with Abraham Lincoln, had her arm dislocated by a racist streetcar conductor, petitioned the government to make western lands available to freed blacks, and made countless speeches on behalf of African Americans and women. In 1875, she retired to her home in Battle Creek, Michigan, where she remained until her death.

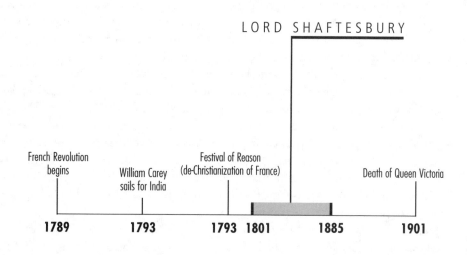

LORD SHAFTESBURY

| French Revolution begins | William Carey sails for India | Festival of Reason (de-Christianization of France) | | Death of Queen Victoria |

| 1789 | 1793 | 1793 | 1801 | 1885 | 1901 |

ACTIVISTS

Lord Shaftesbury

(Antony Ashley Cooper)

GODLY ENGLISH STATESMAN

> *"Social reforms, so necessary, so indispensable, require as much of God's grace as a change of heart."*

When the great English statesman William Wilberforce died in 1833, one of those who attended his funeral was Antony Ashley Cooper, later Lord Shaftesbury. In the words of biographer John Pollock, "Thus the two crusades and the lives of two great social reformers touched briefly and symbolically ... an end and a beginning." If Wilberforce was one of the greatest Christian politicians of his era, Shaftesbury was one of the greatest of his.

Cold home

Unlike Wilberforce, Shaftesbury was a devout Christian when he became a Member of Parliament in 1826. He felt God had called him "to devote whatever advantages he might have bestowed ... in the cause of the weak, the helpless, both man and beast, and those who had none to help them."

He didn't receive this faith from his parents, though. Born the son of the sixth earl of Shaftesbury, he was raised in a home devoid of parental affection. Virtually all he knew of love he experienced through the kindness of a maid named Maria Millis. It was to her that he later traced the beginning of his evangelical Christianity.

Two years into Parliament, Shaftesbury commenced his efforts to alleviate the injustices caused by the Industrial Revolution, which included acts that prohibited employment of women and children in coal mines, provided care for the insane, established a ten-hour day for factory workers, and outlawed employing young boys as chimney sweeps.

Privately he promoted the building of model tenements (on his own estate) and "ragged schools" for waifs. For years he served as president of the British and Foreign Bible Society. He ardently supported the London City Mission, the Church Missionary Society, and the Young Men's Christian Association. He was associated with 33 philanthropic organizations in his life.

His commitment to spread the gospel led him to start a movement to hold religious services in theaters and music halls. Controversy ensued, forcing him to defend the movement in the House of Lords against charges that Christianity would be compromised if it were associated with scenes of frivolous entertainment.

His brother's keeper

The driving force of all this social activity was his faith. Some of the more important guiding principles expressed in his writings include:

- "By everything true, everything holy, you are your brother's keeper."
- "Creed and color, latitude and longitude, make no difference in the essential nature of man."
- "Social reforms, so necessary, so indispensable, require as much of God's grace as a change of heart."
- "What is morally right can never be politically wrong, and what is morally wrong can never be politically right."
- "No man ... can persist from the beginning of his life to the end of it in a course of generosity, [or] in a course of virtue ... unless he is drawing from the fountain of our Lord himself."

Though he had high ideals, as a legislator, Shaftesbury was a realist. He often agreed to compromises to win ground for his causes. For example, he wanted the Board School curriculum to include Bible teaching: "The teaching of the Bible," he argued, "should be essential and not an extra." The problem was how exactly to teach it—by which denomination's interpretation? Since church groups were unable to agree on a syllabus for religious instruction, a compromise was reached: the Bible would be taught but not according to the formularies of any church. Shaftesbury considered such teaching "a meager, washy, pointless thing," but it was better than no Bible instruction at all.

Shaftesbury's lifelong commitment to the welfare of his fellow Brits was once described as "his hopeless pertinacity." He was pertinacious—but hopeless, no.

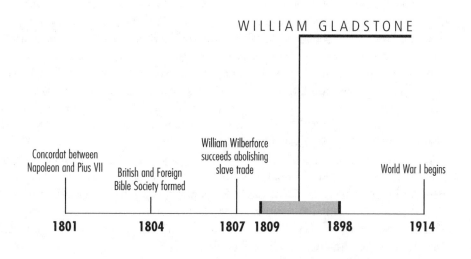

WILLIAM GLADSTONE

Concordat between Napoleon and Pius VII	British and Foreign Bible Society formed	William Wilberforce succeeds abolishing slave trade			World War I begins
1801	1804	1807	1809	1898	1914

ACTIVISTS

William Gladstone

PRIME MINISTER OF IMPECCABLE MORALS

"My political or public life is the best part of my life: it is that part in which I am conscious of the greatest effort to do and avoid as the Lord Christ would have me do and avoid."

For William Gladstone, service in political life was a "most blessed calling." He once said to Queen Victoria, "My political or public life is the best part of my life: it is that part in which I am conscious of the greatest effort to do and avoid as the Lord Christ would have me do and avoid."

Holy and contentious politics

He was raised in an evangelical home, and as a young man, he dedicated his life to Christ. Before embarking on a political career, he seriously considered taking holy orders. But when he entered Parliament in 1832, he never looked back. His political career lasted over 60 years.

He served as president of the board of trade, secretary for the colonies, Chancellor of the Exchequer, and for four different terms, the prime minister. Among his many achievements, he disestablished the Church of Ireland to free Roman Catholics from having to pay taxes to the Anglican church, supported an Irish land act that protected the peasantry, and achieved important reforms—competitive admission to the civil service, vote by secret ballot, abolition of sales commissions in the army, educational expansion, and court reorganization.

In spite of such success, he was a controversial figure. He was disliked by Queen Victoria and had many political rivals, including the great Benjamin Disraeli. Over many years, Gladstone gradually abandoned the traditional Tory beliefs on the importance of rank and privilege—beliefs Disraeli ardently championed. As their differences widened, Disraeli's antipathy for Gladstone increased.

When Gladstone became Chancellor of the Exchequer, Disraeli (the previous chancellor) refused to give him the traditional robes of office. Gladstone repeatedly asked for them, and Disraeli repeatedly sent evasive responses. (The robes never were sent, and today they are displayed in Disraeli's home at Hughenden Manor.)

The ideals that informed Gladstone's public philosophy were rooted in Judeo-Christian morality. Among them, he believed:

• "The duties of governors [political officials] are strictly and peculiarly religious.... Individuals ... are bound to carry throughout their acts the spirit of the high truths they have acknowledged."

• Politics was a "most blessed calling," and Parliament a place where Christian principles could be applied to the "numerous measures of the time."

• "The value of liberty [is] an essential condition of excellence in human things."

• "Christianity [has] established the duty of relieving the poor, the sick, [and] the afflicted."

Renaissance man

Gladstone's interests and gifts ranged beyond politics. He was a superb linguist and classical scholar. He was also a prolific author, frequently contributing to reviews and magazines. Articles on a variety of topics, including poetry, constitutional politics, economics, and church history, flowed from his pen.

He loved the outdoors and believed in vigorous exercise. Moreover, though great demands were placed upon him, he often made time for personal philanthropy. In later years, he wrote several works in defense of the Christian faith. He once publicly debated the famous agnostic T. H. Huxley over the creation narrative in the Book of Genesis.

"The grand old man" retired from political life in early 1894. He traveled widely and continued to write on a variety of subjects. Following his death in 1898, he was buried in Westminster Abbey. Of all of the many tributes offered in his memory, perhaps the shortest and simplest was the most eloquent. He was, Lord Salisbury stated, "a great Christian man."

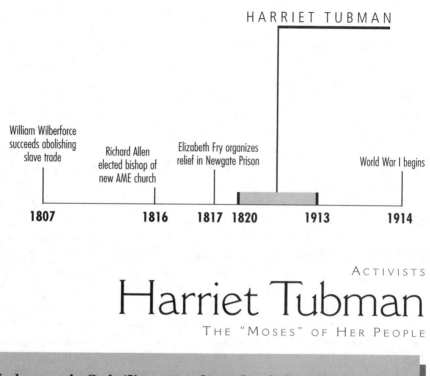

HARRIET TUBMAN

William Wilberforce succeeds abolishing slave trade

Richard Allen elected bishop of new AME church

Elizabeth Fry organizes relief in Newgate Prison

World War I begins

| 1807 | 1816 | 1817 | 1820 | 1913 | 1914 |

ACTIVISTS

Harriet Tubman

THE "MOSES" OF HER PEOPLE

"I always tole God, 'I'm gwine [going] to hole stiddy on you, an' you've got to see me through.'"

In 1831 a Kentucky slave named Tice Davids made a break for the free state of Ohio by swimming across the Ohio River. His master trailed close behind and watched Davids wade ashore. When he looked again, Davids was nowhere to be found. Davids's master returned to Kentucky in a rage, exclaiming to his friends that Davids "must have gone off on an underground road." The name stuck, and the legend of the underground railroad was born.

It was another two decades before the underground railroad became a part of the national consciousness, mostly because of the heroic exploits of the underground railroad's most celebrated "conductor."

Black Moses

Harriet Tubman was raised in slavery in eastern Maryland but escaped in 1849. When she first reached the North, she said later,

295

"I looked at my hands to see if I was de same person now I was free. Dere was such a glory ober eberything, de sun came like gold through de trees and ober de fields, and I felt like I was in heaven."

Tubman was not satisfied with her own freedom, however. She made 19 return trips to the South and helped deliver at least 300 fellow slaves, boasting "I never lost a passenger." Her guidance of so many to freedom earned her the nickname "Moses."

Tubman's friends and fellow abolitionists claimed that the source of her strength came from her faith in God as deliverer and protector of the weak. "I always tole God," she said, "'I'm gwine [going] to hole stiddy on you, an' you've got to see me through.'"

Though infuriated slaveholders posted a $40,000 reward for her capture, she was never apprehended. "I can't die but once" became her motto, and with that philosophy she went about her mission of deliverance.

She always made her rescue attempts in winter but avoided actually going into plantations. Instead she waited for escaping slaves (to whom she had sent messages) to meet her eight or ten miles away. Slaves would leave plantations on Saturday nights so they wouldn't be missed until Monday morning, after the Sabbath. It would thus often be late on Monday afternoon before their owners would discover them missing. Only then did they post their reward signs, which men hired by Tubman would take down.

Because her rescue missions were fraught with danger, Tubman demanded strict obedience from her fugitives. A slave who returned to his master would likely be forced to reveal information that would compromise her mission. If a slave wanted to quit in the midst of a rescue, Tubman would hold a revolver to his head and ask him to reconsider.

Asked whether she would actually kill a reluctant escapee, she replied, "Yes, if he was weak enough to give out, he'd be weak enough to betray us all and all who had helped us, and do you think I'd let so many die just for one coward man?"

She never had to shoot any slave she helped, but she did come close with one: "I told the boys to get their guns ready, and shoot him. They'd have done it in a minute; but when he heard that, he jumped right up and went on as well as anybody."

Tubman said she would listen carefully to the voice of God as she led slaves north, and she would only go where she felt God was leading her. Fellow abolitionist Thomas Garrett said of her, "I never met any person of any color who had more confidence in the voice of God."

Tubman became a friend of many of the best-known abolitionists and their sympathizers. John Brown referred to her in his letters as "one of the best and bravest persons on this continent—General Tubman as we call her."

During the Civil War, Tubman served as a nurse, laundress, and spy with Union forces along the coast of South Carolina. After the war, she made her home in Auburn, New York, and, despite numerous honors, spent her last years in poverty. Not until 30 years after the war was she granted a government pension in recognition of her work for the Federal Army.

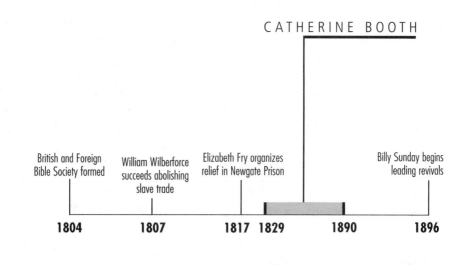

CATHERINE BOOTH

British and Foreign Bible Society formed	William Wilberforce succeeds abolishing slave trade	Elizabeth Fry organizes relief in Newgate Prison		Billy Sunday begins leading revivals
1804	1807	1817 1829	1890	1896

ACTIVISTS

Catherine Booth

COMPELLING PREACHER AND CO-FOUNDER OF THE SALVATION ARMY

> *"If the Word of God forbids female ministry, we would ask how it happens that so many of the most devoted handmaidens of the Lord have felt constrained by the Holy Ghost to exercise it?... The Word and the Spirit cannot contradict each other."*

They were unlikely evangelists. Eighteen-year-old Rose Clapham stood with her colleague, Jenny Smith, and invited hundreds of world-weary coal miners in Yorkshire, England, to a meeting in the local theater. At that 1878 meeting, Rose, an uneducated factory worker, persuaded 700 men to make decisions for Christ—140 of which became the first members of a new church.

Rose was but one of the new "Hallelujah lasses" who were making the Salvation Army one of the most effective missions in England. Who inspired these young, working-class women to minister in such an unusual way? Catherine Booth, co-founder of the Salvation Army.

Liberating gospel

Catherine was raised in the pious and sheltered world of small-town Victorian England, and her mother was a model of Methodist piety. In her teenage years, Catherine suffered from a spinal curvature and was forced to lay in bed months at a time. She read voraciously, especially the writings of Charles Finney and John Wesley, and she not only became assured of her own salvation but also gained a glimmer of her own calling to public ministry.

When people suggested that a woman's place was in the home, she wondered if the Christian church, which preached a liberating gospel to both men and women, could keep women from expressing their manifold ministry gifts. She eventually concluded that a false interpretation of Paul's comment about women keeping silent in church had resulted in "loss to the church, evil to the world, and dishonor to God."

In the early 1850s, she met and married William Booth, a young preacher who was making a name for himself. When she shared her emerging convictions with her new husband, he said, "I would not stop a woman preaching on any account." But he added that neither would he "encourage one to begin."

Her book, *Female Ministry*, soon followed, a short, powerful defense of American Phoebe Palmer's holiness ministry. It was not a plea based on natural rights or other feminist themes of the day. Instead, she founded her argument on the absolute equality of men and women before God. She acknowledged that the Fall had put women into subjection, as a consequence of sin, but to leave them there, she said, was to reject the good news of the gospel, which proclaimed that the grace of Christ had restored what sin had taken away. Now all men and women were one in Christ.

In responding to her critics, she asked, "If the Word of God forbids female ministry, we would ask how it happens that so many of the most devoted handmaidens of the Lord have felt constrained by the Holy Ghost to exercise it?... The Word and the Spirit cannot contradict each other."

Counsel for the defense

Catherine herself, however, had yet to venture to preach or teach publicly. That occasion finally came in 1860, when she first preached during an evening Army service. Her abilities were soon apparent, and her reputation spread.

Her hearers were taken with her gentle manner as well as her powerful appeal. One of her sons later remarked, "She reminded me again and again of counsel pleading with judge and jury for the life of the prisoner. The fixed attention of the court, the mastery of facts, the absolute self-forgetfulness of the advocate, the ebb and flow of feeling, the hush during the vital passages—all were there."

Or as another man put it, "If ever I am charged with a crime, don't bother to get any of the great lawyers to defend me; get that woman."

Though she cared for a household of six at the time (she eventually raised eight children), her preaching schedule increased. She soon felt the pressure: "I cannot give time to preparation unless I can afford to put my sewing out. It never seems to occur to anybody that I cannot do two things at once." On top of that, her husband began falling ill, so she added the administration of the Army to her duties—and thus she grew into her matriarchal role as "the Army Mother."

Small wonder, then, that hundreds of "Hallelujah lasses," as they made their way in the wretched streets and alleys of industrial England, saw the Army Mother as their mentor. And no wonder that the once-lukewarm William, in drafting his Orders and Regulations for the Army, incorporated statements like these: "Women shall have the right to an equal share with men in the work of publishing salvation."

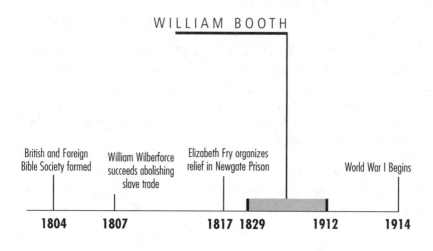

WILLIAM BOOTH

British and Foreign Bible Society formed	William Wilberforce succeeds abolishing slave trade	Elizabeth Fry organizes relief in Newgate Prison		World War I Begins
1804	**1807**	**1817 1829**	**1912**	**1914**

ACTIVISTS

William Booth

FIRST GENERAL OF THE SALVATION ARMY

> *"I seemed to hear a voice sounding in my ears, 'Where can you go and find such heathen as these, and where is there so great a need for your labors?'"*

After he died, 150,000 people filed by the casket, and 40,000, including Queen Mary, attended his funeral. It was a remarkable end for a man born into poverty and who worked in the midst of poverty his whole life.

But William Booth was a remarkable man, who was given the title "The Prophet of the Poor." He is best known today as founder and first general of the Salvation Army.

Pawnbroker's apprentice

Booth was born in relative poverty, in Sneinton, a suburb of Nottingham, England. His parents were not religious and at best laboring class, with little education. His father, "a Grab, a Get," by William's definition, died when William was just 14. By that time, William was helping to earn the family income as a pawn-broker's apprentice.

Sometime during his fifteenth year, William was invited by a Wesleyan couple to attend chapel, where he was converted. He wrote in his diary, "God shall have all there is of William Booth."

Then came another life-changing experience: he heard an American revivalist who led "a remarkable religious awakening" at Nottingham's Wesleyan Chapel. The rush of souls to hear the gospel led Booth to see that "soul-saving results may be calculated upon when proper means are used for their accomplishment." Booth went on to make a life-long commitment to the scientific revivalism methods of Charles G. Finney.

Booth and a group of friends set out to evangelize the poor. They held nightly open-air addresses, after which they invited people to meetings in cottages. Their use of lively songs, short exhortations calling for a decision for Christ, and visitation of the sick and of converts (whose names and addresses they recorded) anticipated methods Booth would write into Salvation Army Orders and Regulations 30 years later.

When he was criticized for using secular tunes to attract crowds, he replied, "Secular music, do you say, belongs to the devil? Does it? Well, if it did I would plunder him for it, for he has no right to a single note of the whole seven."

When his pastor proposed that William himself prepare for ordained ministry, he accepted, and soon found himself pastor to Reform Methodists in Spaulding, though their disorganized ways repelled him.

During this period, William met Catherine Mumford. Beginning with their second meeting on Good Friday 1852, they entered one of the most remarkable relationships in religious history. They married in a South London Congregational chapel in June 1855.

By 1861 William was finding that "settled ministry" did not suit him, and he resigned. He and Catherine became itinerant evangelists in Wales, Cornwall, and the Midlands, Britain's "burned-over" districts. The Booths preached in naphtha-lit tents on unused burial grounds, in haylofts, in rooms behind a pigeon shop—anywhere to fulfill his famous words, "Go for souls and go for the worst!"

Labyrinth ministry

An invitation for Catherine to preach in London in 1865 led him to accept support from lay-run East London missions as a temporary ministry. East London in the 1860s was, in the words of one writer, "a squalid labyrinth, with half a million people, 290 to the acre.... Every fifth house was a gin shop, and most had special steps to help even the tiniest [children] reach the counter."

After seeing some of East London's gin palaces, he told Catherine, "I seemed to hear a voice sounding in my ears, 'Where can you go and find such heathen as these, and where is there so great a need for your labors?'"

William soon organized his own East London Christian Mission which, by 1870, resembled a Methodist society. His mission failed to attract the "heathen masses," however. So in 1878, he energized it by giving it the name "Salvation Army," an idea he borrowed from the successful British Volunteer Movement. A military structure was installed with "General" William Booth at the top. Military trappings were added over the next couple of years. The idea caught the imagination, and within ten years, the Salvation Army was established in the United States, Canada, and Europe as well.

Booth was single-minded in his zeal. He once said, "While women weep, as they do now, I'll fight; while little children go hungry, I'll fight; while men go to prison, in and out, in and out, as they do now, I'll fight—while there is a drunkard left, while there is a poor lost girl upon the streets, where there remains one dark soul without the light of God—I'll fight! I'll fight to the very end!" His zeal, however, made for less than happy personal relationships, which led to strains and schism especially in the American branch.

Over the years, he created an elaborate social relief system because he believed charity would speed the work of evangelism. In 1890, he published *In Darkest England and the Way Out* (which became a bestseller) to explain his social relief scheme.

At the time of his death on August 20, 1912, the Salvation Army had become a family-run Christian empire, with seven of the Booths' eight children taking leadership posi-

tions. Today, following the pattern established by the first general, the Salvation Army marches on with over 25,000 officers in 91 countries.

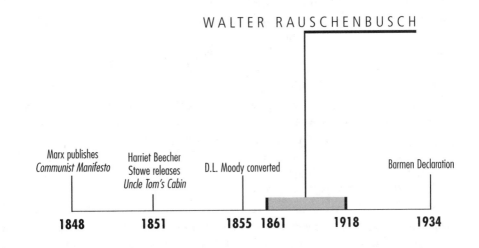

WALTER RAUSCHENBUSCH

Marx publishes Communist Manifesto	Harriet Beecher Stowe releases Uncle Tom's Cabin	D.L. Moody converted			Barmen Declaration
1848	**1851**	**1855**	**1861**	**1918**	**1934**

ACTIVISTS

Walter Rauschenbusch

CHAMPION OF THE SOCIAL GOSPEL

> *"Christ's conception of the kingdom of God came to me as a new revelation. Here was the idea and purpose that had dominated the mind of the Master himself.... I found ... this new conception ... strangely satisfying. It responded to all the old and all the new elements of my religious life."*

It was the hottest selling religious book for three years after it was published in 1907; all told, some 50,000 copies were sold. More important than popularity was impact. As nationally known New York preacher Harry Emerson Fosdick put it, the book "struck home so poignantly on the intelligence and conscience ... that it ushered in a new era in Christian thought and action."

The book was Walter Rauschenbusch's *Christianity and the Social Crisis*, and the book catapulted Rauschenbusch and his "social gospel" into the nation's consciousness, a message he had been honing for some 20 years, since his first pastorate.

Two conversions

Rauschenbusch was born in Rochester, New York, to a Lutheran-missionary-turned-German-Baptist. "I was brought up in a very religious family, and I thank God for it," he said. "We had household religious service every day." After a period of rebelliousness in youth, he said, "I came to my Father, and I began to pray for help and got it. I got my own religious experience." Though he later interpreted this conversion experience through the lens of theological liberalism, he valued this "tender, mysterious experience," as he called it, his entire life.

He was schooled in Germany and then the United States, and after a vocational struggle, he decided: "It is now no longer my fond hope to be a learned theologian and write big books," he wrote at the time. "I want to be a pastor, powerful with men, preaching to them Christ as the man in whom their affections and energies can find the satisfaction for which mankind is groaning."

In 1885 he became pastor of the Second German Baptist Church in New York City, located at the edge of a depressed area known as Hell's Kitchen. Here the young pietistic pastor confronted unemployment, poverty, malnutrition, disease, and crime. "Oh, the children's funerals! they gripped my heart," he later wrote. "That was one of the things I always went away thinking about—why did the children have to die?" He immersed himself in the literature of social reform and began to participate in social action groups.

Slowly his ideas took shape. He had come to the pastorate "to save souls in the ordinarily accepted religious sense" but not all the problems he confronted could be addressed in this way. Though his friends urged him to give up his social work for "Christian work," he believed his social work was Christ's work.

Rauschenbusch sought to combine his old evangelical passion (which he never abandoned) with his new social awareness. He adopted critical approaches to the Bible and identified himself with liberal theologians like Albrecht Ritschl and Adolf Harnack. The kingdom of God became the theme by which he pulled together his views on religion and science, piety and social action, Christianity and culture. "Christ's conception of the kingdom of God came to me as a new revelation," he wrote. "Here was the idea and purpose that had dominated the mind of the Master himself.... I found ... this new conception ... strangely satisfying. It responded to all the old and all the new elements of my religious life."

Rauschenbusch was an optimist. He never believed society could become perfect, but he saw humankind as progressing swiftly toward the kingdom. He embraced socialism but not as an ideology; he simply felt that socialists generally had the most practical answers to the social questions of his day.

He worked out the implications of new thinking with a group of other young Baptist ministers in the Brotherhood of the Kingdom, which met annually (and eventually included many of the nation's leaders in its ranks). In 1897 he joined the faculty of his alma mater, Rochester Theological Seminary, and was able to read and lecture more deeply on social themes. When *Christianity and the Social Crisis* was published, his ideas reached a larger audience.

During the last ten years of his life, further writings followed (*Christianizing the Social Order, A Theology of the Social Gospel,* and his most widely circulated work, *The Social*

Principles of Jesus), as well as constant speaking engagements. He impressed audiences and readers alike with his economy of words, illuminating metaphors, fairness toward those with whom he disagreed, and a disarming sense of humor (some of it pointed at himself).

He loved Germany, hated militarism, and was deeply troubled by the outbreak of World War I. As patriotism swept the U.S. and all things German became repulsive, Rauschenbusch's popularity declined, and even more when, after the war, liberalism came under attack by neo-orthodox thinkers like Karl Barth and Reinhold Niebuhr.

Though subsequent historical events showed Rauschenbusch to be overly optimistic, he still towers above other advocates of the social gospel. "His writings," said Martin Luther King, Jr., "left an indelible imprint on my thinking," and his understanding of the kingdom of God continues to appeal to those who want to combine evangelical passion with social justice.

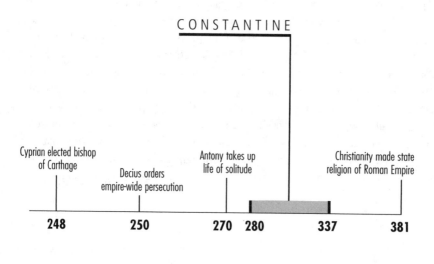

CONSTANTINE

Cyprian elected bishop
of Carthage

Decius orders
empire-wide persecution

Antony takes up
life of solitude

Christianity made state
religion of Roman Empire

248   250   270 280   337   381

RULERS

Constantine

FIRST CHRISTIAN EMPEROR

> "*I have experienced this in others and in myself, for I walked not in the way of righteousness.... But the Almighty God, who sits in the court of heaven, granted what I did not deserve.*"

The first *Life of Constantine* describes its subject as "resplendent with every virtue that godliness bestows." This praise-filled biography came from the hand of Eusebius, bishop of Caesarea in Palestine, and perhaps Constantine's greatest admirer. It is the classic image that prevailed in Eastern Christianity for more than a thousand years.

Historians now debate whether "the first Christian emperor" was a Christian at all. Some think him an unprincipled power seeker. What religion he had, many argue, was at best a blend of paganism and Christianity for purely political purposes.

Certainly, Constantine held to ideals we no longer share. He knew nothing of religion without politics or politics without religion. Yet he clearly believed he was a Christian, and he looked back to a battle at the Milvian Bridge, just outside the walls of Rome, as the decisive hour in his newly found faith.

Field vision

Of Constantine's early years, we know only that he was born in Illyria, a region in the Balkans. His father, Constantius Chlorus, was already a Roman official on the rise. Helena, the daughter of an innkeeper and Constantius's wife, gave birth to Constantine around A.D. 280 in Naissus, just south of the Danube. By the time Constantine was 31, he was in line to become emperor of the western empire—and more.

In the spring of 311, with 40,000 soldiers behind him, Constantine rode toward Rome to confront an enemy whose numbers were four times his own. Maxentius, vying for supremacy in the West, waited in Rome with his Italian troops and the elite Praetorian Guard, confident no one could successfully invade the city. But Constantine's army was already overwhelming his foes in Italy as he marched toward the capital.

Maxentius turned to pagan oracles, finding a prophecy that the "enemy of the Romans" would perish. But Constantine was still miles away. So, bolstered by the prophecy, Maxentius left the city to meet his foe.

Meanwhile, Constantine saw a vision in the afternoon sky: a bright cross with the words BY THIS SIGN CONQUER. As the story goes, Christ himself told Constantine in a dream to take the cross into battle as his standard.

Though accounts vary, Constantine apparently believed the omen to be a word from God. When he awoke early the next morning, the young commander obeyed the message and ordered his soldiers to mark their shields with the now famous Chi-Rho.

Maxentius's troops fled in disarray toward the surging Tiber. The would-be emperor attempted to escape over the wooden bridge erected to span the stream, but his own army-turned-mob, pressing through the narrow passage, forced him into the river, where he drowned by the weight of his armor.

Constantine entered Rome the undisputed ruler of the West, the first Roman emperor with a cross in his diadem.

Wavering believer

Once supreme in the West, Constantine met Licinius, the ruler of the Balkan provinces, and issued the famous Edict of Milan that gave Christians freedom of worship and directed the governors to restore all the property seized during the severe Diocletian persecution.

Eusebius in his *Church History* recorded the Christian jubilation: "The whole human race was freed from the oppression of the tyrants. We especially, who had fixed our hopes upon the Christ of God, had gladness unspeakable."

Constantine's faith was still imprecise, but few questioned its authenticity. In 314 Constantine sent a message to the assembled bishops at the Council of Arles. He wrote about how God does not allow people "to wander in the shadows" but reveals to them salvation: "I have experienced this in others and in myself, for I walked not in the way of righteousness.... But the Almighty God, who sits in the court of heaven, granted what I did not deserve."

For a decade, though, he wavered. For example, on the Arch of Constantine, which celebrates his Milvian Bridge victory, pagan sacrifices usually depicted on Roman monuments are absent. Then again, there are still no Christian symbols, and Victory and the Sun God are honored.

He had no desire to impose his newfound faith as a state religion. "The struggle for deathlessness," he said, "must be free." He seemed to begin where his father left off: more or less a monotheist opposed to idols, and more or less friendly toward Christians. Only through the years did his Christian convictions grow.

Public relations expert

In 323 Constantine triumphed over Licinius and became the sole ruler of the Roman world. The victory enabled Constantine to move the seat of government permanently to the East, to the ancient Greek city of Byzantium (now Istanbul). He enlarged and enriched the city at enormous expense and built magnificent churches throughout the East. The new capital was dedicated as New Rome, but everyone soon called the city Constantinople.

Christians were more populous and vocal in the East than they were in Rome, so during the last 14 years of his reign, "Bullneck" could openly proclaim himself a Christian. He proceeded to create the conditions we call "state-church" and bequeathed the ideal to Christians for over a thousand years.

In 325 the Arian controversy threatened to split the newly united empire. To settle the matter, Constantine called together a council of the bishops at Nicea, a city near the capital. He ran the meeting himself.

"You are bishops whose jurisdiction is within the church," he told them. "But I also am a bishop, ordained by God to oversee those outside the church."

Presiding at the council, Constantine was magnificent: arranging elaborate ceremony, dramatic entrances and processions, and splendid services. He was also a gifted mediator, now bringing his skill in public relations to the management of church affairs.

Unfortunately he could not follow abstract arguments or subtle issues and often found himself at a great disadvantage at these councils.

Delayed baptism

Constantine waited until death drew near to be baptized as a Christian. His decision was not unusual in a day when many Christians believed one could not be forgiven after baptism. Since the sins of worldly men, especially those with public duties, were considered incompatible with Christian virtue, some church leaders delayed baptizing such men until just before death.

He gave his sons an orthodox Christian education, and his relationship with his mother was generally happy, but he continued to act as a typical Roman emperor. He ordered the execution of his eldest son, his second wife, and his favorite sister's husband. No one seems to be able to explain fully his reasons.

While many of his actions cannot be defended, he did bid farewell to the old Roman gods and make the cross an emblem of Victory in the world.

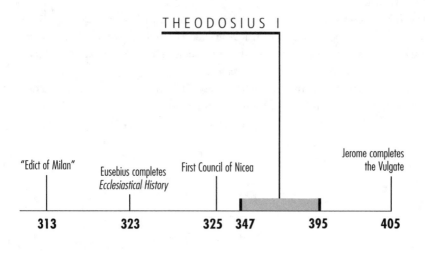

THEODOSIUS I

"Edict of Milan" | Eusebius completes *Ecclesiastical History* | First Council of Nicea | Jerome completes the Vulgate

313   323   325   347   395   405

RULERS

Theodosius I

EMPEROR WHO MADE CHRISTIANITY "THE" ROMAN RELIGION

> "He . . . earned the title 'the Great' because of his devout Christianity."
>
> — Michael Grant

In lists of Roman Emperors, Theodosius is far from the most notable. One historian noted that this son of an emperor killed for high treason "veered disconcertingly between opposites—febrile activity and indolent sluggishness, a simple soldierly life and the splendors of the court." But this little-known emperor forever changed the course of Christian history not in one way, but in two. He used his power to officially enforce orthodox Christianity, but ended up placing his power under that of the church, setting a standard for more than a millennium.

Military man

The blond, elegant Theodosius began his imperial career in the usual manner. He was born in northwest Spain, to a father who was a talented military commander. Theodosius learned his military lessons by campaigning with his father's staff in Britain and elsewhere.

After being crowned emperor in the East (379), he continued to battle German tribes in the north, but finally worked out a unique arrangement with them: for exchange of land and provisions, their soldiers would serve under the Roman banner when needed. It was a novel idea for the time, an arrangement that later emperors would depend on more and more.

To pay for this expanded army, however, Theodosius raised taxes brutally. "No man shall possess any property that is exempt from taxation," he decreed. City magistrates, who were responsible for collecting taxes, were flogged if they failed to levy taxes efficiently.

Yet it wasn't just tax dodgers that caught his attention, but heretics and pagans as well.

Emperor for Christ

Early in his reign, during a serious illness, Theodosius had accepted Christian baptism. In 380 he proclaimed himself a Christian of the Nicene Creed, and he called a council at Constantinople to put an end to the Arian heresy (which, contrary to Nicene doctrine, claimed Jesus was created), which had divided the empire for over half a century. One hundred and fifty bishops gathered and revised the Nicene Creed of A.D. 325 into the creed we know today. Arianism has never made a serious challenge since.

Having won that victory, Theodosius tried to ram through his choice for patriarch of Constantinople, but the bishops rebelled and demanded he appoint a bishop from a short list they created. It was the first of many instances in Theodosius's reign in which the church got the better of him.

The most famous example came in 387: When the city of Thessalonica rioted because a favored charioteer was imprisoned (for homosexuality), Theodosius ordered revenge: a chariot race was announced, citizens gathered in the arena, the gates were locked, and soldiers were set upon the crowd. By the end of the day, 7,000 had perished.

Ambrose, the bishop of Milan who was a spiritual and political adviser to Theodosius, was furious. He refused to give Theodosius Communion until the emperor performed public penance: he must put aside his royal garments, don a shroud, and publicly plead for God's mercy.

When Theodosius consented, it marked a new chapter in the history of church and state. For the first time, a secular ruler submitted to the church. Less than a century earlier, emperors were trying to wipe out the church.

Turning the tables

Theodosius, for his part, tried to reverse that legacy by persecuting heretics and pagans. Arians and Manichaeans (dualists) were condemned and driven underground. One edict prohibited public discussion of any religious questions! Finally, in 391, pagan temples were closed and pagan worship forbidden. Later Roman historians, like Zosimus, looked back on this Christianization of the empire as the cause for the fall of Rome (a charge Augustine refuted in his *City of God*).

Theodosius ended his reign by defeating political enemies in the West, so that by late 394, he stood alone as emperor of a once-more united empire. The moment was brief, however, as Theodosius was dead within five months.

JUSTINIAN I AND THEODORA I

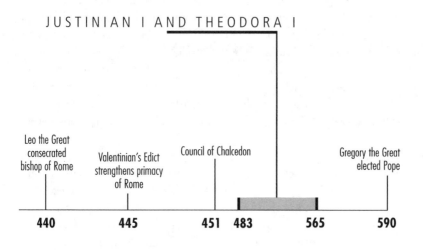

Leo the Great consecrated bishop of Rome	Valentinian's Edict strengthens primacy of Rome	Council of Chalcedon			Gregory the Great elected Pope
440	445	451	483	565	590

RULERS

Justinian I and Theodora I

GREATEST BYZANTINE RULERS

There are two great gifts which God, in his love for man, has granted from on high: the priesthood and the imperial dignity"
—Justinian I

What many previous emperors before had failed to do, "we have decided now to grant to the world, with the help of Almighty God," announced the ambitious Justinian I with his wife, Theodora. Not content to plaster over an empire cracking and peeling with age, he intended to do nothing less than completely remake the Roman Empire—legally, militarily, architecturally—and unite it once more into a glorious kingdom. And in large measure he succeeded.

Farmer and performer

Justinian was born Flavius Peterus Sabbatius, the son of a farmer whose childless uncle was on his way to becoming Emperor Justin I. Justinian was called to the capital in his teens and given the best education possible. He became a member of Justin's inner circle, took a variation of his name, and became

Justin's most influential adviser.

Justinian was meticulous, patient, and by nature solitary. He could also persevere, sustaining long-range plans in spite of serious reverses—though he became unnerved when in danger. He needed so little rest, he was known by his subjects as "the emperor who never sleeps."

When Justinian was crowned in 527, he named as co-regent his young wife Theodora. She was 15 years his junior and his opposite in nearly every way. She was social, witty, supremely self-confident, and never lost her head in a crisis. He adored her, and she was his most important adviser.

She had come to the crown from the gutter. Her parents were performers, the lowest strata of free society. Her father died when she was a child, and she took to the stage to earn a living. Most actresses were also prostitutes, and whispers to that affect followed her all her life.

When she became a Christian, she gave up her former life for spinning wool. In 522, she met Justinian, who was so enamored with her, he changed the law so that actresses could marry into high society. The following year, he married her.

Church and state

Justin longed to reunite the empire partly because of his philosophy of church and state. "There are two great gifts which God, in his love for man, has granted from on high: the priesthood and the imperial dignity," he wrote. "The first serves divine things, while the latter directs and administers human affairs; both, however, proceed from the same origin and adorn the life of mankind."

If both church and state perform their duties well, a "general harmony will result." It was in pursuit of this general harmony that Justinian enlisted his efforts.

Justinian sent his armies to take Africa back from the weakened Vandals in 533. He concluded a peace treaty with his Persian rivals to the east and conquered one Arabic or Slavic kingdom after another. In 535 he invaded Italy and fought the Goths for 25 years until they had been ejected and the peninsula virtually destroyed. By the end of his reign, Justinian had very nearly restored the boundaries of Roman Empire at its height—but at the cost of an empty treasury.

In 528 Justinian established three imperial law schools and appointed a commission to reorganize the legal system. He created what has become known as the Code of Justinian—the *Corpus Juris Civilis*—part of the authoritative statement of Roman law that was gradually accepted throughout Western Europe.

The Code contained much that was unapologetically Christian. "It is right that those who do not worship God correctly should be deprived of worldly advantage too," said Justinian, so the laws made life difficult for heretics and unbelievers. He also closed the famous university at Athens, a center of pagan thought, and prosecuted the heretical Montanists.

But to the faithful he was benevolent. He made it easier to free Christian slaves, gave more legal rights to women and children, made divorce harder, and reduced the number of capital crimes.

Unsatisfying compromise

Still, Justinian sought to unite his empire in religious matters. The most bothersome division for Justinian was between the orthodox Christian believers and the Monophysites. Orthodox believers, who honored the conclusions of the Council of Chalcedon, said Jesus had two natures in one person. Monophysites said Jesus had one nature, his divinity having swallowed up his humanity like a "drop of wine in the ocean." Justinian believed the dispute was a misunderstanding and wanted to reconcile the parties.

But more than theology was at stake. The Monophysites, centered in Egypt, controlled the grain exporting regions of the empire. And then there was Justinian's beloved Theodora: a Monophysite.

In 544 Justinian published a tract, known as "The Three Chapters," in which he tried to find ground for compromise, but this satisfied nobody. Even after forcing his views through a church council, the Second Council of Constantinople (553), the issues were left unresolved.

Great builder

Throughout his 38-year reign, Justinian erected magnificent buildings around the empire—25 basilicas in Constantinople alone, including the Sancta Sophia ("Holy Wisdom"), the crowning jewel of Byzantine architecture.

When Justinian died, the Mediterranean was once again an imperial lake. But the empire was never really united and began dismantling within two years. Nonetheless, the reign of Justinian and Theodora ranks as the greatest in Byzantine history.

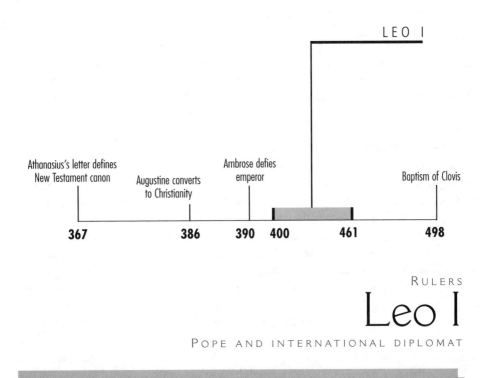

LEO I

Athanasius's letter defines New Testament canon

Augustine converts to Christianity

Ambrose defies emperor

Baptism of Clovis

367   386   390 400   461   498

RULERS

Leo I

POPE AND INTERNATIONAL DIPLOMAT

"As the primacy of the apostolic see is based on the title of the blessed Peter, ... no illicit steps may be taken against this see to usurp its authority."

During his papacy, Leo I condemned heretics, convinced emperors to call councils, and then ignored certain rulings of those councils—all in an effort to make the bishop of Rome the uncontested head of the church. But it was a conversation with the infamous Attila the Hun and the Vandal general that probably did his cause the most good.

No more "first among equals"

By the time history is aware of Leo, he was a proud nobleman of Roman or Tucsan heritage. (As pope he forbade the elevation to bishop of any former slaves, as "such baseness" would pollute the Holy service.) He was an influential deacon deeply involved in civil and ecclesiastical affairs, and he opposed heresy. Leo convinced Pope Celestus I to hear his brief against the Nestorians, and he helped to stiffen Pope Sixtus I's resolve against Pelagians.

His succession to the papacy came "as a matter of course." In

315

his elevation address, he sounded a major theme of his reign: the primacy of the "Chair of Peter" above all other bishops.

"The firmness given by Christ the rock to him who himself was made the rock passes to his heirs," he argued, "and wherever their firmness appears, the power of the Shepherd is manifest." Leo abandoned the traditional doctrine that the bishop of Rome was "first among equals" and declared that he spoke as Peter: "Believe that it is he himself, whom in our office we represent, who is speaking."

Authority of Peter

As pope, Leo continued to fight heresy and, at the same time, to extend his authority. In 443 he disciplined Hilary of Arles, who was outside imperial borders, for practicing too much independence, and in 445 he gained imperial recognition of his rights inside the empire: "As the primacy of the apostolic see is based on the title of the blessed Peter, ... no illicit steps may be taken against this see to usurp its authority."

Over the next few years, he talked Emperor Valentinian III into enforcing civil penalties against the Manichaeans. Similarly, the bishop of Spain began stamping out the Priscillians at Leo's request. His most important case began as an appeal by a monk accused of teaching that Christ had only a divine nature—the Monophysite heresy.

Leo repudiated the monk, Eutyches, in a long letter (the "Tome of Leo") and appealed to Emperor Marcian—an old friend who had just assumed office—to call a church council. More than 500 bishops gathered at Chalcedon, a suburb of Constantinople, in 453. They condemned Eutyches and denounced the Monophysities.

But Canon 28 did not please Leo: it gave the bishop of Constantinople the title of "patriarch" and made his office second only to the bishop of Rome. With the emperor residing in Constantinople and most Christians living in the East, Leo reasoned it was only natural that the influence of the bishop of Constantinople would grow. Leo simply refused to recognize the canon.

Facing down the conquerors

During these years, the empire in the West was crumbling, and "barbarian" armies were taking advantage of Rome's weakness. In 452, when the Huns threatened Rome, Leo went out to meet their leader, Attila, "the Scourge of God," and convinced him to withdraw to beyond the Danube.

When three years later, the Vandal general Gaiseric marched on Rome, Roman soldiers panicked, murdered the emperor, and fled the city. Leo met with Gaiseric and begged for mercy, noting that the city had fallen without a struggle and that only civilians remained. He asked that the Vandal not slaughter the people nor burn their homes. Gaiseric listened silently, then spurred his horse away, calling over his shoulder, "Fourteen days looting." Two weeks later the Romans held a solemn service of thanksgiving for the city having been spared.

Leo's leadership in these political crises helped begin the long process by which the bishop of Rome became the most powerful Western figure in the Middle Ages. This, along with his vigorous pursuit of doctrinal purity and administrative savvy, have led to his being called, with only two other popes, "the Great."

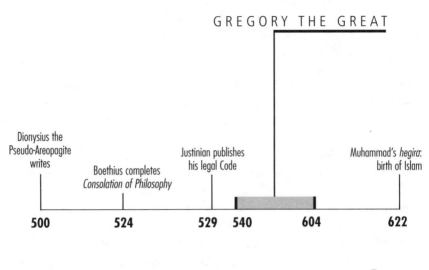

GREGORY THE GREAT

Dionysius the
Pseudo-Areopagite
writes

Boethius completes
Consolation of Philosophy

Justinian publishes
his legal Code

Muhammad's *hegira:*
birth of Islam

| 500 | 524 | 529 | 540 | 604 | 622 |

RULERS

Gregory the Great
"SERVANT OF THE SERVANTS OF GOD"

"Act in such a way that your humility may not be weakness, nor your authority be severity. Justice must be accompanied by humility, that humility may render justice lovable."

Gregory, before he became pope, happened to see some Anglo-Saxon slaves for sale in a Roman marketplace. He asked about the race of the remarkable blond men and was told they were "Anglos." "Not Anglos, but angels," he was said to reply. As a result, it is said, Gregory was later inspired to send missionaries to England.

Though apocryphal, the story shows a devout Gregory concerned about the spread of Christian faith. But this was but one facet of Gregory's extraordinary talent and energies.

Noble beginning

Gregory was descended from Roman nobles with a strong legacy of Christian faith. He was related to two previous popes (Felix III and Agapitus I), his aunts were nuns, and his parents joined cloisters in their later years. He was raised in Rome when it was only a shell of its former glory.

By the age of 30, he was the chief administrative official of the city, responsible for finances, police, provisioning, and public works—an experience that helped him hone his administrative skills and, together with his personal wealth, gave him the opportunity to create six monasteries.

Yet Gregory remained dissatisfied, and upon his father's death in 574, he converted his house into a monastery and retired to a life of contemplation and prayer. During these years, the happiest in Gregory's life, he began a detailed study of the Scriptures. Here he also ruined his health with fasting, a sacrifice that would precipitate his early death.

Called again to service

His administrative skills did not remain unappreciated. In 577 Pope Benedict appointed Gregory one of the seven deacons of Rome, and Pope Pelagius II sent him to Constantinople in 578 as representative to the imperial court, then later recalled him to serve as his confidential adviser.

In 589 a flood destroyed the grain reserves of Rome, instigating a famine and then a plague that swept through Rome and killed Pope Pelagius. Gregory was elected to succeed him. Though he had tried to refuse the office, once elected, he went to work with vigor.

To deal with the famine, Gregory instituted a city-wide penance, fed people from the church's granaries, and organized systematic relief for the poor.

Gregory then set himself reforming the church. He removed high officials "for pride and misdeeds," enforced celibacy, replaced lay officers with monks, and initiated a reorganization of "the patrimony of Peter," the vast land holdings of the church. The efficient and humane management of these estates brought in the revenue necessary to run the church as well as perform tasks the imperial government was neglecting.

An attack by the Lombard invaders in 592 and the inaction of the imperial representative forced Gregory to negotiate an end to the siege of Rome. When the imperial representative broke the truce in 593, Gregory purchased a separate peace treaty with tributes from the church coffers. By this time in Roman history, the pope had become the unofficial civil ruler of Italy, appointing generals, arranging relief, rallying cities to the defense, and paying the salaries of soldiers.

Pastoral care

Gregory also was actively concerned about the work of priests. He wrote a book of instruction for bishops, On Pastoral Care, in which he wrote, "Act in such a way that your humility may not be weakness, nor your authority be severity. Justice must be accompanied by humility, that humility may render justice lovable." It became a manual for holy life throughout the Middle Ages.

Gregory believed preaching was one of the clergy's primary duties, and he conducted a preaching tour of area churches. His Homilies on the Gospels was published in 591 and widely used for hundreds of years.

In 593 Gregory published his Dialogues, a history of the lives of Italian saints, as well as his sermons on Ezekiel and the Song of Songs. In 595 he published his allegorical exposition on Job, *Moralia*, and made changes to the liturgy. His interest in church music has been honored, as well: his name has been given to the plainsong ("Gregorian chant") that developed over the next few hundred years.

His frequent correspondence across the world shows him well aware of evangelistic opportunities in Britain. So it is not surprising that in 596 he sent Augustine, along with 40 monks, on a mission to "this far corner of the world."

Diverse legacy

Gregory set a high mark for the medieval papacy. He defended the primacy of the chair of Peter against even the smallest slight. He reconciled many independent bishops to Rome by humble appeals, not defending his personal rights but those of the institution. He was the first pope to call himself *Servus Servorum Dei*, "the servant of the servants of God," a title still in use today.

The administrative framework he set in place for the management of church lands made possible the development of the Papal States. His encouragement of the monastic life, his friendship with the kings of Spain and Gaul, and his deferential yet independent relationship with the emperor set a pattern for church-state relations for centuries.

He is one of the four great Latin doctors of the church (along with Ambrose, Augustine, and Jerome), and upon his death he was named a saint by popular acclaim.

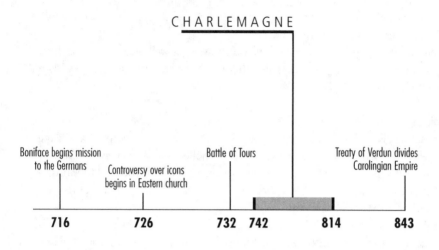

CHARLEMAGNE

| Boniface begins mission to the Germans | Controversy over icons begins in Eastern church | Battle of Tours | | Treaty of Verdun divides Carolingian Empire |

716   726   732 742   814   843

RULERS
Charlemagne
CHRISTIAN RULER OF A "HOLY" EMPIRE

> *"Our task [as secular ruler] is externally, with God's help, to defend with our arms the holy Church of Christ against attacks by the heathen from any side and against devastation by the infidels."*

Pepin III, King of the Franks, knelt with his sons to be anointed by Pope Stephen III in conscious imitation of the anointing of King David by the prophet Samuel. And like David's son Solomon, Pepin's son Charles would preside over a renowned cultural and religious flowering.

Expanding borders

Charles received his education from his mother and the monks of Saint Denis. He could speak and read Latin and his native Germanic tongue, but he never learned to write, though he tried to his entire life. He mastered the military and political arts close to his father's throne.

When Pepin died in 768, Charles was in his mid-20s: vital, energetic, and at six feet three-and-a-half-inches tall, he towered over his subjects. When his brother, Carloman, died in 771, Charles was left as sole ruler of the Franks.

Charles's early reign was marked by incessant warfare, which expanded his control in all directions. His longest wars (772–785) were in an area just below modern Denmark, against the Saxons. As he conquered, he converted them to Christianity at the point of the sword.

Pope Hadrian then asked for his help in the south, calling on Charles to deliver him from the Lombards. Charles obliged and quickly compelled the Lombard king to retire to a monastery. He took the crown for himself in 774, and now ruled over much of what is modern Italy. During an Easter visit to Rome that year he was greeted by the pope with the words; "Behold another Constantine, who has risen in our times."

Charles's 778 campaign against the Spanish Moors did not go as well and he was forced to withdraw. (An unimportant defeat in the Pyrenees formed the theme of the heroic epic, *The Song of Roland*, one of the most widely read poems of the Middle Ages.) Charles was determined to establish a secure border south of the Pyrenees, and he finally did so in 801, when he captured Barcelona.

In the meantime, he had turned his attention to the southeast border of his lands and conquered and absorbed Bavaria. Looking southeast, he pushed farther east along the Danube River into the territory of the Avars. His defeat of these fierce warriors not only netted him 15 large wagons of gold and silver but highlighted his political and military superiority to the Byzantine Empire to the east.

New Roman emperor

His triumph culminated on Christmas 800, when in one of the best known scenes of the Middle Ages, Pope Leo III crowned Charlemagne "Emperor of the Romans."

Charles told his biographer that he attended the service unaware that the pope was going to do this, but modern historians discount this as overly modest. In addition to complex political reasons for wanting the title, Charles had theological reasons. Charles was also a great student of Augustine, much taken with his idea of the *City of God*. He believed the church and state should be allied as forces in the unification of society.

Charles delineated the roles of state and church in a letter to Pope Leo: "Our task [as secular ruler] is externally, with God's help, to defend with our arms the holy Church of Christ against attacks by the heathen from any side and against devastation by the infidels and, internally, to strengthen the Church by the recognition of the Catholic faith. Your share, Most Holy Father, is to support our army with hands upraised to God, as did Moses in ancient days, so that the ... name of our Lord Jesus Christ may be glorified throughout the world."

Charles, then, believed the title, "Emperor of the Romans," made him the successor of the Roman emperors. (Never mind that the Byzantine emperors had thought the same of themselves for centuries!)

Defender of the Church

Charles took seriously his mission to "internally strengthen the church." Indeed, within his kingdom he was far more influential in church affairs than was the pope.

Charles appointed and deposed bishops, directed a revision of the text of the Bible, instituted changes to the liturgy, set rules for life in the monasteries, and sent investigators to dismiss priests with insufficient learning or piety. He had his deacon, Paul, publish a collection of homilies for use throughout the kingdom, instructing him to "peruse the writings of the Catholic fathers and, as in a flowery meadow, pick the choicest blooms and weave a single garland of all that can be put to use."

Charles also took an active interest in the two main religious controversies of his era, adoptionism (which held that Jesus was not "God from God" but was adopted as God's son during his lifetime) and iconoclasm (which condemns icons as idolatry). In his reforms, Charles showed that, like Constantine, he believed he was overlord of the church.

Education was also carefully tended. The partially illiterate Charles believed that success in his political and religious reforms depended on learning: "Although doing right is better than knowledge, knowledge comes before doing." Charles was a patron of scholars,

creating a school for his many children in the palace and accumulating an impressive library. The only copy of many classical texts we have today came from the pens of monks he set to work. He required each cathedral and monastery to set up a school and compelled the children of nobles to attend (who might otherwise have considered this beneath them).

Charles's government helped set the feudal system deeply in place. His armies were made of nobles, bound to him by oaths and granted tracts of land to support themselves and their soldiers. He published his laws in "capitularies," and sent them throughout the realm by *missi dominici*, pairs of inspectors who made sure his orders were obeyed in castles and churches.

This energetic political, cultural, and religious reform, is today known as the Carolingian Renaissance and is one reason Charles was given the appellation, "Great," in Latin, Charlemagne.

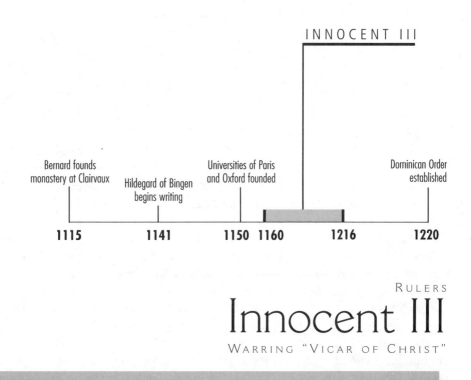

INNOCENT III

| Bernard founds monastery at Clairvaux | Hildegard of Bingen begins writing | Universities of Paris and Oxford founded | | | Dominican Order established |

| 1115 | 1141 | 1150 | 1160 | 1216 | 1220 |

RULERS

Innocent III

WARRING "VICAR OF CHRIST"

"Verily the representative of Christ, the successor of Peter, the anointed of the Lord, the God of Pharaoh set midway between God and man, below God but above man, less than God but more than man, judging all other men, but himself judged by none."

When England's King John refused Pope Innocent's appointee for archbishop of Canterbury in 1208, Innocent placed the nation under interdict; the church would not marry, baptize, or bury anyone. John retaliated by expelling most of the bishops, but that only made matters worse. Innocent excommunicated the king, declared the throne vacant, and invited the French to invade. John finally recognized Innocent as his superior in 1213. But even then the pope had a quarrel—he declared the *Magna Carta* void because John had entered into it without his consent.

Such was the power of Innocent III, the first pope regularly to style himself the "Vicar of Christ."

Born to rule

Lotario Scotti was born into a noble Italian family and sent to the finest schools. He studied theology in Paris and canon law in Bologna. He was entrusted with important tasks by Popes Lucias III and Gregory VIII. At 30, his uncle, Pope Clement III, made him a cardinal. The day after Pope Celestine III died, Innocent became one of the youngest men ever selected to sit in Peter's Chair. He was quickly ordained as a priest and the next day consecrated Innocent III.

Innocent was born to rule; he was exceptionally gifted in intellect, will, and leadership. He was the foremost church lawyer of the age. Still, he had a combative spirit and was prone to fits of depression.

He began his reign by purging church officials not loyal to him and by curbing excesses of his own household. Plates of gold were exchanged for wood, and nobles from royal families were replaced by monks. He reasserted control over the papal estates, though after an attempt on his life, he gave his family charge of key cities.

Universal ruler

Innocent saw the pope as feudal overlord of all secular rulers—"not only over the universal church, but the whole world." He thought of his office in a semi-Divine light: "Verily the representative of Christ, the successor of Peter, the anointed of the Lord, the God of Pharaoh set midway between God and man, below God but above man, less than God but more than man, judging all other men, but himself judged by none."

The death of Holy Roman Emperor Henry VI in 1197 gave him the opportunity to put this theory into practice by arbitrating between the rivals for the imperial throne. He conceded the right of the imperial electors to select a candidate, but he insisted he make the final appointment. He first selected Otto of Brunswick, who promised to recognize the enlarged Papal States and renounce any claim to the assets of deceased church officials. When Otto invaded Italy (breaking his promise to Innocent), Innocent excommunicated him and installed his own ward, Frederic II, as Holy Roman emperor.

Innocent could truthfully declare that kings held their crown by virtue of the "grace of God and of the pope." He maneuvered European monarchs like pawns on a chess board and accepted the gift of countries like Spain and Hungary as matters of course. He compelled Philip of France to take back the wife he divorced. Innocent corresponded with the eastern emperor about reunion until the Fourth Crusade was diverted on its way to Egypt and ended up sacking Constantinople in 1204. Turning the *fait accompli* to his best advantage, Innocent set up a Latin rite church in the ruins.

Reformer

The thirteenth century was a time of religious ferment, which saw the eruption of sects—orthodox, heretical, and schismatic—reacting to church corruption. After trying persuasion with the heretical Albigensians, Innocent declared a bloody crusade against them. More than 15,000 peasants were slaughtered in one town alone.

Innocent instituted a wide-ranging series of church reforms. Clergy excesses from luxurious clothing to drunken carousing were attacked. He promoted honest business practices in the church, encouraged provincial and national councils, required bishops to visit

Rome every four years, restored observation of rules in religious orders, and encouraged the foundation of schools. During his reign, he recognized and gave patronage to two newly established reform groups, the Franciscans and the Dominicans. He issued over 6,000 decrees and formalized many of his reforms with the Fourth Lateran Council—where the term "transubstantiate" (meaning, the bread of Communion becomes the real body of Christ) was first officially used.

Innocent died of recurring fevers on a trip to settle a dispute between Pisa and Genoa, a dispute he feared would hinder his next crusade.

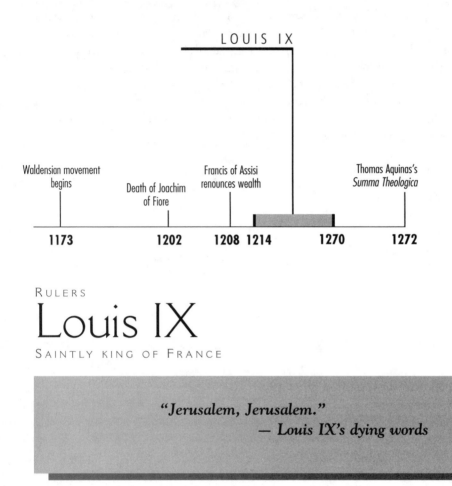

LOUIS IX

Waldensian movement begins	Death of Joachim of Fiore	Francis of Assisi renounces wealth		Thomas Aquinas's *Summa Theologica*
1173	1202	1208	1214	1270 1272

RULERS

Louis IX

SAINTLY KING OF FRANCE

> *"Jerusalem, Jerusalem."*
> *— Louis IX's dying words*

He didn't act like a king. He wore hair shirts and visited hospitals, sometimes emptying the bedpans. He collected relics and built a chapel to house them.

Such unkingly behavior was one reason Louis IX developed the reputation as the most Christian of rulers.

Teenage Christian king

Born the fourth of 11 children to King Louis VIII and Queen Blanche, Louis became heir to the throne after his three older siblings died. Blanche raised her son to be strictly religious: "I love you, my dear son, as much as a mother can love her child," she once said to him, "but I would rather see you dead at my feet than that you should ever commit a mortal sin." At age 12, prepubescent Louis found himself king, with a devout but smothering mother at his side.

At 20 he married Margaret of Provence ("a girl of pretty face, but prettier faith"), to whom he quickly became devoted. She bore him 11 children. When he left on a crusade, he took his wife and children along.

Louis lived his faith, and his reputation spread. The Latin emperor of Constantinople gave Louis the Crown of Thorns in 1238, and Louis built the magnificent Sainte Chapelle to house this relic of Christ's crucifixion.

In 1242 Henry III of England invaded Angevin. Louis managed to drive off the English king but contracted an infection that almost killed him. He vowed if he got well, he would do what men of nearly every generation in his family had done for 150 years: he would lead a crusade.

Failed crusade

With 36 ships loaded with 15,000 men, their horses, and supplies, Louis headed for Egypt, the center of Muslim power and the doorway to Jerusalem. After capturing Damietta, he led his army inland toward Cairo. But an epidemic forced Louis to retreat. The king suffered so badly from dysentery that he cut a hole in the back of his pants and marched with the rear guard.

Louis and part of the army were captured before making it back to the ships. Their ransom was so high, it reportedly took two days to count the gold. When one of Louis's officials bragged about cheating the Muslims, the king angrily ordered the ransom paid in full.

The defeat plunged him into despair and deeper piety. He blamed himself for the loss, believing God was punishing him for his sins. He began dressing plainly, eating simply, and helping the poor. Instead of going home, Louis took his army to Palestine, where they built walls and towers around several coastal cities. He stayed four years, returning to France only upon hearing of the death of his mother, who had been ruling in his absence.

Dying on a bed of ashes

Back home, Louis redoubled his penance and his efforts to create a holy nation. He systematized customary law, recorded cases as precedents, and replaced trial by combat with the examination of witnesses under oath. He outlawed usury (lending money at an excessively high rate), ordered blasphemers to be branded on the lips, and forbade feudal lords to make private war on one another.

All feudal lords made a show of charity and good works. What made Louis different was his humility and perseverance. Every year, he went to the abbey of Saint Denis barefoot and bareheaded. Louis not only served the poor at his table, but he and his sons washed the feet of the beggars. He was especially generous to the widows of crusaders. Louis had a special passion for sermons, then just coming into vogue, and he encouraged the preaching friars, repeating his favorite homilies to those at his table. Queen Marguerite's confessor records that she would often get up at night and cover the king with a cloak while he was at his lengthy prayers, because he did not notice the cold.

Twenty-two years after his first crusade, Louis tried to redeem himself with another.

He landed in Tunis, in northern Africa, in the heat of the summer of 1270. Dysentery or typhoid quickly swept through the unsanitary camp. Louis fell ill and died while lying penitently on a bed of ashes, whispering the name of the city he never won: "Jerusalem, Jerusalem." He soon became the only king of France named a saint by the Roman Catholic Church.

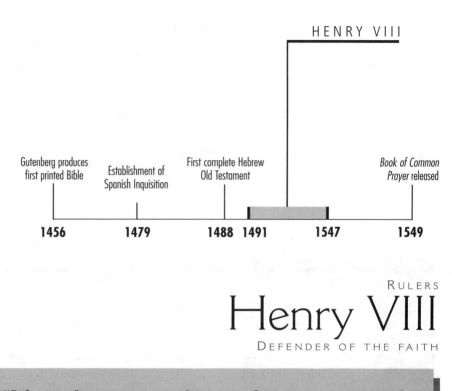

HENRY VIII

| Gutenberg produces first printed Bible | Establishment of Spanish Inquisition | First complete Hebrew Old Testament | | | Book of Common Prayer released |

1456   **1479**   **1488**   **1491**   **1547**   **1549**

RULERS

Henry VIII

DEFENDER OF THE FAITH

> *"I do not choose anyone to have it in his power to command me, nor will I ever suffer it."*

Many consider Henry to have been a dilettante king, letting his ministers run the country while he hunted stag. In truth he was actively involved in the details of anything that he judged important. Henry demanded the facts be boiled down to their essence. Then he would listen to the issues and make a quick decision, often in the time it took him to dismount from his horse.

The most important decision of his reign, however, he struggled with for years. But once he determined his course, he followed it with a flurry of decisions that forever changed his country.

An auspicious beginning

Henry was born the second son of Henry VII. He was intelligent, handsome, physically powerful, talented in music, and an avid hunter and sportsman. He was sole ruler of England and the richest man in the world at 18 years of age.

To cement England's alliance with Spain, Henry wed the Spanish king's aunt, Catherine of Aragon (also the widow of his brother). When Henry defeated France and Scotland in successive battles, his popularity soared. Over the next decade, Henry made and broke peace treaties, stood for election as Holy Roman Emperor, engaged in the power politics of Europe, and turned his attention to religion.

Henry had always been a religious man. He heard mass five times a day unless he was hunting (then he could only hear three). He was also deeply interested in theological disputes. In 1521, with Lutheranism infecting the English universities, Henry wrote *Defense of the Seven Sacraments* against Luther. A beleaguered and grateful pope rewarded him with the title "Defender of the Faith."

Producing an heir

By 1526 Henry began to seek ways to end his marriage with Catherine. The alliance

with Spain was restricting his international intrigues, he had fallen in love with 19-year-old Anne Boleyn, and, most importantly, Catherine had failed to give him a male heir (she did give birth to a daughter, Mary). England had recently survived a bloody and costly civil war; Henry needed a male heir to insure a peaceful succession upon his death.

Getting an annulment was fairly easy in the sixteenth century—if both parties wanted one. But Catherine was unwilling and sought the support of her nephew, Emperor Charles V. The emperor didn't want to see his aunt disgraced and routed the pope's troops. Pope Clement, seeing the score, had no choice but to refuse Henry the annulment.

When Anne became pregnant in 1532, Henry moved ahead on his own. He had already forced the clergy to submit to his supremacy in all ecclesiastical matters. Now he married Anne in secret, had his new archbishop of Canterbury, Thomas Cranmer, declare his marriage to Catherine invalid, and crowned Anne queen in 1533. Henry and the church teetered on the brink of schism.

A fight for control

When the pope threatened excommunication, Henry plunged ahead. He passed one act forcing all to recognize the children of his new marriage as heirs to the throne. Then he passed another making him the "supreme head" of the church in England. He dissolved monasteries, redistributing their property to his nobles to reinforce their loyalty. Monks who resisted were executed, and the money from their treasuries went into his coffers.

Still, in an era of Reformation, his church reforms were conservative. He appeared to want a Catholic church—just one that was always loyal to him and to England. "I do not choose anyone to have it in his power to command me, nor will I ever suffer it," he once said. So while he broke from Rome, he continued to uphold transubstantiation and demanded clerical celibacy.

Meanwhile, Henry tired of Anne because she had only produced a girl—Elizabeth. He trumped up charges of infidelity against her, had her beheaded, and then married Jane Seymour. After she gave birth to a son (Edward), she died. Henry married three more times before he died.

Henry's break from Rome was fundamentally over control of the English church. Though he instituted some Protestant measures during his reign (like putting English Bibles in all the churches), and though he always supported his Protestant-leaning archbishop of Canterbury, Cranmer, Henry sided with Rome on key issues of doctrine and practice.

But the events he set in motion would not permit England to return to the past. During the reign of his son, Edward VI (1547–53), England turned staunchly Protestant. After a brief return to Catholicism under Mary I (1553–1558), his daughter Elizabeth I set England on a permanently Protestant course.

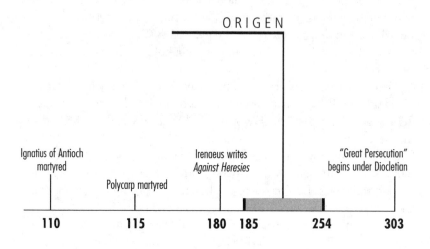

ORIGEN

Ignatius of Antioch
martyred

Polycarp martyred

Irenaeus writes
Against Heresies

"Great Persecution"
begins under Diocletian

110   115   180 185   254   303

SCHOLARS AND SCIENTISTS

Origen

BIBLICAL SCHOLAR AND PHILOSOPHER

> *"We who by our prayers destroy all demons which stir up wars, violate oaths, and disturb the peace are of more help to the emperors than those who seem to be doing the fighting."*

This third century "religious fanatic" gave up his job, slept on the floor, ate no meat, drank no wine, fasted twice a week, owned no shoes, and reportedly castrated himself for the faith. He was also the most prolific scholar of his age (with hundreds of works to his credit), a first-rate Christian philosopher, and a profound student of the Bible.

Child prodigy Origen Adamantius ("man of steel") was born near Alexandria about A.D. 185. The oldest of seven children in a Christian home, he grew up learning the Bible and the meaning of commitment. In 202 when his father, Leonidas, was beheaded for his Christian beliefs, Origen wanted to die as a martyr, too. But his mother prevented him from even leaving the house—by hiding his clothes.

To support his family, the 18-year-old Origen opened a grammar school, copied texts, and instructed catechumens (those seeking to become members of the church). He himself studied under the pagan philosopher Ammonius Saccas in order to better defend his faith against pagan arguments. When a rich convert supplied him with secretaries, he began to write.

Bible student and critic

Origen worked for 20 years on his *Hexapla*, a massive work of Old Testament analysis written to answer Jewish and Gnostic critics of Christianity. An examination of Biblical texts, it had six parallel columns: one in Hebrew, and the other five in various Greek translations, including one he found at Jericho in a jar. It became an important step in the development of the Christian canon and scriptural translation, but unfortunately it was destroyed. So massive was it that scholars doubt anyone ever copied it entirely.

This first Bible scholar analyzed the Scriptures on three levels: the literal, the moral, and the allegorical. As he put it, "For just as man consists of body, soul, and spirit, so in the same way does the Scripture." Origen, in fact, preferred the allegorical not only because it allowed for more spiritual interpretations, but many passages he found impossible to read literally: "Now what man of intelligence will believe that the first and the second and the third day ... existed without the sun and moon and stars?" In any event, Origen's method of interpretation became the standard in the Middle Ages. Origen's main work, *De Principiis* (*On First Principles*), was the first systematic exposition of Christian theology ever written. In it he created a Christian philosophy, synthesizing Greek technique and biblical assumptions. Add to these massive works his homilies and commentaries, and it's clear why he was reputed to have kept seven secretaries busy and caused Jerome (c.354–420) to say in frustrated admiration, "Has anyone read everything that Origen wrote?"

Heretical church father?

Origen has always been controversial. His reported self-mutilation, in response to Matthew 19:12 ("... there are eunuchs who have made themselves eunuchs for the sake of the kingdom of heaven....") was condemned as a drastic misinterpretation of the text. In Palestine he preached without being ordained and was so condemned by his bishop, Demetrius. When on a second trip, he was ordained by the same bishops who had invited him to speak the first time, Demetrius sent him into exile.

While some of his writings are thought to have been hypothetical, Origen did teach that all spirits were created equal, existed before birth, and then fell from grace. Furthermore, "those rational beings who sinned and on account fell from the state in which they were, in proportion to their particular sins, were enslaved in bodies as punishment"—some demons, some men, and some angels. He also believed that all spirits, even Satan, could be saved. "The power of choosing between good and evil is within the reach of all," he wrote.

Most notably, however, Origen described the Trinity as a hierarchy, not as an equality of Father, Son, and Spirit. And though he attacked Gnostic beliefs, like them, he rejected the goodness of material creation.

Three centuries after his death, the Council of Constantinople (553) pronounced him a heretic: "Whoever says or thinks that the punishment of demons and the wicked will not be eternal ... let him be anathema."

Some contend that Origen was merely trying to frame the faith in the ideas of his day; still his works were suppressed following his condemnation, so modern judgment is impossible.

Despite such condemnation, Origen said, "I want to be a man of the church ... to be called ... of Christ." His *Contra Celsum*, in fact, is one of the finest defenses of Christianity produced in the early church. Answering the charge that Christians, by refusing military service, fail the test of good citizenship, he wrote, "We who by our prayers destroy all demons which stir up wars, violate oaths, and disturb the peace are of more help to the emperors than those who seem to be doing the fighting."

The authorities, however, were not convinced: in 250 the emperor Decius had Origen imprisoned and tortured. He was deliberately kept alive in the hope that he would renounce his faith. But Decius died first and Origen went free. His health broken, Origen died shortly after his release.

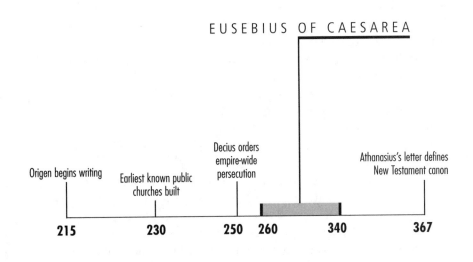

EUSEBIUS OF CAESAREA

Origen begins writing

Earliest known public
churches built

Decius orders
empire-wide
persecution

Athanasius's letter defines
New Testament canon

215   230   250   260   340   367

SCHOLARS AND SCIENTISTS

Eusebius of Caesarea

FATHER—AND MAKER—OF CHURCH HISTORY

"I feel inadequate to do [church history] justice as the first to venture on such an undertaking, a traveler on a lonely and untrodden path."

Imagine writing a comprehensive history of the church's last three centuries. Now imagine no one has ever written such a history before, so there's no single collection of key documents, no books profiling key figures, no chronology of major events, not even a fixed system of dates. When Eusebius, bishop of Caesarea, undertook such an effort, he felt trepidation: "I feel inadequate to do it justice as the first to venture on such an undertaking, a traveler on a lonely and untrodden path," he wrote in his introduction to the *The Church History* (or *Ecclesiastical History*). "But I pray that God may guide me and the power of the Lord assist me, for I have not found even the footprints of any predecessors on this path, only traces in which some have left various accounts of the times in which they lived."

For this ten-volume work, Eusebius is known as "the father of church history." But in his day, he was as much a maker of history as a recorder of it.

Persecuted

There was once a biography of Eusebius, written by his successor as Caesarea's bishop, but like so many other documents, it is lost. So we know nothing for certain about this historian's early life. He was probably born in Palestine, certainly baptized at Caesarea and ordained a presbyter (elder) under his teacher and friend, Pamphilus. So closely did he follow this Origen devotee that he called himself Eusebius Pamphili, son of Pamphilus.

But in 303 came Diocletian who ordered his "great persecution," and Pamphilus was martyred within seven years. Eusebius too, was imprisoned but managed to avoid his mentor's fate. Around 313, about the time of Constantine's Edict of Milan, Eusebius became bishop of the Palestinian city. There he continued work on his church history, which he began during the persecutions. He also wrote a 15-volume refutation of paganism called *Preparation*, and *Demonstration of the Gospel*, demonstrating Christ's fulfillment of Old Testament prophecy; he also completed his *Chronicle* of world history.

Eusebius's history was not written simply to record the deeds of the church after Christ's ascension; he wanted to show that Christianity, with Constantine's conversion, was the pinnacle of humanity's long climb. The church had been an oppressed minority, but now it could enter a period of peace.

Peace seeker

Just as Eusebius was writing about Christianity's defeat of paganism, one of its greatest threats was developing on the inside. Arius, a presbyter from Libya, was gaining followers around the empire, teaching, "There was a time when the Son was not." Egyptian bishop Alexander and his chief deacon, Athanasius, fumed at the teaching. The argument spread throughout the empire, promising to rip the church in two. Constantine—God's chosen instrument, as Eusebius saw him—called the Council of Nicea to close the fissure.

Since his earliest days with Pamphilus, Eusebius was enthralled with the teachings of Origen, who has been criticized for 1,800 years for his belief that the Trinity was a hierarchy, not an equality. So Eusebius was less concerned with Arius's heresy than the threat of disunity in the church. When Arius was censured, Eusebius—who thought the entire debate brought Christianity the "most shameful ridicule"—was among the first to ask that he be reinstated.

At the Council of Nicea, Eusebius (whose name means "faithful") attempted to mediate between the Arians and the orthodox. But when the council was over and Arius was anathematized, Eusebius was reluctant to agree with its decision. He eventually signed the document the council produced, saying, "Peace is the object which we set before us." But a few years later, when the tables flipped and Arianism became popular, Eusebius criticized Athanasius, hero of the council. He even sat on the council that deposed him. Eusebius wasn't himself an Arian—he rejected the idea that "there was a time when the Son was not" and that Christ was created out of nothing. He simply opposed anti-Arianism.

As the Arian controversy continued to rage, Eusebius stayed in Caesarea—declining a promotion to become bishop of Antioch—and wrote. Among his most famous writings of this period was another history: a praise-filled *Life of Constantine*, his adored political leader.

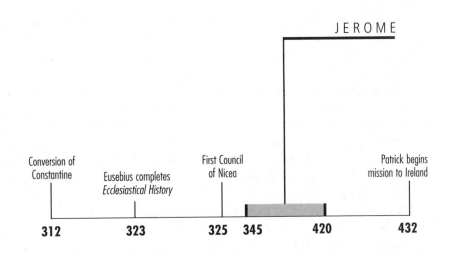

JEROME

Conversion of
Constantine

Eusebius completes
Ecclesiastical History

First Council
of Nicea

Patrick begins
mission to Ireland

312   323   325   345   420   432

SCHOLARS AND SCIENTISTS

Jerome

BIBLE TRANSLATOR WHOSE VERSION LASTED A MILLENNIUM

> *"Make knowledge of the Scripture your love.... Live with them, meditate on them, make them the sole object of your knowledge and inquiries."*

Eusebius Hieronymus Sophronius, thankfully known as Jerome, was probably the greatest Christian scholar in the world by his mid-30s. Perhaps the greatest figure in the history of Bible translation, he spent three decades creating a Latin version that would be the standard for more than a millennium. But this was no bookish egghead. Jerome was also an extreme ascetic with a nasty disposition who showered his opponents with sarcasm and invective.

From Cicero to scorpions

Jerome was born to wealthy Christian parents in Stridon, Dalmatia (near modern Ljubljana, Slovenia), and educated in Rome, where he studied grammar, rhetoric, and philosophy. There he was baptized at age 19.

Like other students, Jerome followed his studies with travel. But instead of discovering the sensuous pleasures of the empire,

Jerome found himself drawn to the ascetics he met along the way, including those in Trier (now in southwest Germany) and Aquileia, Italy, where he joined a group of elite ascetics. Among them was Rufinius, famous for his translations of Origen's works. The group disbanded around 373, however, and Jerome resumed his travels, this time taking "an uncertain journey" to become a hermit in the Holy Land.

Exhausted, he only made it as far as Antioch, where he continued his studies of Greek. He even studied under Apollinarius of Laodicea (who was later condemned as a heretic for teaching Christ had only human flesh, not a human mind or will). But his Greek studies were interrupted by a dream—one of the most famous in church history—during Lent 375: dragged before a tribunal of God, he was found guilty of preferring classic pagan literature to Christian: "Ciceronianus es, non Christianus," (You are a follower of Cicero, not of Christ) said his judge.

Shaken, Jerome vowed never to read or own pagan literature again. (More than a decade later, however, Jerome downplayed the dream and again began reading classic literature.) He then shuffled off to the Syrian desert, rediscovering the joys of an ascetic "prison, with none but scorpions and wild beasts for companions." He settled in Chalcis, where the rigors of this life were exhausting. He begged for letters to stave off his loneliness, hated the harsh desert food, and could not find peace.

"Though I was protected by the rampart of the lonely desert, I could not endure against the promptings of sin and the ardent heat of my nature," he later wrote. "I tried to crush them by frequent fasting, but my mind was always in a turmoil of imagination."

Still, he learned Hebrew from a Jewish convert, prayed and fasted, copied manuscripts, and wrote countless letters. Despite his repeated assurances that he was happy in Chalcis, he returned to Antioch after a few years—shortly after other hermits began to suspect Jerome was a secret heretic (for his views on the Trinity, which, some argued, emphasized the unity of God at the expense of the three persons).

Sharp-tongued secretary

By then, Jerome was recognized as an important scholar and monk. Bishop Paulinus rushed to ordain him as priest, but the monk would only accept it on the condition that he would never be forced to carry out priestly functions. Instead, Jerome plunged himself into scholarship, especially that of the Bible. He attended exegetical lectures, examined Gospel parchments, and met other famous exegetes and theologians.

In 382 he was summoned to Rome to be secretary and one possible successor to Pope Damasus. But during his short three-year stint there, Jerome offended the pleasure-loving Romans with his sharp tongue and blunt criticism. As one historian put it, "He detested most of the Romans and did not apologize for detesting them." He mocked the clerics' lack of charity ("I have not faith and mercy, but such as I have, silver and gold— that I don't give to you either"), their vanity ("The only thought of such men is their clothes—are they pleasantly perfumed, do their shoes fit smoothly?"), their pride in their beards ("If there is any holiness in a beard, nobody is holier than a goat!"), and their ignorance of Scripture ("It is bad enough to teach what you do not know, but even worse ...

not even to be aware that you do not know").

He even bragged of his influence, declaring, "Damasus is my mouth." Those who might have supported him, though already skeptical of his interest in "correcting" the Bible, were put off when one of his female disciples died during a severe fast. When Damasus died in 384, Jerome fled "Babylon" for the Holy Land.

Creator of the Vulgate

A wealthy student of Jerome's founded a monastery in Bethlehem for him to administer (it also included three cloisters for women and a hostel for pilgrims). Here he finished his greatest contribution (begun in 382 at Damasus's instruction): translating the Bible into everyday Latin (later to be called the Vulgate, meaning "common"). Though there were Latin versions available, they varied widely in accuracy.

"If we are to pin our faith to the Latin texts," Damasus had once written to him, "it is for our opponents to tell us which, for there are almost as many forms as there are copies. If, on the other hand, we are to glean the truth from a comparison of many, why not go back to the original Greek and correct the mistakes introduced by inaccurate translators, and the blundering alterations of confident but ignorant critics, and, further, all that has been inserted or changed by copyists more asleep than awake?"

At first Jerome worked from the Greek Old Testament, the Septuagint. But then he established a precedent for later translators: the Old Testament would have to be translated from the original Hebrew. In his quest for accuracy, he consulted Jewish rabbis and others.

One of the biggest differences he saw between the Septuagint and the original Hebrew was that the Jews did not include the books now known as the Apocrypha in their canon of Holy Scripture. Though he still felt obligated to include them, Jerome made it clear that he thought them to be church books, not fully inspired canonical books. (Reformation leaders would later remove them entirely from their Bibles.)

After 23 years, Jerome completed his translation, which Christians used for more than 1,000 years, and in 1546 the Council of Trent declared it the only authentic Latin text of the Scriptures. Sadly, the text of the Vulgate that circulated throughout the Middle Ages was a corrupt form of Jerome's work, encumbered by copyists' errors. (In the late sixteenth century, corrected editions were published.)

Jerome's work became so widely revered that until the Reformation, translators worked from the Vulgate; not for a thousand years did scholars again translate directly from the Greek New Testament. And ironically, Jerome's Bible added impetus to the use of Latin as the Western church's language, resulting centuries later in a liturgy and Bible lay people could not understand—precisely the opposite of Jerome's original intention.

For Jerome, however, his scholarship gave him an appreciation of the Word of God he carried for the rest of his life: "Make knowledge of the Scripture your love.... Live with them, meditate on them, make them the sole object of your knowledge and inquiries."

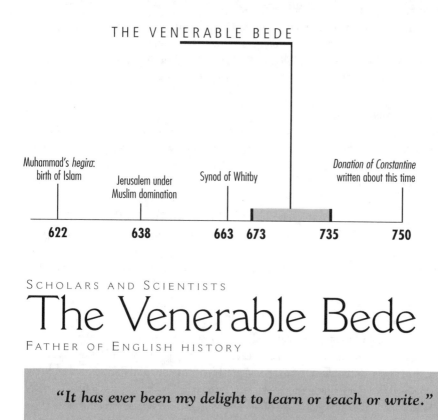

THE VENERABLE BEDE

Muhammad's *hegira*: birth of Islam	Jerusalem under Muslim domination	Synod of Whitby		Donation of Constantine written about this time
622	638	663	673	735	750

SCHOLARS AND SCIENTISTS

The Venerable Bede

FATHER OF ENGLISH HISTORY

> *"It has ever been my delight to learn or teach or write."*

At age 7, Bede was given to the monks of Wearmouth Abby as an oblate. He never left. "From that time, I have spent the whole of my life within that monastery, devoting all my pains to the study of the Scriptures, and amid the observance of monastic discipline and the daily charge of singing in the church, it has ever been my delight to learn or teach or write."

Indeed: Bede completed some 40 works in his busy life, none more important than *History of the English Church and Its People.* Bede ranks not only as the first English historian, but also one of the best.

Hardest working man in the business

More specifically, the young Bede was given over to the care of the abbot Benedict Biscop, a learned man with refined tastes, who introduced Bede to the world of beauty and scholarship. Bede's love for church liturgy was cemented during an early tragedy, when all the monks but Benedict succumbed to the plague and Bede and his abbot alone labored together to continue the services until others could be sent to support them.

For the adult Bede, life was an continuous round of devotion and study. His fellow monks testify to his character, as one put it, "I can with truth declare that I never saw with my eyes or heard with my ears anyone return thanks so unceasingly to the living God."

Bede, for his part, only qualified his reputation as a hard working scholar: "I really don't work 'night and day,' but it is quite true that I do toil hard to reach a right judgment on all that I read."

Bede was a renaissance scholar: He wrote on grammar, mathematics, poetry, church music, rhetoric, and science, both for a general audience and for his own pupils. One of his students, Alcuin, went on to become an influential figure in the court of Charlemagne.

Still, it is his English history that is best known and most treasured today. His interest in the topic began with curiosity about the correct date to celebrate Easter, and Bede is the first historian to use the A.D. (from the Latin *anno Domini*, "in the year of our Lord") system of dating. His history ranges from 55 B.C. to A.D. 731, and without it, we would know little of the early centuries of Christianity in Britain, especially the history of Celtic Christianity, early missions to the Continent, and the definitive Synod of Whitby (during which the Celtic church submitted itself to Rome).

His thoroughness and accuracy are the book's strengths, and considering the limitations of the day, Bede's achievement is remarkable: he quoted some 144 separate works and no doubt consulted even more. He asked traveling monks to consult Vatican archives for him, and evidence came to him from many witnesses scattered over Europe. And he exhorted his copyists to preserve his citations—"since I do not want to be thought a thief in putting down as mine what is really theirs."

Though remembered as a historian, Bede's chief delight was in the study of Scripture. Four-fifths of his writings were on biblical interpretation. These include commentaries on the Pentateuch, the Gospels, Acts, and Revelation. On his deathbed he translated the Gospel of John from the Latin into English, which one English biblical scholar called the "opening scene of the ... history of the English Bible."

He died on the floor of his cell where he regularly prayed, and just before he died, he was heard chanting the Gloria.

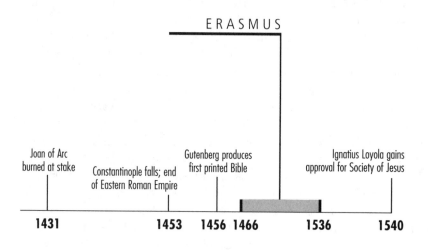

Joan of Arc burned at stake	Constantinople falls; end of Eastern Roman Empire	Gutenberg produces first printed Bible		Ignatius Loyola gains approval for Society of Jesus	
1431	**1453**	**1456**	**1466**	**1536**	**1540**

SCHOLARS AND SCIENTISTS

Erasmus

PIOUS HUMANIST WHO SPARKED THE REFORMATION

"Would that the farmer might sing snatches of Scripture at his plough and that the weaver might hum phrases of Scripture to the tune of his shuttle, that the traveler might lighten with stories from Scripture the weariness of his journey."

"When I get a little money I buy books," wrote Erasmus of Rotterdam, who took the name Desiderius in his adult life. "If any is left ... I buy food and clothes."

This illegitimate son of a Dutch priest lived in search of knowledge, in pursuit of piety, in love with books, and oppressed by the fear of poverty. Along the way, his writings and scholarship started a theological earthquake that didn't stop until western European Christendom was split.

No fan of monasticism

Born in Rotterdam, orphaned by the plague, Erasmus was sent from the chapter school of St. Lebuin's—which taught classical learning and the humanities—to a school conducted by the monastic Brethren of the Common Life. He absorbed an emphasis on a personal relationship with God but hated the severe rules of monastic life and the intolerant theologians. They intended to teach humility, he later recalled, by breaking the pupils' spirits.

But he was poor, and both he and his brother had to enter monasteries; Erasmus decided to join the Augustinians. He wanted to travel, gain some academic elbow room, and leave behind the "barbarians" who discouraged him from classical studies. And as soon as he was ordained a priest in 1492, he did, becoming secretary to the bishop of Cambrai, who sent him to Paris to study theology.

He hated it there too. The dorms stank of urine, the food was execrable, the studies mechanical, and the discipline brutal. But he was able to begin a career in writing and traveling that took him to most of the countries of Europe. Though he often complained of poor health, he was driven by a desire to seek out the best theologians of his day. On a trip to England in 1499, he complained of bad beer, barbarism, and inhospitable weather, but he also met Thomas More, who became a friend for life.

On the same trip he heard John Colet teach from the Scriptures, not the layers of commentaries he had studied in Paris. Colet, who would later become the dean of St. Paul's, encouraged the Dutch scholar to become a "primitive theologian" who studied Scripture like the church Fathers, not like the argumentative scholastics.

Thereafter Erasmus devoted himself to the Greek language, in which the New Testament was written. "I cannot tell you, dear Colet, how I hurry on, with all sails set, to holy literature," he soon wrote to his new friend. "How I dislike everything that keeps me back, or retards me."

The result was his most significant work: an edition of the New Testament in original Greek, published in 1516. Accompanying it were study notes as well as his own Latin translation—correcting some 600 errors in Jerome's Vulgate.

In the preface, Erasmus said he undertook the project so everyone could finally read the Bible: "Would that these were translated into each and every language.... Would that the farmer might sing snatches of Scripture at his plough and that the weaver might hum phrases of Scripture to the tune of his shuttle, that the traveler might lighten with stories from Scripture the weariness of his journey."

Two of the most noteworthy praises of Erasmus's work came from Pope Leo X and from a German monk named Martin Luther—who, one year later, would launch the Protestant Reformation.

"Foolish" critic

Before that turning point—which would eventually consume the humanist (which at the time meant student of the humanities, not one who praises humanity above all else)—Erasmus became famous for his other writings. And there were plenty for him to be famous for. By the 1530s, between 10 and 20 percent of all the books sold had his byline.

He said he wrote to "correct the errors of those whose religion is usually composed of ... ceremonies and observances of a material sort and neglect the things that conduce to piety." He became famous for his biting satire, *In Praise of Folly*, which attacked monastic and ecclesiastic corruption. He lambasted miracles supposedly performed by images, indulgences, and what he felt were useless church rites.

The books brought him fame, as did his Bible. This and his attacks on a church caught Luther's attention, who wrote asking for support.

Between Scylla and Charybdis

The two never met, but their fates were entwined for all history. Erasmus's enemies accused him of inspiring the schismatic Luther. And indeed, Erasmus found much he liked in the German's writings, describing him to Leo X as "a mighty trumpet of gospel truth." At the same time, he privately told his printer to stop printing Luther's writings because he didn't want his own efforts tangled with the Reformer's.

For four years, Erasmus pleaded moderation to both sides. But when pressed, he sided with the pope. "I am not so made as to fly in the face of the Vicar of Christ," he assured Leo.

Still, he hated the bickering and intolerance of both sides: "I detest dissension because it

goes both against the teachings of Christ and against a secret inclination of nature. I doubt that either side in the dispute can be suppressed without grave loss. It is clear that many of the reforms for which Luther calls are urgently needed."

His mediating position, however, didn't satisfy either side: "My only wish is that now that I am old, I be allowed to enjoy the results of my efforts," he wrote. "But both sides reproach me and seek to coerce me. Some claim that since I do not attack Luther I agree with him, while the Lutherans declare that I am a coward who has forsaken the gospel."

Indeed, Luther attacked him as a Moses who would die in the wilderness "without entering the promised land." And the Roman Catholic church forbade his writings. "Had I not seen it, nay, felt it myself," he wrote, "I should never have believed anyone who said theologians could become so insane."

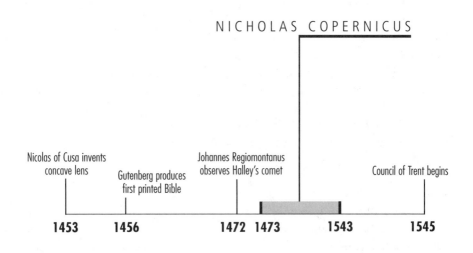

NICHOLAS COPERNICUS

Nicolas of Cusa invents concave lens	Gutenberg produces first printed Bible	Johannes Regiomontanus observes Halley's comet			Council of Trent begins
1453	1456	1472	1473	1543	1545

Nicholas Copernicus

REVOLUTIONARY ASTRONOMER

> *"[It is my] loving duty to seek the truth in all things, in so far as God has granted that to human reason."*

"The two great turning points of the Reformation age, the Lutheran and the Copernican, seem to have brought mankind nothing but humiliation," wrote historian Heiko Oberman. "First man is robbed of his power over himself, and then he is pushed to the periphery of creation."

In contrast to Luther, however, Nicholas Copernicus was not one to make bold, public gesture; instead he spent his life in relative quiet, hesitant to publish his revolutionary views until his very last days. And yet Copernicus, as much as Luther, revolutionized how Europeans thought of themselves, their world, and their God.

World-class scholar

Copernicus was born in Torun, in eastern Poland, where his father was an influential businessman. Copernicus studied first at the University of Cracow, where he first took an interest in astronomy ("most beautiful and most worth knowing," he said), and then moved on to the University of Bologna to study Greek, mathematics, and more astronomy. At Bologna he fell in with scholars who agreed that Aristotle's cosmology was too inelegant—in Copernicus's words "no sure scheme for the movements of the machinery of the world which has been built for us by the Best and Most Orderly Workman of all."

After a brief visit home to be installed as canon (a permanent salaried staff position in a cathedral), he returned to Italy to complete his doctorate of law and to study medicine at the University of Padua. In 1506 he returned to Poland, and though only in his early thirties, he was said to have mastered all the knowledge of the day in mathematics, astronomy, medicine, and theology.

Astronomy as hobby

As a canon, he served as confidant and secretary to his uncle, the bishop, and as a physician to the poor. Though weighed down with administrative and medical duties, he found time to formulate his ideas on astronomy into a booklet he called his *Little Commentary* (1512). He was not treading popular ground, since medieval theologians had nearly made it a point of orthodoxy that the earth was the center of the solar system, proof that humankind was the center of God's attention. Copernicus knew that "as soon as certain people learn that ... I attribute certain motions to the terrestrial globe [that is, that the earth moved around the sun], they will immediately shout to have me and my opinion hooted off the stage...." Still he considered it his "loving duty to seek the truth in all things, in so far as God has granted that to human reason."

In 1514 the pope asked if he could help revise the calendar. Copernicus replied that "the magnitude of the years and months ... had not yet been measured with sufficient accuracy." But he took this as a personal challenge and turned his tower apartments into a night observatory. His daylight hours were spent on his official duties with the sick, in administration, and guiding the diocese through a war between the Teutonic Knights and the King of Poland.

Eventually Copernicus passed on his official responsibilities to younger men and settled into semi-retirement in his private observatory. This might have been the end of a full life had not a young Lutheran mathematician and disciple visited the old astronomer. Copernicus, invigorated by the encounter, finally agreed to publish theories he'd been developing for a lifetime. In his *On the Revolutions of the Celestial Spheres* (1543), he appealed to the pope to judge between him and the "idle talkers" who "although wholly ignorant of mathematics ... distorting the sense of some passage in Holy Writ to suit their purpose ... attack my work."

His work passed into the hands of the less courageous. His editor inserted an anonymous preface indicating that the work was a mathematical construct to better explain the motions of the planets, not a description of how the solar system actually worked.

Copernicus's ideas (though anticipated by some ancient astronomers, he discovered in his studies) were too much for contemporaries; even a revolutionary like Martin Luther found it impossible to believe the sun, not the earth, anchored the solar system.

It wasn't until Galileo (1564–1642) that Copernicus's ideas were seen for what they were—a revolution in how humankind conceived of itself. For some this implied that de-centered earth was an insignificant speck to a distant God; others, though, marveled that the creator of a now infinite universe would lavish such attention on a planet that seemed to stand at the periphery of all creation.

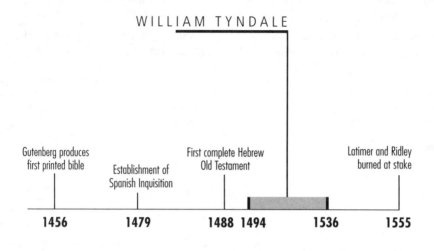

WILLIAM TYNDALE

Gutenberg produces first printed bible	Establishment of Spanish Inquisition	First complete Hebrew Old Testament		Latimer and Ridley burned at stake	
1456	**1479**	**1488**	**1494**	**1536**	**1555**

SCHOLARS AND SCIENTISTS

William Tyndale

TRANSLATOR OF THE FIRST ENGLISH NEW TESTAMENT

> *"Let it not make thee despair, neither yet discourage thee, O reader, that it is forbidden thee in pain of life and goods, or that it is made breaking of the king's peace, or treason unto his highness, to read the Word of thy soul's health—for if God be on our side, what matter maketh it who be against us, be they bishops, cardinals, popes."*

William Tyndale could speak seven languages and was proficient in ancient Hebrew and Greek. He was a priest whose intellectual gifts and disciplined life could have taken him a long way in the church—had he not had one compulsion: to teach English men and women the good news of justification by faith.

Tyndale had discovered this doctrine when he read Erasmus's Greek edition of the New Testament. What better way to share this message with his countrymen than to put an English version of the New Testament into their hands? This, in fact, became Tyndale's life passion, aptly summed up in the words of his mentor, Erasmus: "Christ desires his mysteries to be published abroad as widely as possible. I would that [the Gospels and the epistles of Paul] were translated into all languages, of all Christian people, and that they might be read and known."

It would be a passion, though, for which Tyndale would pay dearly.

Genius translator

He was a native of Gloucester and began his studies at Oxford in 1510, later moving on to Cambridge. By 1523 his passion had been ignited; in that year he sought permission and funds from the bishop of London to translate the New Testament. The bishop denied his request, and further queries convinced Tyndale the project would not be welcomed anywhere in England.

To find a hospitable environment, he traveled to the free cities of Europe—Hamburg, Wittenberg, Cologne, and finally to the Lutheran city of Worms. There, in 1525, his New Testament emerged: the first translation from Greek into the English language. It was quickly smuggled into England, where it received a less-than-enthusiastic response from the authorities. King Henry VIII, Cardinal Wolsey, and Sir Thomas More, among others, were furious. It was, said More, "not worthy to be called Christ's testament, but either Tyndale's own testament or the testament of his master Antichrist."

Authorities bought up copies of the translation (which, ironically, only financed Tyndale's further work) and hatched plans to silence Tyndale.

Meanwhile Tyndale had moved to Antwerp, a city in which he was relatively free from both English agents and those of the Holy Roman (and Catholic) Empire. For nine years he managed with the help of friends to evade authorities, revise his New Testament, and begin translating the Old.

His translations, it would turn out, became decisive in the history of the English Bible, and of the English language. Nearly a century later, when translators of the Authorized, or King James Version, debated how to translate the original languages, eight of ten times, they agreed that Tyndale had it best to begin with.

Betrayal

During these years, Tyndale also gave himself methodically to good works because, as he said, "My part be not in Christ if mine heart be not to follow and live according as I teach." On Mondays he visited other religious refugees from England. On Saturdays he walked Antwerp's streets, seeking to minister to the poor. On Sundays he dined in merchants' homes, reading Scripture before and after dinner. The rest of the week he devoted to writing tracts and books and translating the Bible.

We do not know who planned and financed the plot that ended his life (whether English or continental authorities), but we do know it was carried out by Henry Phillips, a man who had been accused of robbing his father and of gambling himself into poverty. Phillips became Tyndale's guest at meals and soon was one of the few privileged to look at Tyndale's books and papers.

In May 1535, Phillips lured Tyndale away from the safety of his quarters and into the arms of soldiers. Tyndale was immediately taken to the Castle of Vilvorde, the great state prison of the Low Countries, and accused of heresy.

Trials for heresy in the Netherlands were in the hands of special commissioners of the Holy Roman Empire. It took months for the law to take its course. During this time, Tyndale had many hours to reflect on his own teachings, such as this passage from one of his tracts:

"Let it not make thee despair, neither yet discourage thee, O reader, that it is forbidden thee in pain of life and goods, or that it is made breaking of the king's peace, or treason unto his highness, to read the Word of thy soul's health—for if God be on our side, what matter maketh it who be against us, be they bishops, cardinals, popes."

Finally, in early August 1536, Tyndale was condemned as a heretic, degraded from the priesthood, and delivered to the secular authorities for punishment.

On Friday, October 6, after local officials took their seats, Tyndale was brought to the cross in the middle of the town square and given a chance to recant. That refused, he was given a moment to pray. English historian John Foxe said he cried out, "Lord, open the King of England's eyes!"

Then he was bound to the beam, and both an iron chain and a rope were put around his neck. Gunpowder was added to the brush and logs. At the signal of a local official, the executioner, standing behind Tyndale, quickly tightened the noose, strangling him. Then an official took up a lighted torch and handed it to the executioner, who set the wood ablaze.

One other brief report of that distant scene has come down to us. It is found in a letter from an English agent to Lord Cromwell two months later.

"They speak much," he wrote, "of the patient sufferance of Master Tyndale at the time of his execution."

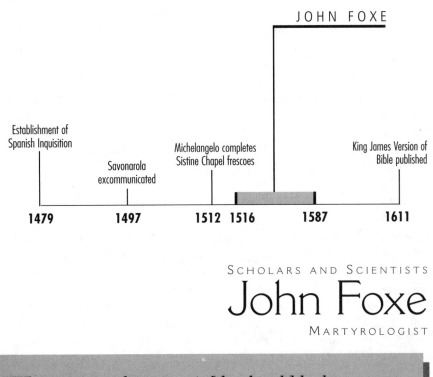

JOHN FOXE

| Establishment of Spanish Inquisition | | Michelangelo completes Sistine Chapel frescoes | | King James Version of Bible published |

Savonarola excommunicated

| 1479 | 1497 | 1512 1516 | 1587 | 1611 |

SCHOLARS AND SCIENTISTS

John Foxe

MARTYROLOGIST

> *"What storms and tempests it [the church] hath overpast, wondrous it is to behold."*

The works of church historians rarely influence history itself, but John Foxe's *Acts and Monuments of Matters Happening to the Church*—commonly known as *Foxe's Book of Martyrs*—is the exception that proves the rule.

"It is hard to overemphasize the impact his *Acts and Monuments* had the 20 years following its 1563 publication," writes historian David Loades. "By the second edition (1570), it was part of the national myth.... Foxe provided both a history and theology for the triumph of the Reformation."

Wonders to behold

Foxe's life itself was shaped by trials. He lost his father as a youth, and his relationship with his stepfather remained cool. At Oxford his brilliance and "indefatigable zeal and industry" earned him a master's degree and a fellowship, but when he cast his lot with emerging Protestantism, he lost his fellowship, his family disowned him, and, turning to tutoring, he found it difficult to find steady work.

Finally, the family of the executed Earl of Surrey hired him to educate the earl's newly orphaned children, and because of the political climate, hid him in the house. During the reign of Edward VI (1547–1553), he was able to live openly, and he began work on a history of the persecution of Reformers.

When Catholic Mary ascended the throne, Foxe fled to the Continent. There he met John Knox and other Protestant refugees, supporting himself as a printer. In 1554 Foxe published his research in a Latin martyrology of 212 pages. Mary's persecution of English Protestants, many of whom were Foxe's friends, forced him to begin a revision immediately.

With Protestant sympathizer Elizabeth's accession to the throne, Foxe returned to England and to the service of one of his former pupils, now the Duke of Norfolk. He worked with printer John Day to produce in 1563 an English version of his masterwork, now about 1,800 pages. It was a striking volume with extensive documentation, stirring narrative, and horrifying woodcut illustrations, including accounts of many of the 300 martyrs of Mary's reign. Foxe wanted to demonstrate to readers how the church, despite all manner of trial and persecution, "hath yet endured and holden its own! What storms and tempests it hath overpast, wondrous it is to behold."

Factual errors and a polemic style, however, made it controversial, especially regarding his treatment of the previous English queen: "We earnestly pray that the annals of no country, Catholic or pagan," Foxe wrote, "may ever be stained with such a repetition of human sacrifices to papal power, and that the detestation in which the character of Mary is holden may be a beacon to succeeding monarchs to avoid the rocks of fanaticism!" Foxe's writings were one reason the Catholic queen became known as "Bloody" Mary.

Since the book contained dramatic accounts of so many Protestant martyrs, it worked as a powerful support for Elizabeth's Protestant establishment. The 1570 edition (revised and enlarged to some 2,500 pages, covering the history of persecution from the early church on) was ordered displayed in every church, common hall, and college.

Historian Douglass Campbell commented, "When one recollects that until the appearance of *Pilgrim's Progress* the common people had almost no other reading matter except the Bible and *Foxe's Book of Martyrs*, we can understand the deep impression that this book produced. Those who could read for themselves learned the full details of all the atrocities performed on the Protestant reformers; the illiterate could see the rude illustrations of the various instruments of torture, the rack, the gridiron, the boiling oil, and then the holy ones breathing out their souls amid the flames."

After his patron died, Foxe's finances became precarious. Though twice offered livings in Anglican churches, he refused because of his Puritan leanings. He wore himself away with hard work to the point that friends did not recognize him on the street. But before he died, he had produced two more editions of his mammoth work and more than 30 other published pieces, and he had conducted a full schedule of preaching and good works.

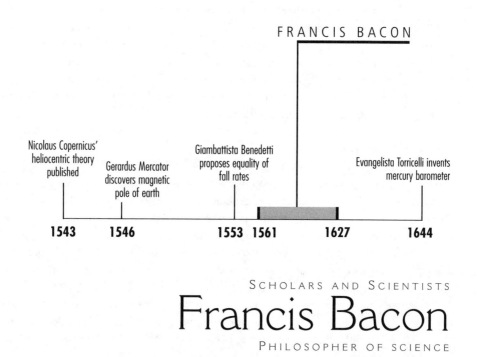

FRANCIS BACON

Nicolaus Copernicus' heliocentric theory published	Gerardus Mercator discovers magnetic pole of earth	Giambattista Benedetti proposes equality of fall rates		Evangelista Torricelli invents mercury barometer
1543	**1546**	**1553 1561**	**1627**	**1644**

Francis Bacon

PHILOSOPHER OF SCIENCE

> *"Knowledge is the rich storehouse for the glory of the Creator and the relief of man's estate"*

Francis Bacon was a devout Anglican remembered for his public failure and a great scientific mind. Perhaps, as he said, the "best of men are like the best of precious stones, wherein every flaw ... [is] noted more than in those that are generally foul and corrupted."

Years of frustration

Bacon had a wonderful start. His father was a high official serving Queen Elizabeth, and his mother was a woman of keen intelligence. But Francis was bored with his tutors and appalled by the scholastic disputation that passed for science. He dropped out of Cambridge at 15, and his father got him an appointment to serve the ambassador to France. These youthful privileges were stripped away in 1579 when his father died, leaving him precious little. He returned to school with renewed purpose, becoming a barrister, a Member of Parliament, and a law professor in the next seven years. But he was satisfied neither with his honors nor his income.

His efforts at advancement were stymied, mainly because the queen didn't like him. But she did like his patron, the Earl of Essex. Essex treated Bacon like a son and was a good mentor until he led a revolt. Elizabeth appointed Bacon to a minor post in the prosecution of his friend, but he threw himself into the case with fervor. Alexander Pope called him "the wisest, brightest, meanest of mankind," but Bacon wrote to Essex that he must prefer the good of his country to their friendship.

Years of achievement

The ascension of King James marked a new beginning for Bacon. This ruler liked him, and his rise to the peak of political power was dizzying. In 1607 he was solicitor general, then clerk of the star chamber, attorney general, lord keeper of the seal, and in 1618, lord chancellor. During this period he also published his most famous literary works. The *Instauratio Magna* (Great Revival) was to be nothing less than a comprehensive theory of knowledge. He only completed two parts, but in these he summed up the extent of learning and the deficiencies in human understanding, and he proposed a new science based on experimentation, inductive reasoning, and the betterment of the human condition.

The House of Commons lodged a corruption complaint against him in 1620. He pleaded guilty, noting that although he was "the justest judge," he had partaken in "the abuse of the times." Within a year, he had been stripped of his offices, broken financially, and ruined politically.

He retired to his writing. He introduced the essay form to the English language and completed *The New Atlantis*, which mixed his scientific approach and his Christian beliefs. Bacon divided knowledge into philosophy, or natural knowledge, and divinity, or inspired revelation. Though he insisted that philosophy and the natural world must be studied inductively, he argued that where religion is concerned, we can only study arguments for the existence of God. Knowledge of God's nature, action, and purposes can only come from special revelation. But Bacon also believed that knowledge was cumulative, that study encompassed more than a simple preservation of the past. True study, he said, will ultimately help mankind. "Knowledge is the rich storehouse for the glory of the Creator and the relief of man's estate," he wrote. "A little philosophy inclineth man's mind to atheism, but depth in philosophy bringeth men's minds about to religion."

In 1626 he stopped in the snow to conduct an experiment on the preservation of food, fell ill, and died on Easter Sunday. In his will, he included this final prayer: "When I thought most of peace and honor, thy hand [was] heavy on me, and hath humbled me, according to thy former loving kindness.... Just are thy judgments upon my sins.... Be merciful unto me for my Savior's sake, and receive me into thy bosom."

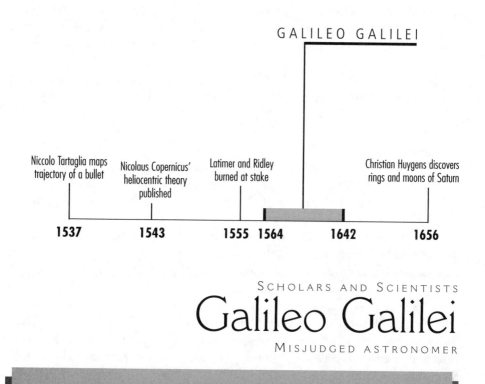

GALILEO GALILEI

Niccolo Tartaglia maps trajectory of a bullet	Nicolaus Copernicus' heliocentric theory published	Latimer and Ridley burned at stake		Christian Huygens discovers rings and moons of Saturn
1537	**1543**	**1555** **1564**	**1642**	**1656**

SCHOLARS AND SCIENTISTS

Galileo Galilei

MISJUDGED ASTRONOMER

"God is known by nature in his works, and by doctrine in his revealed word."

Galileo Galilei, though famous for his scientific achievements in astronomy, mathematics, and physics, and infamous for his controversy with the church was, in fact, a devout Christian who saw not a divorce of religion and science but only a healthy marriage: "God is known by nature in his works, and by doctrine in his revealed word."

Irritating young genius

Galileo never got his university degree. He studied for four years and dropped out, then studied on his own for two years, living as a tutor and publishing solutions to complex problems. This brilliance got him the chair of mathematics at the University of Pisa, where he immediately made enemies. The "natural philosophers" of his day made their discoveries debating the works of Aristotle. Galileo believed in observing nature under controlled

355

conditions and describing the results mathematically. This difference alone created friction, but Galileo humiliated his enemies with public demonstrations of their errors—for example, Galileo proved, contra Aristotle, that bodies of different weights would fall at the same velocity. His enemies ran him off in two years. Friends got him the chair of mathematics at Padua, a more progressive institution, which he occupied for 18 years. These were his happiest and most productive days, during which he explored physics in ways that were to bear much fruit.

Detoured by the telescope

In 1609 Galileo heard of a device to make distant objects appear closer, and the applications of such an instrument were immediately obvious to Galileo. He quickly put together a telescope and displayed it to the Venetian Senate, which was so impressed, it immediately doubled his salary. That winter he turned his telescope on the sky and made some astounding discoveries. In complete contravention of accepted beliefs, he saw that the moon was not a smooth sphere, that Jupiter had moons, and that Venus had phases, indicating it orbited the sun. He published a small pamphlet describing his observations in 1610. It made him world-famous.

At 46, after 20 years of quiet study, he was now in demand. Lured to Tuscany with a grand salary, Galileo abandoned his wife and put his daughters in a convent. He made a triumphant visit to Rome, where the papal court vied to do him honor. The head of church astronomers confirmed his discoveries, and Jesuit astronomers jostled to look through the telescope.

But his academic enemies were not finished. They induced Dominican friars to preach on such texts as "Ye men of Galilee, why stand ye gazing up into heaven?" and cast Galileo's views—especially his support of the Copernican discovery that the earth revolved around the sun—in the worst possible light. The feeling in Rome was that Copernicus's views would be more devastating to the church than those of Luther or Calvin. Pope Paul V ordered the Inquisition to look into the matter.

Trials and silence

Galileo contended that proper interpretation of Scripture would agree with observed fact. The "Book of Nature," written in the language of mathematics, would agree with the "Book of Scripture," written in the everyday language of the people. Besides, the "Bible teaches men how to go to heaven, not how the heavens go," and that it would be "a terrible detriment for the souls if people found themselves convinced by proof of something that it was made then a sin to believe."

But the Inquisition ruled against him in 1616. This was not as unreasonable as it appears. His position flew in the face of common sense and 1,500 years of academics. It violated the accepted laws of physics. The star parallaxes demanded by this system could not be observed (and would not be until 1838). The Inquisition condemned the Copernican system and forbade Galileo from teaching it as fact.

But Galileo the scientific combatant never gave up. When a friend was elected pope in 1623, Galileo went to see him, but Urban VIII would not lift the injunction for fear of undermining church authority. Galileo did obtain permission to write about "the systems of the world," both Ptolemaic and Copernican, as long as he discussed them non-committally and came to the conclusion dictated to him in advance by the pontiff—that is, that man cannot presume to know how the world is really made because God could have brought about the same effects in ways unimagined by him, and he must not restrict God's omnipotence.

So Galileo embarked on his *Dialogue Concerning the Two Chief World Systems* (1632). As soon as it came out, with the full and complete imprimatur of the censors, it was greeted with applause and cries of praise from every part of Europe as a literary and philosophical masterpiece. But even though formally noncommittal, it clearly championed the Copernican system and featured a dull defender of Ptolemy in whom the pope saw too much of himself.

Galileo was called back before the Inquisition in 1633. A document was produced (later proved a forgery by historians) that said Galileo had promised not to write about the Copernican system whatsoever. The old fighter, now 70, was ordered to renounce publicly his teachings and submit to house arrest.

In his last years, he published a compendium of his earlier work in physics—*Dialogue Concerning Two New Sciences*, his greatest achievement—and shortly thereafter went blind.

It wasn't until 1981 that the Catholic church ordered a commission to look into Galileo's case, and another 11 years before the commission acknowledged the "errors" of Galileo's judges.

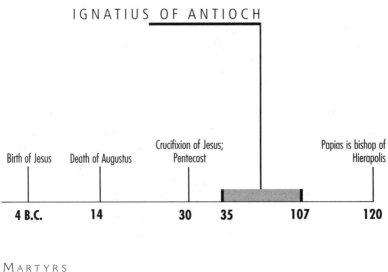

IGNATIUS OF ANTIOCH

| Birth of Jesus | Death of Augustus | Crucifixion of Jesus; Pentecost | | Papias is bishop of Hierapolis |

4 B.C.   14   30   35   107   120

MARTYRS

Ignatius of Antioch
EARLIEST POST-NEW TESTAMENT MARTYR

> *"Now I begin to be a disciple.... Let fire and cross, flocks of beasts, broken bones, dismemberment ... come upon me, so long as I attain to Jesus Christ."*

Ignatius was going to die. He knew it. He wanted it. The only possible problem, as he saw it, was meddling Christians.

"I fear your kindness, which may harm me," he wrote to Roman Christians hoping to free him. "You may be able to achieve what you plan. But if you pay no heed to my request, it will be very difficult for me to attain unto God." And that was truly Ignatius's goal: to imitate "our God Jesus Christ" in death. If Christians really wanted to do something, they should pray that he would remain faithful. "If you remain silent about me, I shall become a word of God. But if you allow yourselves to be swayed by the love in which you hold my flesh, I shall again be no more than a human voice."

That Ignatius truly wanted to die was about as much as we know about his martyrdom. It's not even known for certain that he was killed, though that's likely.

As the second (or third) bishop of Antioch, one of the most important churches of the day, he was certainly one of the most prominent Christians of the time immediately succeeding the apostles. But Antioch was also home to some religious debates, and while Ignatius denounced division as "the beginning of evil," the bishop engaged in debate with tenacity.

To the Magnesian church (near Ephesus) he wrote scathingly of the Ebionites, who demanded the keeping of Jewish regulations. "It is outrageous to utter the name of Jesus Christ and live in Judaism." Similar attacks were launched against the Docetists, who believed Christ only appeared to be human. Anyone believing such nonsense that Christ only seemed to suffer could not truly be called a martyr, he asserted.

He was probably arrested on the charge of "atheism"—denial of the Roman gods— and was taken from Antioch to Rome by an escort of ten soldiers. At nearly every stop, he met leaders of local churches, and during the trip he penned, with the help of a secretary, seven letters.

Though most famous for being one of the church's earliest martyrs, his letters also served to record the rapid development of church hierarchy. "Follow, all of you, the bishop, as Jesus Christ followed the Father," he wrote to Polycarp's church at Smyrna (now Izmir, Turkey). "Wherever the bishop appears, there let the people be, even as wheresoever Christ Jesus is, there is the catholic church. It is not lawful apart from the bishop either to baptize or to hold a love-feast [church meal]," he continued in his letter to Smyrna. The instruction is also remarkable because it is the first recorded use of the phrase "catholic [meaning, universal] church." (He was also the first outside the New Testament to speak of Jesus' virgin birth.)

The details of Ignatius's death are lost to history, but not his desire to have his life count for something: "Now I begin to be a disciple.... Let fire and cross, flocks of beasts, broken bones, dismemberment ... come upon me, so long as I attain to Jesus Christ."

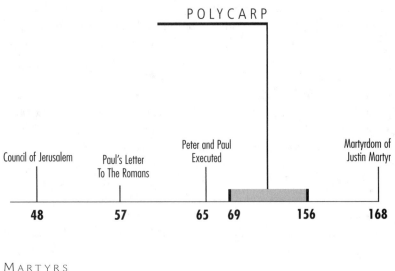

POLYCARP

| Council of Jerusalem | Paul's Letter To The Romans | Peter and Paul Executed | | | Martyrdom of Justin Martyr |
| 48 | 57 | 65 | 69 | 156 | 168 |

MARTYRS

Polycarp

AGED BISHOP OF SMYRNA

> "He who grants me to endure the fire will enable me also to remain on the pyre unmoved, without the security you desire from nails."

Polycarp had been a Christian since he was a child, but the Romans didn't get around to killing him until he was in his eighties. Whatever the reason for the delay, it is still the first recorded martyrdom in post-New Testament church history.

Uneducated but direct

He lived during the most formative era of the church, at the end of the age of the original apostles, when the church was making the critical transition to the second generation of believers. Tradition has it that he was personally discipled by the apostle John and that he was appointed as bishop of Smyrna (in modern Izmir in Turkey) by some of the original apostles.

In his later years, he tried to settle disputes about the date to celebrate Easter, and he confronted one of the church's most troublesome heretics, the Gnostic Marcion, calling him "the first born of Satan," when he ran into him in Rome. Polycarp was also responsible for converting many from Gnosticism. His only existing writing, a pastoral letter to the church at Philippi, shows he had little formal education, and was unpretentious, humble, and direct.

Such traits are especially evident in the account of his martyrdom, which was written within a year of his death. It is not clear exactly why he was suddenly, at age 86, subject to arrest, but when he heard Roman officials were intent on arresting him, he decided to wait for them at home. Panic-stricken friends pleaded with him to flee, so to calm them, he finally agreed to withdraw to a small estate outside of town. But while in prayer there, he received some sort of vision. Whatever he saw or heard, we don't know. He simply reported to his friends that he now understood, "I must be burned alive."

Roman soldiers eventually discovered Polycarp's whereabouts and came to his door. When his friends urged him to run, Polycarp replied, "God's will be done," and he let the soldiers in.

He was escorted to the local proconsul, Statius Quadratus, who interrogated him in front of a crowd of curious onlookers. Polycarp seemed unfazed by the interrogation; he carried on a witty dialogue with Quadratus until Quadratus lost his temper and threatened Polycarp: he'd be thrown to wild beasts, he'd be burned at the stake, and so on. Polycarp just told Quadratus that while the proconsul's fire lasts but a little while, the fires of judgment ("reserved for the ungodly," he slyly added) cannot be quenched. Polycarp concluded, "But why do you delay? Come, do what you will."

Soldiers then grabbed him to nail him to a stake, but Polycarp stopped them: "Leave me as I am. For he who grants me to endure the fire will enable me also to remain on the pyre unmoved, without the security you desire from nails." He prayed aloud, the fire was lit, and his flesh was consumed. The chronicler of this martyrdom said it was "not as burning flesh but as bread baking or as gold and silver refined in a furnace."

The account concluded by saying that Polycarp's death was remembered by "everyone"—"he is even spoken of by the heathen in every place."

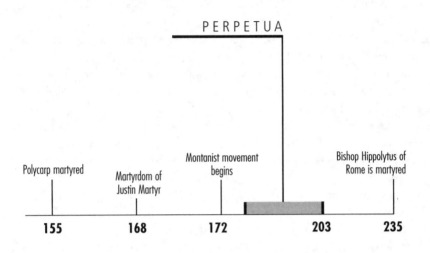

PERPETUA

Polycarp martyred	Martyrdom of Justin Martyr	Montanist movement begins		Bishop Hippolytus of Rome is martyred
155	168	172	203	235

MARTYRS

Perpetua

HIGH SOCIETY BELIEVER

"It will all happen in the prisoner's dock as God wills, for you may be sure that we are not left to ourselves but are all in his power."

We have little idea what brought Perpetua to faith in Christ, or how long she had been a Christian, or how she lived her Christian life. Thanks to her diary, and that of another prisoner, we have some idea of her last days—an ordeal that so impressed the famous Augustine that he preached four sermons about her death.

Perpetua was a Christian noblewoman who, at the turn of the third century, lived with her husband, her son, and her slave, Felicitas, in Carthage (in modern Tunis). At this time, North Africa was the center of a vibrant Christian community. It is no surprise, then, that when Emperor Septimius Severus determined to cripple Christianity (he believed it undermined Roman patriotism), he focused his attention on North Africa. Among the first to be arrested were five new Christians taking classes to prepare for baptism, one of whom was Perpetua.

Her father immediately came to her in prison. He was a pagan, and he saw an easy way for Perpetua to save herself. He entreated her simply to deny she was a Christian.

"Father do you see this vase here?" she replied. "Could it be called by any other name than what it is?"

"No," he replied.

"Well, neither can I be called anything other than what I am, a Christian."

In the next days, Perpetua was moved to a better part of the prison and allowed to breast-feed her child. With her hearing approaching, her father visited again, this time, pleading more passionately: "Have pity on my gray head. Have pity on me, your father, if I deserve to be called your father, if I have favored you above all your brothers, if I have raised you to reach this prime of your life."

He threw himself down before her and kissed her hands. "Do not abandon me to be the reproach of men. Think of your brothers; think of your mother and your aunt; think of your child, who will not be able to live once you are gone. Give up your pride!"

Perpetua was touched but remained unshaken. She tried to comfort her father—"It will all happen in the prisoner's dock as God wills, for you may be sure that we are not left to ourselves but are all in his power"—but he walked out of the prison dejected.

The day of the hearing arrived, Perpetua and her friends were marched before the governor, Hilarianus. Perpetua's friends were questioned first, and each in turn admitted to being a Christian, and each in turn refused to make a sacrifice (an act of emperor worship). Then the governor turned to question Perpetua.

At that moment, her father, carrying Perpetua's son in his arms, burst into the room. He grabbed Perpetua and pleaded, "Perform the sacrifice. Have pity on your baby!"

Hilarianus, probably wishing to avoid the unpleasantness of executing a mother who still suckled a child, added, "Have pity on your father's gray head; have pity on your infant son. Offer the sacrifice for the welfare of the emperor."

Perpetua replied simply: "I will not."

"Are you a Christian then?" asked the governor.

"Yes I am," Perpetua replied.

Her father interrupted again, begging her to sacrifice, but Hilarianus had heard enough: he ordered soldiers to beat him into silence. He then condemned Perpetua and her friends to die in the arena.

Perpetua, her friends, and her slave, Felicitas (who had subsequently been arrested), were dressed in belted tunics. When they entered the stadium, wild beasts and gladiators roamed the arena floor, and in the stands, crowds roared to see blood. They didn't have to wait long.

Immediately a wild heifer charged the group. Perpetua was tossed into the air and onto her back. She sat up, adjusted her ripped tunic, and walked over to help Felicitas. Then a leopard was let loose, and it wasn't long before the tunics of the Christians were stained with blood.

This was too deliberate for the impatient crowd, which began calling for death for the Christians. So Perpetua, Felicitas, and friends were lined up, and one by one, were slain by the sword.

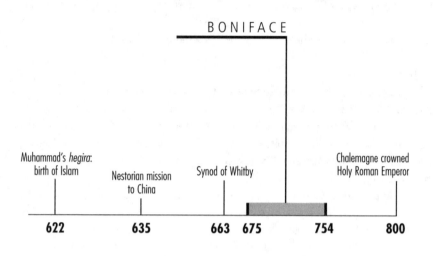

BONIFACE

Muhammad's *hegira*: birth of Islam	Nestorian mission to China	Synod of Whitby		Chalemagne crowned Holy Roman Emperor
622	635	663 675	754	800

MARTYRS

Boniface

APOSTLE OF GERMANY

> *"You seem to glow with the salvation-bringing fire which our Lord came to send upon the earth."*
> — *Gregory II to Boniface*

His first job as a missionary was a failure. Wynfrith (or Winfrid) had wanted to be a traveling evangelist ever since missionary monks had visited his family's home when he was five years old. He'd given up his noble parents' secular dreams for him back in Wessex, England. And he'd given up a successful life as a Benedictine monk—having written the first Latin grammar produced in England, several poems, and a treatise on metrics.

Now in his early forties, Wynfrith wanted to be a missionary, particularly one to Friesland (in the northern Netherlands). But the Frisians were in revolt, and Wynfrith had to come home without converts.

While he'd been away, his abbot had died—and Wynfrith had been elected to replace him. It was a high honor, but Wynfrith still wanted to be a missionary. He sailed away from England for the last time, this time bound to meet the pope in Rome.

Pope Gregory II confirmed Wynfrith's call to missions, remarking, "You seem to glow with the salvation-bringing fire which our Lord came to send upon the earth." After receiving assurances that the English monk would use the Roman, not Celtic, formula for baptism, he commissioned Wynfrith to evangelize both those "led astray ... and now serve idols under the guise of the Christian religion" and those "not yet cleansed by the waters of holy Baptism." The pope also changed Wynfrith's name to Boniface—"good works"—named after a Roman Christian martyred in the Arian controversy.

Zealous axe-wielder

He returned to Friesland and Germany, evangelizing and suppressing heresy. While establishing churches and Benedictine monasteries, he destroyed idols, baptized heathens, and opposed "ambitious and free-living clerics." His zeal against heresy often led to ruthless, severe action. He demanded that two heretical missionaries not only be excommunicated, but imprisoned in solitary confinement. Even among sympathetic historians today, he has a reputation as "difficult, prickly, and tactless."

He was equally zealous in his mission against paganism. At Geismar, he found a huge sacred oak tree, a shrine to Thor. He immediately took an axe to it. After only a few blows, the tree toppled to the ground, breaking into four pieces and revealing itself to be rotted away from within.

"A great throng of pagans who were there cursed him bitterly among themselves because he was the enemy of their gods," wrote Boniface's biographer, Willibald. "When the pagans who had cursed saw this, they [stopped] cursing and, believing, blessed God." Boniface used the oak to build a chapel, which became the center of his new monastery.

As he continued to clash with pagans, heretics, and even fellow orthodox Christians (like the bishop of Mainz, who reportedly was trying to claim the regions evangelized by Boniface as his own), he became convinced that ecclesiastical reform was an integral part of evangelization. No church councils had been held in the Frankish realm for decades before his arrival. Boniface convened five between 742 and 747. At Boniface's prodding, the councils adopted strict regulations for the clergy and condemned local heretics. Eventually, Boniface himself was appointed archbishop of Mainz, replacing his rival.

Missionary again

After a few years of administration, Boniface again felt Friesland calling him, a land "he had once deserted in body but never, indeed, in his heart," according to Willibald. In his late seventies, he resigned his post to head north once again. Once again, he and his followers roamed the countryside destroying shrines, building churches, and baptizing thousands.

One group of these new converts was due to arrive at Dorkum on the River Borne. But while Boniface and his 52 companions awaited the neophytes, a gang of pagan predators arrived on the shore seeking loot. Though he had earlier traveled under the armed protection of the Frankish ruler, he was now far beyond its reach. Boniface, at his first synod, had ensured that clergy would not carry arms, so all he had to defend himself was the book in his arms, which he used as a shield.

The new Christians, who had fled upon seeing the raiders, returned to find Boniface and his companions slaughtered. Next to their bishop lay a copy of Ambrose's writings on *The Advantage of Death*, with two deep slashes in it. The book is still on display in Fulda, Germany.

Actually, Boniface spent a small percentage of his life as a missionary. His historical significance is found more in his strong advocacy of Roman order in the church, his reform of the Frankish churches, his uniting churches in southern and central Germany, and his revitalizing nominal Christians in northern Europe. But he thought of himself mainly as a missionary, as did countless others. From the eighth century to the eleventh, he became one of missionaries' top role models.

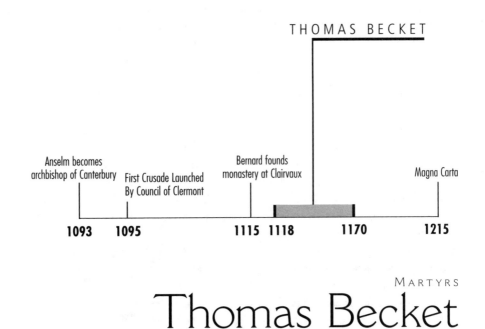

THOMAS BECKET

Anselm becomes archbishop of Canterbury	First Crusade Launched By Council of Clermont	Bernard founds monastery at Clairvaux			Magna Carta
1093	**1095**	**1115**	**1118**	**1170**	**1215**

Thomas Becket

MURDERED ARCHBISHOP OF CANTERBURY

> *"For the name of Jesus and the protection of the church I am ready to embrace death."*

In this century, the Nobel laureate T.S. Eliot dramatized Thomas Becket's martyrdom in his play *Murder in the Cathedral*, and Jean Anouilh's play *Becket* was turned into a an Oscar-winning film. In the Middle Ages, Becket's reputation was even more spectacular. His shrine in the Canterbury Cathedral was for centuries one of the most popular pilgrimage destinations in Europe (and the destination of poet Geoffrey Chaucer's pilgrims in his *Canterbury Tales*).

In spite of Becket's stature then and now, few people today know his story, a tale that bristles with ironies and reversals worthy of major plays and motion pictures.

One heart and one mind

Becket was the son of a French merchant who had settled in London. He studied for the priesthood in England and France and became archdeacon of Canterbury in 1154, where his administrative and leadership gifts became quickly evident. Contemporaries described Thomas as tall and thin, with dark hair and a pale face that flushed in excitement. His memory was tenacious, and he excelled in argument and repartee.

Such traits impressed Henry II, who in 1155 appointed Becket chancellor of England, and Becket immediately began employing his extraordinary gifts in the service of the king, solidifying the king's power throughout the land. In this work, the two became close friends. Contemporaries spoke with wonder of the relations between chancellor and sovereign, who was 12 years his junior, and people declared, "They had but one heart and one mind."

When the Canterbury archbishop Theobald died in 1161, Henry forced Becket's nomination as replacement. It was clear the king hoped to rely on his close ties with Becket to bring the church into submission with the rest of his realm. But Becket balked because, as he told Henry, "I know your plans for the church; you will assert claims which I, if I were archbishop, must needs oppose." But Henry had his way and Becket was installed.

When Becket became archbishop, he devoted himself to being the church's leader with the same energy he had shown working for Henry. As chancellor he had given himself to spiritual disciplines, but now as archbishop, he increased his devotion to fastings, use of hair shirts, protracted vigils, and prayer.

Soon the former friends were clashing as each sought to do his duty. A critical break came in the disputes over the Constitutions of Clarendon (1164), which specified the extent of state control over church and clergy, and tried to assure that clergy accused of serious crimes would be tried by the state, not by the church, as had been the custom. (The custom had also been to let clergy off with light sentences—reprimands or defrocking—even for such crimes as murder.) Under pressure, Becket at first submitted, but then he recanted, insisting on the right of the church to judge its own clergy. This led to a fierce struggle, and Becket was exiled in France for six years.

Meanwhile, Henry worried about who would succeed him and arranged for his son Henry to be crowned in 1170 by the archbishop of York. This was a violation of the rights of Canterbury to preside over the coronation. Eventually Henry had to yield, and a reconciliation with Becket was arranged.

Becket returned to England and at once began to excommunicate bishops who had executed the king's commands. This infuriated the quick-tempered king.

On December 29, 1170, four of the king's knights went to Canterbury and confronted the archbishop in his own cathedral during a Vespers service (but it is unclear whether they did so under Henry's direct orders or out of loyalty). To their angry question, "Where is the traitor?" Becket boldly replied, "Here I am, no traitor, but archbishop and priest of God."

They tried to drag him from the church but were unable, and in the end, they slew him where he stood. As he died, he said, "For the name of Jesus and the protection of the church, I am ready to embrace death."

Europe was shocked by the murder. The pope forced Henry to do penance at Becket's tomb, and Becket was canonized by Pope Alexander III in 1173, an extraordinarily brief space of time. Miracles were soon reported at the site, and devotion to the shrine swelled—until 1538, when Henry VIII destroyed it, with nearly all the other shrines in England.

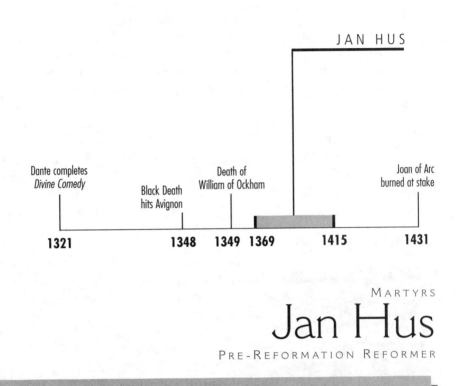

JAN HUS

Dante completes *Divine Comedy*	Black Death hits Avignon	Death of William of Ockham		Joan of Arc burned at stake
1321	**1348**	**1349 1369**	**1415**	**1431**

MARTYRS

Jan Hus

PRE-REFORMATION REFORMER

> *"Lord Jesus, it is for thee that I patiently endure this cruel death. I pray thee to have mercy on my enemies."*

Early in his monastic career, Martin Luther, rummaging through the stacks of a library, happened upon a volume of sermons by Jan Hus, the Bohemian who had been condemned as a heretic. "I was overwhelmed with astonishment," Luther later wrote. "I could not understand for what cause they had burnt so great a man, who explained the Scriptures with so much gravity and skill."

Hus would become a hero to Luther and many other Reformers, for Hus preached key Reformation themes (like hostility to indulgences) a century before Luther drew up his 95 *Theses*. But the Reformers also looked to Hus's life, in particular, his steadfast commitment in the face of the church's cunning brutality.

From foolishness to faith

Hus was born to peasant parents in "Goosetown," that is, Husinec, in the south of today's Czech Republic. (In his twenties, he shortened his name to Hus—"goose," and he and his friends delighted in making puns on his name; it was a tradition that continued, especially with Luther, who reminded his followers of the "goose" who had been "cooked" for defying the pope).

To escape poverty, Hus trained for the priesthood: "I had thought to become a priest quickly in order to secure a good livelihood and dress and to be held in esteem by men." He earned a bachelor's, master's, and then finally a doctorate. Along the way he was ordained (in 1401) and became the preacher at Prague's Bethlehem Chapel (which held 3,000), the most popular church in one of the largest of Europe's cities, a center of reform in Bohemia (for example, sermons were preached in Czech, not Latin).

During these years, Hus underwent a change. Though he spent some time with what he called a "foolish sect," he finally discovered the Bible: "When the Lord gave me knowledge of Scriptures, I discharged that kind of stupidity from my foolish mind."

The writings of John Wycliffe had stirred his interest in the Bible, and these same writings were causing a stir in Bohemia (technically the northeastern portion of today's Czech Republic, but a general term for the area where the Czech language and culture prevailed).

The University of Prague was already split between Czechs and Germans, and Wycliffe's teachings only divided them more. Early debates hinged on fine points of philosophy (the Czechs, with Wycliffe, were realists; the Germans nominalists). But the Czechs, with Hus, also warmed up to Wycliffe's reforming ideas; though they had no intention of altering traditional doctrines, they wanted to place more emphasis on the Bible, expand the authority of church councils (and lessen that of the pope), and promote the moral reform of clergy. Thus Hus began increasingly to trust the Scriptures, "desiring to hold, believe, and assert whatever is contained in them as long as I have breath in me."

A political struggle ensued, with the Germans labeling Wycliffe and his followers heretics. With the support of the king of Bohemia, the Czechs gained the upper hand, and the Germans were forced to flee to other universities.

The situation was complicated by European politics, which watched as two popes vied to rule all of Christendom. A church council was called at Pisa in 1409 to settle the matter. It deposed both popes and elected Alexander V as the legitimate pontiff (though the other popes, repudiating this election, continued to rule their factions). Alexander was soon "persuaded"— that is, bribed—to side with Bohemian church authorities against Hus, who continued to criticize them. Hus was forbidden to preach and excommunicated, but only on paper: with local Bohemians backing him, Hus continued to preach and minister at Bethlehem Chapel.

When Alexander V's successor, the antipope John XXIII (not to be confused with the modern pope by the same name), authorized the selling of indulgences to raise funds for his crusade against one of his rivals, Hus was scandalized and further radicalized. The pope was acting in mere self-interest, and Hus could no longer justify the pope's moral authority. He leaned even more heavily on the Bible, which he proclaimed the final authority for the church. Huss further argued that the Czech people were being exploited by the pope's indulgences, which was a not-so-veiled attack on the Bohemian king, who earned a cut of the indulgence proceeds.

Scripture rebel

With that Hus lost the support of his king. His excommunication, which had been tacitly dropped, was now revived, and an interdict was put upon the city of Prague: no citizen could receive Communion or be buried on church grounds as long as Hus continued his ministry. To spare the city, Hus withdrew to the countryside toward the end of 1412. He spent the next two years in feverish literary activity, composing a number of treatises. The most important was *The Church*, which he sent to Prague to be read publicly. In it he argued that Christ alone is head of the church, that a pope "through ignorance and love of money" can make many mistakes, and that to rebel against an erring pope is to obey Christ.

In November 1414, the Council of Constance assembled, and Hus was urged by Holy Roman Emperor Sigismund to come and give an account of his doctrine. Because he was promised safe conduct, and because of the importance of the council (which promised significant church reforms), Hus went. When he arrived, however, he was immediately arrested, and he remained imprisoned for months. Instead of a hearing, Hus was eventually hauled before authorities in chains and asked merely to recant his views.

When he saw he wasn't to be given a forum for explaining his ideas, let alone a fair hearing, he finally said, "I appeal to Jesus Christ, the only judge who is almighty and completely just. In his hands I plead my cause, not on the basis of false witnesses and erring councils, but on truth and justice." He was taken to his cell, where many pleaded with him to recant. On July 6, 1415, he was taken to the cathedral, dressed in his priestly garments, then stripped of them one by one. He refused one last chance to recant at the stake, where he prayed, "Lord Jesus, it is for thee that I patiently endure this cruel death. I pray thee to have mercy on my enemies." He was heard reciting the Psalms as the flames engulfed him.

His executioners scooped up his ashes and tossed them into a lake so that nothing would remain of the "heretic," but some Czechs collected bits of soil from the ground where Hus had died and took them back to Bohemia as a memorial.

Bohemians were furious with the execution and repudiated the council; over the next several years, a coalition of Hussites, radical Taborites, and others refused to submit to the authority of the Holy Roman emperor or the church and fended off three military assaults. Bohemia eventually reconciled with the rest of western Christendom—though on its own terms (for example, it was one of the few Catholic regions that offered Communion of both bread and wine; the rest of Christendom simply received the bread). Those who repudiated this last compromise formed the *Unitas Fratrum* ("Union of Brethren"), which became the foundation for the Moravian Brethren (Moravia is a region in the Czech Republic), who would play an influential role in the conversion of the Wesley brothers, among others.

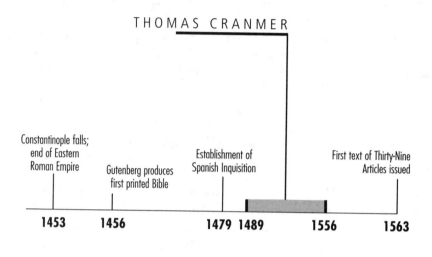

THOMAS CRANMER

Constantinople falls; end of Eastern Roman Empire — **1453**

Gutenberg produces first printed Bible — **1456**

Establishment of Spanish Inquisition — **1479 1489**

First text of Thirty-Nine Articles issued

1556

1563

MARTYRS

Thomas Cranmer

GENIUS BEHIND ANGLICANISM

> *"Blessed Lord, who hast caused all holy Scriptures to be written for our learning; grant that we may in such wise hear them, read, mark, learn, and inwardly digest them...."*

Thomas Cranmer, seated in an Oxford cell before a plain wooden desk, weary from months of trial, interrogation, and imprisonment, tried to make sense of his life. Before him lay the speech he was to give the next morning, a speech that repudiated his writings that had denied Catholic teaching.

Also before him was another speech, in which he declared the pope "Christ's enemy and antichrist."

Cranmer has often been accused of waffling, if not hypocrisy, but the decision he made the next morning—as much as his most famous and lasting work, *Book of Common Prayer*—settled the matter of where he really stood on the Reformation.

From scholar to public figure

Cranmer was born 66 years earlier in Aslacton, Nottinghamshire. He attended Cambridge, became a fellow of Jesus College in 1510, and was ordained a priest. He threw himself into his studies, becoming an outstanding theologian, a man of immense, though not original, learning. In about 1520, he began joining other scholars who met regularly to discuss Luther's theological revolt on the Continent.

Cranmer's reform leanings remained merely academic until he was drawn into the politics of the day. In August 1529, King Henry VIII happened to be in a neighborhood Cranmer was visiting, and he ended up conversing with the king. Henry had been trying to figure out how to divorce his first wife, Catherine of Aragon, in order to marry his new love, Anne Boleyn. The king, impressed with Cranmer's reasoning, commanded Cranmer to write a treatise backing the king's right to divorce and then made Cranmer one of his European ambassadors.

In this capacity, Cranmer made a trip to Germany, where he met Lutheran reformer Andreas Osiander—and Osiander's niece, Margaret. Osiander's Reformed theology and his niece so appealed to Cranmer that, despite his priest's orders, he married her in 1532. Because of the complex political situation in England, however, he kept his marriage a secret for years.

In August 1532, the aged archbishop of Canterbury died, and by March of the next year, Cranmer was consecrated as the new archbishop. Cranmer immediately declared the king's marriage to Catherine of Aragon void from the beginning; he then declared valid the marriage to Anne Boleyn (which had secretly taken place in January).

Cranmer believed in royal absolutism, that his primary duty was to obey the king, God's chosen, to lead his nation and church. Time and again in Henry's rocky reign, Cranmer was ordered to support religious policies of which he personally disapproved, and he always obeyed the king.

In 1536, he became convinced by rather dubious evidence that Anne had committed adultery, and he invalidated the marriage. In 1540, he ruled that Henry's proposed marriage to Anne of Cleves was lawful—and when Henry sought a divorce six months later, Cranmer approved it on the grounds that the original marriage was unlawful!

But Cranmer wasn't a lackey. Time and again, Cranmer alone of all Henry's advisers pleaded for the lives of people who fell out of royal favor, like Sir Thomas More, Anne Boleyn, and Thomas Cromwell. He even publicly argued against Henry's *Six Articles*, designed to move the country back in a Catholic direction. But when the *Six Articles* were approved by Parliament, he went along with the king's policies.

For his part, Henry intervened for Cranmer when court politics threatened Cranmer's position and life. And it was Cranmer for whom Henry asked on his deathbed.

Reform and reversals

With the accession of Edward VI in 1547, Cranmer's time arrived. The young king's guardian, Edward Seymour, Duke of Somerset (and his successor, the Duke of Northumberland), began to make the Church of England decidedly Protestant.

Cranmer took the chief role in directing doctrinal matters. In 1547 he published his *Book of Homilies*, which required clergy to preach sermons emphasizing Reformed doctrine. He composed the first *Book of Common Prayer*, only moderately Protestant, in 1549, followed in 1552 by a second that was more clearly Protestant. Cranmer also produced the *Forty-Two Articles* (1553), a set of doctrinal statements that moved the

Church of England even further in a Reformed, Calvinist direction.

These documents became critical to the formation of Anglicanism, and the *Book of Common Prayer* (BCP), though revised over the years, still retains Cranmer's distinctive stamp and is used by millions of Anglicans worldwide. The *BCP* contains some of the most well-known prayers in Christendom, including:

"Blessed Lord, who hast caused all holy Scriptures to be written for our learning; grant that we may in such wise hear them, read, mark, learn, and inwardly digest them, that by patience and comfort of thy holy Word, we may embrace, and ever hold fast, the blessed hope of everlasting life, which thou hast given us in our Savior Jesus Christ. Amen."

After Edward VI died in 1553, Cranmer supported Protestant Lady Jane Grey (great-niece of Henry VIII) as the new sovereign. But Lady Jane Grey was deposed within nine days, and Mary (Henry's devoutly Catholic daughter by Catherine of Aragon) triumphantly entered London.

Immediately, Parliament repealed the acts of Henry VIII and Edward VI and reintroduced heresy laws. Mary's government began a relentless campaign against Protestants. Cranmer was charged with treason and imprisoned in November 1553. After spending nearly two years in prison, Cranmer was subjected to a long, tedious trial. The foregone verdict was reached in February 1556, and in a ceremony carefully designed to humiliate, Cranmer was degraded from his episcopal and priestly offices and handed over to be burned at the stake.

A weary and depressed Cranmer, hoping to avoid the stake, was convinced that he should submit even to a Catholic sovereign and repudiate the Reformation. He signed a document that said, "I confess and believe in one, holy, catholic visible church; I recognize as its supreme head upon earth the bishop of Rome, pope and vicar of Christ, to whom all the faithful are bound subject."

Still, the government believed Cranmer must be punished for the havoc he had wreaked. He would still be burned at the stake—after making one more profession of his Catholic faith.

On the day of his execution, Cranmer was led into a church, and when it was his turn to speak, he drew out a piece of paper and began to read. He thanked the people for their prayers and then said, "I come to the great thing that troubleth my conscience more than any other thing that I ever said or did in my life." Referring to the recantations he had signed, he blurted out, "All such bills which I have written or signed with my own hand [are] untrue."

Loud murmurs sped through the congregation, but Cranmer continued, "And as for the pope, I refuse him as Christ's enemy and antichrist, with all his false doctrine. And as for the sacrament—"

Cranmer was immediately dragged from the stage and out to the stake. The fire was kindled and quickly the flame leapt up. Cranmer stretched out his right arm and hand into the flame and held it there as he said, "This hand hath offended." Only once did he withdraw it to wipe his face, and then he returned it until it had burned to a stump. Praying, "Lord Jesus, receive my spirit!" he died.

Within two years, Elizabeth I ascended the English throne and moved the church back in a Protestant direction, revising Cranmer's 42 Articles to 39, and adopting his *Book of Common Prayer* as the guide to worship. Today Anglicanism is the expression of faith for 51 million worldwide.

HUGH LATIMER & NICHOLAS RIDLEY

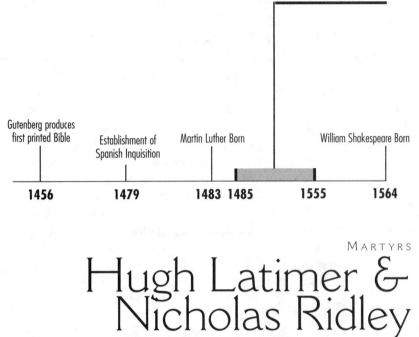

Gutenberg produces first printed Bible	Establishment of Spanish Inquisition	Martin Luther Born		William Shakespeare Born
1456	1479	1483 1485	1555	1564

MARTYRS

Hugh Latimer & Nicholas Ridley

ENGLISH REFORMERS WHO DIED TOGETHER

"Be of good comfort, Mr. Ridley, and play the man! We shall this day light such a candle, by God's grace, in England, as I trust never shall be put out."

Their lives didn't coincide much, but in their deaths, they stood side by side, perhaps the most well-known martyrdoms of the Reformation.

Early on it was clear that Nicholas Ridley had one of the finest minds in England. After attending Cambridge and the Sorbonne in Paris, he settled down to a scholarly career at Cambridge. About 1534, he first showed interest in Protestantism, and in 1537, he was appointed the chaplain to reform-minded Thomas Cranmer, archbishop of Canterbury. In the 1540s, when a Roman Catholic reaction set in during Henry's reign, Ridley was suspected of heresy, but during the Protestant reign of Edward VI, he was appointed bishop of Rochester, and then bishop of London as well.

Ridley used his influence to further the Protestant cause. His impact on the emerging *Book of Common Prayer* is seen especially in the section on the Eucharist. Christ's sacrifice was not "repeated," as in the Catholic liturgy; instead, worshipers offered a "sacrifice of praise and thanksgiving."

As bishop of London, he had stone altars replaced by wooden tables for observing Communion, which caused an uproar among Catholics in the city. He also instituted pastoral work in the city, aiding the poor and founding hospitals and schools.

When Roman Catholic Mary Tudor became queen upon Edward's death, Ridley was imprisoned in the Tower of London. He was joined by Hugh Latimer and Thomas Cranmer, and all three were taken to Oxford, where their "heretical" opinions were examined. When given an opportunity to recant his views, Ridley declined.

Hugh Latimer started out as a passionate Catholic. During his years at Cambridge University (he enrolled in 1506), he gained a reputation both as an ascetic and extraordinary preacher. Upon receiving a degree in theology in 1524, he delivered a lecture in which he assailed German Lutheran Philip Melanchthon for his high view of Scripture.

HUGH LATIMER

Among Latimer's listeners, though, was Thomas Bilney, a leader of a society of Protestants at Cambridge. After the lecture, Bilney asked Latimer to hear his confession. The startled Latimer, believing his lecture had converted the evangelical, readily complied. The "confession," however, was a stealthily worded sermon on the comfort and confidence the Scriptures can bring. Latimer was moved to tears—and to Protestantism.

Latimer's sermons now targeted Catholicism and social injustice. He preached boldly, daring in 1530 to utter a sermon before the strong-armed Henry VIII that denounced violence as a means of protecting God's Word. For this he won the king's respect.

This farmer's son soon became one of Henry's chief advisers after the king's break with Rome. Appointed bishop of Worcester, he supported Henry's dissolution of the monasteries. However, when he opposed the king's *Six Articles* (Henry's retreat from Protestantism), he was put under house arrest for six years.

He was given his freedom during the reign of Edward VI, and he flourished as one of emerging Protestantism's leading preachers. But with the ascension of Mary, he was again imprisoned, tried, and along with Ridley, condemned to death.

A tale of two martyrs

According to John Foxe, in his famous *Book of Martyrs* (officially titled, *Acts and*

Monuments), Ridley arrived at the field of execution first. When Latimer arrived, the two embraced and Ridley said, "Be of good heart, brother, for God will either assuage the fury of the flame, or else strengthen us to abide it." They both knelt and prayed before listening to an exhortation from a preacher (as was the custom before an execution for heresy).

After the sermon, one of the officials pleaded, "Mr. Ridley, if you will revoke your erroneous opinions, you shall not only have liberty so to do, but also your life."

"Not otherwise?" said Ridley.

"If you will not do so," replied the official, "there is no remedy: you must suffer for your deserts."

"Well," concluded Ridley, "so long as the breath is in my body, I will never deny my Lord Christ and his known truth. God's will be done in me."

The blacksmith wrapped a chain of iron around the waists of Ridley and Latimer. When the wood about Ridley's feet was lit, Latimer said, "Be of good comfort, Mr. Ridley, and play the man! We shall this day light such a candle, by God's grace, in England, as I trust never shall be put out."

As the fire rose Latimer cried out, "O Father of heaven, receive my soul!" and he died almost immediately. Ridley however, hung on, with most of his lower body having burned before he passed away.

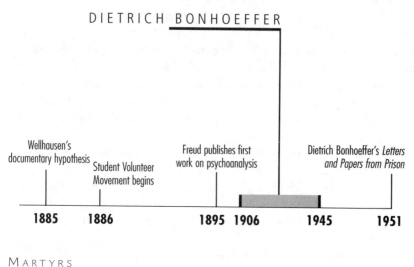

DIETRICH BONHOEFFER

Wellhausen's documentary hypothesis

Student Volunteer Movement begins

Freud publishes first work on psychoanalysis

Dietrich Bonhoeffer's *Letters and Papers from Prison*

1885 **1886** **1895 1906** **1945** **1951**

MARTYRS

Dietrich Bonhoeffer

GERMAN THEOLOGIAN AND RESISTER

> *"Cheap grace is preaching forgiveness without requiring repentance, baptism without church discipline, Communion without confession.... Cheap grace is grace without discipleship, grace without the cross, grace without Jesus Christ, living and incarnate."*

"The time is fulfilled for the German people of Hitler. It is because of Hitler that Christ, God the helper and redeemer, has become effective among us.... Hitler is the way of the Spirit and the will of God for the German people to enter the Church of Christ." So spoke German pastor Hermann Gruner. Another pastor put it more succinctly: "Christ has come to us through Adolph Hitler."

So despondent had been the German people after the defeat of World War I and the subsequent economic depression that the charismatic Hitler appeared to be the nation's answer to prayer—at least to most Germans. One exception was theologian Dietrich Bonhoeffer, who was determined not only to refute this idea but also to topple Hitler, even if it meant killing him.

From pacifist to co-conspirator

Bonhoeffer was not raised in a particularly radical environment. He was born into an aristocratic family. His mother was daughter of the preacher at the court of Kaiser Wilhelm II, and his father was a prominent neurologist and professor of psychiatry at the University of Berlin.

All eight children were raised in a liberal, nominally religious environment and were encouraged to dabble in great literature and the fine arts. Bonhoeffer's skill at the piano, in fact, led some in his family to believe he was headed for a career in music. When at age 14, Dietrich announced he intended to become a minister and theologian, the family was not pleased.

Bonhoeffer graduated from the University of Berlin in 1927, at age 21, and then spent some months in Spain as an assistant pastor to a German congregation. Then it was back to Germany to write a dissertation, which would grant him the right to a university appointment. He then spent a year in America, at New York's Union Theological Seminary, before returning to the post of lecturer at the University of Berlin.

During these years, Hitler rose in power, becoming chancellor of Germany in January 1933, and president a year and a half later. Hitler's anti-Semitic rhetoric and actions intensified—as did his opposition, which included the likes of theologian Karl Barth, pastor Martin Niemoller, and the young Bonhoeffer. Together with other pastors and theologians, they organized the Confessing Church, which announced publicly in its Barmen Declaration (1934) its allegiance first to Jesus Christ: "We repudiate the false teaching that the church can and must recognize yet other happenings and powers, personalities and truths as divine revelation alongside this one Word of God...."

In the meantime, Bonhoeffer had written *The Cost of Discipleship* (1937), a call to more faithful and radical obedience to Christ and a severe rebuke of comfortable Christianity: "Cheap grace is preaching forgiveness without requiring repentance, baptism without church discipline, Communion without confession.... Cheap grace is grace without discipleship, grace without the cross, grace without Jesus Christ, living and incarnate."

During this time, Bonhoeffer was teaching pastors in an underground seminary, Finkenwalde (the government had banned him from teaching openly). But after the seminary was discovered and closed, the Confessing Church became increasingly reluctant to speak out against Hitler, and moral opposition proved increasingly ineffective, so Bonhoeffer began to change his strategy. To this point he had been a pacifist, and he had tried to oppose the Nazis through religious action and moral persuasion.

Now he signed up with the German secret service (to serve as a double agent—while traveling to church conferences over Europe, he was supposed to be collecting information about the places he visited, but he was, instead, trying to help Jews escape Nazi oppression). Bonhoeffer also became a part of a plot to overthrow, and later to assassinate, Hitler.

As his tactics were changing, he had gone to America to become a guest lecturer. But he couldn't shake a feeling of responsibility for his country. Within months of his arrival, he wrote theologian Reinhold Niebuhr, "I have made a mistake in coming to America. I must live through this difficult period in our national history with the Christian people of Germany. I will have no right to participate in the reconstruction of Christian life in Germany after the war if I do not share the trials of this time with my people."

Bonhoeffer, though privy to various plots on Hitler's life, was never at the center of the plans. Eventually his resistance efforts (mainly his role in rescuing Jews) was discovered. On an April afternoon in 1943, two men arrived in a black Mercedes, put Bonhoeffer in the car, and drove him to Tegel prison.

Radical reflections

Bonhoeffer spent two years in prison, corresponding with family and friends, pastoring fellow prisoners, and reflecting on the meaning of "Jesus Christ for today." As the months progressed, be began outlining a new theology, penning enigmatic lines that had been inspired by his reflections on the nature of Christian action in history.

"God lets himself be pushed out of the world on to the cross," he wrote. "He is weak and powerless in the world, and that is precisely the way, the only way, in which he is with us and helps us. [The Bible] ... makes quite clear that Christ helps us, not by virtue of his omnipotence, but by virtue of his weakness and suffering.... The Bible directs man to God's powerlessness and suffering; only the suffering God can help."

In another passage, he said, "To be a Christian does not mean to be religious in a particular way, to make something of oneself (a sinner, a penitent, or a saint) on the basis of some method or other, but to be a man—not a type of man, but the man that Christ creates in us. It is not the religious act that makes the Christian, but participation in the sufferings of God in the secular life."

Eventually, Bonhoeffer was transferred from Tegel to Buchenwald and then to the extermination camp at Flossenbürg. On April 9, 1945, one month before Germany surrendered, he was hanged with six other resisters.

A decade later, a camp doctor who witnessed Bonhoeffer's hanging described the scene: "The prisoners ... were taken from their cells, and the verdicts of court martial read out to them. Through the half-open door in one room of the huts, I saw Pastor Bonhoeffer, before taking off his prison garb, kneeling on the floor praying fervently to his God. I was most deeply moved by the way this lovable man prayed, so devout and so certain that God heard his prayer. At the place of execution, he again said a prayer and then climbed the steps to the gallows, brave and composed. His death ensued in a few seconds. In the almost 50 years that I have worked as a doctor, I have hardly ever seen a man die so entirely submissive to the will of God."

Bonhoeffer's prison correspondence was eventually edited and published as *Letters and Papers from Prison*, which inspired much controversy and the "death of God" movement of the 1960s (though Bonhoeffer's close friend and chief biographer, Eberhard Bethge, said Bonhoeffer implied no such thing). His *Cost of Discipleship*, as well as *Life Together* (about Christian community, based on his teaching at the underground seminary), have remained devotional classics.

Subject Index